P9-CFV-600

The Road to Confederation

The Road
to Confederation

THE EMERGENCE OF CANADA:

1863-1867

Donald Creighton

1964

MACMILLAN OF CANADA

TORONTO

© DONALD CREIGHTON 1964

All rights reserved—no part of this book may be reproduced in any form without permission in writing from the publisher, except by a reviewer who wishes to quote brief passages in connection with a review written for inclusion in a magazine or newspaper.

Printed in Canada by the T. H. Best Printing Company Limited

Acknowledgements

By gracious permission of Her Majesty the Queen, I have been able to make use of material relating to Canadian Confederation in the Royal Archives, Windsor Castle; and for this privilege I am very grateful. I am under obligation to Admiral of the Fleet the Earl Mountbatten of Burma, who kindly permitted me to examine certain documents on British colonial policy in the Palmerston Collection.

I owe much to archivists and librarians in Canada and England, and I should particularly like to express my thanks for generous assistance to the following persons and institutions: Dr. W. Kaye Lamb and the staff of the Public Archives of Canada, especially Mr. W. G. Ormsby, formerly head of the Manuscript Division; Dr. C. Bruce Fergusson and his assistants in the Public Archives of Nova Scotia; Dr. A. G. Bailey and the staff of the University of New Brunswick Library; Miss W. D. Coates of the National Register of Archives, England; Dr. George MacBeath of the New Brunswick Museum; Mr. Maurice P. Boone of the Legislative Library, Fredericton; Miss Jean Gill of the Charlottetown Public Library; Dr. J. J. Talman of the Library of the University of Western Ontario; the staff of the Legislative Library, Toronto.

My colleague, Professor J. M. S. Careless, whose *Brown of The Globe: Statesman of Confederation* has so greatly enlarged our understanding of British American union, has made available a manuscript memoir of Sir William Howland, and I should like to thank him for the opportunity of using this evidence. Professor G. R. Cook, also a colleague in the Department of History, read a number of my chapters and gave me the benefit of his judgment on certain problems of interpretation; and I am grateful to him and to his wife, Eleanor, who kindly helped me with the task of proof-reading. Professor P. G. Cornell, of Waterloo University, put his special knowledge of the period at my disposal; and Professor P. B. Waite, of Dalhousie University, whose *The Life and Times of Confederation, 1864-1867* has done so much to illuminate the Confederation years, supplied several references and replied to inquiries. I should like to express my appreciation of their help.

I am under particular obligation to Professor W. L. Morton of the University of Manitoba, who has generously permitted me to use some of his own material on the Confederation period.

I am greatly indebted to the Canada Council for a grant that enabled me to give an uninterrupted year of study and writing to this book.

Finally, I should like to record my gratitude to the University of Toronto, and especially to the President, Dr. C. T. Bissell, the Dean of Arts and Science, Professor V. W. Bladen, and the Chairman of the Department of History, Professor J. M. S. Careless. The interest they have shown in my work and the assistance they have given me have been a constant encouragement.

D. G. CREIGHTON

Contents

Illustrations

The photographs of Samuel Leonard Tilley and of the delegates to the Quebec Conference are from the New Brunswick Museum, Saint John. The photograph of the Confederation Chamber, Charlottetown, was supplied by the National Film Board. The others are from the Public Archives of Canada.

MAPS (*by Geoffrey Matthews*)

PHOTOGRAPHS

Between pages 20 and 21

Between pages 52 and 53

Frederic Bowker Terrington Carter, Newfoundland
J. Ambrose Shea, Newfoundland
Hector Louis Langevin, Province of Canada
William McDougall, Province of Canada
Thomas D'Arcy McGee, Province of Canada
Sir Charles Hastings Doyle, General Officer Commanding,
     Nova Scotia
Sir William Fenwick Williams, Lieutenant-Governor of
     Nova Scotia
Lord Monck and household, Rideau Hall, Ottawa, 1866

The Road to Confederation

CHAPTER ONE

Maritime Initiative

I T WAS the enthusiasm of Gordon of New Brunswick that gave the movement its real start. There was, of course, nothing new about the idea; the political union of the three Maritime Provinces – Nova Scotia, New Brunswick, and Prince Edward Island – had long been a respectable, if not a very fashionable, subject of discussion. Maritime politicians had talked about it with an air of polite respect and thoughtful public spirit. Two Maritime governors – Lord Mulgrave of Nova Scotia and Sir John Manners-Sutton, Gordon's predecessor in New Brunswick – had been its earnest advocates. But Manners-Sutton had long before gone on to his next colonial assignment in Trinidad; Mulgrave was to return to England in the autumn of 1863 to succeed to his father's title of Marquess of Normanby; and no Maritime politician had shown the slightest sign of risking his popularity by taking up Maritime union as a cause. It remained an academic, politically unprofitable proposal, which had never acquired much convinced support, and had never aroused any popular enthusiasm at all. Very possibly it might have languished and died of inanition if Gordon had not taken the most strenuous methods to revive it. He brought to the task all the enthusiasm of his youth, the zeal of his ardent temperament, and the assurance – which was very considerable indeed – of the superior political wisdom of his own views.

In 1861, when he first came out to New Brunswick, Arthur Hamilton Gordon was still a comparatively young man, not yet thirty-two years old, with a long, narrow, melancholy countenance, a thick black beard, and a pair of watchful and brooding eyes. He was the son of the 4th Earl of Aberdeen, who had been Prime Minister of Great Britain from 1852 to 1855 and whose administration had been ruined by the tragic misfortunes of the Crimean War. Both the 4th Earl and the formidable William Ewart Gladstone were 'Peelites' – followers of Sir Robert Peel in his breach with the main body of the Conservatives over the Repeal of the Corn Laws; and Gladstone regarded Aberdeen with a reverence even more profound than that which he accorded his first leader, Sir Robert. Young Gordon had served as his father's private secretary during Aberdeen's term of office. Gladstone naturally knew 'Arthur' well, and looked on him with affectionate interest; and in 1858, when he set out on his mission to examine the state of the British protectorate in the Ionian Islands, he invited the young man to accompany him as his private secretary.[1] Their association on this survey had a permanent and unfortunate effect upon Gladstone's opinion of Arthur; and the deterioration in their relations began in Brussels on their way down to the Mediterranean, where there occurred a curious and significant episode, which Gladstone never completely forgot – or forgave. King Leopold of the Belgians, wishing to do all the honours to the visiting English statesman, invited Gladstone to a great state dinner, and young Gordon, as Aberdeen's son, was included in the invitation. At the appointed hour, one of the King's own carriages arrived to take the English visitors to the palace, and Gladstone seated himself in it with dignity. Five minutes went by. No Arthur. Ten minutes. No Arthur. Finally, after more than a quarter of an hour, the complacent young man appeared, without apology, nonchalantly explaining that he could not find the right waistcoat. They were terribly late. The King and the whole company had obviously been waiting. But young Gordon was completely unabashed. He offered no apologies. He made no attempt to take the blame for the embarrassed and indignant Gladstone.[2]

In 1858, at the time of the Ionian Islands adventure, the political future of the Peelites looked cloudy and uncertain. But in 1859, Gladstone, manfully overcoming his strong moral objections to Lord Palmerston, and incidentally ensuring the success of his own future political career, decided to join with the Whigs; and, as a result, the Peelites entered the new Palmerston government in force. Young Gordon's political friends and patrons were now securely established in the seats of the mighty; and next year, when Aberdeen died, confiding Arthur to Gladstone's care, there was every prospect that something would be done for the young man. Gladstone took his responsibilities for Arthur seriously; but, after the Ionian Islands mission, he possibly would have preferred to discharge his trust at a comfortable distance. Very fortunately, young Gordon's new ambitions coincided very nicely with Gladstone's private preferences. As a result of his Ionian Islands experience, he decided that he would like a career in the British colonial service.

Nothing could be more easily arranged. The spacious British Empire of the mid-nineteenth century offered a pleasingly varied selection of jobs; and, for his first appointment, Gordon was offered a choice of the governorship of either Antigua or New Brunswick.[3] It would probably have been much better if he had chosen Antigua, which was a Crown colony in the West Indies, where the governor really governed, and where representative institutions had not yet been heard of. As it was, he decided upon New Brunswick, which had had a legislature for over three-quarters of a century and which, even more regrettably, had actually been granted responsible government. In New Brunswick the governor merely reigned and the Executive Council really ruled; and the Executive Council was now dominated by typical representatives of a new *parvenu* class of lumber merchants and shopkeepers who a generation before had overcome the old Loyalist oligarchy of squires, professional men, and civil servants. The original New Brunswick, 'the Province of the Loyalists', 'the most gentlemanlike on earth', had in fact been submerged in a torrent of immigrants, chiefly 'famine' Irish. New Brunswick politics, 'the politics of the timber trade', had degenerated into a hard, shrewd game in which the main factors seemed to be a narrow self-interest and a suspicious parochialism.

From the first, Gordon's feelings about New Brunswick were decidedly mixed. He loved the provincial capital, the sleepy little town of Fredericton, its gracious cathedral church, the

winding, lovely St. John River with the rich intervale lands
spread out on either side, and, beyond the horizon of low hills,
the deep and lonely pine forests of the north.⁴ Camping and
hunting, with only a few carefully selected companions and
guides, canoeing along the meandering rivers with only the
sounds and silences of the pine woods about him, were pleasures
of which he never tired. 'My summers are delightful,' he reported happily. His winters, which brought sleigh-rides, tuneful
with tinkling bells and joyous with wind and sun and effortless
speed, could be delightful also; but, though they were sometimes
exhilarating, they could also be very cruel. What he loathed
and dreaded most at first – and what sometimes brought actual
physical illness – was the appalling cold of winter. 'The dreaded
winter is now closing in fast,' he wrote sombrely in mid-October
1862;⁵ and six months later, in March and April 1863, he was
still noting, with angry incredulity, temperatures as frigid as
thirty-two degrees below zero and deep, unbroken expanses of
snow.⁶ Often, when he watched the huge, gleaming drifts from
his study window, or heard the wind scream down from the
north-west, or felt the draughts along the halls of Government
House, he thought, with a pang of resentful envy, of Antigua
and those other numerous British colonies that basked in tropical or sub-tropical warmth. He explained sardonically that he
preferred to live in a 'locality where the earth was not invisible
for half the year, even if there was the risk of yellow fever and
cholera'.⁷ In March 1863, when the snow was still deep on the
ground, and he had been 'ill and suffering' with the cold, he
frankly asked to be transferred to Trinidad.⁸ The Colonial Secretary, to whom all these complaints and importunate demands
were addressed, was the Duke of Newcastle, another Peelite
member of Palmerston's cabinet. Newcastle had a tart, matter-
of-fact way with troublesome governors; but he was also inclined
to take the lenient Peelite view of old Aberdeen's temperamental son. He told Gordon in May that he hoped soon to be able to
send him to 'some place where zero is unknown'.⁹

This kindly promise did not entirely satisfy Gordon. The
comfort of warmth was by no means all he wanted in life; and
the cold of winter was certainly not the only thing he disliked

about New Brunswick. He had, in fact, a very large capacity for disapproval and criticism. Finding fault was something he did frequently and well; and he found in New Brunswick a wide and open field for the exercise of his talent. The province itself was a dreary, unenterprising, poverty-stricken place which in every respect offered a sharp contrast with the 'wealth, activity and progress' he so admired in Canada. Provincial politics was a sordid business limited by a narrow outlook and parochial jealousies, in which bribery at elections was accepted, vulgar buffoonery in the legislature condoned, and parliamentary corruption complacently regarded as 'smartness'. In the Assembly, almost 'every gentleman of education and position has lost his seat and has been replaced by some ignorant lumberer or petty attorney, or by some keeper of a village grog shop or grocery store'.[10] Even his Executive Council – the responsible government of the province – had, with a few notable exceptions, degenerated into an uncouth, illiterate, needy, corrupt, and intemperate group of men.

Yet these were the creatures who actually governed the province. And he, the Lieutenant-Governor, who was obliged by the conventions of responsible government to act on their advice, wielded only an empty and formal authority. Gordon had a very lofty view of the dignity of his vice-regal office, as well as a high opinion of his own abilities. He instructed the Anglican clergy of the province that, after praying for the Queen, they should petition the deity for 'Thy Servant Arthur'. He would have been decidedly annoyed if he had suspected that it was as 'Thy Servant Arthur' that he was soon to become familiarly and jocosely known in New Brunswick. He might perhaps have been even more deeply offended if he could have dreamed that, long after his honourable career had closed and his life ended, 'Thy Servant Arthur' would be the irreverent nickname by which he would be recalled by the small circle of Canadians who alone remembered his existence.[11] At the time, the clergy no doubt prayed dutifully as requested; but the politicians, far from showing him a similar respect or treating his advice with becoming deference, seemed hardly to bother to pay any attention to him at all. It was absurd, grotesque, monstrous! It was a total inversion of the natural order of things – an enormity to which Gordon never became hardened, which he never ceased to regard with astonishment and indignation. All he could hope to do was, through suggestion and persuasion, to acquire an indirect influence over the deliberations of his ministers; and this was an inactive, devious, humiliating role which he found painfully distasteful to play. 'I wish I had more work,' he wrote enviously, 'for I am fond of it, and . . . I am – if I know myself at all – a far better administrator and director than persuader and influencer.'[12] To retain any influence at all required a constant exercise of tact and forethought, a cheerful acceptance of slights and rejections, a heroic check upon his own temper, and a formal complicity in the doubtful deeds of his advisers. 'I cannot tell you', he wrote to the Colonial Secretary, 'how degraded I often feel at having nothing to do but to give formal effect to their atrocious jobs.'[13] He raged impotently at the shameful futility of his position. He had ideas, he wanted to do things, he liked power, or, as he charmingly put it, 'opportunity for usefulness'. Yet he knew himself to be 'utterly helpless, and that helplessness felt to be a triumph over the past by the people'.[14]

In theory at least, there were two possible remedies for his discontent. He could simply resign and give up his position – or he could attempt to enlarge its scope and alter its character. He could exchange New Brunswick for a nice submissive Crown colony, where the Governor would have an active and positive part to play, and where the climate was agreeably sub-tropical. Or, alternatively, he could stubbornly remain in New Brunswick and try to reform and improve the fundamental conditions of political life in British North America. Of the two courses, the first was more certain and much easier; he could simply accept the first opportunity of a transfer. But the second possibility aroused his ambition and challenged his creative abilities. Many people in England looked on the North American colonies as the *damnosa hereditas* of British imperialism; but Gordon did not share this view. Potentially, British North America was the greatest political community in the Empire. It was true that at the moment the nation of the future stood arrested in frustration and danger. Two-thirds of it was a howling wilderness.

The inhabited part was split up into half a dozen miserable fragments of provinces, of which Prince Edward Island and New Brunswick were the most contemptible. In such tiny governments, such overgrown municipalities, the inevitable pettiness of public issues and the lack of talented and devoted men in public life could not help but make for parochialism, maladministration, and low political morality in every department of provincial life. Badly governed within, the provinces were weak and vulnerable to pressure and danger from without. And their survival, as a collective whole, was now obscurely threatened by the vast continental upheaval that had been begun by the American Civil War.

Gordon had the best of reasons for appreciating just how great the danger of the Civil War could be. He had come out to his post in New Brunswick in the autumn of 1861, when the struggle had not yet lasted six months; and before the year was out Great Britain and the United States were nearly at war. On the 8th of November, on the high seas, Captain Wilkes of the S.S. *San Jacinto* stopped the British mail packet *Trent* and took from her by force two Confederate diplomatic agents, James Murray Mason and John Slidell, and their two secretaries. For this breach of international law and Anglo-American good relations, Great Britain insisted on reparation. A stiff note, whose severity was modified by the dying Prince Albert, demanded an apology and the liberation of the four Southerners. For over a month, while the crucial messages travelled slowly back and forth across the Atlantic, British North America waited tensely, as if for an inevitable explosion. The provinces called out their militia and braced themselves for the encounter; the arrival, in mid-winter, of large reinforcements of imperial troops gave the anxious colonists ample assurance that Great Britain was determined to defend them. A patriotic wave of enthusiasm, which carried both English- and French-speaking Canadians along on its crest, swept through the whole of British North America. In those fearful weeks of December, the provinces, in a sudden blaze of illumination, comprehended their real nature and their true destiny. Roused by the dangers of the *Trent* crisis, they confirmed their identification with Great Britain and declared their determination to fight for their collective independence in North America.[15]

All British North America shared in this mood of decision and resolution; but Gordon and New Brunswick had a special reason for remembering the *Trent*. Most of the transports bearing the imperial reinforcements to Canada failed to ascend the St. Lawrence before it was sealed with ice; and, in the storms and extreme cold of January, about seven thousand British soldiers were triumphantly transported in sleighs through northern New Brunswick to Rivière du Loup in Canada. This mid-winter passage through the province was a co-operative endeavour of both British and British Americans which dramatically expressed their spontaneous feelings of unity and purpose.[16] It showed the province's political conviction and willingness; but it also revealed the weakness and vulnerability, not only of New Brunswick, but of British America as a whole. Throughout the provinces, the militia, upon which so little money had been so grudgingly spent, was weak in numbers and deficient in training. The transport of the British troops through the snow-choked Madawaska Road had proved for all to see how desperately a railway between Canada and the Maritime Provinces was needed.

Captain Wilkes was disavowed, Mason and Slidell were liberated, and the war scare was suddenly over; but neither Great Britain nor British North America was likely to forget the shock of the *Trent* crisis. The thought of the American Civil War and its possible implications lay at the back of Gordon's mind as it lay in the mind of every member of the British governing class, every British administrator in North America, and nearly every British American. It was one reason why responsible people began, in the next few years, to consider various plans for the reorganization of British North America – projects for improved defence, interprovincial trade, better interprovincial communications, and even political union. If the northern provinces were to survive and develop, they must organize and centralize their separate, haphazard, and uncoordinated activities. Political union would supply the impulse for growth and expansion and the strength for defence. It would also – and this was a major

point with Gordon – sweep away all the corrupt and paltry provincial legislatures, and substitute one, or possibly two, British
American parliaments, which would have big affairs to deal
with, and which would attract 'respectable gentlemen' of talent
and public spirit to political life.

'I should like', he told the Colonial Secretary frankly, 'to
prepare the way for the union of the colonies (the paramount
necessity of their future).'[17] The union he wanted was a strong
union – a legislative union; he disliked and distrusted federalism; but, though he always considered that the ultimate object
ought to be a general union of the whole of British America, he
came to believe that a regional union of the Maritime Provinces
would be an important first step, highly desirable in itself, towards the larger scheme. His superior, the Duke of Newcastle,
took much the same view; and they were also in agreement that
both unions ought to be preceded by the construction of an
intercolonial railway from Halifax to Quebec. An intercolonial
railway was equally necessary for either a regional or a general
union. It was the one essential preliminary to the consolidation
of British North America. He concentrated upon its achievement
with enthusiasm and conviction.

⇥⇥⇥ II ≪≪≪

FOR OVER A DECADE now, the people of the Maritime Provinces had speculated hopefully about an intercolonial railway that would unite New Brunswick and Nova Scotia, span the
Appalachian Highlands – the great empty wilderness of northern New Brunswick and eastern Canada – and link Halifax and
Saint John with Quebec and Montreal. For over a decade the
history of the Intercolonial Railway project had been one long,
uninterruptedly gloomy tale of proposals, misunderstandings,
disagreements, refusals, and delays. But in September 1862,
when delegates from the three provinces met in Quebec to discuss the scheme once more, the prospect looked more hopeful
than it had done for a long time. The *Trent* affair and the war
scare of the previous autumn had lent the plan an extreme ur-

gency it had never had before. The British government, though it steadfastly refused to contribute funds to the undertaking, had offered to guarantee the interest on the loan that certainly would be necessary for the construction of the railway. On the basis of this not over-generous but useful offer – which was all they were likely to get – the delegates quickly settled the intractable problem of finances, and decided that Canada should pay five-twelfths and Nova Scotia and New Brunswick three-and-a-half-twelfths each of the cost. Gordon, who, with Mulgrave of Nova Scotia, had gone up to Quebec to be present at the negotiations, returned home delighted with the conference, vastly impressed with that 'splendid country Canada', and hopefully confident of the future of the railway.

From then on, the enterprise began to take on a grimmer and more doubtful appearance. Late in the autumn the delegates went to England to discuss with the British government the terms of the loan and the imperial guarantee of interest. There they were confronted with that awful mid-Victorian presence: British Treasury officials, inspired and directed by the Chancellor of the Exchequer, William Ewart Gladstone. For Gladstone and his permanent staff the business of making things financially difficult for colonies was not only a public duty but also a personal satisfaction. Gladstone insisted firmly that, if Great Britain were graciously to guarantee the loan necessary to finance the railway, a sinking fund must be set up, and the fund's money safely invested in solid, low-interest British government bonds. The Maritimers, Howe and Tilley, who disliked these harsh, rigid terms as much as the Canadians, were prepared to argue the matter through to a settlement; but the Canadians, Howland and Sicotte, after having taken part in the discussions for some time, departed abruptly, and, without returning, packed their bags and sailed for Canada, leaving behind at the Colonial Office a document in which they seemed to repudiate the entire agreement.[18]

A shiver of angry uneasiness went through the Maritimers. Gordon felt it as acutely as anybody. 'It looks very much as if the Canadian government were going to throw over the Intercolonial Railway,' he wrote to Newcastle in January 1863. 'That

Sicotte means to do so if he can is certain; but I still have some faith in Mr. Sandfield Macdonald's comparative honesty.'[19] The fact was that the real intentions of the Canadian government remained exasperatingly obscure. Unlike Nova Scotia and New Brunswick, which in 1863 passed legislation authorizing the expenditures that they had assumed under the agreement of September 1862, Canada did not legislate at all about the Inter-colonial Railway. The Canadian government soon began to press for a preliminary survey of the route, which, it argued, was absolutely essential before the scheme could be carried a single stage further. All this looked very evasive and questionable; but, on the other hand, the Canadian ministry did not appear to have formally repudiated the agreement of the previous September. The Maritimers waited doubtfully, worriedly, yet hopefully. Gordon waited; and as he waited his thoughts kept returning to the subject which by now had become an obsession with him – the maladministration, parochialism, and corruption of re-sponsible cabinet government in a small province like New Brunswick.

On the last day of 1862, he had written a long confidential dispatch to the Colonial Secretary, suggesting that the cure for the political vices of New Brunswick might be found in a legislative union with its neighbours.[20] Maritime union was, he thought, an effective remedy for a great evil. It was a cause worthy of fighting for. Yet he did not immediately follow up his suggestion. He did nothing publicly or privately to start a move-ment for Maritime union until the summer. In June he crossed Northumberland Strait to Charlottetown and spent a few days as the guest of the Lieutenant-Governor, George Dundas, and his wife, in the Island's Government House, a lovely, white colonial building, with tall, graceful pillars and an air of quiet elegance.[21] Mrs. Dundas was a pretty woman, with a sweet smile and a gracious manner; and, like most other people, Gordon found her charming. Dundas, who was ten years older than Gordon, was an ex-soldier who had sat in the House of Commons for some years as Member for Linlithgow. Gordon wrote him down condescendingly as 'no Solomon' though with some 'quiet sense'; and he was quick to take advantage of this obvious opportunity of discussing the merits of his new project with a fellow Governor and with the Island politicians whom he met for the first time around the Dundas dinner-table. A feeling of parochial exclusiveness dominated Prince Edward Island's attitude to the rest of British North America; and a recent debate in the Assembly on unions – federal or legislative, Maritime or general – had proved clearly how reluctant the Islanders were to surrender even a part of their precious autonomy to some larger political organization.[22] Most of the public men who might have been invited to Government House to meet Gordon would probably have disliked his proposal; but, as it happened, there were at least three among those he met who must have shown more than a polite interest in his ideas, who might even have voiced a guarded approval of his particular scheme of Maritime union.

Colonel John Hamilton Gray, the retired army officer who was premier of the province, had already put himself on record in the recent debate as a believer in a general British North American union. Gray's principal political rival was George Coles, the veteran Liberal leader, the grizzled victor of the fight for responsible government. Coles was now presenting himself as the uncompromising opponent of the Island's chief economic and social curse, the huge property rights of the absentee landlords; and in the recent debate he had vehemently declared that he was ready to accept any union, federal or legislative, provided it would give Prince Edward Island sufficient political support and financial assistance to banish 'the baneful influence of the Cunards' and the other absentee proprietors for ever.[23] In Coles's view, union – any kind of union – was simply a means to a more important end; but W. H. Pope, the Provincial Secretary in Gray's Conservative government, and another likely guest at the Dundas dinner-parties, might have agreed with Gordon that Maritime union was valuable in its own right. It was true that, in the March debate in the Assembly, he had favoured a general British American union and had looked doubtfully on the smaller project; but, in the meantime, he may have been coming closer to the belief he voiced so strongly only a little later, that Maritime union was desirable for itself and as a useful precursor to the larger scheme. Suave, persuasive, ingratiating, Pope had an astonishing capacity for convincing others – and perhaps himself – that his own private views were an accurate reflection of general public opinion.

Very probably he helped to convince Gordon. At any rate, it was in Government House, Charlottetown, that Gordon reached the astonishing conclusion that 'the leading men there are heartily desirous of being united with New Brunswick and Nova Scotia. . . .'[24] The revelation was an inspiring one. The insularity, mental as well as physical, of the Islanders was notorious; and, as Gordon himself told Newcastle, he had anticipated that 'the strongest resistance' to the idea of Maritime union would come from Prince Edward Island. Now, on what was surely the very best authority, it seemed that these assumptions were wrong; '. . . the leader of the government assured me', he wrote to the Colonial Secretary, 'that there would be no difficulty in securing its adoption by the legislature'; and the leader of the opposition, he reported, 'spoke in much the same sense'.[25] Gordon had talked with some of the very few Island politicians who were willing, for one reason or another, to look beyond the narrow limits of their domestic politics; and his incurable inclination to wishful thinking, his complacent readiness to assume the acquiescence of others in the wisdom of his own opinions, did the rest. He returned to New Brunswick in the highest of spirits. He had scarcely known such a moment of elation since his arrival in the province two years before. Dimly but enticingly there was opening up before him a way by which he might at last perform a great creative act of statesmanship for British North America. With every prospect of success, he could put himself at the head of a movement for the legislative union of the Maritime Provinces; the one great supposed obstacle to the scheme had turned out, on closer inspection, to amount to nothing. It was a wonderful opportunity – a much more wonderful opportunity than he had recently been disposed to think he would ever be granted in New Brunswick. And, once back in Fredericton, he lost no time in setting the whole plan before his Provincial Secretary and Premier, Samuel Leonard Tilley.

Tilley was one of the least likely persons to share Gordon's romantic enthusiasm or moral disapproval; but Gordon realized that he could get nowhere without Tilley's support. Besides, within limits (there were always strict limits to Gordon's favourable appreciation of any colonial) he respected Tilley.[26] He had picked Tilley out as virtually the only intelligent, reliable, and 'gentlemanlike' member of the very unsavoury and none too scrupulous group of advisers that made up his Executive Council. A Saint John business man, the senior partner in a firm that dealt largely in proprietary medicines, Tilley kept something of the counting-house approach to politics, and showed a touch of the shopman in his affable and ingratiating manner. He was short and slight in person, clean-shaven where so many of his contemporaries were heavily bearded, with a bright, quick, sharp eye, rosy cheeks, and a ready and cheerful smile. While many of the politicians of his generation practised an inflated and clumsy oratory, Tilley talked plain good sense in a laconic, terse, unemphatic manner. His specialty was finance; his arguments were buttressed with statistics. He treated politics as a series of concrete, prosaic problems which could best be solved in a matter-of-fact, business-like way. One was not likely to suspect the dreamer, the visionary, or the idealist in Samuel Leonard Tilley. Yet there had been one curious dramatic aberration in the unpretentious pedestrianism of his career – one glaring exception which either proved the rule of his character or demonstrated its hidden contradictions.

Tilley was a rigid teetotaller. He became, in his modest way, an evangelist for total abstinence. In the end, this led him to an idealistic action, which, in the hard-drinking New Brunswick of the mid-nineteenth century, was so egregiously preposterous as almost to warrant a certification for insanity. In 1855, when Provincial Secretary in a Liberal government – New Brunswickers called them the 'Smashers' – Tilley had persuaded the legislature to enact a law totally prohibiting the sale of intoxicating liquors in the province. This cost Tilley his seat in the Assembly, and the 'Smashers', office. They surrendered power to their opponents, the Conservatives, who were now affectionately renamed the 'Rummies' by a grateful New Brunswick electorate.[27] The evangelist Tilley had learnt a sharp lesson in practical politics that he was not likely to forget; but, on the other hand, he never ceased to preach total abstinence or to believe in the ultimate necessity of total prohibition. Final defeat was something that he did not like to acknowledge. There was a strong streak of perseverance, of hopeful persistence, in his character; and, during reverses or in retreat, he had proved himself to be extremely agile and resourceful. The débâcle of the prohibition law might very well have ruined his career. But it did nothing of the sort. He had been Premier of New Brunswick now for half a dozen years.

When Gordon portentously revealed his project for Maritime union, Tilley inspected it in his usual cool, matter-of-fact fashion. Like most of his contemporaries who thought about the matter at all, he could see that a great nation might some day rise in British North America; but that possibility, like his beloved prohibition, was probably something for the dim future. In the meantime, there were some essential preliminaries: more interprovincial trade and better interprovincial communications were needed. The idea of a British American customs union had an obvious appeal to Tilley; and he had already succeeded Joseph Howe as the principal champion of the Intercolonial Railway. Obviously these schemes served a British North American union better than a merely Maritime union; and Tilley had never shown much interest in a reunited Acadia. But Gordon's incredible news from Prince Edward Island put a different face on the matter; and Tilley assumed that in Nova Scotia, where Tupper was a declared advocate of Maritime union, there must be some support for the project. He agreed with Gordon that here was an opportunity that could be exploited. A few days later Gordon was writing one of his copious confidential dispatches, describing for the Colonial Secretary's benefit the unanimous unionist sentiment in Prince Edward Island and the prospects of success in Nova Scotia, and hopefully announcing his intention of laying the foundation of the union scheme that very summer and autumn.[28]

⇒⇒ III ⇐⇐

IT WAS ON THE 6th of July, 1863, that Gordon wrote his confidential dispatch. The newspapers that day were full of the thrilling details of a terrible battle fought between Federal and Confederate forces at a little place called Gettysburg, some-where in south-eastern Pennsylvania. For days, editors were kept busy printing and interpreting the vivid stream of telegrams, dis-patches, and commentary that flowed in from the United States. For weeks they kept returning at intervals to the absorbing editorial task of speculating upon the battle's probable signifi-cance for the future. To British North Americans, Gettysburg was something more than an exciting spectacle upon soil which, however near, was still foreign. They could not consider it with detachment as an event from whose consequences they were completely isolated. During the last two years, they had been recurrently aware of the possibility that, in various ways – some vaguely sinister, some extremely dangerous – they might become involved in the fortunes of the American Civil War. At times it seemed as if the whole future of British America might be bound up in its outcome.

The *Trent* crisis had been a terribly bad beginning for Anglo-American relations during the Civil War; but even before Captain Wilkes made his seizure they had begun to deteriorate. Great Britain never accorded diplomatic recognition to the Southern Confederacy; but in the spring of 1861, at the beginning of the war, when Lincoln imposed a blockade on Southern ports, the British government issued a proclamation of neutrality, thereby implicitly recognizing the South's belligerency. This, though it was the only possible course, was deeply disconcerting and annoying to the Northerners. The cool detachment of neutrality surprised and hurt them. What they wanted, and expected, was sympathy, approval, moral support, and hearty applause. They felt, as Americans have felt since about every one of their wars, whether 'hot' or 'cold', that they were engaged in a great moral struggle, a majestic conflict over principles in which the future of democracy and liberty were at stake, and in which right and virtue were on their side and evil and injustice on that of their enemies. British neutrality, they suspected, had been conceived in blind, malevolent, anti-Northern prejudice, and would certainly favour the South. They were more than ever confirmed in this opinion when, in the summer of 1862, 'vessel 290' escaped from Laird's dock at Birkenhead, in England, heavily armed itself at sea as a Confederate cruiser, assumed a name soon destined to become notorious, the *Alabama*, and began a spectacular career of destruction on Federal shipping.

British Americans, despite their proximity to the United States, had lived, and were living, their own life. Their political pulses did not beat to the same rhythm as those of the Americans; their political ideas were based on different principles and shaped by different experience. The Northern conception of the war as a great crusade for democracy and humanity never really won their acceptance; they tended rather to think of it as an ordinary struggle for power, with faults as well as virtues on both sides. At first they were puzzled and disillusioned by Lincoln's insistence that the war was being fought, not to end slavery, but to preserve the Union. When, fifteen months later, the Emancipation Proclamation finally did appear, it was frequently criticized as a political action, unprincipled and hypocritical, which would likely end in a race war.[29] The terrible slaughter, the corruption, the sudden wealth, and the presidential despotism which, as the war went drearily on, seemed to be among its most distinguishing marks, disturbed or repelled British Americans. Some, who were interested in grand continental strategy, saw in the break-up of the Union and the establishment of a new balance of power in the North American continent the best promise of the future greatness of British America.[30] Many more were impressed not so much by the opportunities as by the terrible dangers of a continent in dissolution. The Northern press, led by the New York *Herald*, began early and continued intermittently to threaten retaliation on the provinces for their own sins and those of the Motherland. Dislike of American resentment against Great Britain, fear of often-asserted American continental ambitions, fear that both these powerful urges would in the end express

themselves in the invasion and conquest of British America –
these were deep-seated feelings that nourished a quiet, persistent
hostility to the Northern cause.

By the summer of 1863, when Lee started north on his invasion
of Pennsylvania, anti-Northern feeling in British America was
fairly strong and widespread. A few important newspapers –
the *Globe* in Toronto, the *Herald* and *Le Pays* of Montreal, the
Morning Freeman in Saint John – upheld the Federal cause; but
most of the urban dailies and tri-weeklies, whether Liberal or
Conservative in politics, favoured the South. When the news of
Lee's northward movement arrived, editors looked forward to its
probable consequences with eager and confident expectation.
The invasion, the Montreal *Gazette* assured its readers, was no
mere raid.³¹ 'The North may very well shake and quiver,' reflected
the Toronto *Leader* complacently.³² Even the excited and triumphant telegrams announcing a Northern victory, which soon
began to arrive, did not disturb this confidence too seriously.
The news from the South puzzled and disappointed the British
Americans; but newspaper editors offered ready explanations
that minimized the importance of the battle and depreciated
Federal success. The reports from the battlefield were conflicting,
bewildering; it was impossible to tell exactly what had happened;³³ and one could be certain that the vainglorious Northern
newspapers had grotesquely exaggerated the results. 'The Yankee
press has such a monstrous talent for lying', the Halifax *British
Colonist* remarked, 'that it would be gross folly to believe, in all
its minutiae, anything which it publishes.'³⁴ Lee, it was conceded
grudgingly, had possibly experienced a repulse; but a repulse
was far from being a decisive defeat; and even the *Globe* agreed
with the other newspapers that Northern commanders showed
a singular inability to exploit their successes to the full.³⁵ The
war, a succession of bloody and inconclusive battles, would go
on; '... and the repulse of General Lee is neither the annihilation
of the Southern Confederacy, nor significant of such an even-
tuality.'³⁶

Yet a slight but perceptible shift in public opinion had taken
place. Up to that point, the general assumption – almost the
general conviction – had been that the South was bound to win

the war. Now, for the first time, there appeared at least the possibility that in the end it might lose. 'The retreat of Lee,' reflected the *Globe*, 'the capture of Vicksburg, the idea that the great rebel army of the Potomac may be thoroughly scattered and destroyed and the war ended at a single stroke, will give immense vigour to the Northern forces.'[37] This optimistic opinion that the war might be brought to a sudden close found very few believers. The Montreal *Gazette* implied that it might conceivably end in the conquest of the Confederacy; but it insisted that the road to Northern victory would be extremely long and difficult.[38] By the autumn, the Saint John *Morning News* was reassuring its readers that 'the conquest of the South appears to be as far distant as ever'.[39] The British American sense of security, now partly resting upon a belief in the Confederacy's capacity for resistance and survival, was disturbed but not seriously unsettled. The concern for defence, which had troubled British America ever since the *Trent* crisis, was renewed, rather than greatly increased. New Brunswick, in the legislative session of 1863, had already trebled its small appropriation for defence; and in the autumn, Canada, responding at length to the urgings of its Governor General, Lord Monck, passed measures reorganizing the militia, establishing military schools, and increasing the volunteer force to a total of thirty-five thousand men.

Defence had been slightly improved. But apart from this there were few signs of any great intensification of the existing concern for the future of British North America. The Intercolonial Railway scheme rested in suspense. There were as yet no rivals for Gordon's plan of a Maritime union.

⫸⫸⫸ IV ⫷⫷⫷

THE NEXT FEW WEEKS were among the happiest that Gordon ever spent in New Brunswick. Life had suddenly acquired a new meaning. His position as Governor, which he so often complained was empty, trivial, and degrading, had for the first time taken on a real importance. He dropped his request for transference to a sub-tropical Crown colony; he waived his right to a

leave of absence in the autumn of 1863. 'This move', he wrote
to Newcastle, referring to the campaign for Maritime union,
'rather changes my wishes as to my own removal for I should
certainly like to carry through the measure after having set it
going.'[40] 'I have given up the idea of coming home this autumn,'
he wrote, several weeks later. 'The union scheme, if it is to come
to anything, will require much management, and I cannot risk
its failure by absence.'[41] For the first time he was occupied and
busy, and radiantly happy in his busyness. It seemed to him that
he was more popular and more powerful in the province than he
had ever been before. His authority, which he knew was indirect,
could only be exercised through others, and might 'collapse with
a grand crash' at any moment, had been accepted by his advisers
in a matter of the highest political importance. He drafted plans
for the union and was full of hope that it might be carried out
in the winter of 1863-4.[42] He saw himself, prominent, active, and
influential, as the first governor of Acadia. 'You may think', he
wrote to the Colonial Secretary, 'I have written too much as if I
were the Governor of the new Province. Of course, as, if effected,
it will be very much my work, I should not think it an unnatural
appointment. . . .'[43]

At the Colonial Office, Gordon's copious confidential dispatches made a very favourable impression on the Minister and
his subordinates. If Gordon's reports were approximately
accurate, then the youngest governor had certainly discovered
a genuine popular movement, hitherto mysteriously hidden, but
apparently powerful, in favour of Maritime union. It was a
cardinal principle of mid-Victorian British colonial policy – a
principle to which Newcastle himself heartily subscribed – that
the initiative in all important internal changes in the colonies
must lie with the colonists themselves. 'I am very glad to see',
Newcastle wrote in a minute on Gordon's dispatch of the 6th of
July, 'that this important question is being taken up seriously
by the people themselves.' His preferred order of priorities, he
realized, would have to be changed. Since the Intercolonial
Railway scheme seemed now so full of difficulties, and Maritime
union had such excellent prospects of success, legislative union
must precede, not follow, the construction of the railway. A

CHARLES TUPPER
Nova Scotia

SIR RICHARD
GRAVES MACDONNELL
*Lieutenant-Governor
of Nova Scotia*

Government House, Halifax

Provincial Buildings, Halifax

JONATHAN MCCULLY
Nova Scotia

JOSEPH HOWE
Nova Scotia

cautious endorsement of Gordon's scheme was certainly in order. 'I shall be glad to learn', Newcastle formally replied on the 31st of July, 'that you have taken all prudent means, without committing the home government beforehand, to bring about a proposal from the Lower Provinces for a legislative union.'[44]

Gordon was delighted. He now had the blessing of the Colonial Office and the promised co-operation of Prince Edward Island. All that he lacked was the assurance of the support he and Tilley expected from Nova Scotia; and this came late in September when Charles Tupper, on his way back to Halifax from Quebec, stopped off for a few hours in Saint John, and he and Gordon and Tilley talked over the Maritime union project. Tupper, who was Provincial Secretary and effective Premier of the new Conservative government at Halifax, wore his usual positive air of well-being, assurance, and decision. At forty-two he was still a relatively young man, personable enough in appearance, with a round, youthful countenance, good, well-formed features, and luxuriant dark hair and beard. His forcefulness, his vehemence, his unshaken confidence and determination, had their ultimate source in a powerful frame, robust good health, and a literally inexhaustible physical vitality. Years before, when he was still a youth in his 'teens, sailing for the first time across the Atlantic to attend medical school at Edinburgh, he had taken on the tough, insolent mate of the brigantine on which he travelled and had given him a terrific mauling.[45] There was always something of the pugilist in politics about Tupper. In the last general election he had knocked Joseph Howe completely out of the ring of provincial affairs; and he radiated some of the physical exuberance of a successful prize-fighter. He was ready to take on all comers. He knew what he wanted, he had positive opinions on a great variety of subjects, and he could wear down and flatten many an opponent by the sheer shattering force and endless verbosity of his style of argument.

Tupper, in his expansive, aggressive way, was more likely to be immediately attracted to ambitious projects than Tilley. Tupper had already delivered public lectures in support of both Maritime union and general British North American union.[46] In his view, Maritime union was valuable in its own right as well as useful as a preliminary stage in the making of a united British North American nation. He was prepared to be sympathetic when Gordon began to sketch the outlines of his scheme. It was a highly tentative, provisional plan, which simply provided that the first united 'Acadian' legislature was to be an amalgamation of the existing provincial parliaments and left most of the details of the union to this body. The one really concrete recommendation in this hazy outline was clearly inspired by Gordon's dawning realization that unionist sentiment in Prince Edward Island, however unanimous it had seemed to him, might have to be strengthened by some special concession. His first suggestion was that the Island be exempted from taxation for railways which were, of course, all on the mainland. But Tilley and Tupper did not think this proposal very practicable, and they did not believe that the Islanders would look on it as a very powerful inducement. Instead they proposed that the first legislature of the united province should be committed in advance to the purchase of all the outstanding rights of Prince Edward Island's absentee proprietors. And this – a very compelling concession indeed – was duly incorporated in Gordon's plan.[47]

In general, therefore, Tupper found nothing serious to object to in Gordon's plan. On the other hand, he did not particularly like the method the Lieutenant-Governor proposed for carrying it into operation. Gordon's strategy, which sought to avoid the vulgar and obstreperous Maritime assemblies as much as possible, was to arrange a meeting of the three Maritime premiers and to work out in private a preliminary agreement for the union of the provinces. This agreement was then to be presented to the three provincial legislatures in the form of an address to the Queen, praying Her Majesty to establish the desired legislative union by act of the Imperial Parliament. It was an undemocratic plan, which stressed government leadership, cut down debate and public discussion to a minimum, and allowed the widest latitude for viceregal influence. Tupper demurred. Lord Mulgrave, the Lieutenant-Governor of Nova Scotia, had just left the province to return to England; and he had been succeeded, as a temporary 'Administrator', by General Hastings Doyle, the Commander of the Forces. Tupper's relations with Lord

Mulgrave had been none too pleasant, and he had little relish for viceregal influence. He quickly proposed an alternative plan. He suggested that, instead of a small meeting of three premiers, there should be held a fairly large conference, to which each Maritime government, duly authorized by its legislature, would send a small contingent of delegates, chosen both from government and opposition, and from the legislative council as well as the legislative assembly.

Gordon instantly began to feel a marked distaste for Charles Tupper. This was not an unusual experience for the Lieutenant-Governor of New Brunswick when confronted by provincial politicians with ideas of their own; and the main result of his widening acquaintanceship among the public men of British North America was the progressive enlargement of the scope of his disapproval. Tupper, he informed the Colonial Office, was a man possessed of but 'very moderate abilities, considerable obstinacy, and a large share of vanity'. Tupper's scheme of a conference was 'highly objectionable'; it was 'calculated rather to raise fresh difficulties than to smooth down existing ones', he told Tupper firmly.[48] The Nova Scotian Premier apparently listened with becoming deference to the Governor's arguments; and, in the end, Gordon reported, it was agreed that the plan he had originally proposed should be followed. The three premiers – Tilley, Tupper, and Gray of Prince Edward Island – were to meet as soon as possible in private and devise a scheme for a legislative union. Gordon assumed, as a matter of course, that the meeting would take place in Fredericton.

Up to this point – it was now the end of September – the 'movement' for Maritime union had not been a popular movement at all. It had, in fact, been a very private, beneficent conspiracy, hatched by only four plotters – Gordon, Tilley, Tupper, and the Duke of Newcastle. Almost nobody outside this tiny circle had the faintest idea that a plan for a legislative Maritime union was under discussion by the heads of governments. In the newspapers there was no clamour for union, no debate about it, no discussion on it, hardly even a favourable mention of it. This utter silence, and the lack of interest it seemed to suggest, might have continued indefinitely, if it had not been for the shocking and infuriating revelation that broke suddenly over the Maritime Provinces in the early autumn. Late in September, the Canadian government suddenly cleared up the exasperatingly hazy ambiguity in which their Intercolonial Railway policy had lain ever since the previous December. By a Minute of Council of the 18th of September, 1863, the Canadian government announced that the agreement of September 1862 was 'terminated', had been 'abandoned', and that negotiations for a new agreement must start all over again.[49]

The great betrayal, which the Maritimers had been uneasily expecting and dreading, and which they had tried to reassure themselves could not conceivably happen, was now manifest. A great, shrill, mounting chorus of consternation, outrage, and fury arose on every hand. The Maritime newspapers explored the ample but straining limits of the English language in their search for the proper vocabulary of vituperation. They differed only – and not very significantly – in the violence of their verbal onslaught and in the depths of their moral indignation. The Canadians were false, faithless, perfidious, and corrupt political tricksters whose conduct was reprehensible in the most outrageous degree. They had 'resorted to the most despicable subterfuges' and had 'glaringly falsified solemn pledges'.[50] Henceforth no trust whatever could be placed in Canadian assurances. Canada had proved ready and willing to sacrifice 'every principle of honour, manliness, and fair dealing, resort to the most corrupt and dishonourable artifices, injure the public credit, and render the very name of their Province a by-word and a reproach'.[51] 'So gross a breach of faith, so wantonly perpetrated,' one newspaper summed up the indictment, 'it would be difficult to find precedent for in the history of nations.'[52]

Gordon made himself the principal official mouthpiece of Maritime indignation at the great Canadian betrayal. 'Such a disavowal of contractual obligations between independent nations', he wrote acidly to Monck on the 7th of October, 'would, I do not hesitate to say, be probably followed by a suspension of diplomatic relations.'[53] In this letter, which Newcastle thought very regrettable, Gordon expressed, in his usual outspoken fashion, the angry sense of revulsion from Canadians, the bitter feeling of estrangement from Canada, which had suddenly possessed the Maritimers. If this was how Canadians behaved, they wanted nothing to do with them. 'The perfidy of Canada, as manifested in her recent relations with Nova Scotia and New Brunswick, completely severs the incipient sympathy that was rapidly obtaining between her and these continental Provinces.'⁵⁴ Maritime self-respect, if nothing else, required that Nova Scotia and New Brunswick should turn away from Canada 'as from a stranger'. 'All that remains', declared one newspaper vindictively, 'is to leave the Canadians to themselves and the tender mercies of the Northern States . . .'.⁵⁵ 'It is all up,' the Halifax *Morning Chronicle* asserted bluntly, 'and the sooner we of the Lower Provinces begin to think and act for ourselves, independent of Canada, the better.'⁵⁶

The Canadian repudiation of the agreement of 1862 and the bitter sense of alienation from Canada which followed in the Maritime Provinces had a deep but short-lived effect upon Maritime thoughts and plans. All hopes of the immediate construction of the Intercolonial Railway were wrecked. The thought of any association – let alone political union – with Canada left the Maritimers disgusted and angry. And, finally, their resentful feeling of estrangement from Canada provided the strong emotional basis of a new found sense of solidarity among themselves. They drew together out of their revulsion from Canada. 'Now that the union of the British American Colonies, as a group, is no longer a project which men of the present generation can hope to see accomplished,' said the *Morning Chronicle*, 'the next best thing for the Maritime Provinces is that their public men should devote their serious consideration to the practicability of consolidation upon a smaller scale.'⁵⁷ In the weeks that followed, the *Morning Chronicle* made itself the chief advocate of 'consolidation upon a smaller scale', or Maritime union. It supported such a scheme in a series of editorials, concocted a draft constitution for the union, and faithfully reported the opinions of other newspapers on the subject.⁵⁸ Some were indifferent, a few opposed, a number were either interested or favourable; and, in any case, Maritime union as a possible project had received more publicity than it had ever had before.

From Gordon's point of view, the crisis in the relations of Canada and the Maritime Provinces could hardly have come at a more fortunate time. Maritime union had ceased to be a private conspiracy of four people. It had become a public issue, openly discussed and strongly supported. It even showed some not very conclusive signs of becoming a popular movement. The Duke of Newcastle had said how glad he was 'to see that this important question is being taken up seriously by the people themselves'. For the first time, his pleasant assumption bore some relation to the truth.

➤➤➤ V ◄◄◄

WITH ALL THIS encouragement and support, Gordon ought to have found the path of his advance growing smoother and easier. But in fact, to his amazement and disgust, his difficulties, instead of lessening, seemed mysteriously to grow bigger and more numerous. The next stage in the movement towards union was the meeting of the three premiers. Everything in his plan depended upon it; and, in his fond enthusiasm, he had assumed that the only point to be settled about this vital conference was the simple question of a suitable date. Gradually, painfully, he began to realize his mistake. After two months of persistent effort, he had to face the possibility that the invincible parochialism and jealous separatism of the Maritime Provinces might actually prevent their three premiers from agreeing upon a place for the meeting![59] Gordon affected to regard these 'trifling differences' with contempt; he swore that he would not be balked by 'form or punctilio'. But a strong stand required unified and enthusiastic support, and unified and enthusiastic support seemed curiously lacking.

Late in the autumn, long after he had first told Tilley, he finally laid his union scheme before his Executive Council, and discovered that, although no open opposition was likely, there were certainly several ministerial dissenters.[60] From Halifax, General Hastings Doyle reported that his ministers were definitely not 'heart and soul' in the union movement yet.[61] Gordon's gay confidence in quick success began to dwindle; and it was at this point that Newcastle, who had become rather bored with his young Lieutenant-Governor's tiresome mixture of temperament, ambition, and self-esteem, administered a most depressing lecture on the realities of colonial politics. 'As you appear to have changed your mind,' he wrote tartly, 'both as to coming home and as to removal to a warmer climate, under an impression that a union of the Lower Provinces is close at hand and that you would probably succeed to the united government if you remain where you are, I think it is only fair to curb your enthusiasm by pointing out that, so far from you having "set the measure going", it has been constantly agitated for more than ten years, and more than once has appeared quite as near being accomplished as it does now.'[62] Obviously, Newcastle continued with gloomy realism, the process of unification would be a long one, and by the time it was over he himself would probably be out of office and the governorship would be the gift of someone else.

In December, when Gordon's enthusiasm was already sinking and Maritime union was running into all kinds of apathy and obstruction, an event occurred that drove it out of men's minds completely. Early on the afternoon of Saturday, the 17th of December, the astonished Haligonians observed two Federal American men-of war entering Halifax harbour, and along with them, in tow, another, an apparently captured vessel. This was the passenger steamer *Chesapeake* which had been accustomed to ply the coastal run between Portland and New York, and which ten days before had been captured by a group of Confederates, or Confederate sympathizers, including a number of British Americans. Colonel John C. Braine and Vernon Locke, who led the group, had acquired a letter of marque from the government at Richmond and they planned to turn the *Chesapeake* into a Confederate privateer, with the ambition of preying upon Northern commerce.[63] Inexperienced in navigation and continually short of coal, the 'pirates' failed to make a clean escape, and the *Chesapeake* was hunted down and captured by American warships in British American waters, at Sambro harbour, close to Halifax. Now she lay at anchor, guarded by the Federal gunboats, in full view of the city; and for three hours Captain A. G. Clary of the U.S.S. *Dacotah* gave the provincial authorities no explanation of the presence of these strange vessels in their waters. Finally, when a messenger had been sent to make inquiries, Clary reported that his ships were the *Dacotah* and the *Ella and Annie,* and that he had put into Halifax harbour to deliver the captured steamer *Chesapeake* to the provincial officers before going on to Portland. He told the truth, and nothing but the truth, in this first report. He did not, however, tell the whole truth. The whole truth was that the Americans had also captured three Nova Scotians, including George Wade, one of the 'pirates', and held them in irons aboard ship. Doyle and Tupper were annoyed at this concealment of the truth, and even more annoyed at the 'flagrant violation of neutral rights' which the Americans had committed in making prisoners of the three Nova Scotians inside British American territorial waters. They demanded the 'unconditional surrender' of both the *Chesapeake* and the prisoners.[64]

'Suppose,' General Hastings Doyle is alleged to have asked, 'suppose he [Clary] refuses and attempts to leave the port with Wade on board.'

'In that case,' Tupper replied, 'you must sink his vessel from the batteries.'[65]

For about an hour on Sunday, the 18th of December, Doyle, Tupper, and the cabinet waited in tense unease; but Clary's reply, promising to deliver both the steamer and the prisoners the next day, ended their anxious uncertainty. It was arranged that Wade, because of his illegal arrest, was to be formally discharged by the provincial officer, as soon as he had been delivered by the Americans; but a police constable, with a warrant authorized by Doyle and the Mayor of Halifax, was waiting on the dock to rearrest him for piracy. The Queen's Wharf was crowded – crowded with Haligonian friends of the Confederacy; and, as the *British Colonist* had remarked six months before, just after the battle of Gettysburg, 'it is needless to deny that nearly everybody in this community comes under that description'.[66] Swiftly, unexpectedly, in the brief moment of his liberation, Wade jumped into a small boat that was lying in readiness beside the wharf, the two fishermen at its oars pulled away with frantic speed, the police constable was prevented by Southern sympathizers from firing his pistol, and Wade made good his escape.[67]

For nearly three months, the *Chesapeake* affair and the trials that grew out of it continued to interest and excite the Nova Scotians and the New Brunswickers. The Haligonians who had helped Wade to escape from the Queen's Wharf were let off with mild reprimands and their leader with a small fine.[68] Colonel Braine and some of his comrades were arrested in Saint John and charged with piracy and murder; but the decision of the Magistrate's Court, that they be extradited to the United States, was appealed, and John Hamilton Gray, one of the most eloquent of the provincial lawyers, agreed to act as counsel for the prisoners. Before Judge W. J. Ritchie, they produced evidence to show that they were commissioned belligerents, not pirates, and that the capture of the *Chesapeake* had been an act of war.[69] In the end they were discharged; and there could be no doubt that in Saint John, as well as in Halifax, the freeing of the captors of the *Chesapeake*, and of all who had aided and abetted them, was extremely well received.

In popular estimation the *Chesapeake* affair had had a happy ending. The American State Department, even the Northern press, did not make a great deal out of it. But it was a highly dangerous episode none the less. It presented, for the first time in a serious way, what was likely to become a problem of increasing importance for the British Americans; and it also revealed how defective, for one reason or another, were their means of coping with it. As the Civil War went on, as the efforts of the Confederacy to defend itself grew more desperate, Southerners or Southern sympathizers might very well attempt to use British North America as a base to distract the conquering North by means of raids or privateering. The British provinces would likely find it difficult to protect themselves against such compromising plots. Their police and militia were ill equipped to detect and prevent unneutral conspiracies. And – most important of all –

their citizens were not really neutral. Most British Americans were pro-Southern, or, at least, anti-Northern. The North was resentfully aware of this; and since it expected the whole English-speaking world to be identified with its crusade, it refused to accept or tolerate this anti-Northern feeling.

In the meantime, while the Maritimers watched the *Chesapeake* trials in crowded court-rooms, Gordon's darling project, Maritime union, was slipping deeper down the well of public forgetfulness. Circumstances changed distractingly, new proposals were advanced, and the attention and interest of the Maritimers shifted in sympathy. On the one hand, Canada was recovering something of its lost prestige by taking unexpected and energetic action to revive the Intercolonial. On the other hand, many New Brunswickers were forgetting their angry disappointment of last autumn in their rapt absorption in a dazzling new scheme – the extension westward of their provincial railway, called by the pompous name of the European and North American Railway, to the American border and American railway connections. 'Western Extension', which was rapidly acquiring a large following in south-western New Brunswick, was coming into open competition with the Intercolonial Railway; but at this dangerous moment in its history the Intercolonial project was suddenly resuscitated, and by its alleged destroyers, the Canadians themselves. 'Rather than risk the loss of another year,' Monck telegraphed to Gordon on the 19th of February, 'the Canadian government is about to proceed with the survey of the line of the Intercolonial Railway at its sole cost.'[70] Early in March, Sandford Fleming, the Canadian government engineer, arrived at Rimouski and began his toilsome snowshoe journey through the winter forest to the Restigouche.[71] Canada had regained the initiative and was proving her good faith; she was demonstrating the fact that, although she had rejected one Intercolonial agreement, she had not given up the Intercolonial Railway scheme. Halifax newspapers, which only a while ago had been busily denouncing Canada's 'tergiversation', were now commenting favourably on Canadian enterprise. In New Brunswick there was less-favourable comment, and an occasional cynical flick at the Canadian change of heart.[72] Too many New Brunswickers had shifted their gaze from the north, where the Intercolonial Railway would run, to the south-west and the American border. The Intercolonial would serve either a Maritime union or a British American union. Western Extension would strengthen New Brunswick's orientation towards the United States.

As public interest in Maritime union perceptibly waned, Gordon's ardour for his pet project also cooled, though for very different reasons. He felt himself being manoeuvred, forcibly and relentlessly, out of his fancied position of leadership. His own scheme had been wrecked by his incredible failure to convene a meeting of the three premiers. Tupper's plan of a fairly large conference, authorized by the three legislatures, with delegates specially chosen for the purpose, was obviously the device that was certain to be adopted for the discussion of Maritime union. Gordon tried vainly to regain executive initiative by sending a copy of his suggested 'bases' of union to General Doyle for consideration by the Nova Scotian cabinet. He was bluntly informed that all such plans were the proper business of the delegates at the future conference.[73] He raged, with angry futility, against this 'decided encroachment on the province of the executive government'. He predicted furiously that the proposed conference was 'the best means which could be adopted for raising every possible difficulty and putting off to an indefinite period any real decision on the question'.[74] It was all quite useless. His scheme had been taken over – quite definitely for the worse – by these grubby Maritime politicians and he had lost the power to influence events. Four months ago, he had given up his leave of absence on the ground that the union scheme would 'require much management'. How much 'management' would he be permitted to give it now? As early as the 18th of January, 1864, he wrote to the Colonial Secretary, renewing his request for leave, and announcing that he hoped to sail for England by the middle of April.[75]

⇒⇒ VI ⇐⇐

GORDON, the 'author' of Maritime union, had grown resentfully depressed about the prospects of his scheme. The public attitude to the project had definitely changed. No large body of Nova Scotians were watching with eager expectation when, on the 28th of March, Tupper moved in the Assembly for power to appoint not more than five delegates to confer with representatives from New Brunswick and Prince Edward Island 'for the purpose of arranging a preliminary plan for the union of the three provinces under one government and legislature'. This resolution, which assumed the desirability of union and simply provided for its planning, went about as far as it was possible to go; but, despite this, or perhaps because of it, the motion was not regarded as a party measure. It did not arouse much opposition; but it failed equally to awaken much enthusiasm, or even much interest. Tupper, in his speech, supported Maritime union partly for its own sake and partly as a significant step towards a general British North American union, which he held out as the ultimate goal, but which at the moment he considered unattainable. A fair number of the speakers who took part in the Assembly debate followed Tupper's lead. They declared frankly that they would have been much better pleased with a proposal for a general union. Without enthusiasm, they added that they would accept a single Maritime legislature as a step in the right direction.[76]

On the 9th of April, less than a fortnight after the Nova Scotian legislature had authorized the appointment of delegates, the same subject was brought up at Fredericton. Gordon had hoped that a resolution couched in identical terms would be submitted in the three provincial parliaments; but, to his chagrin and annoyance, it was his own province that first got out of step. The motion submitted by Tilley simply empowered the Executive to appoint delegates 'for the purpose of considering the subject of the union of the three provinces under one government and legislature'. This studiously non-committal resolution was supported, as a non-party measure, by Colonel J. H. Gray – the slightly younger namesake of the Premier of Prince

Edward Island – who had defended the *Chesapeake* 'pirates' in the Saint John trial. In his speech Gray relied chiefly on the uninspiring argument that Maritime union had long engaged public attention and that perhaps it would be a good idea to settle the question one way or the other, it apparently didn't matter which. A. J. Smith, a disaffected 'Smasher' now in opposition, announced that he had no serious objections to the motion, since he did not believe it would 'come to anything'. One member thought the conference would not do much good, another believed it could not do much harm; but, although Tilley's attitude was lukewarm, and only one speaker was a convinced Maritime-unionist, the resolution passed the Assembly and subsequently the Legislative Council. The New Brunswickers were detached and sceptical; but they had just enough interest in Maritime union to be willing to make the slight effort of holding a conference about it.[77]

Even this small risk seemed almost more than Prince Edward Island was ready to take. The debate in the Island Assembly, which took place on the 18th of April, revealed the most determined and uncompromising opposition to the very idea of Maritime union. The irony of Gordon's preposterous assumption that the leading men of the Island were 'heartily in favour' of union was now revealed in all its mockery. The government itself would go no further than to propose the appointment of delegates 'for the purpose of discussing the expediency of a union of the three provinces'; and the Premier, J. H. Gray, justified this limited objective in a rambling, half-hearted, and equivocal speech. 'This', he declared, 'is as far as I deem to be prudent for us to proceed at the present.'[78] It was certainly not very far; but it was further than a good many Assemblymen had the slightest desire of going. The Provincial Secretary, W. H. Pope, who had definitely become a unionist now, analysed the various benefits of a united Acadia, though he would clearly have preferred a general British American union.[79] Another daring speaker showed dissatisfaction with Prince Edward Island's 'paltry' separate existence, and hoped for a more spacious future. There were only a few faint signs of a wider outlook; and they were quickly swallowed up and lost in the Assembly's prevailing mood of parochial complacency and suspicion.

A long line of speakers rose to insist that legislative union would bring many important disadvantages, without any compensating advantages whatever, for Prince Edward Island. On the one hand, they were absolutely certain that union would not aid defence, lessen religious strife, settle the land problem, or bring in new capital for economic growth. On the other hand, they were equally sure that it would saddle the Island with the heavy debts of the mainland provinces, commit it to the support of expensive mainland public works, increase taxation, and give the province a totally inadequate representation in the united legislature. The difficulty of getting across the Strait of Northumberland in winter-time – of leaping 'from ice-berg to ice-berg' – was repeatedly advanced as a serious objection to union, not because it would prevent Bluenoses and New Brunswickers from getting to the Island, but because it would impede Islanders in crossing to the mainland. The union conference would not be regarded as too objectionable if it were held at Charlottetown. Even union itself might be considered, provided the Island were given the same representation in the united legislature as either of its far more populous sister provinces, and provided also that Summerside or Charlottetown were made the capital of the union. 'If the Provinces of Nova Scotia and New Brunswick were to be annexed to Prince Edward Island,' Colonel Gray summed up the general feeling, 'great benefits might result to our people; but if this Colony were to be annexed to these Provinces, the opposite might be the effect.'[80]

In the end, the Premier's motion was carried, but – in sharp contrast with procedure in the other provinces – as a party measure and after a division. George Coles, the leader of the opposition, failing sadly to play the role of ardent unionist for which Gordon had confidently cast him, spoke for an opposition amendment to defer the whole matter. Since, he argued, the debate had clearly shown the complete absence of any real support for the project, the appointment of delegates would be 'bogus'.[81] Gray, roused by Coles's taunting accusation of disbelief in his own proposal, tried to clarify his position in a second speech, and wrapped his support up in the same impossible conditions. Those who voted for the motion did so because it had now become a party question, and because they thought it would be offensively rude to refuse out of hand a mere invitation to attend a conference. The plea of 'common courtesy' helped to carry Gray's motion. And in the Legislative Council, after what Attorney General Edward Palmer described as a 'dull and languid' debate, the resolution also carried, though by a smaller majority.[82]

It was done. A conference on Maritime union could now legally be held. But the manner of its authorization did not promise very much. It had been strongly resisted in one province, and accepted without any enthusiasm and with a good deal of sceptical indifference in the other two. If the conference itself had been made possible in this half-hearted, unenthusiastic, and mutinous fashion, what hope was there that it would ever establish a union? The omens were certainly not very favourable; but, on the other hand, the three provinces had actually got so far as to agree – which they had never done before – to hold a meeting to discuss the subject. Governor Gordon, still diplomatically hopeful, put the best possible face upon the matter. He told the New Brunswick legislature that he had learned with 'much pleasure' of its decision to take part in the proposed conference. He wrote to Doyle and Dundas 'venturing' to suggest that the conference should be held towards the end of July or the beginning of August.[83] Then, having only begun to make preparations, and tacitly giving up any idea of 'management', he set out on the 12th of April for his leave of absence in England. He was, in fact, in such a hurry to get away that he sailed before the final day of the legislative session. A little muddle of untied ends remained behind him. He had failed to name the five New Brunswick delegates to the approaching conference. Both the place and the date of the meeting were still undecided.

During the whole of May and June, this state of completely suspended activity continued. The Maritime Provinces were now governed by the uncommunicative Dundas at Charlottetown, and by two mere administrators, General Doyle at Halifax, and Colonel J. A. Cole, the officer commanding the imperial forces in New Brunswick, at Fredericton. The administrators

were stop-gap appointees who naturally assumed that it was not
their business to start anything important; and Dundas was
temperamentally disinclined to take the initiative at any time.
Early in May, after his Legislative Council had finished its debate on union, he replied to Gordon's letter suggesting a time
for the conference. There was no objection, he reported, to late
July or early August as a suitable time; but he then added an
ominous qualification. 'This will, however,' he hinted darkly,
'in a measure depend upon the place decided upon for the
meeting of the delegates.'[84] It was fairly obvious what was happening. The Executive Council of Prince Edward Island was
making its second move in the popular game of insisting upon
the centrality of the Island in the whole project of Maritime
union. In effect, Colonel Gray and his colleagues were threatening that if the conference was not held at Charlottetown, Prince
Edward Island might not take part in it.

Either Colonel Cole did not trouble to read between the lines
of this letter, or, if he saw its implications, he decided that it was
not up to him to do anything about the matter. He did not reply
to Dundas's letter. May had gone by. June was rapidly going;
and it was not until the 22nd of June – a date which the Canadians were to think memorable for quite a different reason –
that the new Lieutenant-Governor of Nova Scotia finally arrived
in Halifax. He was Sir Richard Graves MacDonnell, Knight
Bachelor, a fifty-year-old professional colonial administrator,
with a hooked nose, a ruddy complexion, plentiful side-whiskers,
an air of experience and assurance, and a sardonic gleam in his
eye. Mulgrave had thought highly enough of MacDonnell to
recommend him as his successor; but Doyle, an anglicized Irishman who enjoyed a bit of slightly malicious gossip at the expense of his fellow countryman, set down the man who had
dethroned him rather severely as a middle-class snob. Mac-
Donnell, he reported chattily to Gordon, had had the bad taste
to be born the son of a poor Irish clergyman with a large family.
The poor clergyman subsequently became Provost of Trinity
College, Dublin, and improved his social standing in the process; and young Richard, who had passed his boyhood in genteel

Anglican squalor, grew to manhood in what Doyle described as 'the worst school in the world, viz., second-rate Dublin snobs'. MacDonnell, Doyle considered, was '*au fond* a charlatan'; but he admitted that he possessed 'a good deal of the off-hand cleverness of my countrymen'.[85]

It was a rather severe judgment. MacDonnell had a quick, critical mind and a sharp tongue. For the past twenty years he had been travelling around the British imperial circuit, and he had held a variety of senior administrative posts in Africa, the West Indies, and Australia. His travels had given him a large fund of knowledge and experience, a slightly bored, slightly cynical attitude to most things except colonial governors in general and himself in particular, and a strong conviction that the British colonial service ought to be, above all else, a satisfactory career for its members. He expected to make his influence felt in the discussions in the Nova Scotian Executive Council, and later he was to speak his mind freely in public about the iniquitous 'spoils system' which both political parties practised in their administrative appointments. He had come to Nova Scotia with instructions to forward the cause of Maritime union; but it was a cardinal principle of the colonial service, to which Mac-Donnell heartily subscribed, that a governor – particularly a governor newly installed in office – should almost never do anything in a hurry. For over a fortnight, MacDonnell did nothing about Maritime union.

Then, on the 9th of July, he received a curious letter from Viscount Monck, Governor General of Canada. Monck wrote to inform him that the Canadian government wished to send a delegation of its own to the conference which Nova Scotia, New Brunswick, and Prince Edward Island proposed to hold. 'The object of the Canadian government', Monck explained, 'is to ascertain whether the proposed union may not be made to embrace the whole of the British North American Provinces.' He hoped that his self-invited Canadians would be welcome; and he politely asked to be informed of the place and date which had been fixed for the meeting.[86]

MacDonnell considered the letter. It was a curious, unexpected request. This new delegation might prove an embarrassment to the Maritime conference. What were these unpredictable Canadians up to now?

CHAPTER TWO

The Astonishing Agreement

THE LETTER that Monck wrote to MacDonnell was the first great result of a major crisis in Canadian politics. On the 30th of June, the very day on which the letter was sent, the three Reform members in a new coalition government – the 'Great Coalition' – had been sworn in at Quebec; and it was this coalition that had invited itself to the conference on Maritime union in order to submit to the Maritimers the very different proposal of a general British North American confederation. In Canada – a province long ridden by venomous and relentless party politics – the making of a coalition government was in itself an astounding occurrence. A coalition government which declared its intention of proposing a radical change in the political organization of British America was an even more startling phenomenon. The two together constituted such a violent departure from the order of nature in Canadian public affairs as to seem either monstrous or miraculous. Some Canadians were doubtful, a few were annoyed, many were pleased, and a good number were uplifted with hope for the future as they had never been before. In some respects their views of the strange event differed widely; yet their most profound impression was common to all. They were surprised, puzzled, bewildered. What did the Coalition portend? How had it come into being? The whole prodigious affair was baffling in the extreme. But the most incredible part of it was undoubtedly the unaccountable conduct of George Brown.

In 1864 George Brown was forty-five years of age. He had first been elected to the Canadian Assembly in 1851; and his first ten

39

years in parliament had made him perhaps the most famous, if not the most notorious, man in Canadian public life. A great, tall, raw-boned, red-haired man, with a frame of apparently great strength and superabundant vitality, a set of passionate convictions on a wide variety of subjects, a large capacity for moral indignation and critical invective, and a gift for vehement and indiscreet utterance, he had stamped the impress of his powerful personality upon the consciousness of Canadians more deeply and ineffaceably than perhaps any other Canadian public man of his generation. For ten years, he had been the flaming evangelist of Upper Canadian sectionalism – the fearless defender of the rights, and the uncompromising avenger of the wrongs, of Canada West. For French-speaking, Roman Catholic Canada East, he had become the living embodiment of Protestant bigotry and fanaticism; for Conservatives of both Canada East and Canada West, he had grown to be the most formidable and dreaded of their critics and accusers. In parliament and in his extremely popular newspaper, the Toronto *Globe*, he had attacked the Tory party, not only for its reliance on French-Canadian votes and its subservience to Lower Canadian pressures, but also – in a sweepingly comprehensive denunciation – because of its corruption, its injustice, and its flagrant violation of the constitution. Finally, to cap it all, he had quarrelled so violently on a personal matter with John A. Macdonald, the Conservative leader of Canada West, that they had completely ceased to speak to each other. Yet it was this man – this apparent personification of party politics and sectional hatreds – who had taken the initiative in forming a coalition government with the very men he had never ceased to denounce as criminals. What had happened? Had he proved himself a betrayer of his principles and a traitor to his party? Was he – as some Conservatives affected to assume – simply a repentant sinner who had finally found his way to salvation? Or was he really rising to the stature of a great statesman who, flinging aside partisan politics and personal dislikes, was about to become the saviour of his country?

Brown had, in fact, performed the greatest act in his political career. But its purposes and meaning were not nearly so mysterious as some Canadians thought or pretended to believe. A change had taken place in Brown; but it had been a slow, not a sudden one. He had not been 'born again' in June 1864; but, three years before, a curious metamorphosis of his character had begun.[1] In 1861, almost exactly at the end of the first decade of his public career, its stormy and controversial period ended in his defeat in the general election of that year. A pause succeeded – a significant pause, marked by a sequence of events, some only accidentally linked, which together seemed to suggest that Brown's course had veered in a new direction. After his defeat at the polls, he became seriously ill, endured a long and depressing convalescence, returned for the first time, after an exile of a quarter-century, to pay a visit to England and his native Scotland, met Thomas Nelson, an old school friend, in the streets of London, and accepted an invitation to spend a few days in the Nelson home, Abden House, in Edinburgh. There he met Anne Nelson, Thomas Nelson's sister, an extremely attractive, intelligent, and cultivated young woman, who had the bookish interests of the publishing family to which she belonged and who had travelled widely in Europe. Up to that moment, the three great enthusiasms of Brown's bachelor existence had been the *Globe* newspaper, of which he was the proprietor, the Free Church of Scotland in Canada, and Canadian – particularly Upper Canadian – politics. Now he fell suddenly and deeply in love with Anne.

The metamorphosis of George Brown had reached its final and astounding stage. The earlier phases had been inconspicuous and preparatory. Now the transformation was revealed in all its completeness. In October 1862, Brown's brief, eager courtship ended in the announcement of his engagement to Anne. In November they were married. Before the year was out, the middle-aged but ardent husband had brought his bride back to Toronto; and there, in January 1864, their first child, Margaret, was born. George's thoughts, his plans, his hopes, his apprehensions – every mental and physical activity of his being – seemed focused, in complete obsession, upon this small, adorable private world that had been miraculously created for him. Anne's letters, the photographs she had had taken of herself and baby 'Maggie', the holiday they planned to spend together in Scotland in the summer of 1864, the new house Brown was buying on Wellington Street, and the carpets, wallpapers, curtains, and furniture with which he hoped to make it delightful for his little family – these were the subjects that filled his mind to the exclusion of almost everything else. He was conscious – joyously conscious – of his obsession. He freely acknowledged his insatiable hunger for his new home life, and the infinite happiness that the presence of his wife and daughter brought him. 'If you only knew', he wrote to Anne, 'how greedily I read all you tell me about yourself and little Maggie, you would not grudge giving me an account of all your daily doings.'[2]

Yet Brown had taken a step – an important step – that seriously belied the completeness of his contented absorption in his new domestic existence. After two years' absence from the Canadian legislature, he had gone back to parliamentary life. Elected for the constituency of South Oxford in the by-election of March 1863, he had repeated this easy triumph in the general election of the following summer. An inner compulsion – strong and perhaps irresistible – had driven him back to Canadian politics. It was impossible for him to extinguish completely and for ever an interest that had burned so ardently and consumed so much of his energy for so long a time. But the unobtrusive and unprovocative Brown who sat in the eighth parliament was obviously a very different man from the aggressive and uncompromising leader who had dominated the Reform party in the 1850s. 'I find a wonderful change in my feelings about all this since the olden time,' he confided to Anne at the beginning of his first election campaign in South Oxford.[3]

In the Assembly, both his position and his attitude to it had altered. The great Brown who had once been invited to form a provincial government was not now even a junior member of the ministry. The flaming partisan of yesteryear found himself looking on with a cool, critical, occasionally bored and restless feeling of detachment. John Sandfield Macdonald, the Upper Canadian Reform leader and joint premier of the Province of Canada, had never won much of his respect or personal regard; and he was not likely to mourn the downfall of the Sandfield Macdonald–A. A. Dorion government very deeply. Yet it was

not simply that he was critical – or jealous – of the new Reform
leaders, or that he felt discouraged about the present state and
the future prospects of the Reform party. It was rather that he
was tired of the petty partisanship of both parties, and weary of
the miserable intrigues and manoeuvres into which Canadian
politics had degenerated as a result of the failure of the Province
to grapple with the fundamental problem of its political life.

Very often, during the long, dragging weeks of the late winter
and spring of 1864, he was sorely tempted to leave Quebec, re-
join Anne and Maggie, and be quit of Canadian politics for ever.
'I hate this parliamentary work,' he wrote passionately home to
his wife, 'because it keeps me away from you. Twenty times a
day I fancy myself by your side with our baby on your knee. I
put my arm round your neck, and look into your eyes, and kiss
you with my whole heart. And then I think what a fool I am to
be here. And then come thoughts of the country, and public
duty, and the newspaper, and so I give a great grumph, and turn
away from the subject. What I would give to be able to set out
for Toronto this afternoon, never to return! And yet, what
hinders me? Are the reasons sufficient? Ought I not to break
through the meshes and be off?'[4] He could never be sure. Between the irrepressible longing to be back in Toronto with
Anne and the grumbling sense of duty that tied him to the
Assembly at Quebec a confused and indecisive battle was being
waged all the time. In the end, what kept him chained to his
desk in the front row of the government side was an obscure
feeling of obligation, not to his party but to the Province, and
above all to its Upper Canadian division, a stubborn hope that
he might yet be able to do something that would liberate Canada
– and in particular free his own section, Canada West – from the
rigid and paralysing constitutional framework in which she was
imprisoned.

During his whole parliamentary career, he had been notoriously the most trenchant and most persistent of all the critics of
the wretched constitution of the united Province of Canada. In
form, the Province was a unitary state; but he knew that in fact
it was a particularly unworkable and inequitable federal system.
Its division into two sections, Canada West and Canada East,

signified much more than mere administrative convenience.
Canada West was predominantly English-speaking and Protestant; Canada East, French-speaking and Roman Catholic. The
two sections had formerly been the two separate provinces of
Upper Canada and Lower Canada; they were still often called
by their old names; and now in the united Province of Canada
they possessed exactly the same political strength. Despite its
substantially and increasingly larger population, Canada West
still had the same number of members in the provincial Assembly as Canada East; and, in Brown's judgment, this equality of
representation not only inflicted a great wrong on Canada West
but also made effective government virtually impossible in the
Province as a whole. Parity, he was convinced, was a pernicious
weapon that enabled and encouraged each section to fight for its
own economic interests, political prestige, and distinctive institutions and customs. Parity had reduced Canadian politics to a
state of permanent sectional conflict, in which, he felt absolutely
sure, Canada West had been the chief loser and sufferer. The
French Canadians, sticking firmly together in the largest single
bloc, had dominated the Conservative party; and the Conservative party, holding office for most of the last ten years, had
yielded to French-Canadian pressures, accepted French-Canadian
ideas, and extended French-Canadian influence.

The losses and injuries that Canada West had suffered as a
result of sectional parity and French-Canadian domination had
been the major themes of Brown's impassioned harangues during the 1850s. But chronic governmental instability, as well as
continued sectional warfare, was a principal feature of the Canadian system; and by 1864, Brown, like many other people, was
disgusted with the intolerable agitations of Canadian politics.
Parties, though they tried, of course, to appeal to each division
and to attract both French Canadians and English Canadians,
displayed an inveterate tendency to become strong in one section
only to grow weaker in the other; and as a natural result they
had reached, during the last half-dozen years, an apparently permanent state of approximate equality. If the Conservatives had
held office rather longer than their Reform opponents, it was
only by the narrowest of margins. The business of getting in

power and staying in power consumed everybody's time, exhausted everybody's energies, and led absolutely nowhere. For the sake of power – as Brown knew only too well – governments shirked responsibility, avoided action, evaded contentious issues, constantly intrigued for support, and yet ended up, with increasing frequency, in defeat by the smallest handful of votes. Since 1860, there had been two general elections; but they had brought no real improvement. By March 1864, the Reform government headed by Sandfield Macdonald and A. A. Dorion was obviously tottering to its fall.

During the 1850s Brown had tried to reform this maddening state of affairs by winning the party game and gaining a sectional victory for Canada West. Representation by population, the sovereign remedy he had so repeatedly prescribed in the 1850s, would have preserved the united Province and enabled Canada West to dominate it by means of an additional ten to twenty seats. But representation by population, by itself alone, was a revolutionary reform that French Canada would never accept willingly and English Canada could hardly impose by force. He had become aware of this; but the knowledge had not weakened his conviction that, in some fashion or other, this fundamental inequity of the constitution must be righted. Sectional parity was the ultimate source of all the constitutional ills of Canada. Sectional parity must be ended and justice given to the vastly superior numbers of Canada West. His purpose had not changed. His final goal remained exactly the same. Yet his views on ways and means had grown less partisan and dogmatic. He hoped to lift the issue of constitutional reform above party politics and give it its rightful independent status as the most important question in Canadian public life. The best way to begin, he thought, was to persuade the Assembly to set up a fairly large and representative select committee that could undertake for the first time a really thorough and impartial study of the problem.

On Monday, the 14th of March, he rose to defend his motion for the appointment of a select committee of nineteen on constitutional reform.[5] His manner was conciliatory; the wording of his involved and cumbrous resolution was much more adroitly politic than it would have been earlier. He knew that he could count upon the backing of the Upper Canadian Reformers; but the Conservatives were another matter, and, since the basis of his strategy was to gain the approval of the whole House, he tried not unskilfully to win over the opposition.[6] The bulk of his resolution was a long quotation from a letter that three Conservative ministers, A. T. Galt, G. E. Cartier, and John Ross, had written to the Colonial Secretary in 1858 in support of the scheme of British North American federation which the then Conservative government of Canada had sponsored. This quotation, the main theme of which was the evils that flowed from the unreformed Canadian constitution, became the text of the hour-long sermon Brown preached that night to the Assembly. It was an earnest appeal from experience to reason. There were no complaints, tirades, charges, or denunciations. He simply asked the House to agree that a great evil existed for which a remedy must be found.[7] He made no attempt to advocate either of his own particular solutions to the problem – representation by population, or a federal union of Canada East and Canada West. He gave no indication of which remedy he preferred; he would, he said, consider any and all proposals with sympathy and candour. All he tried to do that night was to review, simply but forcibly, the chronic and intolerable difficulties of the present position and to urge the Assembly to seek earnestly for a possible way out.

'I was delivered from my responsibility on the representation question last night,' he wrote to Anne, 'having spoken out my whole mind on the subject.'[8] He had spoken with great seriousness; and he was a little disconcerted by the reception which this revelation of his 'whole mind' received. Like many another party politician turned national statesman, he was slightly discomfited to realize that everybody did not instantly take him as seriously as he took himself. The Conservatives seemed perversely indisposed to distinguish between the new Brown and the old, to recognize the statesmanlike sincerity and impartiality of the new Brown's proposal. They probably regarded the proposed committee as a new but transparently recognizable device for still another tiresome ventilation of the grievances of Canada West. Instead of admitting the importance of the subject and debating Brown's motion on its merits, they fell back on the well-worn party tactic of ridiculing the personal inconsistencies of the mover of the motion. Cartier laughed at Brown for admitting so belatedly his apparent approval of the Conservative federal policy of 1858;[9] John A. Macdonald twitted him for his abandonment of that great single panacea – representation by population.[10] 'John A.', Brown wrote to Anne disgustedly, 'was especially mean and contemptible.'[11] The 'wretched course' the Tories took in the debate disappointed and exasperated him; but he did not give up hope. His resolution did not come to a vote, and the whole subject was simply postponed to another day.

In the meantime, Canadian politics plunged again into one of its favourite specialties, a ministerial crisis. On the 21st of March, after desperate but vain efforts to form a coalition with the Conservatives, the Sandfield Macdonald–A. A. Dorion government resigned. Ten days later, after repeated attempts to arrange a combination with a broader base in the House, the Conservatives, under the nominal leadership of old Sir Etienne Taché, took office once again.[12] The new government, with the veterans John A. Macdonald and George E. Cartier as its obvious principals, was drawn largely from the old Conservative group and had the old Conservative following. It was, in fact, a government very much like its predecessor. It would administer affairs in much the same way, and by the same tiny majorities. And it faced the same fate.

On the same day, the 31st of March, the House adjourned until May.

⇒⋙ II ⋘⇐

O N   T H E   M O R N I N G of the 11th of May, George Brown arrived back in Quebec. It had taken him over two nights and a day to make the train journey from Toronto to the capital.[13] Forty miles east of home a breakdown of the locomotive brought the first long delay, and at Belleville a derailed and smashed freight train blocked the line for hours. He was already a day late when he reached Montreal and started out on the second, exasperatingly circuitous part of his journey. From Montreal, the main line of the Grand Trunk Railway – the old St. Lawrence and Atlantic – ran south-eastward towards its terminus at Portland, in the state of Maine. Passengers for Quebec changed trains at Richmond, in the Eastern Townships, and the Grand Trunk's north-eastern branch line brought them to Lévis, across the river from the capital. Early on the morning of the 11th, Brown stood on the dock at Lévis, waiting for the ferry, and looking over the St. Lawrence at the rock of Quebec. The sheer cliffs, crowned by the Grand Battery, the Citadel, and that severely plain and patently economical building, the temporary house of the legislature, soared up before him.

For most people, the only attraction of Quebec lay in the grandeur of its setting.[14] It was an old, shabby, and neglected town, with narrow, irregular streets paved with worn and broken planks and lined with squat or narrow houses, built often of depressingly grey stone and crowded tightly together.[15] It had rained very heavily just before Brown arrived, and the cab that carried him from the riverside up Mountain Street to the Upper Town laboured through streets that seemed like filthy ditches, choked with a mixture of mud and powdered planks. It was much pleasanter in the Upper Town, for there the houses were newer and more modish and the open squares and still surviving gardens gave the newly-arrived visitor a sense of airy space. But the air that May morning was chill, decidedly colder than it had been in Toronto, and as he drove along Brown noticed to his surprise that dirty dwindling patches of snow still lingered in corners and at the foot of walls.

For Brown, as for most of the Canadian parliamentarians, the first vexatious task after arrival was the search for lodgings. Usually only the ministers of the day leased or bought houses, and most of the members were temporary residents who lived in rooming-houses or hotels. At the beginning of each session there was invariably stiff competition for the most desirable places, with dozens of legislators rushing about from one to another of a few select private establishments or descending upon the town's two possible hotels, the Russell House and the St. Louis.

Brown, a distinctly late arrival, found his two favourites – Mrs. Steele's and Mrs. Langlois's boarding-houses – completely full, and in the end he had to take refuge in a room in the St. Louis Hotel.[16] There, despite the pleasant appearance of balmy spring weather, his depression, restless impatience, and disillusionment with most things political speedily returned. The only thing that gave meaning to his exile from Anne and his imprisonment in this dreary little town was the hope of constitutional reform; and on the 19th of May, when the adjourned debate on his motion for a constitutional committee was resumed, he could not repress his anxiety, or conceal how desperately eager he was for success.

'I feel a very great desire to carry my motion,' he wrote to Anne during the dinner interval in the debate. 'I would give a good large sum to carry it. It would be the first vote ever carried in parliament in favour of constitutional change – and even that would be some satisfaction after my long fight for it.'[17] His own opening speech was deliberately unprovocative.[18] Dreading aroused tempers and acrimonious recriminations, he made no attempt to reply to John A. Macdonald's personal charges; and, to his surprise and delight, the debate continued on the reasoned level on which he had launched it – 'a capital debate', he thought it, 'calm, temperate, and to the point'. The principal government spokesmen, Macdonald, Cartier, and Galt, as well as Reform leaders like Holton and Dorion, voted individually against the resolution; but the government as a whole did not oppose it, and among the parliamentary rank and file there was enough suppressed longing for a better state of things to carry the motion by the unexpected majority of fifty-nine to forty-eight.[19] Brown had got his way and his committee. Next day it met, with eighteen of its twenty-one members present; a sub-committee was appointed to draft a series of propositions for discussion, and they got down to work.[20]

In the meantime, while the committee men gravely considered the problem of the constitution, the new Conservative government was rushing down its short and unspectacular course to disaster. Its estimated majority, as George Brown pointedly reminded the Assembly on the 19th of May, was two; and want-of-confidence motions, always a favourite form of constructive parliamentary activity in the Canadian legislature, were, in this case, as likely as they ever had been to produce results. The government survived the first attempt to overthrow it; but its margin of safety was so narrow that within a short while the opposition was busily preparing for another frontal attack. The state of the House, with its evenly balanced forces, was a constant invitation to rivalry and intrigue. All that was necessary was for one or two members to change sides, and the pleasing spectacle of a defeated ministry would be the inevitable result. 'We have sixty-four and the Speaker,' Brown reported to his wife, 'the Ministry have sixty-four; and Dunkin [a Conservative] is with us in heart but wants the pluck to say so publicly.'[21] With such hopeful prospects of success, the Reform opposition redoubled its efforts; and on Monday, the 13th of June, they decided that they were ready for the test. 'The opposition are talking very confidently today', wrote the correspondent of the Toronto *Leader*, 'of their ability and their intention to defeat the government tomorrow. They say they will receive the votes of two members who have thus far supported the government and that this will give them a majority of one.'[22]

The session, in any case, was drawing to a close; business was being wound up; and, as it happened, George Brown was due to report on the 14th for his constitutional committee. The weather had turned suddenly hot. Only a few days before, Quebec's brief, laggard, but lovely spring had ended in the onrush of a blazing northern summer. The new legislative buildings, planted in a commanding position at the edge of Cape Diamond, lay open to the full glare of the sun; and the Assembly room was oppressively warm when Brown rose to make his report soon after the three o'clock opening on Tuesday, the 14th of June. Without explanations or amplifications – which would have been dangerous at this stage – he presented the committee's findings. The report was brief and very general; but at least it cleared the way for a real settlement of Canada's political difficulties by the simple but conclusive method of removing all the impossible or ineffective proposals that had been cluttering up the discussion of the subject for years. The impracticable remedies – such as the double majority – which were impossible of realization, and the desperate remedies – such as representation by population or dissolution of the union – which would have solved the problem by shattering the province, were both rejected. The committee came down strongly in favour of a federal system, though it made no attempt to decide what kind of federal union should be adopted. 'A strong feeling', Brown's report declared, 'was found to exist among the members of the committee in favour of changes in the direction of a federative system, applied either to Canada alone, or to the whole British North American Provinces, and such progress has been made as to warrant the committee in recommending that the subject be again referred to a committee at the next session of parliament.'[23]

The report ended, Brown sat down, and Galt, the Minister of Finance, rose to move the House into committee of supply. At this point the crisis broke. Antoine Aimé Dorion, the French-Canadian Reform leader, got up to present the expected want-of-confidence amendment. This was the supreme moment of the session; it was also a telling illustration of the petty futility of Canadian politics. Dorion and his friends could find no real cause for dispute in the present policies of the new Conservative government. They had to go back into the past – a long way back, in fact. Dorion's amendment censured the government for a financial transaction which had taken place in 1859, and for which A. T. Galt, as Minister of Finance in the then Conservative administration, was responsible.[24] The transaction, though technically doubtful, was five years old. The government that authorized it had been out of office since May 1862. It was true that John A. Macdonald and Cartier, as well as Galt himself, had been members of that earlier Conservative ministry, and were now in power again. But this was the only link between the past offence and the present government – the rather feeble justification of this much-delayed act of retributive justice.

The ministry, of course, accepted the amendment as a challenge to itself, and the final struggle began.[25] The galleries were crowded and tense. People had come expecting trouble and they were not disappointed. Hour after hour, the angry, futile debate over the five-year-old past went doggedly on. The long June day grew old. The lamps were lit; and with every moment the burden of the heavy, sultry atmosphere in the great room seemed to deepen oppressively. It was not until half past eleven that the vote came. Sixty members voted in favour of Dorion's amendment; fifty-eight voted against it.[26] The government had been defeated by two votes on a want-of-confidence motion. There was a ripple of excitement among the spectators; and a few minutes later, when Macdonald moved adjournment for the day, the motion was carried amid opposition cheers. But members on both sides of the House had been through this experience too often to feel very deeply either the joy of victory or the bitterness of defeat. After only two and a half months, another government had fallen. And in everybody's mind was the question – the question which, from the very frequency of its repetition, had become more painfully difficult to answer – what was to happen next?

Brown thought an answer must be found. In the few moments of excited movement and discussion that followed the adjournment, a great decision was rapidly taking shape in his mind. The coincidence of the ministerial crisis and his committee's report – the confrontation of the chronic disease with its only effective remedy – seemed almost a providential invitation – even a providential command. He had looked forward, but without much interest or enthusiasm, to just such a crisis as had occurred that night. He had assumed that it would be followed by another general election; and a few weeks ago he had informed Anne that he would not again be a candidate and that, with the end of this parliament, he would be free of public life for ever. Yet now he hesitated. Surely the moral of tonight's crisis was plain for everybody to read? Would not the Reformers see that they had just as little chance as the Conservatives of maintaining stable government in the existing Assembly? Could not both parties be brought to realize that another general election would be very unlikely to result in a positive decision, one way or the other? Was it possible to take advantage of this new breakdown of government to form a combination of parties that would be strong enough to undertake constitutional reform?

That night, and the next morning, Brown sought out and

ALBERT JAMES SMITH
New Brunswick

SAMUEL LEONARD TILLEY
New Brunswick

ARTHUR HAMILTON GORDON, *Lieutenant-Governor of New Brunswick* (light suit),
SIR CHARLES HASTINGS DOYLE (at his right), *and* STAFF

Government House, Fredericton

Provincial Buildings, Fredericton

ROBERT DUNCAN WILMOT
New Brunswick

JOHN HAMILTON GRAY
New Brunswick

talked earnestly with two supporters of the beaten Conservative government, J. H. Pope and Alexander Morris.[27] Morris, a minor prophet of British North American union who had written and lectured on the subject years before, was a particularly appropriate confidant. Brown's message was simple but portentous. The crisis, he argued earnestly, ought to be utilized 'in settling for ever the constitutional difficulties between Upper and Lower Canada'. He added that he would be prepared to co-operate with the existing or any other administration that would deal with the question promptly and firmly, with a view to its final settlement. Morris and Pope immediately asked if they might inform John A. Macdonald and Galt of Brown's offer. Brown gave the required permission. He knew, as Pope and Morris went off, that his proposal would at least reach two key members of the defeated Conservative government.

⋙ III ⋘

MEANWHILE, the government had already met and decided upon its first step. It was a conventional, party decision, which disregarded the speculations and tentative approaches of the past few months though the ministers were perfectly aware of them. Ever since the beginning of the new year, there had been more rumours of coalitions and more talk of constitutional reform than there had been for a long time before. In mid-March, before it gave up the struggle and resigned, Sandfield Macdonald's Reform government had tried to effect a union with the Conservatives;[28] and the Conservatives, concentrating particularly upon the somewhat detached and powerful figure of George Brown, had made similar efforts to win Reform support.[29] The work of Brown's committee, in which several Conservative leaders had taken part, had brought up again for consideration all the possible methods of escape from the impasse of Canadian politics; and the defeated ministers, though none of them possessed Brown's single-minded determination to effect reform, were almost as weary as he was with the endless and profitless agitations at Quebec. John A. Macdonald, in particular, felt a growing anxiety to get back to his abandoned legal practice while there was yet time; and for over a year he had been trying to extricate himself from the possessively loyal clutches of his devoted followers and to retire into private life.[30]

Yet all these considerations, if they were examined, were thrust aside for the present. The cabinet decided to follow routine procedure, and to ask for a dissolution and an appeal to the people; and next morning, the 15th of June, Sir Etienne Paschal Taché, the titular head of the government, waited on the Governor General to present his colleagues' collective advice. Taché, a silver-haired veteran of seventy who had emerged from semi-retirement to bring the prolonged ministerial crisis of March to a close, was an urbane and dignified old ambassador; and the cabinet's case for a dissolution – which was later reduced to writing – had at least a plausible appearance.[31] He admitted that last night's adverse vote must be interpreted as implying the withdrawal of the Assembly's confidence in the government; but he pointed out that Dorion's motion was 'in its terms a censure on an administration not now existing for an official act which occurred five years ago'.[32] He and his colleagues, he argued, had been defeated in a factious attack on an administrative misde-meanour of the past; but the Assembly had given them support for all their current measures. The country would surely confirm that support. The ministry could appeal to the country with confidence. There was all the more reason for making such an appeal, since the present parliament had been elected before the defeated ministers had taken office and they had therefore had no chance of going to the people on their record.

Sir Charles Stanley, 4th Viscount Monck, the Governor General of Canada, listened with interest but also with reserve. A large, loosely built, heavily bearded man, deliberate, temper-ate, but tenacious in his mental processes, he was not immediately convinced of the wisdom of his minister's advice. He had been Governor General of Canada since the autumn of 1861; and these years, contentious yet curiously barren of achievement, had taught him a lot about Canadian politics. He was not an original or profound political philosopher; but he had a clear eye for facts and a readiness to learn from experience. His caustic critic

Arthur Gordon had said that he never appeared 'to see anything with his own eyes';[33] and although Monck denied that he had prophesied that he would be the last Governor General of Canada, his views on the future of the British Empire were probably the conventional views of the Little-Englander governing class of his day. On the other hand, as he said himself, his opinions did not include 'getting rid of the colonies against their will or interests' – which, in Canadian circumstances, meant keeping them a very long time indeed;[34] and meanwhile he viewed British North America more accurately, because much more objectively, than Gordon would ever try to do or be capable of doing. To Gordon, who had little direct experience in British affairs, colonial political behaviour fell deplorably short of the lofty standards that were upheld at Westminster. But Monck, who had been a Member of Parliament and knew something of the seamy side of nineteenth-century British politics, dismissed these complacent comparisons in his usual downright, matter-of-fact fashion. He suspected that 'jobs' were frequently perpetrated in Canada; but he reminded Gordon with cheerful realism that it was 'perfectly well understood in the [British] House of Commons that those who support the Ministers in the evening are entitled to favours at the Treasury in the morning'.[35] Of the 'purity' of Canadian elections he did not feel he could speak with so much certainty; 'but', he said flatly, 'I believe it to be quite equal to that which prevails at home, though I am afraid that is not putting it very high'.[36]

Monck's experience made him highly sceptical of fashionable but dubious generalizations about British North American politics. It also enabled him to see where some of the main Canadian troubles really lay. His range was narrow; but he grasped firmly and tenaciously what lay within it. He had reached the conclusion that – whatever might have been true of the past – the two major Canadian political parties were not now divided by any significant differences of opinion on any important public issue. The twelve-month history of the eighth parliament, with its successive Reform and Conservative governments, and its unbroken governmental incapacity, seemed to him to prove his point. 'During this period,' he wrote of the time following the general election of June 1863, 'no question involving any great principle or calculated to prevent politicians on public grounds from acting in concert had been raised in parliament.'[37] The conclusion that followed from these facts seemed simple enough to Monck's practical and straightforward mind; politicians on both sides must be persuaded 'to throw aside personal differences and to unite in the formation of a government strong enough to advance the general interests of the country'.[38] Lord Monck hoped to make that appeal himself – and with success. He saw himself as the inspiration of an effective 'amalgamation of parties'. All he wanted was a chance of carrying out his plan. He thought he had found such an opportunity in the resignation of the Macdonald-Dorion ministry in March; but after more than a week's struggle with the jealous and obstinate partisans of Canadian politics, he had had to admit himself beaten. Now, less than three months later, a second, equally good, chance had been given him.

He wanted very badly to take advantage of it. His Council had just advised a dissolution and a general election. Ultimately, if all other courses of action proved impossible, he could not decline that advice; but to accept it immediately, on Taché's first oral request, would be to throw away his chance. What was needed, by himself and everybody else concerned, was time – time in which party animosities, heated again by the personal accusations of yesterday's debate, would have a chance to cool – time in which the idea of a coalition of parties, tactfully promoted and powerfully aided by himself, could make its appeal to both Reformers and Conservatives. Time was absolutely essential. There must be at least a brief delay. And he saw an easy – and easily defensible – way in which such a respite could be gained. He informed the waiting Taché that he was not prepared to give an immediate answer to his request. He pointed out that a second general election in a single year, with no reasonable assurance of a more decisive result than on the first occasion, was a burden and an expense which did not carry their own justification. He was ready, he said, to consider the proposal on its merits. And, as a preliminary, he asked Taché to put the cabinet's reasons for suggesting the dissolution in writing.

This was the sobering news that the Premier carried back to his colleagues. Early in the afternoon, Council held another session;[39] and a brief paper, setting out the government's case for a general election, was drafted and dispatched to Government House.[40] Then it was three o'clock and time to meet the Assembly. There was no news whatever to communicate. John A. Macdonald, rising in his place in the front row, to the right of Speaker Wallbridge, had only the briefest, barest, and most uninformative message to give the House. He and his colleagues, he announced, considered that their position had been so seriously affected by the adverse vote of the previous evening that they had decided they must communicate with the Governor General.[41] It was a tantalizing fragment of information; and as soon as Macdonald had finished and had moved the adjournment, John S. Macdonald, the Reform leader, was quickly on his feet, protesting against this cavalierly unenlightening message and demanding more information. These were routine opposition tactics and John A. Macdonald was ready with the routine government reply. He reminded Sandfield Macdonald of the executive councillor's oath not to divulge advice until authorized to do so. Then he sat down again. And the episode was apparently over.

Yet it was not, for – somewhat surprisingly – Brown rose to speak. And Brown, who might have been expected to deliver a smashing attack against a secretive and scheming government that was trying desperately to cling to office despite its well-merited rejection by the House last night, was, in actual fact, employing an entirely different kind of language. He said briefly that he supported Sandfield Macdonald's request for information in principle; but he then went on in a fashion that suggested an entirely different attitude to the government's silence and the enforced pause in the business of the House. He felt, he said, 'that in the position of great gravity in which the honourable gentlemen opposite were now placed, they should be allowed every fair opportunity to consider what course they should pursue'.[42] They would surely have to ask themselves whether another general election would bring any useful results – to examine other possible ways out of the political stalemate. He hoped, he said, that they would take the fullest time for this serious consideration.

What was Brown up to? A note of concern – even of sympathetic concern – was unmistakably suggested in his brief comment. What did it mean? Did it imply that Brown was willing to play a separate part, independently of the other Reform leaders, in the present ministerial crisis?

→≫ IV ≪←

FOR JOHN A. MACDONALD, Wednesday, the 15th of June, was a day of shocks and surprises. Pope and Morris related their strange conversations with Brown; and Brown himself, as if in public support of his own private suggestion, had emphasized the government's need of time for the consideration of all possible alternatives to a dissolution. There could be no doubt about the facts or their implications. An extraordinary offer – an offer which might very well change the whole course of Canadian history – had unquestionably been made. Why should not he, Macdonald, explore it? The government had advised the Governor General to dissolve the legislature; but Monck had declined to follow the advice immediately, had asked for the reasons, in writing, for another appeal to the people, and was no doubt now composing a reply to the government's argument. There was time to find out what Brown really intended, and Macdonald's every instinct urged him to take advantage of it. In his own fashion – a fashion less passionate, impulsive, and impatient – he was just as weary of the meaningless gyrations of Canadian politics as was his great rival. He had agreed with the government's recommendation of a general election, but without enthusiasm. For many months he had been trying to be quit of general elections for ever. He was in a particularly restless, receptive, and experimental mood.

He acted swiftly. The next day was Thursday, the 16th of June; and that afternoon, as the three o'clock hour for opening drew closer, the hot and humid Assembly room was again rapidly filling up with people. There, in the middle of the gangway, was the tall, dominating figure of George Brown. Casually, Macdonald edged his way towards him. A word with Brown here, in the crowded Assembly chamber, would be far more likely to pass unnoticed than a formal meeting at Brown's hotel or Macdonald's house. Quietly, swiftly, he explained that Brown's statements to Morris and Pope had been reported to him. Would Brown have any objection to meeting him and Galt and talking the matter over? Brown replied, 'Certainly not'.[43] In a minute, the apparently casual encounter was over. In a minute more, the two men had returned to their places, the Speaker had taken the chair, and the day's brief business began. Later, Morris, the faithful go-between, changed this tentative engagement into a definite appointment. Macdonald and Galt were to call on Brown at his hotel, the St. Louis, at one o'clock on Friday.

The next move was obvious. Without delay, the Taché-Macdonald government met and considered what proposals its two emissaries should make to the incredible George Brown. Nearly four years before, in the summer of 1858, another Conservative government had decided upon a general British North American federation as its policy; and now Taché and his colleagues agreed to stick to this plan. In all probability, they had little difficulty in making up their minds. It was true that the membership of the Taché-Macdonald government of 1864 differed markedly from that of the Cartier-Macdonald government of 1858; but, on the whole, the new ministers strengthened rather than weakened the support for a general federal union. Thomas D'Arcy McGee, the Irish ex-rebel who had become a strong believer in monarchy and parliamentary government, had been preaching British North American union in both Canada and the Maritime Provinces;[44] and although Taché himself had probably not as yet formed any very positive opinions, the Taché connection in general was thought to favour confederation, and Sir Etienne's nephew, J. C. Taché, co-founder with Hector Langevin of *Le Courrier du Canada*, had as early as seven years before written a long series of articles in favour of a general federal union.[45] It was not these new-comers, however, but Macdonald, Cartier, and Galt, the leaders in 1858, and equally the dominant figures in 1864, who really determined

Conservative government policy in those June days. In the minds of Galt and Cartier, the financier and railway magnate and the corporation lawyer, there was no hesitation and no uncertainty at this crucial moment. Only three months before, in the first debate on Brown's motion for a constitutional committee, they had both shown openly and unmistakably that they still clung to the policy of 1858.[46]

Macdonald was the only member of the triumvirate who may have felt some momentary doubts. Like his colleagues, he believed that the only possible federation was a federal union of the whole of British North America. But he saw union chiefly as strength and as expansion; and now he was full of unhappy doubts that expansion by means of federation would never give a transcontinental British American union the strength he craved for it. The American Civil War, now at the beginning of its fourth year, had planted in him a nagging disbelief in the power of federation ever to create a really 'great empire' for the British colonies in North America. While both Cartier and Galt had signed the report of Brown's committee, which recommended a federal solution for Canada's difficulties, Macdonald had declined to put his name to it;[47] and three months earlier, when the Assembly had first debated Brown's proposal, he had frankly argued that, instead of planning for a federal union, British North America should have a legislative union 'in fact, in principle, and in practice'.[48] At these words, Cartier had openly interrupted his colleague. 'That is not my policy', he had declared bluntly; and the House had laughed.[49]

Macdonald's doubts about federalism and his preference for legislative union were real; but they were valid only so long as the question of union stayed in the realm of theory. He was, in all probability, never very much impressed by Brown's committee as a means of achieving constitutional reform. In his opinion, a committee report was an academic exercise which would be recorded – and probably buried – in the *Journals* of the Assembly. But Brown's offer of political support belonged to the far different category of political realities. With its promise of an absolutely omnipotent majority in the legislature, it instantly removed the whole speculative business of British American union to the sphere of action, where rigid theories were out of place, and compromises were essential. Macdonald lived for the action of practical politics; and he knew as well as Cartier, and better than Brown, that practical politics is the art of the possible. Brown's offer spoke to his sure instinct for political diplomacy and management. It roused his vast hopes for a great transcontinental British North America.

On the night of Thursday, the 16th of June – the eve of the incredible interview with Brown – the plan that Macdonald and Galt would propose was clear. What would happen at the conference nobody knew. In a day, the whole political future of Canada might be completely altered. And for the small group of people – less than a score, in all probability – who knew of the visit that Galt and Macdonald intended, the last half of the 16th of June was a strange time, full of suspense, uncertainty, and surmise. The day was stiflingly hot. It was over ninety in the shade that Thursday. And at night – it could hardly have happened more appropriately for the anxiously waiting ministers – there was a reception and ball at Spencer Wood, the Government House that stood a little way out of town, off the Montreal road.

During the morning the ladies of the viceregal household had been making wreaths and garlands of flowers and evergreens for the walls of the ballroom; and – what was less decorative but comfortably practical – the large veranda had been swathed in 180 yards of fine white muslin, carefully tacked to floor and ceiling to keep out the mosquitoes. The legislative councillors and assemblymen of Canada, led by the French Canadians, were enthusiastic, hearty, and indefatigable dancers. The band of the 17th Regiment provided the music; and although the ballroom was warm with the gathered heat of the day, the veranda with its gay lights and muslin protection was deliciously cool for promenades between dances. No ball ever ended very early at Quebec, but finally they were all gone with the exception of two tireless visitors, including, of course, that joyous extrovert, George Cartier. The last dance was a highly energetic, acrobatic affair, in which only gentlemen took part, and Cartier was clearly jumping higher than his companions.[50]

>>> V <<<

I T WAS ABOUT ONE O'CLOCK on Friday when Macdonald and
Galt walked into the St. Louis Hotel and up to Brown's room.
That morning, the Governor General's reply to the cabinet's
request for a dissolution had been finally delivered.[51] Monck had
agreed to accept the government's advice, but he also urged his
ministers, at length, to consider the possible alternative of forming a strong coalition. Macdonald and Galt could feel that they
had the Governor's blessing, as well as Brown's own invitation,
for their talk; but the first few minutes of the interview were stiff
and awkward with remembered hostilities, and, after a few rather
formal preliminaries, they got down to business. They invited
Brown's aid 'in strengthening the administration with a view to
the settlement of the sectional difficulties of Upper and Lower
Canada'.[52] Obviously, this invitation had to be clarified in two
important ways before Brown could accept it and before Macdonald and Galt would be satisfied with his acceptance. How
would Brown and his political friends 'strengthen' the government? What plan would be adopted to 'settle' the sectional
difficulties of Upper and Lower Canada?

Part of Brown was sick of politics. All of him recoiled in hor-
ror from joining openly with political enemies whose crimes he
had been denouncing for a decade. He disliked the thought of
taking office, and much preferred to give independent, outside
support to a Conservative government pledged to reform. But
Macdonald shrewdly suspected that Brown's presence in the
ministry was the only certain guarantee of the loyalty of the
Reformers of Canada West; he wanted a coalition, in which
Brown and one or two other Reform leaders would be ministers.
They argued over this point for some time without reaching any
agreement; and then Brown, who found the problem of Reform
support distasteful and embarrassing, changed the subject and
plunged at once into his own passionate interest, the nature of
the solution of Canada's sectional difficulties. Eagerly he put the
great, leading question to Galt and Macdonald; and Galt and
Macdonald replied promptly that their remedy was a federal
union of the whole of British North America.[53]

Brown shook his head gravely. British North American union would come, he agreed, and come perhaps before very long; but at the moment it was impossible, and the solution of Canada's troubles could not wait. The best remedy, he went on in answer to Macdonald's and Galt's question, was 'parliamentary reform based on population, without regard to a separating line between Upper and Lower Canada'.[54] This was 'representation by population' in its original, harsh, unqualified form. The mere proposal of this notorious solution was a striking illustration of the fact that deep within the new Brown – the public-spirited and magnanimous Brown, reborn of the pangs of tribulation and love – there lurked, unchanged and implacable, the old, unregenerate sectional leader. As his speeches advocating the constitutional committee proved, he saw the Canadian problem chiefly in terms of what he himself called 'the representation question'. His main purpose was to end the inequity of sectional parity; and his first choice was the simple, drastic method he had proposed over ten years before. Now it was Macdonald's and Galt's turn to say no. They said it firmly and decisively. No government could carry 'Rep. by Pop.' against the opposition of Canada East. And this impossibility was so apparent that even Brown's own committee had been forced to recognize it.

The three men sitting in the uninspiring hotel bedroom – Brown intense and passionately serious, Galt stoutish, expansive, bursting with ideas and plans, Macdonald adroit, affable, and unemphatic – had reached the crucial point of their discussion. The period of preliminary manoeuvring for position was over. A compromise must be found. The two Conservatives, not perhaps without a slight feeling of malicious satisfaction, decided to use the Brown committee as a device against its author. Might not this constitutional committee's report offer a possible basis of agreement? In a kind of desperation they began to debate this suggestion; and, after a good deal of discussion, they reached the conclusion that 'a compromise might probably be found in the adoption either of the federal principle for all the British North American Provinces, as the larger question, or for Canada alone . . .'.[55] Politically there was a good deal to be said for this compromise, for it combined the Conservative plan of 1858 with the scheme for a federal union of the Canadas alone, which had been adopted by the Reform Convention in 1859. But, though the two plans were not mutually exclusive, a government would have to start with one or the other. Which was to come first? It was the fundamental problem of policy, and they were still arguing earnestly about it when they realized that it was nearly three o'clock, and that the Assembly was about to meet. They had not finished; but they were pleased and excited by their progress. They were so confident, indeed, that they authorized Macdonald to reveal the fact of the negotiations to the House.

The Assembly had already endured two of the briefest, most baffling, and most unsatisfactory sessions in its existence; but once again the members turned up in full force, and the public galleries were crowded. In his most laconic fashion – the mere facts themselves were eloquent enough – Macdonald announced that the Governor General had that morning agreed to a dissolution of parliament. The ministers, however, he continued, were anxious to avoid an election and to end the province's sectional difficulties, and they had begun discussions with a prominent member of the opposition – the member for South Oxford – in the hope of finding an agreed principle for reform on which a stronger government could be based.[56] Dorion was quickly on his feet, protesting that the ministry was using the threat of dissolution to bully the House into submission to its wishes. Obviously the Reform party was at odds with itself once more, and Dorion and his friends from Canada East would probably oppose any union of parties that might be reached in the next few days. But this did not seriously weaken the tremendous import of Macdonald's news. It could not spoil the dramatic announcement that Brown now rose to make. He was sure, he said, referring to Dorion's charge, that the members would acquit him of any desire to aid the government in coercing the House. Only the pressure of the most extreme circumstances, he declared, could ever have justified negotiations between such old and inveterate opponents as the Conservative ministers and himself. But the circumstances of Canadian politics – the sectional hostility, the feeble governments, the inconclusive elections – were extreme. And at last the pressure for reform had become irresistible.[57]

After a last assurance to the doubtful, Brown sat down. The Speaker rose. There was a great roar of applause; and Dufresne, one of the French-Canadian members, quickly crossed the floor of the House to shake Brown's hand. Then they were all shaking hands. They were crowding about Brown, talking, laughing, cheering, excitedly speculating. Dorion, Holton, and their adherents from Canada East looked mystified and put out. A few Conservatives affected to believe that the negotiations were simply another clever party manoeuvre in the endless game of Canadian politics. 'That cock will never fight,' said one old Tory of the projected coalition. 'It's one of John A.'s *coups*,' cried one Conservative triumphantly. 'We have them in a trap now.'[58] There was astonishment on all faces, doubt and disapproval on a few. But there was something else as well – an unmistakably delighted expression of relief from the burden of the past, of hope for the promise of the future.

→≫ VI ≪←

IT WAS a strenuous week-end, in more ways than one. Brown did not get to bed until well past one o'clock on Friday.[59] On Saturday, there were repeated and prolonged conferences; and that night Lord Monck gave a dinner-party, to which George Brown was invited, and privately – and also somewhat prematurely – described by his host to the members of the viceregal household as a prospective minister. The company sang a French-Canadian, and then a 'Christy' minstrel, song in chorus, with Cartier – that 'funniest of little men', Frances Monck thought him – carrying the solo part of the *chanson* in his high pitched, hearty fashion.[60] On Sunday, the negotiations were officially called off, but Brown's worried sense of obligation and his unhappy state of indecision robbed him of much of his sleep on Sunday night.[61] It was his supreme moment of power and it brought with it his heaviest load of responsibility. He carried the whole burden of the talks for the Reform side, while the ministerial delegation, in the meantime, was being steadily recruited. Cartier, as was only appropriate, joined the discussions on Saturday; Taché, who was away from Quebec for the week-end, took his place at the conference table on Monday. But Brown bore his weight of responsibility alone; and, for a person of his nervous sensibility, the pace and pressure of the negotiations became exhausting in the end.

The two problems – the nature of the political settlement and the form that Brown's support was to take – still confronted them intractably. But by Saturday night the question of policy at least had been determined. Brown, whose driving purpose was to see justice done to Canada West, fought hard to make the federal union of the two Canadas alone the first objective of the new government. The smaller federation was much the easier of the two, and much the more urgent; the inclusion of the Maritime Provinces and the North West Territories could be left to the future. But the Conservative ministers, with the hope and promise of a nation before them, were not content to wait for the future. They told Brown firmly that they declined to waive 'the larger issue' of the general British North American union. In the end, the two projects were combined in one long, awkward sentence of the 'Ministerial Explanations'; but it was also declared that a mission would be sent to seek the consent of the Maritime Provinces; and, in the explanations the ministers gave later to the House, they made it clear that their first attempt would be to create a British American federation.[62] The coming conference on Maritime union, which gave Canada an opportunity of promoting the larger scheme, strengthened the argument of the Conservatives. On the first of the two crucial issues, Brown had to give way.

The second question – perhaps even more formidable in its difficulty – remained. Were the Reformers to join the new government, or were they merely to give it outside support? If they joined, how many places were they to have in the coalition and was Brown himself to accept office? With his whole being, Brown revolted against the thought of joining a new administration; but, on the other hand, he knew very well that there must be guarantees for the satisfaction of Upper Canada, and he realized only too clearly that, for a good many party members, the only satisfactory guarantee would be Reform representation led by himself, in a coalition government. His first proposal, that six of the twelve portfolios in the coalition government should be given to Reformers, was preposterous in the light of Dorion's opposition, and the Conservatives firmly rejected it. His second request, however, for four out of the six Upper Canadian places, was a good deal more reasonable, for well over half the sixty-five Upper Canadian seats in the Assembly were held by Reformers.[63]

Canada West was Macdonald's dominion in the government; and Macdonald determined the government's reply. He refused to concede Brown's request. He was willing, he said, to give half of the six Upper Canadian ministerial posts to the Reformers, but further than that he would not go. He insisted that his followers from Canada West would simply not accept a reduction of the Conservative membership in the cabinet to two; and he made it quite clear that, so long as he remained in the ministry, he would not be content to give up his leadership of the Upper Canadian division. If he stayed, he was determined to keep his senior position; but, at the same time, as he reminded Brown and his colleagues, he had long been anxious to retire, and, with Taché's permission, he would willingly resign, if that would help the arrangements.[64] Yet this was an impossible suggestion. In the government everybody was thinking of, Macdonald was indispensable. If Brown was essential to him, he was equally essential to everybody in the room, including Brown himself.

By the evening of Monday, the 20th of June, the negotiations were over. On Tuesday, the results were submitted to the two party caucuses. The Conservatives gave their approval readily enough. In the Reform caucus there was a strong minority that favoured giving the new government independent support from outside; but the majority believed that direct Reform representation in the cabinet was necessary, and, moreover, was willing to accept, as a minimum, the Conservative offer of three portfolios.[65] On Tuesday evening, when Brown met the government representatives for the penultimate time, he might very well have concluded an agreement; but, in fact, for more than another twelve hours, he continued to fight a stubborn rear-guard engagement, partly because he thought the Conservative offer of three departments ungenerous (the Governor General agreed with him), but mainly because he felt, on his own part, an almost invincible repugnance to taking office. The Conservative spokesmen stubbornly declined to give up the 'principle of equality' in the Upper Canadian division of the cabinet; and they assured Brown, with the utmost earnestness, that his presence in the coalition was a *sine qua non*.[66] The words were still ringing in Brown's ears when he went to bed that night. He knew that he would have to enter the coalition ministry. The pressures within himself, as well as those from outside, were propelling him irresistibly along the hard and difficult path of duty which he dreaded. 'You will see', he wrote a little later to Anne, 'that the meeting [the caucus] passed a resolution urging me to go into the government, but that did not influence me much. Private letters from many quarters did far more. And the extreme urgency of the Governor General did still more. . . . The thing that finally determined me was the fact, ascertained by Mowat and myself, that unless we went in the whole effort for constitutional changes would break down, and the enormous advantage gained by our negotiations would probably be lost.'[67]

Brown's prolonged hesitation and the frantic last-minute composition of the 'Ministerial Explanations' delayed the opening on Wednesday, the 22nd of June. It was four o'clock before the Assembly began its session. Macdonald and Cartier, in English and French, announced the formation of the Coalition and read the long, detailed account of the negotiations of the past five days.[68] Dorion and Holton asked pertinent and embarrassing questions. A sharp little debate developed. Then Brown rose to speak. By now it was five o'clock. Those golden, late-afternoon moments of one of the longest, richest days of the summer of 1864 were, in reality, the last moments of the old familiar existence of the Canadian legislature. And it was fitting that Brown, who by his generous initiative had made the coming revolution possible, should say the last word of explanation and justification. The strain, the doubts, and the painful regrets of the last few days had left him very emotionally disturbed. He was terribly conscious of the political enormity, the monstrous offence – in the eyes of ordinary, party-minded men – of the action he was taking. To many he must have seemed to be betraying his principles, repudiating his political past, breaking the united Reform party in two.

Rather laboriously, he tried to argue that the Reform Convention of 1859 would have accepted the idea of British American federation if it had seemed feasible at the time, and that, in any case, the Coalition was pledged to a federal union of the Canadas.[69] He told the House the painful truth that, at every stage of his negotiations with the Conservatives, he had informed his Lower Canadian friends of what he was doing, and tried, and failed, to win their agreement. Only the desperate political crisis in which the province stood, he declared, could ever have induced him to join with his old enemies and risk the charges of disloyalty from some of his old friends. But sectional animosities had at last made it utterly impossible for the government of the province to be carried on any longer with peace, harmony, and usefulness. '. . . Mr. Speaker,' he cried – and his whole cause lay in the one sentence – 'party alliances are one thing, and the interests of my country are another.'[70]

This was Brown's supreme moment. He had brought about the end of the old order, and the uncertain beginning of the new. Within a week, in as rapid a fashion as possible, the legislature completed its sessional business. On the 30th of June, just after the prorogation, the three new Reform ministers, George Brown, Oliver Mowat, and William McDougall, were sworn into office. On the same day Lord Monck sent off two important communications – one a dispatch to the Colonial Secretary, informing him of the formation of the Coalition government, and the other a letter to the lieutenant-governors or administrators of the Maritime Provinces, asking permission for a delegation from Canada to attend the approaching conference on Maritime union.

From that moment the two projects of British American federation and Maritime union came into open competition with each other.

CHAPTER THREE

First Responses

T HE FORMATION of the Coalition government and the
announcement of its policy of general federation created
an enormous sensation throughout British North America. In his very first meeting with Macdonald and Galt in the
St. Louis Hotel, Brown had predicted that people would be
scandalized by the unseemly spectacle of such mortal enemies as
himself and John A. Macdonald acting together. The storm of
comment that broke after the 22nd of June certainly proved him
right. The mere fact of the existence of the Coalition was in itself
a shock. The policy of British American union, and the acceptance of the 'federal principle' – now deeply suspect after three
years of civil war in the United States – as the means of achieving
it, were equally sensational. In Canada, where the Coalition had
the awful appearance of a political revolution, people had first to
digest and then recover from this affront to their ingrained partisan feelings. In the Maritime Provinces, where Canadian party
politics were regarded mainly with exasperation and disapproval,
it was the policy of the Coalition, its adoption of federalism, that
immediately attracted interest. From every point of view, the
astounding event of the 22nd of June compelled attention and
demanded thought. All over British North America, the hum
of discussion and argument grew gradually louder. The great
debate, which was to last three years and to form the most vital
episode in the intellectual history of British North America,
began to get under way.

In the Maritime Provinces, Monck's letter of the 30th of June
and the news, which soon became public, that the Canadians

wished to attend their conference, had an immediate and remarkable effect. Up to this point, the Maritimers appeared to have completely forgotten Maritime union. Except in Prince Edward Island, where the response had been distinctly hostile, the scheme had aroused neither popular enthusiasm nor dislike. It had, in fact, been received with majestic indifference by the greater part of the population. All during the late spring and early summer, the newspapers had had almost nothing to say about the proposed conference. The politicians had made no preparations for it; the very place and date of the meeting were still undecided. The resolutions authorizing the conference might merely have remained the record of pious intentions; but, unfortunately, the Canadians had seen them, had taken them literally, and for their own purposes had asked to be invited. Clearly, something would have to be done at once. On the 9th of July, the day that Monck's letter had reached Halifax, the executive councils of both Nova Scotia and New Brunswick met hurriedly; and MacDonnell and Cole wrote to the Governor General, assuring him that the Canadians would receive a cordial welcome at the conference, though MacDonnell added the pointed reminder that their participation in it must be entirely unofficial.[1] Dundas of Prince Edward Island, who disliked haste, preferred to act always on advice, and probably could not get his Executive Council together, sent no reply at all as yet.

Obviously, the belated arrangements for the conference would now have to be made. A time and place would have to be decided, and the Maritime delegates nominated, for this British American family gathering. Tupper, though his natural inclination was to retain the Nova Scotian initiative in the project, sensibly realized that it would be best to leave the most difficult of these decisions to the two junior provinces. The end of July – Gordon's proposed date for the conference – was out of the question now, and Gordon himself, somewhat curiously, was still lingering in England. Nobody would object, Tupper assumed, if the meeting were postponed until the 1st of September. The really dangerous question was the place. Tupper had heard from W. H. Pope, the virtually unique Island enthusiast for Maritime union, who was eager to have the conference held in either Nova Scotia or New

Brunswick. But Tupper was not convinced by Pope's well-meant plan of broadening the restricted mental outlook of his fellow Islanders by a junket to the mainland. Edward Palmer, the Island's Attorney General, a declared opponent of Maritime union and a power in the Gray government, had also written to Tupper, giving advice the exact opposite of Pope's. The conference, Palmer had urged, should be held at Charlottetown; and Tupper knew that Governor Dundas significantly agreed with his Attorney General. 'I confess I have a strong impression', he wrote to Tilley, 'that our difficulty is likely to be with the Island and that our presence there would not do any harm.'[2]

It was the danger of Island opposition rather than the risk of Canadian interference that troubled Tupper. His chief, Mac-Donnell, was perturbed by the probable complications resulting from the Canadian visit. The 'wider question' of British American federation seemed premature to him, and he believed that the smaller project of Maritime union was all that could be managed for some time to come.[3] Such misgivings did not affect the robust Tupper. If the prospect of the Canadian invasion awakened either his hopes or his fears, he gave very little sign of it; he probably assumed that the 'official' business of Maritime union was to be the real business of the conference. Opposition was to be expected from Prince Edward Island, and persuasion would certainly be necessary: 'I know you are a host in yourself in the persuasion line,' he told Tilley.[4] The first obvious step in the task of mollifying the Islanders was to hold the conference at Charlottetown. At any rate, Nova Scotia would accept any choice. The two junior provinces could decide the matter between them.

In this strain, MacDonnell wrote officially to Dundas and Cole, suggesting tactfully that he saw 'some advantages in the selection of Charlottetown' as the place for the conference,[5] but leaving the choice of both time and place to the two other governments. Then, having given a shake to the file marked 'Maritime union' in order to clear the dust from it, he decided that the most agreeable and instructive way in which a newly-appointed Lieutenant-Governor of Nova Scotia could pass the middle weeks of summer was to go on a cruise of exploration along the coasts of the province and visit its harbours, coal-mines, and gold-fields. Without waiting for replies from Cole and Dundas, but leaving a series of addresses to which letters could be forwarded, he boarded the government schooner *Daring* and put out to sea. He continued, nevertheless, to feel slightly concerned about the approaching conference. Ought he to have gone so far as to recognize an irregular, unofficial discussion of British American federation? It was extremely annoying to be pushed too far by creatures like colonial politicians; and, to protect himself, he wrote to the Colonial Secretary, asking for confirmation of his actions, or further instructions.[6] He also waited hopefully for letters from Cole and Dundas; but he found none at his different forwarding addresses. Cole later explained that he had not written because he confidently expected Gordon's return, and, most unaccountably, Gordon had not yet turned up.[7] Dundas, who, in the matter of correspondence, seemed to feel that a day lost was a day gained, had just not bothered to write.

The sea voyage brought MacDonnell close to the uncommunicative Dundas; and on Sunday, the 24th of July, the *Daring* put into Charlottetown harbour. MacDonnell stayed only a night in the Island's Government House. But his brief visit seemed to electrify the imperturbably inactive Dundas. He quickly called a meeting of his available executive councillors for a discussion of the conference with the Lieutenant-Governor of Nova Scotia.[8] Next morning MacDonnell left; but the *Daring* was scarcely out of Charlottetown harbour when Dundas was in communication with Cole of New Brunswick; and an exchange of telegrams settled Charlottetown and the 1st of September as the place and date of the meeting.[9] Now that it was certain that Nova Scotia and New Brunswick were coming humbly to the Island rather than the Island going shamefully to the mainland, the Gray government polished off all the arrangements for the conference in an enthusiastic burst of speed, by nominating its own delegates. Finally, Dundas actually got around to answering Monck's letter of the 30th of June. He would, he said, be 'rejoiced' to welcome the Canadians to Prince Edward Island. He also pointed out –

MacDonnell's firmly directing hand is visible here – that the Canadian participation in the conference would have to be unofficial.[10]

There could be no doubt about it. The interference of the Canadians had made the Maritime conference a certainty. It had also succeeded in making it, for the first time, a subject of interested discussion. So long as union appeared to be a purely and exclusively Maritime affair, a prosaic matter of uniting three rather small Atlantic provinces very well known to each other, in a legislative union, the Maritimers took such a tepid interest in the project that they seemed to be quite capable of forgetting all about it for months at a time. The intrusion of the Canadians – a reckless, quarrelsome, and ill-disciplined people – and the insertion of their grandiose federal project, even unofficially, on the agenda paper, dramatically changed the whole character of the conference, vastly enlarged its scope, complicated its issues, and invited or provoked comments, comparisons, and criticisms from the public and the press. From about the middle of July, when the news of the coming Canadian invasion became general, the Maritime newspapers took up the subject of the conference almost as if they had just discovered its existence. The awakening of interest was slower in Prince Edward Island than in the two mainland provinces, for even in summer, when the steamships plying regularly between Charlottetown, Pictou, and Shediac ended the Island's winter isolation, it was hard to rouse the Islanders from the deep repose of their satisfied self-sufficiency. But by August, even a paper or two in somnolent Charlottetown began to join in the general debate.[11]

Yet it was the unofficial, not the official, agenda of the conference that really interested them. The federal union of all the provinces, at once a fascinating and a frightening idea, was the main subject of this new and excited discussion. Maritime union was almost never considered by and for itself, but always in relation to the wider question of general federation. Maritime opposition newspapers, with a new-found belief in legislative union as a practical and sensible project, affected to fear that it might be endangered or superseded by this presumptuous and obviously selfish Canadian scheme. If Canada, 'all riven and distracted with internal strife', the Halifax *Morning Chronicle* exclaimed indignantly, was to be permitted 'to enter this conference with her half-matured Confederation scheme', her presence at the meeting would almost certainly 'distract it and defeat the whole project'.[12] Confederation, the *Chronicle* explained to its readers, was simply a device adopted by the desperate Canadians to settle their chronic sectional strife by lugging the Maritime Provinces into the mess of federalism; and federalism, the Halifax *Acadian Recorder* assured its readers gravely, was the great disintegrating force in politics, the Guy Fawkes lurking beneath the constitution, the sinister solvent of the crumbling republic to the south.[13] Two Saint John newspapers, the independent *Morning Telegraph*, and the opposition *Evening Globe*, though they implied the future possibility of a British American union, thought that the current Canadian campaign for confederation was hasty and premature.[14] Even the Halifax *British Colonist*, in which Tupper's editorial influence was dominant, seemed intimidated by the strength of the opposition to the Canadian plan, and tried to reassure its readers that Maritime union was the real object of the Charlottetown conference and that the Maritime delegates would not be diverted from their true purpose by the persuasions of wily and interested Canadians.[15]

It was only too clear that their distrust of the Canadians, their doubts about federalism, and their defensive attitude towards their own plan of legislative union were all potent forces working against confederation in the Maritime Provinces. Yet, despite all this, Maritimers showed, again and again, that they could not help but feel that their ultimate destiny lay in British American union. Even the sharpest critics of the Canadian plan admitted that everybody had dreamed of 'a future when the British possessions in America should become a great nation'. The Saint John *Morning News* – the paper with which Tilley was usually identified – went further and accepted the Canadian assumption that confederation was the one form of union by which the northern provinces could attain 'that greatness which is their manifest destiny'.[16] Federal union, the *Morning News* argued, was definitely preferable to legislative union.[17] It was the 'bounden duty' of the Charlottetown Conference to examine the

Canadian proposal seriously; and if confederation proved to be a practicable project, it should be undertaken at once, and Maritime union dropped as a probable embarrassment to the grander scheme.[18]

⇾⇾ II ⇽⇽

THE MARITIMERS had leaped at once into a debate on the Coalition's policy. The Canadians had first to get over the shock produced by the Coalition itself. To many of them the union of Reformers and Conservatives brought a long-desired sense of relief from the futile partisanship and weak misgovernment of the past; but to others it meant a shattering of accustomed party habits from which they took some time to recover. The process of recovery was easiest for the Reformers of Canada West. Their old leader, George Brown, who had acted the part of a self-sacrificing patriot in the crisis, was the hero of the hour, and his policies were apparently triumphant. The declared, original purpose of the Coalition was 'the settlement of the sectional difficulties of Upper and Lower Canada'. Representation by population, Brown's first remedy for the province's constitutional disease had been accepted as the basic principle of the proposed federal assembly. The Reformers of Canada West had a good deal of reason for their assumption that the great result of the Coalition was to be the righting of the wrongs of Upper Canada, by traditional Reform policies; and this pleasant impression was at first strengthened by Brown himself and his newspaper, the Toronto *Globe*. During the debate of the 22nd of June, when Dorion had taunted him with abandoning the Reform policy of Canadian federal union for the Conservative policy of British American federation, Brown had pointedly referred his accuser to the 'Ministerial Explanations' where the two projects were ambiguously coupled.[19] Late in July, the *Globe* was still arguing that the federation of the two Canadas ought to come first and that, on grounds of costs alone, 'the advocates of the larger federation are bound in consistency to take the smaller one in the meantime'.[20]

Apart from the Reformers of Canada West, all the other political groups in the province were, in varying degrees, either surprised, disconcerted, troubled, or frankly aghast. The two sections of the Conservative party, the *Bleus* of Canada East and the Liberal-Conservatives of Canada West, found the Coalition itself, and the Coalition's policy, almost equally disturbing. In French Canada, the astonishing spectacle of George Brown joining a ministry headed by his mortal enemies, Cartier and Macdonald, aroused widespread suspicion and alarm. Could any reliance at all be placed on this terrible man's sincerity and goodwill? 'Ah mais', said the Montreal newspaper *La Minerve*, attempting to express the incredulity of many French Canadians, including faithful Conservatives, 'ce n'est pas possible. Quoi, M. Brown, l'ennemi du Bas-Canada, supporter l'administration de MM. Taché et Cartier! Allons donc! C'est une ruse de sa part, tout au moins. Il veut compromettre les chefs de notre parti dans l'espoir de leur arracher plus tard des concessions fatales.'[21]

More might be yielded to Brown in the future. But were not the concessions he had already gained highly dangerous and possibly fatal? It was by no means certain that the powers to be assigned to the 'local governments' in confederation would be sufficient to protect the distinctive culture of French Canada. What was clear – appallingly clear – was that George Brown's dreaded principle of representation by population would form the basis of the proposed federal assembly, and that in that assembly French Canada would be doomed to be a minority for ever. This realization filled many of the stoutest of Cartier's followers with uneasiness; and it was in these irrepressible alarms of their fellow countrymen that the French-Canadian Reformers, the *Rouges*, who had been left in a hopeless minority by the Coalition, saw their best chance of regaining some political support. In the past they had always had the reputation of being liberals, sceptics, anti-clericals, ready to mock the narrow, exclusive conservatism of French-Canadian 'nationality'. Now, in complete and cheerful disregard of their own inconsistency, they unblushingly presented themselves as the only sincere defenders of that 'nationality'. They attacked Taché and Cartier for having accepted Brown's fatal principle of Rep. by Pop. They denounced the *Bleu* leaders for their attempts to disguise the completeness of their surrender. They invited the French-Canadian voters to note the devious methods by which their own ministers had tried to palliate 'le contrat immoral et infâme au moyen duquel ils viennent de vendre leurs compatriotes: c'est la lâcheté la plus insigne dans la trahison la plus noire.'[22] The brazen hardihood of these manoeuvres outraged the *Bleu* editors. 'La presse *Rouge* . . .', reported *La Minerve* in scandalized tones, 'devient nationale, patriotique, dévote même. . . . Franchement, une pareille hypocrisie nous soulève le coeur de dégout.'[23]

Unfortunately disgust and contempt were not enough. The *Rouge* newspapers had put their fingers upon what was a profound and widespread apprehension. It was easy enough to denounce French-Canadian Liberal leaders as time-serving and unprincipled hypocrites; but it was far harder, while the details of the Coalition's federal plan were still undisclosed, to allay fears and re-establish confidence in troubled French Canada. The best plan that the newspapers, French and English, of Canada East could devise was to appeal to the French Canadian to remain patient, not to indulge in premature doubts and criticisms, to suspend judgment until the new constitution was complete; and, in the meantime, to trust faithful leaders like Cartier and Taché, who had proved their fidelity by defending French Canada so ably in the past. After all, the Conservative editors pointed out, the Coalition was three-quarters Conservative; and four out of the six Lower Canadian portfolios were held by French-Canadian ministers.[24] Surely these tested leaders could be relied upon, until it was conclusively proved that they were attempting to betray their fellow countrymen. 'Nos ministres', said *La Minerve* appealingly, 'ont en ce moment une tâche bien lourde et bien difficile à remplir. . . . Ce sont des hommes d'un patriotisme éprouvé. . . . Rangeons-nous en phalange serrée et compacte autour de nos chefs. . . .'[25]

The French-Canadian *Bleus* were not alone in their tremors for the future. The English-speaking Conservatives of both Canada East and Canada West had each their characteristic worries and apprehension. It was true that British North American federation was a Conservative scheme, first announced in

1858; but, since then, the Conservative leaders had preached federalism far less than they had preached preservation of the Canadian union. The Coalition's new federal creed, hastily promulgated and featuring one notorious Reform heresy, left many of the Conservatives in a perplexed and irritable state. And the spectacle of George Brown sitting triumphantly in the cabinet as President of the Council shocked and outraged them almost as much as it had the French Canadians. The Conservatives of Canada West, though most of them loyally followed Macdonald, were disconcerted by the sudden official request 'to take a life enemy to their bosom'.[26] The fuss made over that miserable 'repentant sinner', George Brown, deeply annoyed them. They looked on it as a particularly offensive vulgarization of the parable of the prodigal son. 'The more extreme Ministerialists', the Montreal *Gazette* reported, 'are afraid that one cannot touch pitch and not be defiled; that one cannot have any political intercourse with Mr. George Brown and not make some lamentable sacrifice of principle. . . .'[27]

There was another deep-seated fear, peculiar to the Conservatives of Canada East. If the French Canadians realized that they were certain to be outvoted in the federal assembly, the English Canadians of Canada East were equally and painfully aware that, in their local or provincial legislature, they were doomed to be a permanent minority. For generations they had stood for the economic and political unity of the St. Lawrence valley; and they were troubled by a federal plan that, while it kept the unity of the river's dominion for some purposes, divided it into fragments for others. Only a few days after the Coalition had been formed, the Montreal *Gazette* was already protesting against 'the creation of two, three, or four separate local legislatures for Canada'.[28] Soon the *Gazette* was to become a notable advocate of a strongly centralized federation; but at first, like the *Bleu* newspapers, it urged its readers to suspend judgment and to put their trust in the predominantly Conservative nature of the Coalition. 'We are prepared', it announced, 'to rely on our representative men in the coalition . . . to see that our interests are secured.'[29]

In Canada East, the newspapers provided the only outlet for these varied misgivings; in Canada West, the voters could express their mixed feelings openly through by-elections. By the law as it then was, the three new Reform ministers, Brown, Mowat, and McDougall, having accepted office under the Crown, had to go back to their constituencies for re-election. Both Brown in South Oxford and Mowat in South Ontario were elected by acclamation; but McDougall's candidature in North Ontario was a dubious enterprise from the beginning. Brown had been rather reluctant to accept McDougall as the third Reform nominee in the Coalition cabinet. McDougall was less popular and more vulnerable than the other two; and parliament was barely prorogued when Matthew Crooks Cameron, the defeated Conservative candidate in the last North Ontario election – a Tory whose opposition, at this stage, was more against the 'objectionable' McDougall personally than against the Coalition or its policies – announced that he was going to contest the riding against the new minister. The *Globe* raged that this was a breach of the compact between Reformers and Conservatives and a betrayal of a Coalition minister who had relied on the good faith of the Conservative party. The Conservative *Leader* tartly replied that the Conservatives of North Ontario had not broken a contract they never made and that, in any case, McDougall, a politician 'utterly heartless and corrupt', thoroughly deserved to be defeated.[30] In the end, despite the aid of Brown, Mowat, and John A. Macdonald, all of whom joined in a concerted effort to support the new minister, Cameron beat McDougall by a majority of one hundred votes.[31]

'There is no denying it,' declared the *Globe* angrily, 'the Conservatives have had a party victory in North Ontario.'[32] Brown had warned Macdonald that, if Cameron won, there would be a storm from the Reform side;[33] but the significance of the North Ontario election was a good deal less than the Reformers imagined it to be at the time. Cameron's victory was an expression of Conservative irritation and bewilderment. The first violent feelings of astonishment and dismay that the alliance with Brown had aroused in many Conservatives found release in the vote against McDougall, and exhausted themselves in the process. McDougall found another seat in Lanark. The Conservatives, having had their ill-tempered fling, closed ranks with the Reformers in support of the Coalition. The Canadians, with some doubts and apprehensions, were overwhelmingly in favour of the new government and its programme.

>>> III <<<

IN THE LAST fortnight of July and the first week in August – the fag end of the political year before the holidays started and grouse-shooting began – the British Colonial Office was unusually busy with British North American affairs. Monck's brief dispatch announcing the formation of the Coalition government arrived on Downing Street on the 8th of July. MacDonnell's puzzled communication, with its news of the Canadian request to attend the conference on Maritime union, reached the Colonial Office a fortnight later, on the 1st of August. The Secretary for the Colonies and his permanent advisers were now confronted with a conference whose official and unofficial business differed completely; and they had to make up their minds what attitude to adopt to the unexpected and disconcerting Canadian intrusion, with all the complications it seemed to bring with it. Everybody assumed, of course, that the British government could not possibly try to prevent the Canadian visit, or to force the Maritimers to stick to their official business. In matters of internal reform or political reorganization, the initiative clearly lay with the British North American colonists themselves; and until they made up their minds the United Kingdom government must maintain a stiffly correct attitude of benevolent neutrality. This was Colonial Office orthodoxy; but its profession did not entirely eliminate private views. The Colonial Office officials had come to believe that Maritime union was a sensible, practical, and useful scheme. Newcastle himself, impressed by Gordon's vigorous arguments and confident assurances, had agreed to change the order of his priorities, and to put Maritime union, instead of the Intercolonial Railway, in first place.

In April 1864, however, Newcastle – not an old but a very ill man – resigned his office in the Palmerston cabinet. He was succeeded by Edward Cardwell, a Peelite like his predecessor, an earnest but uninspired and uninspiring man, with all the Peelite copy-book virtues of industry, efficiency, prudence, and conscientiousness. A cool, cautious, exceedingly wary administrator, with few strong political convictions, few real interests, and almost no enthusiasms, he was always capable of seeing at least two sides to a question and instinctively adopted a neutral or negative attitude to most issues.[34] Sir Frederic Rogers, the Permanent Under-Secretary of the Colonial Office, thought his 'fidgets' a great torment.[35] His fellow parliamentarians deplored his lack of forthrightness. Even Gladstone, who was a past master at the difficult business of wrapping a subject up in frustrating layers of qualifications, reservations, and ambiguities, was occasionally exasperated by the way in which Cardwell 'beat about the bush' and 'flinched from the point'.[36]

His attitude to colonial problems was characteristic. He was neither an imperialist nor an anti-imperialist. Either position would have been much too positive and definite for Edward Cardwell's liking. He most emphatically did not want the extension of the Empire; but, on the other hand, he was not particularly eager to hurry on its dissolution. The security of the British American provinces seemed important to him, for here Great Britain was involved; but his interest in the colonies in their own right, as developing overseas communities which might soon become nations, was extremely small. For him British North America was not a potential transcontinental nation but a tangled complex of British problems, commitments, and obligations. His first duty, as he saw it, was to modernize and clarify the imperial relationship, to persuade British America to take up more of the burdens of maturity, and, in the process, to reduce Great Britain's responsibilities on the North American continent.

The particular colonial problem that was uppermost in the minds of the British ministers when Cardwell took over the Colonial Office was the problem of British American – and particularly Canadian – defence. There was, of course, nothing new about this. For a generation Great Britain had been attempting to cut her military costs in North America and to persuade the Canadians to practise the virtues of self-reliance. The efforts were not novel; but as the American Civil War went on they were continued and intensified by a new and anxious determination. The growing estrangement between the United Kingdom and the United States brought home to the imperial government the terrible magnitude of her responsibilities in Canada. While the war lasted, British America was probably safe; but when it ended, whatever the outcome, whether the Confederacy was subjugated or gained its independence, would there not very probably be danger for the British provinces? If the North won the war, it might, flushed with victory, turn upon British America and exact a terrible revenge. If it lost the war, it might 'seek on the St. Lawrence an indemnity for what it has lost on the Potomac'.[37]

In 1863, the capture of Vicksburg and the Union victories of Gettysburg and Missionary Ridge seemed to bring the war – and British American security – closer to their end. In the autumn of that year, Great Britain, its fears and anxieties increased rather than allayed, sent out Lieutenant-Colonel W. F. D. Jervois with instructions to examine and report upon the present state and possible improvement of the Canadian defences.[38] The Canadian government, under the pressure of British persuasion and the vague fear of American dangers, had slightly and reluctantly strengthened its armed forces; but when the Canadians were urged to make a more strenuous effort, they quickly took refuge behind the stone walls of their dependence and colonialism. To the British government, whose pecuniary interests happily coincided with its principles of colonial rule, it seemed obvious that colonies which had enjoyed responsible government for more than a generation should be ready to accept the major burden of their own defence. On their part, the Canadians were equally convinced that foreign policy, and hence defence, was mainly an imperial rather than a colonial responsibility; that if war did come, it would come for imperial rather than colonial reasons, and that, as loyal British subjects, they had a right to expect that Great Britain would defend them, with all her resources, in time of trouble. For some time, an inconclusive and, at times, none too friendly argument over the division of responsibility for defence had been carried on between the Brit-

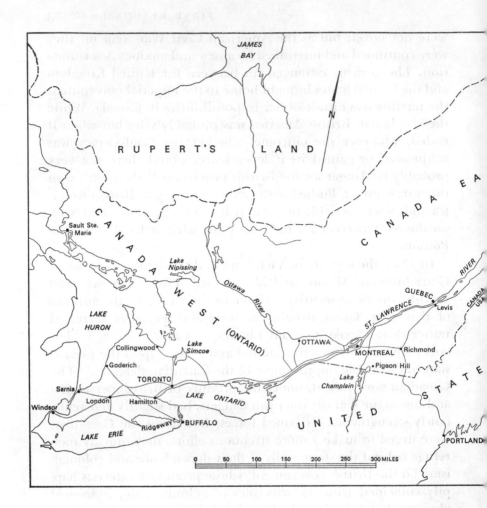

British North America

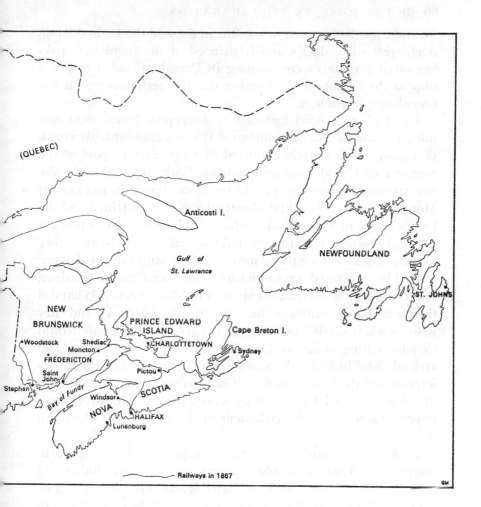

just before Confederation

ish and Canadian governments. But in the end the United Kingdom, wearied of delays and frightened of the monstrous risks her small garrisons were running in Canada, decided to put a stop to the dispute and to seek a definite settlement with the Canadian government.

The basis of this settlement was the report Jervois had submitted to the British government.[39] It was a frighteningly realistic report, for it frankly admitted that the western part of the province of Canada was indefensible. Both imperial and colonial troops, it suggested, should be concentrated in the east, at Montreal and Quebec; and Montreal was to be fortified and the fortifications of Quebec strengthened. Here was a comprehensive and practical plan that shifted the main centre of resistance to the east where it would be most effective, stiffened the defence offered by the armed services with fortifications, and maintained easy communication with the sea and the Royal Navy. What did the Canadian government think of this plan? How far did they wish to see it carried out and what part of the expense would they be willing to incur? The time for decision and action had arrived. And in late July, when the news of the Maritime conference and the Canadian Coalition was arriving, Cardwell was drafting the crucial dispatch by which the British government hoped to force an early settlement of the question of Canadian defence.

Yet how far should this forthright dispatch – this virtual ultimatum – go? How far should it accept British responsibility and offer British assistance for Canadian defence? On this vital question, the Palmerston government was not all of one mind. On the one hand were the Whigs, with the eighty-year-old Prime Minister at their head, who still saw grandeur in the British Empire, and still recognized definite obligations for its defence. On the other hand were the new Liberals, led by Gladstone, the Chancellor of the Exchequer, who thought that this 'very stiff business' could be settled on strictly cost-accounting principles, and who believed that the best solution was simply 'to shift the centre of responsibility' from the United Kingdom to the British American colonies.[40] These doctrinaire anti-imperialist views, so fashionable throughout the governing class at the time, had their adherents in government; but, as Gladstone himself admitted, the cabinet as a whole was not prepared then to act on the revolutionary basis he had suggested; and the Prime Minister himself was utterly opposed to the humiliation of a British withdrawal from North America which might seem to have been inspired by fear of the growing military might of the United States.

'I cannot admit', Palmerston wrote to Russell, the Foreign Secretary, on a proposed change in Cardwell's draft dispatch, 'that it is a question for consideration or division whether our North American Provinces are to be fought for or abandoned. . . . We have those colonies and cannot abandon them without disgrace and dishonour, ministerial and national, and we must do our best to defend them in co-operation with their inhabitants.'[41] In the end, the dispatch that Cardwell sent off on the 6th of August assumed the continuance of British military support, and a British contribution to the new fortifications. It also, however, strongly asserted the principle that Canada's defence 'must ever principally depend upon the spirit, the energy, and the courage of her own people'.[42] Finally, it invited the Canadian government to take the initiative in devising a comprehensive plan of defence.

Canadian defence was a matter for the British cabinet; but British American unions, either legislative or federal, were also likely, and in short order, to become a concern of the British cabinet; and the British cabinet might soon have to decide where, if at all, the weight of its own influence was to be placed. The permanent officials in the Colonial Office could not help feeling that the Canadian plan of a British American federation was premature and speculative. Maritime union, they considered, was much more practicable; and they feared that the only result of the Canadian intrusion on the Charlottetown Conference would be the postponement or frustration of their pet project for the Maritime Provinces. The preferences of the Colonial Office clerks were clear; but it was also becoming clear, in the anxious summer of 1864, that the opinions of a few senior clerks in Downing Street might not prove decisive. Gladstone, a powerful force in the cabinet, evidently considered British commitments in North America a problem of the deepest gravity; and the solution that he was propounding to his colleagues was definitely political as well as military in character.

In July, when the defence issue was under discussion, Gladstone addressed a long printed memorandum on the subject to his colleagues in the ministry. In it he set out at length the imperial philosophy on which his military proposals were based. His main aim was 'to shift the centre of responsibility' in defence from Great Britain to the colonies. The United Kingdom, he insisted, must cease to be a principal in the matter and become an assistant – a willing and generous assistant, but an assistant only. The British American provinces, in order to bear the burden of this increased responsibility, must grow out of the 'sentiment and habits of mere dependencies'; and England must help them to acquire a 'corporate and common feeling'. 'I submit', Gladstone wrote, 'that the true aim of all our measures at this important juncture should be to bring the people of the British North American colonies, regarded in one mass, as nearly to a national sentiment and position as their relation to the British Crown will permit.'[43] If, he concluded, a British American union or federation became a political possibility, the United Kingdom should encourage and assist in its formation 'by every means in its power'.

Gladstone was not interested in a union of the Maritime Provinces. He was concerned with the 'corporate and common feeling' of the British American provinces 'regarded in one mass'. And Gladstone was a Peelite, with whom Cardwell had been long and intimately associated, and whose opinions and general outlook he continued to share. At the crucial moment, the essential connection between Canadian defence and British American political reorganization had been heavily emphasized by a minister whose power and influence were great; and the favourable reception of the Canadian federal plan by the British government was virtually assured before the plan itself had been more than sketched out in its barest essentials. At this stage, however, when he had no more information than the newspapers afforded, Cardwell obviously could not make even a preliminary judgment on the merits of the new proposal. Yet he evidently did not share his advisers' annoyance at the Canadian intrusion on the Charlottetown Conference, or their fear that Maritime union might be delayed or imperilled by the discussion of a general federation. In any case, the British North Americans would have to make up their own minds first. Their two projects – Maritime union and general federation – might follow each other – or combine with each other – or compete with each other.

≫≫ IV ≪≪

Aᴜɢᴜsᴛ had come. The blue, unclouded skies and the blazing sun, under which the legislature had sweltered during the ministerial crisis at Quebec, had kept reappearing, an almost daily miracle, ever since the middle of June. Throughout the province, the long drought had parched and browned the countryside; the woods and grasses were as dry and inflammable as straw. Even before the end of June, there were persistent bush fires in the region of Quebec, and one day a frightening combination of wood-smoke and thunder-clouds had produced an appalling darkness that frightened the whole capital.⁴⁴ A month later, George Brown, writing to his wife, Anne, from Uxbridge, where he had gone to campaign for William Mc-Dougall, in the North Ontario by-election, could see fires burning in near-by fields from the windows of the room in which he sat.⁴⁵

Far away to the south, in the uncertain borderland between the Federal Union and the Southern Confederacy, different and far more terrible fires of conflict had been burning with climactic violence all that summer. Once more, to the horrified dismay of the North, the fortunes of war seemed to have changed. The prospect of an imminent Union victory, which had looked fairly clear in the late summer of 1863, now appeared to be fading. For three months, ever since the beginning of May, the Northern armies had been engaged in a concerted and massive attempt to break the last resistance of the South; and now, after three months of continuous fighting and appalling losses, the goal

looked almost as far away as it had ever done. It was true that in
the south-west, where the wily Confederate General Johnston
had been replaced by the brave but unskilful Hood, the Federal
commander Sherman was closing in rapidly towards the complete
investment of Atlanta. But Grant, after a series of indecisive
and costly battles, had settled down to the siege of Petersburg,
with Lee's Army of Northern Virginia still confronting him defiantly. The defence of Richmond was an amazing demonstration
of the resourcefulness and stubborn endurance of the Confederate forces; Jubal Early's raid towards Washington showed a
flash of the dash and daring of Stonewall Jackson's Shenandoah
Valley campaigns. These very mixed results – the slow and
costly Federal advance had neither broken Confederate resistance nor prevented Confederate reprisals – bred discouragement,
war-weariness, and defeatism in the North. Northern morale
reached what was probably its lowest point in the entire war.

In British North America, this increasingly sombre Union
mood had a marked effect. Sympathy for the South, which, from
the beginning of the war, had been so strong and widespread in
the British provinces, was steadily maintained. British American
newspapers were virtually as hopeful of ultimate Southern success as they had been in 1862, during the flood-tide of the Confederacy's fortunes. The long, doubtful, and bloody conflict of
that summer strengthened the conviction, which a good many
British North American editors shared, that the South was probably invincible and that the North no longer possessed the spirit
and determination to subdue it. The *Leader* of Toronto announced with all possible assurance that 'the independence of
the South is as good as achieved'.[46] The Montreal *Gazette* hoped
that soon 'the mad project of subjugating the South by the
sword will, however reluctantly, be given up'.[47] In any event,
the inconclusive war, which now seemed likely to continue for
some time with little prospect of a Federal victory, would prolong British America's immunity from attack and was visibly
exhausting the North's martial ardour.

If, in the end, the South won its freedom, a new balance of
power on the continent would ensure the permanence of British
America's security. In such circumstances the Union would be

both too exhausted and too intimidated to risk an attempt to gain Northern compensation for Southern losses; and, as the Saint John *Morning News* reflected, the British colonies would not be 'crushed in the coils of the great Federal anaconda'.[48] Unquestionably, a vague, brooding apprehension of trouble with the United States lay at the back of the thoughts of both Maritimers and Canadians at this time; but in the summer of 1864 its effect on their plans for the political reconstruction of British North America was neither direct nor strong. Cardwell's dispatch, requesting a decision on the problem of Canadian defence, did not reach Quebec until late in August; and the Canadian ministry, its attention concentrated almost exclusively upon the federal plan it was to present at Charlottetown, easily decided to postpone consideration of the British government's proposal. Both Maritime union and confederation were to be planned and considered by themselves, largely apart from the dangerous turmoil to the south.

If the Charlottetown Conference was likely to end up as an open competition between confederation and Maritime union, the Maritimers seemed placidly unaware of the prospect, or disinclined to get excited about it. They appeared to be simply waiting without much concern, and even without a great deal of interest, to see what would turn up. Maritime union, if it ever became a reality, would certainly have to be the result of spontaneous and happy inspiration. Drafting a federal constitution was admittedly a more difficult business than planning a legislative union; but Nova Scotia and New Brunswick faced problems – including the Island's obvious reluctance to join a legislative union – that were nearly as serious as those that confronted Canada. But nobody at either Halifax or Fredericton seemed to be giving these matters much thought. Gordon, the vanished champion of Maritime union, had still not returned to New Brunswick. Tilley and Tupper were apparently making no preparations at all for the discussions at Charlottetown. Apart from the admittedly large bait of the proposed purchase of the rights of the absentee proprietors, they had no special inducements to offer Prince Edward Island.

The contrast between this tranquil waiting on events and the strenuous activity in Canada became more striking as the summer wore on. Early in August, the Canadian government began to hold a series of cabinet meetings at which the details of its federal scheme were worked out.[49] There was not too much time. The conference at Charlottetown, at which the Canadians would have to present their proposal, was less than a month away; and, in the interest of its own solidarity, the Coalition was in urgent need of a detailed plan upon which its members could speak with one voice. The question-begging statement in the 'Ministerial Explanations' of the 22nd of June – 'local matters being committed to local bodies, and matters common to all to a general legislature, constituted on the well-understood principles of federal government' – had given the opposition an opportunity, of which it quickly took advantage, to provoke the ministers in both houses into making different and slightly contradictory interpretations of these mysterious phrases. In the end, in order to quiet the uneasiness of both its old and its new supporters, the Coalition was forced to issue a supplementary definition of purpose, which was given by Macdonald in the Assembly on the 23rd of June and by Taché in the Council on the 24th.[50] The local government, this explanatory statement declared, would be entrusted with the protection of 'all local laws, interests, and institutions'. The general or federal government would have the sovereign power and would deal with all problems common to all sections of the federation. The senior branch of the federal legislature would be composed on the principle of the equality of 'each section, state, or province'. The assembly, or popular branch, would be constituted on a popular basis, and representation by population, though not universal suffrage, would prevail.

Beyond this statement of purpose, the ministers refused to be budged. Their stubborn silence stopped debate in the legislature; but it could not quell the inevitably growing public interest in the Coalition's policy, and it could not prevent newspaper comment and discussion, which was already beginning to get under way. Even more important, the ministers themselves, perhaps particularly George Brown, badly needed to be reassured that they could carry their agreement beyond generalities and through the necessary complexities of a detailed federal plan. The cabinet meetings that began on August the 4th were of vital importance; and the harmony which was the essential basis of their success began at once, almost miraculously, to establish itself. George Brown's doubts and fears were left behind in the rapidly ascending curve of his confidence and reassurance. 'Things go on smoothly enough,' he wrote to his wife after the first day's discussion in cabinet.[51] Three days later almost the last residue of apprehension had disappeared. 'I am happy to tell you,' he confided joyfully to Anne, 'that all fear of our compact not being carried out in good faith has pretty well passed from my mind and I now feel very confident that we will satisfactorily and harmoniously accomplish our great purpose.'[52]

Planning a federal constitution was the most important work that the Canadians undertook that summer. It was not, however, the only effort they made to advance the cause of a general British North American union. On August the 4th, the very day when the Coalition ministers were assembling in Quebec for the constitutional discussions, a party of about one hundred Canadians, including assemblymen, members of the Legislative Council, journalists, and other interested citizens, set out, under the leadership of D'Arcy McGee and James Ferrier of the Legislative Council, for a tour of New Brunswick and Nova Scotia.[53] The idea of the visit had been conceived in the early spring; and the Saint John Chamber of Commerce and the City of Halifax had sent their invitations before the Canadian political crisis had occurred in June. Without any question, the tour was informal, unofficial, non-political; and yet, in an odd way, it never seemed quite free of political implications.[54] The Canadians, now committed to confederation, looked a little like missionaries; and Thomas D'Arcy McGee, the one Canadian cabinet minister who accompanied the tourists on their travels, was certainly the man most likely to put his heart into the task of converting the Maritimers to the new Canadian religion. A practised lecturer, a moving speaker, with a style more formal and elegant than Joseph Howe's but equally lightened by touches of wit and humour, McGee was the ideal evangelist of the creed of British American nationalism. It was his creed,

moreover, and had been long before the Coalition had announced it as government policy. He had all the enthusiasm and
conviction of one of the first witnesses for the new faith.

The route the touring Canadians had to follow was another
illustration, on a large scale, of the incredible deficiencies of
British American communications. Since the Intercolonial Railway had not even emerged as yet from the survey stage, they
travelled by the Grand Trunk Railway to Portland, Maine, and
there took ship for Saint John, New Brunswick. It was pouring
rain when the party mustered at Portland, and the deck of the
tossing vessel that bore them northwards was crowded with
makeshift beds and uneasily recumbent forms.[55] But next morning the skies were again a promising blue; and although Saint
John, which they reached on the evening of the 5th of August,
seemed a sprawling and sombre city, with houses built of the
dullest brown bricks or painted the drabbest ochre or slate grey,
there were thousands of citizens waiting on the docks to give
them the heartiest of welcomes.[56]

Next night, Saint John's lavish hospitality had its climax in a
magnificent feast at Stubbs's Hotel; and after a good rest on Sunday the Canadians were off early Monday morning on the steamboat *Anna Augusta* up the St. John River to Fredericton.[57] The
sun shone, the lovely, rich intervale lands spread out before
them on either side, the band of the 15th Regiment played
waltzes and marches, and in between the French Canadians, in
chorus, were singing 'A la claire fontaine' and 'En roulant ma
boule'. On the way up the river, the *Anna Augusta* overtook the
Heather Belle, which was carrying Lieutenant-Governor Gordon, returned at last from his long leave in England, back to
Government House in Fredericton. There was another lavish
dinner that night in the modest Provincial Building in Fredericton, another long succession of toasts and speeches, a brief reception next morning by Governor Gordon, final farewells and
good wishes, and then the Canadians were off again down the
river bound for Saint John.[58]

The next leg of the journey was almost too strenuous. At daybreak on Wednesday, the 10th of August, after far too much
travelling and far too little sleep, the red-eyed and yawning trav-

ellers set out across the Bay of Fundy on the steamer *Emperor*, bound for Halifax. Once again it was evening before the special train, which they had boarded at Windsor, finally steamed into the Nova Scotian capital; and that night the weary Canadians wanted nothing more than to tumble into bed. Halifax, as they viewed it next morning, seemed an old town, a little dingy, like Saint John, with its wooden houses and their dun-coloured paint.[59] There were some signs of quiet opulence, however, in the sombre residences, the public buildings were imposing, and the city had planned a longer list of hospitalities than Fredericton or Saint John. There was a dance on the deck of H.M.S. *Duncan*, a sail around the North-west Arm and Bedford Basin organized by the Halifax Yacht Club, a picnic featuring two mysterious and slightly intimidating Maritime dishes called 'chowder' and 'hodge-podge', and a reception at Government House, graced by Lady MacDonnell, the reigning beauty of the wives of the Governors of British America. The Halifax visit continued into a second week; but its climax really came on the night of Saturday, the 13th of August, when the great public dinner for the Canadian visitors was held in the Drill Shed on Spring Garden Road.[60]

Though at least one Maritime editor, Timothy Anglin of the Saint John *Morning Freeman*, suspected otherwise, spreading propaganda for confederation was not the main object of the Canadian visit. But the tour was in itself an exercise in the coming together of British America. The Canadians were full of their own federal scheme. The Maritimers, now that the Canadian appearance at Charlottetown had been arranged, were curious about the Canadian proposal, and vastly more interested in their own conference than they had ever been before. Maritime-Canadian relations was the inevitable subject of hundreds of private conversations and scores of public speeches; and the big public dinners at Saint John, Fredericton, and Halifax took on the likeness of great oratorical concerts, at which all the performers were simply playing variations on the central theme of unity. D'Arcy McGee was, of course, a frank, outspoken, and passionate advocate of confederation, who used every opportunity that the tour provided to drive his message home. But there were others, even among the more cautious Maritimers, who were willing to speculate about a future British American union, or to declare their readiness to aid in its creation. The unromantic Tilley described his own vision of the populous, prosperous, and united country that British North America was destined to become.[61] Tupper insisted that the whole aspect of the union question had altered now that the Canadians had taken up the cause of confederation. A more comprehensive union was possible than had been dreamed of when the Maritime conference had been arranged; and Tupper declared that he was willing to give this grander scheme his enthusiastic support.[62] Joseph Howe was the last speaker at the Halifax dinner; and he seemed to sum up its happy feeling of comradeship when he declared that he was 'pleased to think the day was rapidly approaching when the Provinces would be united, with one flag above their heads, one thought in all their bosoms, with one sovereign and one constitution'.[63]

The Canadian visit, as the first great convivial British North American occasion, was an unqualified success. It left behind it pleasant memories of good fellowship, a growing interest in the possibilities of future political comradeship, a definite inclination, as Sir Richard MacDonnell judged, 'to merge small politics in larger and more generous views'.[64] Would this vague but pervasive sentiment have any significant influence on the deliberations at Charlottetown in September? Governor Gordon, who disliked federal unions for what he regarded as their inherent weakness and who was already jealous for the success of his Maritime-union scheme, was inclined to dismiss the Canadian visit as a pleasure excursion of no political significance whatever;[65] but Governor MacDonnell took the matter much more seriously, and gave it as his opinion that 'the arrival of so many Canadian visitors at this peculiar moment must be regarded as having had, and as being intended to have had, an influence on the deliberations of the delegates at Charlottetown next month'.[66] He predicted that a general British American union would be much more extensively supported in the Atlantic provinces than was at all probable six months before. Already there were some significant indications of the truth of this estimate. The *British Colonist*, the Halifax newspaper for which Tupper wrote frequently, became an earnest advocate of general union.[67] The Saint John *Morning News*, which had begun its campaign in favour of confederation, even to the exclusion of Maritime union, in July, continued its propagandist efforts vigorously.[68] Finally – and perhaps strangest of all – George Coles, named as one of the Prince Edward Island delegates to the Charlottetown Conference, published late in August his own preferred solution for the problem, which turned out to be an extremely bizarre and muddled scheme for a general British American federation.[69]

⟶⟫ V ⟪⟵

IN THE MEANTIME, while the Canadians were winning a better name and confederation an interested hearing in the Maritime Provinces, the ministers of the Canadian Coalition were labouring away at Quebec to finish their draft constitution for a federal union of British America. At the beginning of August they had held a lengthy series of cabinet meetings on the subject; and at the end of the month, just before their departure for Charlottetown, they put in another three days' hard work in settling the final details of their plan. It was a difficult, delicate work of compromise and adjustment. The ministers sitting around the Council Board under George Brown's presidency consciously represented community interests and values which often varied and were sometimes contradictory. On the one hand, as they knew very well, there was throughout British America a feeling of local patriotism, a sense of provincial identity which, as in French Canada, sometimes took the concrete form of distinctive customs and institutions, and which could also degenerate into a suspiciously ignorant and narrow-minded parochialism. On the other hand, there was the weighty influence of British North America's political inheritance and experience, the preference for monarchical government and the undivided sovereignty of the parliamentary system, the belief in the strength of union, and the fearful distrust of the disruptive force of the federal principle, so terribly exemplified in the United States. One set of influences was pressing for a strongly centralized general government which would play a preponderant role in confederation. Another, more localized and weaker, group of influences favoured a looser federal union in which the local governments would come closer to being co-ordinate with, and independent of, the central government.

The difference between these two points of view appeared clearly, with the simplified and pugnacious clarity of journalism, during the late summer and early autumn of 1864. Since the final explanatory statement of the 24th of June, the government had given no indication of its plan. The field was free for speculation, rival interpretations, and contrasted theories of federalism; and, by the first week in September, four principal Canadian newspapers – the *Globe* and the *Leader* of Toronto and the *Gazette* and *La Minerve* of Montreal – had got themselves thoroughly involved in a violent controversy over the nature of the proposed confederation. *La Minerve*, like the other *Bleu* or Conservative French-Canadian newspapers, quickly took up and firmly stuck to a more purist federal interpretation which stressed the autonomy of the local governments, though only – and this was an important limitation – in the social, cultural, and religious aspects of provincial life. 'Confédération', declared *La Minerve*, early in the summer, 'signifie ligue d'Etats indépendants les uns vis-à-vis les autres. . . .' French Canada, it predicted, would be 'maître chez lui en tout qui regarde son économie sociale, civile, et religieuse'.[70]

The response of the centralists to these firm affirmations of the local autonomists gathered force slowly during the summer. At the beginning of August, the *Globe* assured its readers that the framers of the British American confederation scheme were applying the 'federal principle' in a fashion exactly the reverse of that which the United States had followed, and that, as a result, 'the local governments shall be delegated governments and that the "sovereign" power shall be vested in the general or federal government . . .'.[71] This categorical statement, in a newspaper whose proprietor was the most important Reform minister in the new Coalition, naturally aroused comment and provoked rejoinder; but the debate did not really become acrimonious until towards the end of the month, when the Montreal *Gazette*, inspired by a remark of Joseph Howe's, in a report of the dinner given to the visiting Canadians at Halifax, hurled itself eagerly into the battle on the side of unity and centralization. Howe, in a characteristic burst of colloquially exuberant rhetoric, had begged the Canadian visitors not to commit the 'political suicide' of dividing the Province of Canada into two sections as a part of their confederation scheme.[72] This, said the *Gazette* impressively, was sage advice that deserved to be heeded. Public opinion in Canada in favour of unity, it insisted, had been steadily strengthening since the prorogation of parliament. 'An absolute, complete legislative union is perhaps impossible,' the *Gazette* conceded. 'But reaping instruction from the pregnant example of our neighbours, Canadians and Acadians alike will infuse as little of the federal principle into their union when established as will suffice to meet the absolute necessities of the case.'[73]

This was too much for *La Minerve*. It denied the *Gazette*'s assumption that Canadian sentiment in favour of legislative union had been growing. It reiterated its contention that the only confederation acceptable to French Canada would be one in which 'le principe fédéral serait appliqué dans toute son étendue . . .'.[74] This was the already familiar position of the *Bleu* journalists; what was new in *La Minerve*'s latest statement was the stubborn intransigence of the tone in which it was made. The *Gazette* was provoked to declare in reply that, if too great an extension of the federal principle were permitted in the Coalition's plan, the English-speaking Canadians of both sections of the Province would simply reject confederation outright, and, instead, impose representation by population 'pure and simple' upon the Province of Canada alone. 'Unreasonable pretensions and obstinacy on one part', moralized the *Gazette*, 'will beget a similar spirit on the other.'[75] It was only too true. *La Minerve* was soon heroically opposing the 'English league' which the *Gazette* had threatened with an army of French Canadians, united as one man.[76]

While this newspaper battle over the character of the proposed confederation was beginning to get heated, the Coalition cabinet was putting the finishing touches to the plan that it would soon be presenting at Charlottetown. Newspaper opinion was useful to the ministers, for it supplied evidence of the various interests and values which they knew must be safeguarded in their federal scheme. But the outbreak of a really serious public row over the basic principles of union might fatally menace the concord by which alone the Coalition could survive. At that moment the cabinet dreaded an upset more than ever, for, with feelings that combined a vast sense of relief with a growing pride of achievement, the ministers began to realize that they had reached an agreement, of almost incredible completeness and cordiality, upon their basic plan for confederation.[77] For years they had been having long constitutional arguments and getting nowhere; but now, in three series of meetings spread over a little more than two months, they had devised a plan for a British American federal union that was acceptable to them all.

Almost everything had seemed to be against them. They were old and inveterate enemies, divided by unforgettable memories of savage quarrels, by incompatibilities of temperament and character, by conflicts of values, standards, and methods. They were united, not by choice, but by desperate necessity; and although they had got along better together than probably they themselves had expected, their brief association had not been without its ticklish moments. The sensitive Brown, who was probably most likely to be uneasy and uncomfortable in such circumstances, did find his colleagues extremely uncongenial at a few dangerous moments. Once, in a fit of gloom and exasperation, he confided to Anne that as soon as the constitutional settlement was really secure he would not care much how quickly a rupture broke up the Coalition cabinet. And on the 27th of August, at the last Council meeting on the federal plan, when Macdonald turned up late and half drunk, and when he and Brown quarrelled furiously over a proposed settlement of a long-standing dispute between the government and the contractors for the new public buildings at Ottawa, the rupture was only very narrowly averted. 'Do you know,' Brown wrote to his wife, 'you were very near being stripped yesterday of your honours as Presidentess of the Council? Would not that have been a sad affair?'[78]

It would, indeed, have been a 'sad affair', for even the tactics at Charlottetown had been decided upon and the basic plan of confederation was complete. In the main, the plan was the work of the four principals – Macdonald, Cartier, Brown, and Galt; and they had combined to create a strongly centralized federation with a preponderant central government. That this would have been Macdonald's and Galt's wish could have been readily predicted; but Brown's and Cartier's acquiescence in such a scheme was outwardly and on the record less easily understandable. Galt's preference for a strong federation dated back to the abortive Conservative scheme of 1858, of which he had been one of the chief authors. Macdonald's fear of the disruptive force of federalism had grown so great during the American Civil War that he had openly declared himself in favour of a legislative union. Brown, on the other hand, might seem to have been committed to a weak, decentralized federation by the platform adopted by the Reform convention of 1859, and by his own passionate insistence that Canada West must be freed from external control. Cartier, the acknowledged and trusted leader of the majority of the French Canadians, must have appeared almost compelled to support the view, already fairly clearly stated in the *Bleu* newspapers, of the co-ordinate authority that the local governments ought to have in confederation.

Yet this apparent difference of Brown's and Cartier's approach was unreal. In fact, they were bound – Brown even more than Cartier – by their characters, convictions, and careers, to accept Macdonald's plan of a qualified centralization. Cartier was committed by the Conservative party's adoption of the plan of 1858. Brown was committed by his passionate crusade for representation by population. The proposed federal assembly, which was to be constituted on the basis of Rep. by Pop., was in fact the complete realization of his political ideal. In the federal assembly, the members from Canada West would have a considerable majority over those from Canada East; the English-speaking representatives from the federation as a whole would outnumber the French-speaking representatives by over two to one. All that Brown had fought for would be realized in the federal assembly. For him the federal legislature was – and must be – the preponderating power in confederation; and his every instinct urged him to enlarge federal powers and to exalt federal sovereignty. In comparison, the 'local governments', dealing with schools, roads, bridges, and other essentially municipal affairs, would be, Brown assumed, relatively insignificant bodies. They would not need, and did not deserve, the expensive and pompous paraphernalia of responsible government. He was convinced that they ought to be provided with an essentially municipal political organization.

To Cartier, these were extreme, radical, 'republican' conclusions which he was not willing to accept. He would insist upon responsible government, and probably upon a bicameral legislature, at least for Canada East; but, though the dignity of the parliamentary system seemed to him necessary for the local government, a vast range of jurisdiction did not. In his view, French Canada must be enabled to control and regulate the legal system, and the cultural and religious institutions in which her character and experience had been most fully expressed; but he was convinced that she could not, and did not, have any political or economic interests that were distinct or separate from those of the rest of Canada. He had friends, including Galt, among the financial and commercial leaders of Canada East. He was a railway promoter who became a solicitor of the Grand Trunk Railway, an optimistic expansionist who believed in economic growth on a national scale. That the central legislature should control the whole broad range of the political and economic activities of a united British America seemed natural and sensible to him. He was ready to limit the powers of the local governments to the essentially distinctive features of French Canada – its educational system, civil code, and religious institutions.

On Monday, the 29th of August, the Executive Council had a last meeting, and towards evening the Canadian delegation to Charlottetown went on board the government steamer *Queen Victoria*.[79] There were eight of them – the seniors, Cartier, Macdonald, Brown, and Galt, and, in addition, their junior colleagues, Campbell, Langevin, McDougall, and McGee. The *Queen Victoria*, as the viceregal party had found on its cruise to the Saguenay the month before, was hardly a luxury steamer. The cabins were rather small and cramped, the beds hard, and the vibration of the screw all too noticeable.[80] But to the tired Canadian ministers, who had done their work and made all their preparations, the prospect of a completely relaxed and leisurely voyage down the St. Lawrence looked extremely attractive. The day had been hot, but there was a broad awning stretched above the sunny deck under which they could loaf in comfort. A little library of books had been provided. There were chess-boards and backgammon, a large and varied supply of food and drink, and a cook who knew how to make the best use of his materials.[81] That evening, as the sun went down behind them, the Canadians sat out on the deck and watched the gradually receding shores, with the steepled churches and whitewashed cottages of the little straggling French-Canadian villages, and, beyond and above them, growing bolder and more precipitous, the massive and sombre ranges of the Laurentian Highlands. This was the St. Lawrence, the 'River of Canada', as Jacques Cartier had called it; and for generations and centuries ships sailing up and down the river had founded Canada, peopled it, nourished it, brought it danger or succour, and, on a few famous occasions, had utterly changed its destiny. On that late-August evening of 1864, a group of mid-Victorian colonial politicians, in tile hats and frock coats, were setting out, in a small government steamer, on as uncertain and possibly as decisive an enterprise as ever the white-coated and red-coated soldiers of the past had sailed to undertake.

The sun had gone now; and behind, at the horizon, there was only a narrow band of dull rose that faded into pale yellow and changed into an exquisite green and finally darkened into the blue-black of the sky. Ahead were the open waters of the Gulf, and the freshening air, and Charlottetown and the future of Canada.

CHAPTER FOUR

Mission to Charlottetown

THE LITTLE TOWN of Charlottetown stood at the top of a broadening wedge of land between the East or Hillsborough River and the North or Yorke River – stretches of water that were called rivers but that were, in fact, simply long arms of the sea. The harbour lay snugly within the most sheltered part of Hillsborough Bay; and from the row of docks and the low, red-coloured cliffs on either side, the land rose gently upward to a wide, flat expanse, on which the eighteenth-century town-planners had laid out a very regular, symmetrical little town-site. The street names – 'Great George' (George III), 'Queen', 'Prince', 'Kent', 'Grafton', 'Richmond', and 'Pownal' – were eloquently Loyalist in their commemoration of Court and government in the days of the American Revolution. The town was, in miniature, a perfect realization of the planned and ordered eighteenth-century conception of urban life. The streets were generously wide. The network of straight roads – the town was 'all rectangles and red earth', one visitor said – had its planned focus in Queen Square. And the centre of interest on Queen Square was the stone structure of the Colonial Building, which housed the government offices, the legislative library, and the Assembly and Legislative Council.

The Colonial Building represented an impressive effort on the part of a tiny and poor colony. It was a characteristic product of the Greek revival in architecture – simple, dignified, a little heavy in some of its touches, but with some distinctive and interesting features such as its recessed corners. The building was, in fact, a handsome jewel of which a poor family might be proud; but there was no doubt that it shone incongruously in what was admittedly a somewhat tattered and dingy setting. Charlotte-town's eighteenth-century town plan, with its straight lines, perspectives, and centres of interest, might have deserved hand-some and harmonious rows of stone and brick structures; but what it had actually got was straggling and irregular lines of wooden shops and houses, clap-boarded or shingled, and painted in the prevailing and depressing Maritime tones of dull brown or slate grey. It was a small, plain, unpretending, and unprepos-sessing place, isolated, unfrequented, and almost inaccessible for nearly half the year, and cherishing in its most concentrated, quintessential form the jealous and suspicious parochialism that was so characteristic of British North America.

People said disparagingly that nothing could ever happen in Charlottetown. But this charge was utterly untrue. Charlotte-town possessed in itself an almost infinite capacity for excitements, arguments, and controversies. With angry tenant farmers con-stantly attacking absentee proprietors, and embattled Protestants resolutely confronting nearly equal numbers of determined Roman Catholics, the opportunities for political agitation within the colony were almost literally endless. Native feuds and local grievances kept Prince Edward Island politics simmering away fretfully in a state that was always just short of the boiling-point. There was no need, and not much scope, for provocation or excitement from abroad. Few visitors came to Charlottetown, and their arrival seldom made any great stir; few intrusions from the outside world ever diverted the citizens of Charlottetown from their absorbed contemplation of their own affairs. It was this long-unbroken and apparently unbreakable isolation that gave a special importance to the days at the end of August and the beginning of September 1864. On those days two intrusions, two positive invasions from abroad, were to burst through, almost together, upon Prince Edward Island's seclusion. On Tuesday, the 30th of August, Slaymaker and Nichols Olympic Circus (Goodwin and Wilder managers) – the first circus in over twenty years to visit the Island – was to begin a four-day run of per-formances. On Thursday, the 1st of September, the Maritime conference, with its complicated agenda of official and unofficial items, would hold its first meeting in the Legislative Council room in the Colonial Building.

The circus, of course, had already visited lucky places like Halifax and Saint John; but it had not yet come anywhere near the frontier citizens of the North Shore and the still more remote Islanders. To these starved people the attractions that Slaymaker and Nichols had to offer – Nichols himself, 'the great principal trick rider', Mlle Caroline, 'maîtresse de cheval', Mlle Elizabeth, 'premier equestrienne', J. Bart, 'American humourist and world's own clown', together with a troop of acting dogs and monkeys, trick horses, and performing ponies – were simply irresistible.[1] The steamboat companies, realizing their wonderful opportunities, offered special excursion rates from Shediac, Summerside, and Pictou. North-Shore New Brunswickers and Nova Scotians crowded the steamers that crossed Northumberland Strait to the Island; and all over the Island itself little straggling processions of buggies, surreys, and democrats, full of expectant circus-goers of all ages, rumbled down the red, dusty roads towards Charlottetown. The capital was crowded – overcrowded – with visitors. The only comparable influx, the old-timers declared, had come in 1860, at the time of the visit of Edward, Prince of Wales.[2] Charlottetown had only about a dozen small hotels and boarding-houses; and by night of the last day of August most of them were nearly full.

In the midst of all this excitement, almost unnoticed in the eager, pushing crowds, the delegates to the conference began to arrive. The Prince Edward Island government had certainly not planned any elaborate or formal reception for its guests. It was rumoured darkly by the newspapers that some of the ministers wanted to attend the afternoon or evening performances of the Olympic Circus; but, from whatever motives, the cabinet decided that it was quite unnecessary for a governmental reception committee, with the Premier at its head, to go down to the docks to greet the delegates. Instead, W. H. Pope, the Provincial Secretary, the almost solitary Island enthusiast for Maritime union, was appropriately deputed to welcome the visitors. Pope, a suavely correct and courteous person, inclined to be slightly fussy in matters of punctilio, was an obvious choice; but, as things turned out, he became a harassed and overworked deputy host, who received jeering criticism instead of thanks for his efforts.

R. B. Dickey, government leader in the Nova Scotia Legislative Council, came first, alone and unannounced, on the 30th of August. The four other members of the Nova Scotia delegation, with Charles Tupper at their head, reached Charlottetown by the steamer *Heather Belle* late on the next afternoon, Wednesday, August the 31st.[3] The New Brunswick delegates, together with their Lieutenant-Governor, Gordon, whose curious interest in the fate of his project would simply not permit him to stay behind in Fredericton, arrived much later, at about eleven o'clock on Wednesday night, in the crowded steamboat *Princess of Wales*, from Shediac.[4] The hour of the New Brunswickers' arrival was known in advance, W. H. Pope was on hand, and there was a small crowd of welcoming citizens on the dock, and carriages and wagons to take the delegates and their luggage to their lodgings. It was certainly an adequate reception; but unfortunately it seemed to emphasize the mortifying experience the Nova Scotians had endured in the afternoon. Their steamer had arrived late, and probably unexpectedly. Pope, at the moment of landing, was not apparently at his post. 'Not a soul belonging to the government was on the wharf to receive them,' the *Examiner* complained bitterly of the reception of the Nova Scotians, 'there was not a carriage of any kind, not even a truck, to take their luggage to the hotels or boarding-houses; and they were suffered to find out, by rule of thumb, where they could get something to eat and a bed to lie upon.'[5]

Two delegations had arrived. They had found a crowded town, a mixed reception, and one devoted but overworked host. The official conference was assembled. But where were the interlopers from the west? Late next morning, close to noon on the 1st of September, a strange steamer, with an impressive 'man-of-war cut' – the Islanders later came to call her the 'Confederate cruiser' – was seen moving slowly into the harbour.[6] The exciting news spread that the Canadians had arrived; and once again the indefatigable Pope was deputed to present the government's cordial greetings to the visitors. Pope, hurrying conscientiously down to the waterfront, was dismayed to discover that the *Queen*

Victoria had not docked, but was riding easily at anchor some little distance from the wharf. If he was really to welcome the visitors personally, there was only one way in which it could be done. He must get himself rowed out to the Canadian steamer in one of the disreputable small boats which seemed unfortunately to be the only conveyances available. It was undignified, it was dreadfully unbecoming, but the Provincial Secretary, suppressing his cultivated distaste at this monstrous departure from the fitness of things, started bravely out 'with all the dignity he could', 'in a flat-bottomed boat with a barrel of flour in the bow, and two jars of molasses in the stern, and with a lusty fisherman as his only companion, to meet . . . the distinguished visitors from Canada'.[7]

In the meantime, the distinguished visitors from Canada had been preparing their own, more ceremonial landing. The disembarkation, like the steamer from which it was made, would, it was hoped, inspire 'the natives with huge respect for their big brother from Canada'. The Canadians had planned to land dressed in their best; and Pope's heroic gesture of hospitality may not at first have made much impression upon a group of preoccupied delegates who were down in their cabins putting the finishing touches to their *toilettes*. At length, as George Brown proudly recorded, the eight ministers and their secretaries took their seats in the *Queen Victoria*'s two boats, the boats 'were lowered, man-of-war fashion, and being each duly manned with four oarsmen and a boatswain, dressed in blue uniforms, hats, belts, etc. in regular style, we pulled away for the shore . . .'.[8] Somewhere ahead, in the flat-bottomed tub, with the barrel of flour and the jars of molasses, were Pope and the fisherman, somewhat indecorously leading the way.

The Legislative Council chamber in the Colonial Building had been chosen for the conference. It was a handsome room, pleasantly proportioned, with big, well-spaced, sashed windows, Ionic pillars, white and gold *décor*, and, above, a little gallery for the admission of newspaper reporters and a few interested citizens. When the Canadians arrived, the fifteen delegates – except A. A. Macdonald, the Liberal leader in the Island Council, who was kept away by illness in his family – were all assembled and seated at the long mahogany table in the centre of the room. In the circumstances, the coming of the Canadians created a rather overpowering sensation. There was such a formidable crowd of them. The Prince Edward Island government had expected a delegation of four. What they now saw confronting them was a group of eight smiling Canadian ministers, and, in the background, the clerk of the Canadian Executive Council, and John A. Macdonald's two secretaries. The advent of the strange, unofficial contingent, which in numbers did not fall very short of equalling the combined total of official delegates, seemed obviously the crowning moment in the gathering of the conference.

The Prince Edward Island government and its Maritime guests certainly appeared to look on it in this light. They had simply waited, without doing anything, until the Canadians arrived. They had even postponed the business of officially constituting their own conference, though all the Maritime delegates, with one exception, were in their places and ready to begin. The distinction between the 'official' conference on Maritime union, and the 'unofficial' conference on general federation, almost seemed in danger of disappearing before the proceedings actually began. But, despite their apparent awe of their impressive western visitors, the Maritimers took care to observe the constitutional formalities of the occasion.[9] The Canadians, not yet recognized delegates but simply privileged guests, were escorted to the little gallery above. From there they looked on while the Maritimers proceeded to organize their conference, and to elect John Hamilton Gray, the Premier of Prince Edward Island, as its chairman.

The significance of this formality was slightly weakened by its extreme brevity. Once their conference was organized and its chairman chosen, the Maritimers postponed any further action on their official business, and formally invited the Canadians to join with them. In a rather complicated series of introductions, the eight Canadian delegates were presented to the fourteen members of the Maritime conference, with most of whom they were completely unacquainted; and then, after a brisk exchange of hearty banalities, the conference was declared adjourned for the dispatch of business until Friday at ten o'clock. The Cana-

dians, with their new hosts as guides, went away to cope with the
difficult problem of lodgings. George Brown was invited to stay
at the Provincial Secretary's house, a few of his colleagues put up
at the Franklin House, and the rest of the Canadian delegation
remained on board the *Queen Victoria* in the harbour.[10] There
were simply too many delegates. Even Lieutenant-Governor
Dundas, who gave a large dinner-party that night to the members
of the conference, found that the suddenly and largely increased
number of delegates was a little too much for the generous limits
of his dining-room table. He had probably intended to ask them
all. He had to invite only as many as he could 'conveniently
receive'.

That night, while the Dundas dinner-party was in full swing,
the Union Generals Sherman and Thomas, bivouacking after
their final fight with Hood for the possession of Atlanta, heard
the heavy explosions that signified the Confederate abandonment
of the beleaguered city. During the 1860s, two new nations – the
Confederate States of America and the Dominion of Canada,
nations that might have helped and strengthened each other –
emerged on the North American continent. September 1864 saw
the beginning of the first stage in the creation of the Dominion;
September 1864 marked also the opening of the last, desperate
phase in the tragic history of the Confederacy. The capture of
Atlanta was the beginning of Sherman's annihilating march to
the sea, the beginning of the final disintegration of Southern
power. But British Americans did not yet grasp the significance
of what was happening. They did not realize that the war was
coming to an end and that their long immunity from possible
external danger was nearly over. The terrible military attrition
of the last four months, the growing war-weariness in the North,
the approaching presidential election, and the 'peace platform'
of the Democratic party convention, all helped to keep alive the
hope of a negotiated settlement. 'Upon the whole', wrote the
editor of the Saint John *Morning News* on the 29th of August,
three days before the fall of Atlanta, 'the prospect of Southern
independence has never looked brighter than at this moment.'[11]
'We cling firmly to the belief', the Toronto *Leader* affirmed a
fortnight later on the 10th of September, 'that the power of the

Confederacy has not been shaken and that there will be no peace except through war and the separation which will result therefrom.'[12]

The collapse of the South and the restoration of the Union were to have profound effects upon the future northern nation; but the Canadian delegates, who went late and gratefully to bed that night in Charlottetown, were not speculating on the possible consequences of the fall of the Confederacy. They were not even aware of its imminence. They were thinking of their mission and of the triumph their first day in Charlottetown had brought. The Maritimers had invited them to take part in the work of the conference. Obviously they were not wedded to their own small union scheme. They were even ready to postpone its consideration in order to give first priority to the Canadian plan. Their interest in the idea of a great, single British American nation did not need to be awakened; apparently it already existed. They wanted to hear more about this giant collective enterprise, which would have two oceans as its only limits, and in which all the British American provinces would be associated. And tomorrow, at ten o'clock, the Canadians would have the chance to unfold their plan.

⋙ II ⋘

IN PRINCE EDWARD ISLAND, even the extreme heats of summer were tempered by the breezes of the Gulf; but the first few days of September 1864 were exceptional days, unusually warm and sunny for any time of the year. At ten o'clock on the morning of Friday, the 2nd of September, when the delegates assembled at the Colonial Building, the Legislative Council chamber, with its white woodwork and gold decorations, was full of brilliant light. It was also rather full of humanity, for the attendance at the Legislative Council debates in Prince Edward Island did not usually exceed a dozen, and the twenty-three delegates at the Charlottetown Conference were nearly double that number. There was not much more than room for them all as they crowded around the long table and prepared, not to take part in a discussion or a debate, but to listen to the gradual and careful unfolding of a plan. It was an attentive audience, neutral, uncommitted, sceptical, yet curious and interested. The Canadians, on their part, were ready and hopeful. They knew their scheme. Each of the four principals – Macdonald, Cartier, Brown, and Galt – had been assigned a definite part in its exposition. It was their great chance.

'On Friday,' George Brown told his wife, '. . . Canada opened her batteries.'[13] John A. Macdonald and George E. Cartier, the two effective leaders of the Canadian Coalition – for Taché's position as first minister was purely titular and he had not come to the conference – divided the day's exposition between them.[14] Their task, which was logically the first and perhaps the most important of all, was to set out the arguments in favour of the Canadian plan – to prove that confederation was possible, desirable, and even necessary. It was a difficult task, and mainly for a single, fundamental reason: a basic feature of the Canadian plan – its immediacy – was new, unfamiliar, and not immediately convincing to the fourteen Maritimers sitting around the long mahogany table that morning. They were unprepared to accept the need of instant action upon which the urgent Canadians placed so much stress. That the enormous and half-empty territories of British America would some day take the form of a nation was a vague assumption they shared in common. But this stupendous undertaking was usually placed in the future, and often in the quite remote future. In the meantime, life as self-governing provinces of the British Empire, with all the real autonomy in domestic affairs that responsible government had ensured, was a very tolerable state of political existence, with which they were all perfectly familiar, and with which very few – except, apparently, the Canadians – were seriously dissatisfied.

Confederation – the project the Canadians now offered – had obviously been chosen as a middle point between these two poles of thought, a compromise between growing national aspirations on the one hand and rooted provincial habits on the other. But was it a satisfactory compromise? Nothing, at any rate, was more likely to win it an attentive and sympathetic hearing from the Maritimers than the combined persuasive powers of Macdonald and Cartier. Outwardly they were a curious contrast. Cartier was short and stocky, with a square, rather rugged countenance and close-cut hair, *en brosse*. His apparently inexhaustible vitality, his unforced heartiness, made him a natural ambassador. He enjoyed company and talk, songs and parties and dances, with an unabashed, engaging gusto. His voice was rather high-pitched, his manner intense, positive, almost explosive; and his fluent English came tumbling out with cheerful disregard for received idiom and pronunciation. The straightforward candour and vigorous downrightness of all he said were both disarming and impressive. Macdonald's debating style was much more casual, conversational, and unemphatic; but the range of his knowledge and the scope and organization of his ideas were impressive from the beginning; and his tall, spare frame and oddly youthful appearance, his easy, jaunty manner and genial ways, began to win him friends at once. He and Cartier had acted together politically for a decade with never a serious difference. They held many fundamental beliefs in common. Yet, in a fashion that was extremely valuable at that moment, they differed from each other, complemented each other, and together produced a more convincing total effect. Macdonald was the acknowledged advocate of the most strongly centralized federation that could be devised. Cartier, whose first and fundamental duty in political life was to defend the special institutions and distinctive culture of French Canada, stood out, in the eyes of the Maritimers, as a living guarantee that local loyalties and local administration must be permitted to survive.

The two men, who knew each other and their present brief so well, were an extremely effective team. When they had finished their elaborate exposition, the process of the conversion of the Maritimers – a fairly swift process it turned out to be – had been taken a first long stage forward. At three o'clock the conference adjourned; and the proceedings of this first day became a pattern which the subsequent sessions followed. From mid-morning to mid-afternoon, the delegates listened to the gradual revelation of the Canadian plan; for the rest of the day there were entertainments for the whole conference, or its members amused themselves in groups or as individuals. That first afternoon,

W. H. Pope, who had certainly honestly earned his title as senior host, gave a grand *déjeuner à la fourchette*, with oysters, lobsters, and other Island specialties. The evening, which was as balmy as the warmest night of summer, with a great golden full moon high in the sky, was free for any kind of relaxation. Some delegates drove out in carriages into the quiet countryside; others spent the evening boating in the bay. George Brown, lazily reclining in a chair on the balcony of Pope's house, looked out over the moonlit waters of the Strait.[15]

Next morning the Canadians began the second stage of their exposition. They had tried first to justify the immediate creation of a federal union. They now began to describe and analyse the political machinery they had designed for it; and the outline of their financial arrangements – always a dangerously controversial aspect of federalism – came first. Alexander Galt, Minister of Finance in the Canadian Coalition, succeeded his two less specialized seniors, Cartier and Macdonald;[16] and Galt was a magician who, on set occasions and with a great theme to inspire him, could give a spectacularly brilliant performance. The Maritimers naturally compared him with Tilley, who was regarded as their best financier. Tilley, in his sensible, unassuming way, had a strong interest in economic growth and a resourceful dexterity with figures; but his laconic speaking manner, the chief virtues of which were clarity, simplicity, and brevity, was hardly more inspiring than that of a capable accountant. Galt, a large forceful man, whose moody, difficult temperament contrasted oddly with Tilley's even-tempered serenity, was an altogether different person.

Gordon, who talked a good deal with him at Charlottetown, thought Galt 'by far the ablest' of the Canadians.[17] Galt had a strong creative instinct, a vigorous expansionist urge, an infectiously enthusiastic capacity for designing large projects, and an amazing fertility in argument and expedient. This was one of the great moments of his career. He was financing the largest of all enterprises, a transcontinental nation; and he could talk, not only in those sweeping generalities and rhetorical flourishes he liked so much, but also with that wealth of convincing illustrative detail of which he was such a master. All the main features of the

Canadian plan – the assumption by the new general government of all provincial debt (and possibly the device of the debt allowance by which this transference could be equitably carried out), the payments of subsidies, based on population, to the new local governments, and the division of sources of revenue between the federation and the provinces – all were set out as parts of one great, integrated, and coherent whole. Galt knew the plan to which he himself had contributed so much, down to its smallest detail; and he excelled himself in its presentation.[18]

At three o'clock, when Galt's brilliant performance was over and the conference once more adjourned, the Canadians reversed their natural roles as guests in Charlottetown and invited their Maritime colleagues to a luncheon on board the *Queen Victoria*.[19] The 'excellent stores of all kinds' and the 'unexceptionable cook', which, Brown had told his wife, were part of the steamer's equipment, now served a different, semi-political purpose. It was an elaborate luncheon, served in 'princely style'; and – what was perhaps equally important – it came at a peculiarly appropriate time. The first awkward moments of the conference were definitely over. The Canadians had been quickly rescued from the embarrassment of their position and made to feel completely at home. Maritimers and Canadians were now able to fit names to faces without difficulty. Acquaintanceships – some of which developed into life-long friendships and associations – were already in process of formation. The word 'confederation', which, up to forty-eight hours before, had seemed to many a vague and not particularly attractive generalization, had now become charged with precise and massive significance.

Rapidly, naturally, the luncheon on board the *Queen Victoria* began to take on a special character of its own. The afternoon sunlight glittered on the decks. The champagne corks popped merrily. There was a babble of gay talk, and bursts of convivial laughter. It was a hilarious party; and stealing into its hilarity was a warmth of feeling, natural enough for fellow subjects of the Queen, who now began to feel themselves fellow citizens of British America. Cartier and Brown made speeches extolling the future of the new, northern, transcontinental nation;[20] and the spectacle of these two bitter and inveterate enemies singing variations on the same theme of national unity somehow caught the imagination of the onlookers and lifted them into a gay confidence in the future which was as heady as the champagne that bubbled in their glasses. They were British Americans who had always assumed, secretly or openly, that, some day in the future, the British North American provinces would join together to make a united nation. Was this union impossible for their generation to achieve? The Canadians had argued, with messianic fervour, that it could be done at once. They were providing what looked to be a workable plan for bringing it into existence immediately. Why should it not be tried? Was there anyone opposed to making the attempt? 'If any one can show just cause or impediment why the Colonies should not be united in matrimonial alliance,' one of the delegates called out loudly, 'let him now express it or for ever hold his peace.'[21] There was silence while the delegates, with their champagne glasses in hand, smiled and waited. No man appeared to forbid the banns. Then, as George Brown told the story to his wife, 'the union was thereupon formally completed and proclaimed'.[22]

Some hours later, as if one entertainment in the Canadian style were not enough for the day, the conference gathered again for dinner at Colonel Gray's handsome dwelling, Inkerman House, a little distance out from Charlottetown. They were British North Americans now and, in spirit at least, the union was made.

»»» III «««

By MONDAY, when the conference met for its third session, the weather had slightly changed.[23] The lovely midsummer warmth of those first few days of September had ended and it was perceptibly cooler. A stiff wind stirred up occasional clouds of red Island dust; and at night there was comfort in the warmth of an overcoat. On Sunday the delegates had gone to church in dutiful mid-Victorian fashion and spent the afternoon in relaxation; and at ten o'clock on Monday, fortified by his rest and the good discourse that he had heard at the Free Church the day

EDWARD PALMER   GEORGE COLES
Prince Edward Island

EDWARD WHELAN
Prince Edward Island

Queen Street, Charlottetown

Government House, Charlottetown

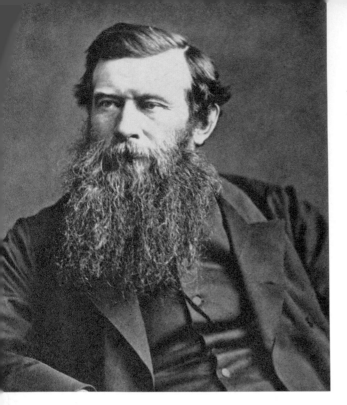

WILLIAM HENRY POPE
Prince Edward Island

JOHN HAMILTON GRAY
Prince Edward Island

before, George Brown rose to continue the elaborate exposition
of the Canadian confederation scheme. In some ways, his share
of the three-day Canadian lecture course on federal union might
have seemed the heaviest of all. He had to explain the Canadian
answers to the two crucial problems of federalism – the constitution of the bicameral federal legislature and the division of
powers between the central and local governments.[24]

There was one main feature of the proposed federal parliament
that was probably perfectly well known to most members of the
conference before Brown so much as opened his mouth that
morning. Throughout British North America, he was famous or
notorious as the determined advocate of representation by
population. The Maritimers were well aware that Rep. by Pop.
was inevitable in the federal assembly, as the Canadians had
conceived it; and the only really uncertain feature of the proposed central legislature was the composition of the upper house
or legislative council. On this vital matter, the Canadian government seemed disposed, though not too explicitly, to follow the
model of the United States. In the supplementary 'Ministerial
Explanations', intended to remove misunderstandings and quiet
fears, which Macdonald and Taché had made on the 23rd and
24th of June, it had been stated that 'one branch of the legislature
must be composed on the principle of equality, each section,
state or province being equally represented therein. . . .'[25]

This, despite a certain confusing redundancy of terms, seemed
to promise provincial equality. But this was not what the Canadians had in mind. Their object was regional, not provincial,
equality; this change, they thought, was dictated by the lessons of
history. They were convinced that states' powers and states' pretensions had caused the break-up of American federalism; and
they believed that general regional needs and interests rather
than particular states' rights should be represented in the British
American upper house. In his long speech on the 5th of September, Brown proposed that the legislative council should be
composed of sixty appointed members – twenty from Canada
West, twenty from Canada East, and twenty from the Maritime
Provinces. Maritime representation would remain exactly the
same, whether the Atlantic provinces entered the confederation

as one government or as three. The Canadians, of course, had every reason to expect that a united Acadia would be created. This, indeed, was the main purpose of the Charlottetown Conference. But the success or failure of Maritime union was not to make any difference in the composition of the legislative council.[26] Regional equality in the upper house became one of the most distinctive and most contentious features of the Canadian plan.

The second major subject with which Brown had to deal that morning was the other crucial problem of federalism – the problem of the division of powers. Here, also, the Canadian cabinet had worked out a fairly complete solution to which, as time would show, it was to cling with great tenacity. The basis of the plan was a single, simple principle, which, like the idea of regional representation in the legislative council, had been derived from the tragic history of the disruption in the United States. The Canadians believed that the states had been fortified and encouraged in their truculent independence by the fatal clause in the American Constitution which provided that all powers not specifically assigned to the central government were reserved to the states or the people. This 'primary error' of the American Constitution must, the Canadians thought, be avoided at all costs. The American principle of division would have to be completely reversed; and in the British North American federation, residuary powers should be granted, not to the provinces, but to the general government.[27]

Theoretically, the method of division could thus have been a very simple one. All that was necessary was to provide a short list of 'local matters' that would be dealt with by 'local assemblies', and then to declare that all remaining legislative power was vested in the federal parliament. Yet the Canadians, somewhat curiously, did not follow this simple method. They may have wished for what was later called 'greater certainty'. They may have feared that the importance of the residuary clause would be reduced if they did not illustrate its vast scope by providing a number of examples. At all events, they complicated the basic simplicity of their plan by drawing up, not only a short list of local powers, but also a considerably longer list of 'general' or 'federal' functions. Both lists were integral parts of the scheme Brown presented that morning and both, quite evidently, had been prepared with great care. Apart from a few minor differences, chiefly of phraseology, they anticipated fairly accurately the final form of the Canadian proposals for the division of powers.[28]

George Brown's was the last of the four set speeches describing the Canadian plan; but on Tuesday, the 6th of September, the conference gave another full day's examination to the Canadian proposals. There were questions that the Maritimers wanted to ask; there were obscure or difficult points that the Canadians wished to explain more fully. This was the crucial session in which serious arguments over special features of the plan might have developed or a general Maritime opposition to the very idea of confederation could have arisen. Yet, in fact, the conference did not get itself locked in dispute over either the principles or the details of the Canadian scheme. For the first time, the proceedings took 'a conversational turn', and a good many delegates spoke;[29] but, on the whole, the Maritimers had astonishingly few additions to propose or changes to submit. George Coles, the Reform leader in Prince Edward Island, apparently suggested that confederation should be accompanied by a special and substantial grant to the Island for the extinction of the rights of its absentee proprietors. Tilley and E. B. Chandler of New Brunswick argued forcibly and persuasively in favour of federal appointment of the judges, as a means of avoiding local political pressures and bad appointments. There was a fairly lengthy discussion – an ominous foretaste of what was to come – of the proposed basis of the composition of the legislative council and the suggested method of the selection of its members; but although a minority of the delegates favoured – and continued to favour – the election of councillors, there was no determined opposition to the principle of regional equality which was the real basis of the Canadian plan.[30]

With this fourth and final session, Canada closed its case for confederation.[31] That evening Governor Dundas and his lady gave a ball and supper at Government House for the delegates,[32] and, as they danced about the white Doric columns of that lofty hall, the Canadians had the best of reasons for feeling, as well as looking, extremely pleased with themselves. They had been generously given the utmost latitude in the presentation of their case; and its reception, through three days of lengthy speeches, could hardly have been more interested. The idea that the northern provinces could unite to form a great and potentially far greater nation had found a ready response among the Maritime delegates; and everything they had said suggested that they found the Canadian plan a practical basis of union. So far, of course, they had committed themselves to nothing, and, as the Canadians knew very well, they had other, 'official' business at Charlottetown on which a decision would have to be reached. They had, in fact, been six days at Charlottetown, and they had scarcely given Maritime union a thought. They must meet – and meet at once – to discuss the project that had brought them there in the first place.

On Wednesday, the 7th of September, the Maritimers assembled alone in the Legislative Council chamber.[33] Their state of mind was extremely divided and uncertain. Maritime union had never been a popular cause. It had been viewed more often with indifference and hostility than with enthusiasm; and now it was very difficult, if not impossible, to judge it solely on its own merits. It could hardly be considered except in relation to the grander project of confederation; and this inescapable necessity could not help but have an influence on the Maritimers' views of their own scheme. On the whole, the Nova Scotians were the most eager and the most united in their desire to press ahead with the Maritime union project. The New Brunswickers, though with some doubts and hesitations, were ready to follow the Nova Scotians into union. But the Prince Edward Island delegation, with the probable exception of only one of its members, W. H. Pope, was utterly and irreconcilably opposed to a union that would mean the abandonment of its own little autonomous legislature.[34] This intransigence destroyed all hope of an easy and rapid accomplishment of a united Acadia; and it left the Maritimers without any obvious alternative course by which they could salvage their own legislative union scheme, and at the same time continue negotiations with the Canadians for a federal British North American union.

It was possible, of course, that Nova Scotia and New Brunswick might join in a partial union, on the assumption – which Lieutenant-Governor Gordon considered a certainty – that Prince Edward Island would very soon change its mind and come begging for admission.[35] But this would mean delay, and the very last thing that the Canadians were prepared to endure was delay. Their announced policy committed them to the federation of the two Canadas if the confederation of British America proved not to be quickly realizable. For Canadians, confederation must come now or be left for the next generation; and to the unhappy and uncertain Maritimers sitting around the Council table that morning, it began to seem certain that persistence in Maritime union was a certain way of ensuring that confederation would not come now. 'I am apt to think, after all,' wrote the correspondent – almost certainly the Nova Scotian delegate, Jonathan McCully – of the Halifax *Morning Chronicle*, 'that the idea of a legislative union of the three will be suspended, at all events for the present. The effort of accomplishing the double organization – both a legislative union of the three and a confederation of the whole at once – would probably tax the power of human effort too heavily.'[36]

By the time the Wednesday session ended, the Maritimers had made up their minds. They had come to the conclusion that Maritime union was a hopeless cause, at least for the moment. Confederation, on the other hand, seemed an inviting prospect, whose possibilities they were ready at least to explore further. They informed the Canadians. George Brown reported to his wife, 'that they were unanimous in regarding federation of all the Provinces to be highly desirable, if *the terms of union could be made satisfactory*, and that they were prepared to waive their own more limited question until the details of our scheme could be more fully considered and matured'.[37] In effect, this announcement ended the Charlottetown Conference. It was adjourned until the 12th of September, at Halifax, and its members were to continue their Maritime tour further; but with the announcement of the 7th of September its real business was finished. Maritime union and confederation had confronted each other as possible associates or potential competitors. Within a week, the delegates had backed away in impatience and relief from the delicate business of making two new constitutions at the same time. Maritime union had been abandoned because it was only partly realizable and because its complications and difficulties might delay or prevent confederation.

Confederation had triumphed. The swift success of the Canadians was astonishing; but it had its limitations nevertheless. All that the Canadian delegation had really gained was the support, conditional and qualified by private reservations, of a small number of prominent Maritime politicians; but beyond this small group was the much larger body of Maritime public men; and beyond them again were the press and the Maritime people. The Charlottetown Conference had held its sessions in private. Privacy permitted the greatest freedom and informality of discussion within the four walls of the Legislative Council chamber; but it also, and inevitably, aroused a large amount of suspicion, resentment, and criticism outside. The Charlottetown newspapermen and the Islanders generally were the first to feel this irritation. The conference was being held in their very midst and they had not the remotest idea what was going on. 'All inquiries of the delegates, touching the scope of their deliberations, are repelled with austere dignity,' complained Edward Whelan of the *Examiner*. '. . . A band of conspirators could not observe more secrecy than they have done.'[38] The Islanders instantly began to think the worst; their own delegates were regarded darkly as suspected traitors. 'There go the men who would sell their country,' was heard on the street when members of the Prince Edward Island delegation passed by.[39]

≫ IV ≪

ONCE the Maritimers had given their answer to the Canadians, the tension broke. For the last day and a half on the Island, the conference relaxed. The Canadians had already entertained the delegates with a party on their steamer; but they had not shown it off to the Charlottetown hostesses – Mrs. Dundas and Mesdames Gray, Pope, Palmer, and Coles, the wives of four of the Island representatives – who, for the past week, had been giving them elaborate luncheons, dinners, and balls. It would be civil to repay their hospitality. It might be politic to prove to Charlottetown women in general that the Canadians were gallant fellows who never forgot the other sex. On Wednesday afternoon, Mrs. Dundas and a large group of ladies were rowed out, in small boats overflowing with crinolines, to the *Queen Victoria*; and the Canadians welcomed them to a *déjeuner* that was as lavish as the first, if slightly less convivial.[40] On Thursday, the more curious and serious-minded delegates, whose interest in the Island and its activities remained unsatisfied, went on a long excursion to the north shore; while other delegates, who felt that they had already had more than enough of sightseeing, stayed in Charlottetown, rested, paid farewell calls, and prepared to depart.[41]

The final and crowning event of the conference was the grand ball, given by the Prince Edward Island government and the leading citizens of Charlottetown, which was held on Thursday night in the Colonial Building. In the brief interval – scarcely more than twenty-four hours – since the conference had quitted the building, a little army of earnest workers had been frantically getting it ready for the party. The Legislative Council chamber, where the delegates had so recently been discussing and arguing, was fitted up as a reception- or drawing-room, and there the Lieutenant-Governor formally received the guests. The Assembly room, the twin of the Legislative Council chamber, which was situated at the other end of the long hall on the first floor, had been transformed into a ballroom, and here the hard-working decorators had achieved their most lavish effects. The arms of Prince Edward Island, in a great transparency, hung over the Speaker's chair. There were large mirrors at each end of the room; flags, evergreens, and flowers decorated the walls and corners. The superintendent of the local gas-works had exercised his utmost ingenuity in devising lighting effects; and in the two tall looking-glasses the sparkling clusters of lights, and the colours of flags, flowers, and swirling crinolines were repeated gaily in endless reflections. There were two bands, assisted by violinists and pianists, so that the music never flagged. If the dancers should happen to do so, there was a most convenient refreshment room in the Legislative Library on the same floor, where tea and coffee were available, as well as quantities of sherry, claret, and champagne. These refreshments were, however, mere appetizers and aperitifs. Downstairs, in the Supreme Court room on the ground floor, where tables were already set out with gleaming white cloths and sparkling cutlery and glassware, supper was waiting to be served.[42]

The night provided a brilliant illustration of the apparently endless vitality of mid-Victorian British North America. It was nine o'clock before the guests began to arrive, and about ten before the Governor, with Mrs. Haviland on his arm, and John A. Macdonald with Mrs. Dundas on his, led the way to the ballroom and the first quadrille began. In Charlottetown, as in Quebec, almost everybody except the really old and decrepit wanted to dance and keep on dancing; but, for the few eccentrics who preferred talk, and for the breathless couples who felt that they needed to sit one out, there was always the refreshment room, where drinks were copiously available, and where D'Arcy McGee, the one man in the party with a truly British North American reputation for wit and humour, kept a large crowd in a pretty continuous roar of laughter.[43] Midnight came and went, while the bands played on with hardly an interval, and it was probably an hour later when the whole company trooped down to the Supreme Court room. Dundas took his place as chairman, and the supper began.

It was a very odd supper, for a ball. In fact, it seemed abruptly to change its character, to transform itself into a ceremonial dinner, and to behave as if it had started at seven or eight o'clock in the evening instead of one o'clock in the morning. The food – beef, hams, salmon, lobster, oysters, salad, pastry, fruits, and wines – came close enough to making up a dinner-party menu; and it was followed by that inevitable appendage of a formal mid-Victorian dinner, an elaborate toast list, which wound its way deliberately and punctiliously in the time-honoured fashion from the toast to the Queen, through toasts to other members of the royal family, the Governors of British North America and the Army and Navy, to the visitors and the 'fraternal feeling' of British North Americans. 'The Goths commenced speech-making,' George Brown wrote sardonically to his wife, 'and actually kept at it for two hours and three-quarters, the poor girls being condemned to listen to it all!'[44] There were others besides the poor trapped women who felt acute fatigue, when the parade of speakers mercifully ended, close to four o'clock in the morning. But, despite their weariness, the Canadians were pleasurably aware of the fact that the speakers, though they tended to skirt the subject of union in a gingerly and general fashion, often showed approval and sometimes flashes of real enthusiasm. Charles Tupper's zeal for confederation might have been expected; but it was interesting to note that Colonel J. H. Gray of New Brunswick was already expatiating, in his fluent and cloudy rhetoric, upon the noble future of a united British America. It was highly reassuring also to hear A. G. Archibald, the leader of the Liberal opposition in the Nova Scotia Assembly and the man who had taken the place in the Nova Scotian dele-gation which Joseph Howe had had to decline, declare without qualification that in his province opposition and government were as one on the subject of union.[45]

Even then, when the applause had died away and the last guest had left the supper-table, the activities of that hectic night were not yet over. There was to be no return through the de-serted streets of Charlottetown to the comfort of familiar beds. The Canadians had offered to take the whole conference on the next lap of its perambulations, across Northumberland Strait to the Nova Scotia mainland; and twenty-three delegates and three Canadian civil servants had to say their good-byes, collect their luggage, and hurry down to the harbour. The *Queen Victoria*, with steam up, was waiting to be gone; but an unusual fog, which was so thick that those two veteran steamers *Heather Belle* and *Princess of Wales* ran aground in the mud of the harbour, blotted out Charlottetown and Hillsborough Bay completely and kept the *Queen Victoria* steady at anchor.[46] It was eight o'clock before the fog cleared and the vessel at last got under way; and then the delegates, who had had too much food and far too little sleep, sat down to a hearty breakfast. The food, the excitements of the last twelve hours, and the magical blue day that emerged from the evaporating mist, kept the party in high spirits until it arrived at Pictou.[47]

Here the delegates separated. A few, including Macdonald, Langevin, and McGee, who prudently realized their limitations and wanted a good rest more than anything else, remained on the steamer and journeyed in a leisurely fashion along the North Shore, through the Strait of Canso, and down to Halifax. The rest of the party, led by such indefatigably curious sightseers as Galt and Brown, disembarked at Pictou and went off on a conducted tour to the coal-mines of New Glasgow.[48] They saw all there was to see at the mines, accepted the substantial 'entertainments' offered by the officials of the mining association, and were driven in coaches across the full width of the Isthmus of Chignecto to Truro. By this time it was midnight and their last reserves of strength were gone. A special train was waiting to take them over the last part of the overland journey to Halifax. It was too much. The mere thought of a special train and more hours of travel aroused nothing but feeble loathing.[49] They collapsed into beds in the Truro hotels, boarded the special train in the morning, and reached Halifax at half past twelve, only a little while after the *Queen Victoria* had come to rest in the harbour.[50]

That afternoon, Saturday, the 10th of September, the conference assembled in the handsomely decorated Legislative Council chamber in the Nova Scotian Province House. It met again on Monday, the 12th, at the accustomed hour of ten o'clock. The first part of this Monday session was taken up with a private discussion held by the Maritime delegates alone; but within an hour the Canadians rejoined their colleagues, and together the 'official' and the 'unofficial' delegates took the one great decision to which their deliberations had led them.[51] Doubt and dissent, half-hidden, partly articulate, did exist among the Maritime delegates; but a formidable group of their principal leaders and spokesmen, fired with the tremendous prospect of nation-building in their own generation, had been veritably swept off their feet. 'We are all in favour of Federation if we can agree on conditions,' Brown summed up the general feeling of the conference at that Monday session, 'and we have good hopes that we can agree on conditions.'[52] With these good hopes high in the ascendant, the delegates decided that a new conference, whose 'official' subject would be the confederation of British North America, including Newfoundland, was to be held at Quebec beginning the 10th of October.

⟫⟫ V ⋘

CONFERENCE closed today,' Macdonald telegraphed to Taché, giving him the portentous news of the approaching gathering at Quebec.[53] It was true that the delegates had ceased their discussions, but their travels and their public speech-making were by no means over. The Maritime people, inclined to be suspicious and critical of this highly secretive and mysterious gathering at Charlottetown, wanted, and deserved, some news. Unfortunately the delegates had nothing very concrete to offer them. The conference had passed no resolutions. No action at all had been taken on the 'official' subject; and the discussions on the 'unofficial' subject of confederation had been so informal and inconclusive that the delegates were still very uncertain how far – if at all – they could be revealed. The Canadian plan, which would become 'official' business only on the 10th of October at Quebec, was scarcely yet in a shape to be made public, even in a summary form. But the theme of union, which had inspired that plan and had captured the imagination of the delegates: surely that could – and should – be discussed? There had been no real opportunity in the tired morning hours of the supper-party at Charlottetown to talk to the Maritimers about the ends and means of British American nationhood. But here, in the capital of Nova Scotia, at a big public dinner, was an ideal occasion.

The rain poured down that night; but the company in the dining-room of the Halifax Hotel was large and apparently enthusiastic. The theme of union ran through everything that was said. Some speakers – Maritimers in particular – approached it a little obliquely, or avoided committing themselves too definitely, or, like Tilley of New Brunswick, expressed no decided preference as between Maritime union and confederation.[54] But the Canadians felt none of these inhibitions; they were promoters who were trying by every device at their command to win popular approval for their plan. Cartier, with his endearing slight mispronunciations and his rambling, inconsequential, but hearty manner, tried to prove how the seaboard and inland provinces needed and complemented each other.[55] Brown, in an elaborate speech, over an hour long and heavily freighted with statistics, set out to demonstrate how the combined human and material resources of the British North American provinces would make a great nation.[56] These speeches, as well as Galt's on financial matters, all concentrated on the possibility – the practicability – of making a federal British North America. Macdonald, who was the first to reply to the toast on 'Colonial Union', chose a rather different approach. His main theme was the character – and in particular the centralized strength – of the proposed federation. This, of course, was the principal feature of the Canadian plan; and of all the speakers that night, Macdonald came closest to a real indiscretion in revealing it. The unified strength of the proposed confederation had become his obsession. 'Now', he said revealingly, 'I see something which is well worthy of all I have suffered in the cause of my little country.... If we can only obtain that object – a vigorous general government – we shall not be New Brunswickers, nor Nova Scotians, nor Canadians, but British Americans, under the sway of the British sovereign.'[57]

If the second half of the work of the Charlottetown Conference was travel, publicity, and promotion, then the dinner at the Halifax Hotel marked only its beginning. The four principal Maritime towns liked to assume that they were on a plane of relative equality (it was the main reason why they could hardly conceive of a common capital); and if a party of British North American politicians began a tour of the Maritime Provinces by stops at Charlottetown and Halifax it was utterly unthinkable that they should not then go on to visit both Saint John and Fredericton. On Wednesday, the 14th of September, after a whole day of delicious rest, the delegates began this final and essential stage of their wanderings, with most of the party going by train to Windsor and across the Bay of Fundy by the steamer *Emperor* to Saint John, while Macdonald, his secretaries, and one or two others boarded the *Queen Victoria* again and cruised back along the North Shore to Shediac.[58] Not all the Canadians were present at the big public dinner the New Brunswickers gave the delegates that night, for Macdonald missed the train at Shediac;[59] but Cartier, Brown, Galt, McDougall, and McGee all joined the long procession of speakers; and the incurably optimistic Brown thought that 'the affair went off splendidly and we made quite an impression on the natives'.[60] There were a few more public avowals of belief in confederation, including a very emphatic one from John Hamilton Gray of Prince Edward Island.[61] There were also a few signs of hesitation and dissent. George Coles, also from the Island, in a ponderously jocular speech, compared his province to a maiden whom Canada had wooed but not yet won.[62] And when the chairman, Gray of New Brunswick, gave the toast to 'colonial union', Timothy Anglin, the fiery editor of the Saint John *Morning Freeman*, remained defiantly in his chair.[63]

It was raining next morning when the steamer took the delegates up the St. John River. Carriages were waiting at Fredericton – as they had not been waiting at Charlottetown – to show the visitors the sights and drive them to their lodgings;[64] and Cartier, Galt, and Brown – Macdonald did not catch up with his colleagues – who were to be the Lieutenant-Governor's guests during their stay in the capital, were brought out in style in the viceregal carriage to what Brown thought of as 'very grand quarters' at Government House.[65] Gordon gave a large dinner-party that night for the members of what he referred to as the 'ambulatory conference'; but he could hardly have given his dinner guests anything like the time that he devoted to the three senior Canadians who were staying the night with him. He pumped Cartier, Galt, and Brown assiduously for news of Charlottetown and details of the Canadian scheme for confederation. He almost certainly offered quantities of valuable advice himself.

It was a curious discussion. On the one hand, with his long, bearded, melancholy countenance and brooding eyes, was Gordon, the man who had hoped ultimately for a legislative union of British America and who had put himself at the head of the movement for the legislative union of the Maritime Provinces. On the other hand, full of their scheme and overjoyed with their reception at Charlottetown, Halifax, and Saint John, were the Canadians, three of the principal authors of a design for a federal union, into which the Maritime Provinces, it was now increasingly assumed, would probably enter as separate provinces. Gordon was convinced that it was the Canadian intervention at Charlottetown which had alone caused the ruin of the Maritime-union project.[66] He was equally certain that a fundamental and fatal weakness lay in the very nature of federalism. As he listened to the excited and talkative Canadians explaining their plan, he thought he saw the inevitable defects emerging clearly. The conflict between the federalists and the provincial-rightists in the division of legislative powers had not ended as conclusively as it ought to have done in the federation's favour. The constitution of the local governments and legislatures had been left extremely vague, perhaps deliberately so. Worst of all, the complete subordination of these local bodies to a central authority that must be paramount if the federation was to be of the slightest value had not been secured at all.[67] Gordon was determined to oppose. So far, federalism had triumphed. It might triumph again at the approaching Quebec Conference. But beyond the conference at Quebec was the British government and the British Parliament; and before that government would accept a federal union and that Parliament enact it, the Crown would surely ask the advice and accept the guidance of its trusted representatives in British America, including himself.

'Mr. Gordon is a man who does his own thinking,' Brown said tolerantly to Cardwell later that autumn.[68] When Cardwell passed the compliment on, Gordon was amused that he had succeeded in concealing so effectively his real feelings – including his feeling of utter abhorrence for that 'dangerous and unscrupulous demagogue' Brown.[69] Next morning, when Cartier, Galt, and Brown set off on the return journey down the river to Saint John, they could have had little idea that the man they had just left behind in Government House was to play such a curious, contorted, and crucially important role in the movement for union on which they had staked their political future. On that last day of the tour, doubts and apprehensions were forgotten in the joyful realization that their mission was over, that it had been an unexpected but tremendous success, and that the solidarity of the Coalition was stronger than ever. 'We have got on very amicably – we Canadians – wonderfully so!' George Brown told his wife.[70] 'Our expedition has been all and more than we could have hoped.'[71]

Now they were eager to be home. A special train carried them from Saint John to Shediac, and there that hard-worked 'Confederate cruiser', the *Queen Victoria*, was waiting for them at anchor. It was midnight and pitch dark when they went aboard; but the steamer put out at once and headed up the Gulf towards the St. Lawrence. If, as they expected, they reached Quebec on the 19th of September, it would be exactly three weeks since they had started out expectantly on their doubtful adventure to Charlottetown. And in exactly another three weeks more from then, all the Maritime delegates would be arriving at Quebec for the second conference which would decide the fate of confederation. Prince Edward Island was dropping behind them down the Gulf. The Charlottetown Conference had become a memory. And all their hopes and expectations were fixed upon Quebec.

CHAPTER FIVE

The Bases of Nationhood

IT WAS very early in the morning of Wednesday, the 5th of October, when young Miss Mercy Coles and her parents got up and made their last hurried preparations for the long journey to Quebec.[1] William Henry Pope and his wife – she had never before been off the Island – were slipping away from their house at the same early hour, while their large family of obstreperous children – 'all steps and stairs', as George Brown described them – and the servants were still deep in slumber. The steamer that bore the little group of travellers across Northumberland Strait to New Brunswick put out from Charlottetown when it was only three o'clock in the morning and still completely dark. A special train was waiting at Shediac; but even so it was getting dark again by the time the five Islanders reached Saint John. And at Saint John one section – much the smaller section – of the Maritime delegation to Quebec was assembling.

All told, the Maritimers were to form a much larger company at Quebec than they had at Charlottetown. Both New Brunswick and Prince Edward Island had appointed two additional delegates; and, while the Nova Scotians and the New Brunswickers had gone unaccompanied to Charlottetown, the Canadians, in an expansive gesture of hospitality, had invited the Maritimers to bring their ladies to Quebec. Five Maritime matrons and nine young and marriageable Maritime daughters gladly accepted this invitation; and these, together with their husbands and fathers, the nineteen delegates, made up a company of over thirty. The Canadian government was thoughtfully sending the *Queen Victoria* down the Gulf of St. Lawrence to bring back as many of its guests as possible;[2] but the *Queen Victoria*, which had carried eight Canadians and their servants comfortably down to Charlottetown, was not quite capacious enough to transport four times that many Maritimers to Quebec.

A division of the large Acadian delegation was unavoidable; and it seemed fair enough that the provinces that had appointed the additional delegates should yield a few places on the *Queen Victoria* and send some of their representatives by the circuitous Portland route. At Saint John the Islanders, Pope and his wife, Coles, Mrs. Coles, and Miss Mercy, met the New Brunswickers, Leonard Tilley and Edward Barron Chandler. Next day they took ship for Portland; but it was not until Saturday, the 5th of October, that they crossed the Canadian border on the long ride up from Portland; and the special train that met them at Richmond for the last lap of the journey did not reach Lévis until half-past five in the evening. The dull October day was darkening into night as they crossed the ferry and toiled up Mountain Street in tiny, crowded cabs to the St. Louis Hotel. It was raining – raining heavily.[3]

In the meantime, the *Queen Victoria* had been making the rounds of the Gulf ports and collecting its Quebec-bound passengers. At Pictou, the steamer's first port of call, the entire Nova Scotian delegation, composed of the same five members that had gone to Charlottetown, came aboard.[4] Tupper brought his wife and daughter. So did Archibald; Miss Dickey accompanied her father. The most surprising addition to the Nova Scotian contingent was, however, the imposing presence of Sir Richard Graves MacDonnell and his beautiful wife. In September, at the time of the Charlottetown Conference, when the Dundases had asked Gordon and MacDonnell to pay them a visit at the Island Government House, MacDonnell had declined the invitation on the ground that 'the presence of an immediate representative of the Crown in any but his own government would rather prejudice than promote harmonious interchange of opinion amongst the delegates . . .'.[5] This important principle of viceregal conduct was now given up, either because MacDonnell wanted to go to Quebec a good deal more than he had wanted to go to Charlottetown, or because he had become aware of the fact that his presence at the Canadian capital was not likely to have any effect whatever upon the deliberations of the conference. In any case, he was not going to stay with the Moncks, who were certain to have enough entertaining to do without the burden of additional house guests. William Collis Meredith, a judge of the Superior Court of Quebec, was an Irish relative of MacDonnell's, and MacDonnell and his wife were going to pay a visit at the Meredith house.[6]

About noon the next day, the steamer put into Charlottetown harbour for the second stop of its leisurely cruise.[7] The Nova Scotians were driven about the town on a brief sightseeing tour, paid a courtesy call on the Dundases, and lunched at Inkerman House with Colonel Gray. The five remaining Island delegates and their two women companions, a sister of T. H. Haviland's, one of the two additional representatives, and Maggie Gray, the Premier's daughter, joined the party, and late in the afternoon they all boarded the *Queen Victoria*. It was ten o'clock at night before the steamer reached Shediac, and the New Brunswickers – a company of nine – did not come aboard until the following morning. None of the delegates had brought his wife; but four pleasurably excited young ladies – two Misses Steeves, a Miss Gray, and a Miss Fisher – eagerly accompanied their fathers. The *Queen Victoria*'s passenger list was now complete, and she stood out from Shediac and struck north for the St. Lawrence River. The fine weather in which the Canadians had sunned themselves on their way down to Charlottetown had completely vanished. The chill winds and the shrouded skies were implacably autumnal; and on Saturday night a violent gale, thick with snow, swooped roaring down the river valley and slowed the steamer's progress to a hesitating crawl.[8] It was not until the early evening of Sunday, the 9th of October, that the *Queen Victoria* finally reached Quebec; and in the fading light the visitors could see that the town and the countryside around it were powdered thick with snow.

The whole company of Maritimers – delegates, wives, and daughters – were to be accommodated, so the Canadian government had decided, at the St. Louis Hotel. Along with the Russell

House, the St. Louis was one of the two best hotels in Quebec. It stood, a square, severely unadorned, rather ugly building, five storeys in height, and flush with the pavement, about half way up St. Louis Street. Its proprietor, Willis Russell, who, with his brother, also ran the Russell House, had decided some time before to close down the St. Louis at the end of the summer season with the idea of carrying out some alterations and re-pairs. The Canadian government, tentatively and quite incon-clusively, had discussed with him the possibility of using the St. Louis for the conference. But these early approaches were not followed up, and Russell, assuming that other provision had been made for the Maritime guests, went ahead with his arrange-ments for the needed alterations and decorating. Then, at the very last moment, just when carpenters, plasterers, and paper-hangers were, by contract, about to descend upon the hotel, the Canadian government suddenly came to life, and frantically begged him to alter his plans and to put his entire hotel at the disposal of their rapidly approaching visitors. In the end, after much heavy persuasion, Russell agreed – though it led him later into a serious row with his building contractors – to keep the St. Louis open, to provide the Maritimers with board and lodging, and, in addition – for the Coalition government was determined to be lavishly hospitable – to serve any refreshments, including wines and spirits, that his guests might desire.[9]

On Sunday night, the 9th of October, the Quebec Conference held its first informal, noisily joyful meeting in the rather shal-low lobby of the St. Louis Hotel. A welcoming bevy of Canadian ministers was in attendance. The Maritimers who had come by train and had arrived on Saturday were eagerly waiting for the other, larger group of Maritimers who had come by steamer and who were expected that very night.[10] 'Such a babble of noise when they came in,' Mercy Coles reported; and such a compli-cated and prolonged series of introductions by which the four new Maritime delegates were presented all round, and the four Canadian ministers who had not gone to Charlottetown were introduced all round, and nearly all the gentlemen had to be presented to the ladies. Mr. Russell's best imported champagne, at $2.50 a bottle, was soon circulating freely; and inside the packed lobby there were light, and warmth, and talk and laughter. Outside, in the muddy, slushy street, it was dark, and raw, and extremely cold. The correspondent of *La Minerve* (he came, of course, from Montreal) had watched the second group of Maritimers arriving at the Quebec docks and gazing curiously about them. They must have thought, he noted cheerfully in his dispatch, that they were in Siberia.[11]

⋙ II ⋘

APART from its magnificent situation, the legislative building at Quebec, in which the conference was to be held, was in no sense imposing. It had been built after the provincial government had reached the agonizing decision to move the capital of the province to Ottawa. If not exactly an unwanted child of the Board of Works, it was certainly not regarded as a departmental favourite. In a few years, when its brief period of glory had come to an end, and parliament and government had migrated to Ottawa, the building was destined to become a post office; and nobody had thought it worth while to spend a lot of money on a building that would have such a prosaic calling and occupy such a humble station in life. It was, in fact, an extremely plain, unadorned structure, built of brick, with a central block and two wings. Flanked by the Grand Battery on one side and Mountain Hill Street and the Prescott Gate on the other, it stood on the very edge of the rock of Quebec. The situation was impressive, the view superb. The whole countryside for miles around, with the great river winding its way onwards towards the sea, lay spread out before the spectator.

Here, a little before eleven o'clock on the morning of Monday, the 10th of October, the thirty-three delegates to the Quebec Conference began to assemble.[12] The room that had been chosen for their sessions, the reading-room of the Legislative Council, was a rather close fit for such a large company. A long, fairly narrow table, covered with red cloth and furnished with an appropriate array of statutes, legislative journals, departmental reports, pamphlets, books of reference, and stationery, ran down the middle of the room; and all around, with not much more than enough room for their chairs on either side, sat the delegates. An elaborate seating plan had been carefully worked out.[13] The chairman of the conference, who as everybody expected was Sir Etienne Taché, sat at the centre of one long side of the table, as at a dinner-party, with the Canadian ministers, Cartier and Galt, on his left, and Macdonald, Campbell, and McGee on his right. Directly opposite Taché was George Brown, flanked by the remaining members of the Canadian cabinet, with McDougall and Cockburn on one side and Mowat, Langevin, and Chapais on the other. Tilley of New Brunswick occupied one end of the table, Gray of Prince Edward Island the other. The New Brunswickers and Nova Scotians grouped themselves about Tilley. The two Newfoundlanders, Ambrose Shea and F. B. T. Carter, as well as the Prince Edward Island delegates, sat at the other end of the table, about Gray.

It was eleven o'clock. All the delegates were in their places. Credentials were presented and the conference was formally convened. On a motion of Gray of Prince Edward Island and Tilley, Taché was elected chairman; and the four provincial secretaries, together with Shea of Newfoundland, were made secretaries of the conference.[14] Taché opened proceedings with a brief benevolent speech; and the delegates then took up the one remaining preliminary matter, which was the question of procedure.[15] Edward Palmer of Prince Edward Island, a tall, stooped man with large, craggy features and a bushy beard, proposed that in all decisions of the conference, except those concerned with points of order, each province should have one vote.[16] Dickey of Nova Scotia, polite, pleasant, but determinedly independent-minded, seconded Palmer's motion. There may have been a hint of anti-Confederate – and anti-Canadian – feeling in the Palmer-Dickey resolution, for Dickey was to become critical of, and Palmer antagonistic to, confederation; but later, when Macdonald suggested that Canada should be given two votes in recognition of its two historic divisions, Palmer readily agreed. The revised rule did not seriously alter the political balance of the conference, for the Maritime Provinces, including Newfoundland, could still outvote Canada, two to one;

but it deepened the ambiguity of the conference's nature and constitution. It was not precisely a conference of provinces, for Canada's two votes – though, of course, they were never split – had been granted because of her division in two sections. It was not exactly a conference of provincial governments either, for, though Canada was represented by its Coalition cabinet, the delegations of the other provinces included, in all cases, members of both government and opposition parties. All that could be said with certainty was that thirty-three prominent and representative public men from five provinces had come together at Quebec to discuss and plan for the future of British America.

Now they were ready and eager to begin, though the details of procedure were not finally settled until the following day. This was the moment for which the Canadians had hoped, worked, and waited. Their great chance had arrived and they felt ready for the task that lay before them as they would not have felt even six weeks before. The dress rehearsal at Charlottetown had given them confidence, and skill, in the exposition of their subject. In Quebec they were on home ground, and they were aware of the sustaining encouragement of their own province. Nothing had occurred during the summer to reduce or weaken the Coalition's overwhelming majority in the legislature; and public opinion, after a few fluttering tremors and hesitations, had come down strongly in favour, not only of the government and its federal scheme in general, but also of the details of confederation as proposed at Charlottetown, so far as these had been made public. A fortnight before, in order to quiet criticisms of the secretiveness of the conference and to test public opinion on the merits of the scheme, the government had prepared a semi-official paper, briefly describing the Charlottetown proposals; and on the 26th of September this was published in the Montreal *Gazette* and *Le Courrier du Canada*, and widely reprinted in other newspapers in the following days.[17]

This communiqué, in both its disclosures and its reticences, was a remarkably astute document. With studious care, it concentrated on practical details and avoided statements of general principle. Its opening theme was that no final decisions had yet been made, and that all was subject to revision at Quebec. It listed possible federal and provincial functions; but it made no mention of the grant of residuary powers to the central legislature. There was no reference to the 'sovereignty' of the national parliament; but equally there was no hint of the 'co-ordinate' authority of federal and provincial legislative bodies. On a number of important issues – such as the constitution of the provincial legislatures, the list of provincial powers, the method of selecting the legislative councillors – there were, the communiqué suggested, different opinions and lots of room for discussion and debate. The federal government would pay the provinces subsidies, in return for its monopoly of the accustomed sources of taxation. It would also take over all provincial debts and assets; and this transference, it was believed, could be managed equitably, since the burden of debt, on a *per-capita* basis, was approximately equal. Finally, the communiqué hinted at the desirability of safeguards for the educational interests of minorities; but it made no mention of guarantees in respect of language. The main thing that Lower Canada would insist upon, the communiqué suggested, was local control of 'the whole body of civil and municipal law'.

This statement, the Canadian ministers knew, had been received with acquiescence – without serious protest, if also without any great enthusiasm. They knew they had the support of their own countrymen; they felt they had almost won the agreement of the Maritimers. And, when Macdonald got up to move the fundamental resolution upon which the whole work of the conference depended, he went back to the phraseology the Maritimers themselves had used on that wonderful Wednesday, September the 7th, when they had first given their answer to the Canadian proposal at Charlottetown: 'that the best interests and present and future prosperity of British North America will be promoted by a federal union under the Crown of Great Britain, provided such union can be effected on principles just to the several Provinces'.[18] Tilley, for the Maritime region, seconded Macdonald's motion; and George Cartier, representing the third great division in the Canadian plan, rose and in his explosive, rambling fashion reviewed once more the main reasons, political and economic, for union – and union now – of British America.

'We all desire that these provinces should be as great as possible,' he concluded simply. 'There is always something better to be done, something greater to be attained.'[19]

When Cartier sat down, the first significant pause in the proceedings arrived. For a moment the Canadians waited expectantly; but if they had any serious doubts about the Maritime response, they were soon reassured. Gray of Prince Edward Island, who had become an ardent unionist even more quickly than his colleague Palmer was becoming a stubborn Anti-Confederate, got up at once to declare that it had been the dream of his life 'to be one day a citizen of a great nation extending from the great west to the Atlantic seaboard'.[20] Gray's speech virtually became the keynote of the discussion that followed. Ambrose Shea and F. B. T. Carter, the unknown delegates from Newfoundland, echoed Gray's enthusiastic acceptance of confederation and enlarged upon the part which the Island might play in it. Coles and Dickey sounded a few discordant notes; but these seemed lost in the general swelling harmony of approval. Mitchell of New Brunswick and Haviland of Prince Edward Island, two of the new delegates, urged a statesmanlike, non-partisan approach to the building of a great united nation. And McCully of Nova Scotia, stressing the same theme, told the conference how his province, if it could have had its first wish, would have preferred a complete legislative union, under a single British American parliament.[21]

That night the Canadian ministry entertained the conference with a dinner at the Stadacona Club. 'If the delegates will survive the lavish hospitality of this great country,' wrote Edward Whelan, the second of Prince Edward Island's new delegates, 'they will have good constitutions – perhaps better than the one they are manufacturing for the Confederation'.[22] The Maritimers seemed impressed by the beginnings of their entertainment; and the Canadians were more than pleased with the way the day's proceedings had gone. Everything looked propitious – everything except the weather. The snow was melting and temperatures had moderated pleasantly. But the clouds above were grey and opaque. And it had started to rain.

⋙ III ⋘

NEXT MORNING at eleven o'clock, when the delegates assembled again in the Legislative Council reading-room, everybody was aware that a crucially important session of the conference was about to begin. Yesterday Macdonald had not spoken in support of his motion; but it was known that he intended to speak on the following day; and it was known, too, that his task would be to describe and analyse the constitutional structure of the proposed confederation. There were only a few brief preliminaries. The chairman, Taché, had a single announcement to make. The rules of procedure were adopted. The four secretaries begged the delegates to appoint an executive secretary in order that they might be free to take an active part in the work of the conference, and recommended Hewitt Bernard, chief clerk in Attorney General Macdonald's department, for the job. The conference complied; and Bernard, an able civil servant who was on friendly terms with Macdonald, knew the Canadian plan intimately, and had gone to Charlottetown, took his place behind a separate small table and began – unfortunately without benefit of shorthand – to keep his records.

Macdonald got to his feet. This was the second time that men had set about founding a federal nation on the North American continent. The two tasks of constitution-making were at least comparable; but the thirty-odd Maritimers and Canadians who faced Macdonald that morning were a very different people from that other generation of North Americans who had adopted the Declaration of Independence and framed the Articles of Confederation and the Constitution of the United States. The British Americans who sat waiting for Macdonald to begin his speech were as far away from the dogmas of the eighteenth-century Enlightenment as they were from twentieth-century obsessions with race, and with racial and cultural separatism. They were mid-Victorian British colonials who had grown up in a political system which they valued, and which they had not the slightest intention of trying to change by revolution. For them the favourite political myths of the Enlightenment did not possess an even quaintly antiquarian interest. They saw no merit in setting out on a highly unreal voyage of discovery for first principles. They would have been sceptical about both the utility and the validity of abstract notions such as the social contract and the natural and inalienable rights of man. The magic formulae of the American and French Revolutions – 'life, liberty, and the pursuit of happiness' and 'liberty, property, security, and resistance to oppression' – would have sounded in their ears like irrelevant and questionable rhetoric. As sober Christians, many of them with a strong evangelical bias, they were bound to reject firmly the doctrine of the perfectability of mankind; and the idea that new institutions and fresh surroundings could make new and better men would have seemed childishly presumptuous and unconvincing to them, despite their nineteenth-century instinct for vigorous enterprise and their nineteenth-century belief in material progress.

God, not government, these British Americans believed, could alone effect the regeneration of mankind. But government, within the limits of the humanly possible, must unquestionably be sovereign. For them, the doctrine of the separation of governmental powers – executive, legislative, and judicial – was a dangerously rigid and over-simplified formula; and they looked upon the American system of constitutional checks and balances as a complicated assemblage of frustrating gadgets. On the evidence as they saw it, the American system did not tend to 'peace, order, and good government' or 'peace, welfare, and good government' – the modest, understated terms in which the aims of government had always been defined in British American constitutional history. On the contrary, the American system seemed to be characterized, all too often, by violent oscillations between the tyranny of the mob and the despotism of the president. The erratic course of the republic had ended now in the hideous carnage of a civil war; and to a great many British Americans the war seemed to be a breakdown not only of American federalism but also of American democracy.

In their view, the consent of the governed and the responsibility of government to the people were infinitely better secured by their own system of parliamentary institutions on the British model. The British constitution, which had outlasted the liberal constitutions of all the new revolutionary republics of both Western Europe and North America, stood then at the apogee of its prestige; and British Americans fully believed what Walter Bagehot was to celebrate three years later – that the 'efficient secret' of the British parliamentary system was responsible, or cabinet, government. Responsible government in British America had been largely won by the efforts of British Americans. It was an essential part of their own political experience; but it had its ultimate origin in the constitutional monarchy of the United Kingdom and was inseparably associated with it. British Americans thought of themselves as British subjects, whose title was not in the slightest diminished by their distance from the centre of Empire. They wished to keep British parliamentary government. They hoped to preserve the British connection.

The prescriptive force of this political inheritance largely shaped the British American conception of their prospective union. There were a great many English-speaking Canadians and Maritimers who believed that if and when their union came it would come far better in a legislative than in a federal form. 'A monarchy', one journalist reasoned, 'looks to a strong central power, from which all authority in the state is derived, and in the name of which all functions of government are exercised.'[23] Great Britain, many people reminded themselves, was itself a 'United Kingdom'; and, over a century and a half before, Great Britain had devised special guarantees for Scottish law and Scottish religion and had reconciled these with the sovereignty of a single national parliament. Why could not British North America build its union in the same way?

Admittedly there were difficulties. The enormous distances of British America would make it hard for 'Red Riverites' and Nova Scotians to make sensible laws about each other's small concerns.[24] The absence of a general system of municipal government in the Maritime Provinces would throw a large mass of petty legislation on the national legislature. Finally – and this seemed the most formidable obstacle to legislative union – there were the special laws and customs of French Canada, and the French-Canadian determination – which most people recognized as legitimate – to defend their distinctive culture. These circumstances, one group of British Americans insisted, made the introduction of the 'federal principle' inevitable. But the 'federal principle', another group of British Americans vehemently replied, was a dangerous and disintegrating principle, which, if it were not drastically restricted and curbed, might prove terribly destructive. How, without extreme peril to the kind of political existence which British America wanted, could parliamentary government and the 'federal principle' be combined?

The Canadian ministry believed it had found an answer to this tremendous puzzle; and it was this answer that Macdonald rose to explain and defend on Tuesday, the 11th of October. His two main themes that morning were the Canadian plan's twin fundamentals. On the one hand, parliamentary institutions must be established securely at the centre of the new federation; and, on the other, the 'federal principle' must be weakened so as to neutralize effectively its centrifugal force. Parliamentary government, Macdonald argued, would enable a united British America 'to work out constitutional liberty as opposed to democracy';[25] and the parliamentary system, in order to realize its purpose, should be restored to its original form and made to conform as closely as possible to the British model. The only serious departure from that model that British North America had ever made was the substitution of popular election for appointment by the Crown in the legislative councils of Canada and Prince Edward Island; and this change, as a potential threat to the primacy of the lower house and thus to ministerial responsibility, could be given up at the appropriate moment of the forming of the union. 'We should keep before us the principles of the British constitution', Macdonald reiterated. '. . . While I do not admit that the elective principle has been a failure in Canada, I think we had better return to the original principle, and in the words of Governor Simcoe, endeavour to make ours an "image and transcript of the British constitution".'[26]

The second major constitutional objective which Macdonald tried to expand that morning was the reduction of the powers of the 'local governments' to the point at which they could not possibly threaten the national parliament's sovereignty. Here, Macdonald was well aware, there were limits, laid down by regional interests or cultural loyalties, beyond which centralization could not be pushed; but he realized equally clearly that, for a variety of important reasons, a strong demand for 'states' rights' could not, and would not, be made in British America. Unlike the successfully revolting Thirteen Colonies that had become the United States, the British provinces had never desired, claimed, nor won sovereign rights by revolution. They could not alter their own constitutions, or make binding contracts among themselves or with foreign powers; and they all freely and fully acknowledged the sovereignty of the British Crown in Parliament. If British North America was to be united in a federation, legislative powers could not be 'delegated' by the provinces to the new federal authority; they could only be redistributed between central and local governments by the imperial Parliament.[27]

There was thus no solid constitutional basis for the claim of 'states' rights' at Quebec. There were no strong impulsions that moved any group of delegates to assert such rights. Maritimers and English-speaking Canadians – many if not most of whom would have preferred a single national government – were prepared to accept federalism as the only feasible way of achieving British American union. French-speaking Canadians, who believed in federation for its own sake, had no intention of attempting to isolate themselves within a self-sufficient and exclusive provincialism. There were a few important things – social customs, cultural and spiritual values – that French Canadians were anxious to have under their own protective control; but in most other human activities – and, in particular, throughout the whole wide range of economic enterprise – they were ready to co-operate in the closest association with English-speaking British Americans. The acceptance of the 'federal principle', against their own political traditions and wishes, was the great concession that the English-speaking delegates at Quebec were prepared to make to French Canada; but they agreed to make it only on the clear understanding that the resulting British American union was to be a strongly centralized federation, a federation radically different from that which had helped to precipitate the American Civil War. Macdonald drove the point home with all the force at his command. 'States' rights' – the reservation by each state of all sovereign powers, 'save the small portion delegated' to the general government – was, he declared, the 'primary error' of the American constitution. 'We must reverse this process', he went on, 'by strengthening the general government and conferring on the provincial bodies only such powers as may be required for local purposes.'[28]

At exactly a quarter past one, as Bernard noted in his minutes, Macdonald finished his speech.[29] There was no debate; and the motion was carried swiftly and unanimously with a burst of applause that could be heard outside the conference room.[30]

⇾⇾⇾ IV ⇽⇽⇽

BY THE MIDDLE OF THE WEEK, when the delegates had provided for the admission of Rupert's Land, British Columbia, and Vancouver Island, and had rejected a final vain attempt by Canada to persuade the Maritime colonies, including Newfoundland, to enter as a single province, the main bases of the proposed federal union had been laid. The conference, though it had not yet advanced beyond generalities, was getting gradually into the swing of its work. The delegates and their wives and daughters were settling down into their hotel, which, if it lacked the spacious splendour of the St. Lawrence Hall in Montreal, was at least pleasantly comfortable. A large and lively company of over thirty, the Maritimers were placed together at a long table in the hotel dining-room; and George Brown, who was the only Canadian minister resident in the St. Louis, usually 'did the honours'. Every night the visitors sat down to what Brown described as 'a company dinner of the first class'; [31] and between meals, Mr. Russell's waiters were flying about, at all hours of the day and night, with tea, coffee, and small collations, as well as unlimited supplies of sherry, port, champagne, and brandy. Then there were dinners at the Stadacona Club, dinners at Spencer Wood, where the Governor General was easy and affable, and, on Tuesday night, a tremendous reception or 'Drawing Room' in the legislative building, which brought a crush of over six hundred people, and was known to be simply the first of a long succession of balls, *déjeuners*, and supper parties that the Canadians intended to shower upon their visitors.[32]

The guests, in the meantime, were acquainting themselves with Quebec's narrow, bewildering streets, and taking the measure of Quebec society and official Quebec entertainment. The Canadian capital, with its large French-speaking population, seemed like a foreign country in which everything looked – and, even more obviously, sounded – strange and outlandish. The Maritimers were interested, amused, impressed, but, for the first few days, slightly on the defensive and very far from uncritical. Edward Whelan's first impression, at the Governor General's reception on Tuesday night, was that the Quebec women were a remarkably plain lot, usually quite short, and almost invariably much too stout. Mercy Coles recorded her opinion that the Maritime women, headed by the handsome Mrs. Tupper, were 'quite a credit to the Lower Provinces'.[33] 'I have seen more pretty girls at a Government House ball in Charlottetown – more at the late banquet in the Province Building there – than I witnessed at the great Drawing Room,' Whelan wrote proudly to the readers of his newspaper, the *Examiner,* in Charlottetown.[34]

It was an uncertain, tentative, non-committal period, in which the conference had not yet grappled with its crucial problems and the Maritimers and Canadians had not yet quite decided what they thought about each other. The weather hardly encouraged conviviality or inspired statesmanship. By this time, in fact, the weather was beginning to get slightly on everybody's nerves. The first few days of rain had been accepted as natural – even desirable –after the prolonged drought of the summer; but soon after that these typical British Americans, who had come by experience to believe that a beautiful autumn was a part of their birthright, were beginning to regard that October in Quebec as a strange and malevolent calamity. It rained. It kept on raining. The steady downpour made getting about town a muddy ordeal and spoilt carriage drives to such obvious tourist attractions as the Plains of Abraham and the Falls of Montmorency. 'The sun has not shone two hours since we arrived,' Mercy Coles exclaimed disgustedly. 'I never was in such a place.'[35] That was on Wednesday when Mercy and some of the other women made a dismally damp expedition to the Indian village at Lorette. And next day the correspondent of *La Minerve* reported mournfully from Quebec: 'Il pleut, il pleut tous les jours.'[36]

At this point, on Thursday, the 13th of October, the polite, preliminary calm of the conference was abruptly broken. Macdonald rose to present a group of resolutions concerning the framework of the new general parliament. The first of these, which simply proposed what everybody expected – a federal legislature of two houses – was, of course, entirely acceptable. The second resolution was quite different and a much more contentious matter. It provided that, for the purpose of forming the upper house or legislative council, British North America should be regarded as consisting of three sections or divisions – Canada East, Canada West, and the four Maritime Provinces together – and that each section should be represented in the legislative council by an equal number of members.[37]

This motion, as the Canadians by this time must have expected, instantly aroused a determined opposition. Despite its seemingly familiar appearance, it contained a highly objectionable innovation. It looked like the plan for the upper house that the Canadians had presented at Charlottetown and against which the Maritimers had not protested too loudly. But in reality it was not the Charlottetown plan at all. In the Charlottetown plan, the term 'Maritime Provinces' had meant Nova Scotia, New Brunswick, and Prince Edward Island; but in Macdonald's new resolution, the Maritime Provinces numbered four and included Newfoundland. To the Canadians, the inclusion of this second island seemed an obvious and logical improvement of their plan. Newfoundland would help to bring the population of the third, or Maritime, region of confederation closer to the level of that of Canada East or Canada West. Newfoundland therefore should logically be crammed into the third regional division of the legislative council. The Canadians, spurred on by their desire for a symmetrical organization on regional lines and by their hope for a great, all-inclusive British American nation, had once again pushed their scheme to its dangerously logical limits.

Legislative Council Chamber, Provincial Building, Charlottetown

The Charlottetown Conference, September, 1864

Left to right	
C. DRINKWATER (secretary)	W. H. STEEVES, *New Brunswick*
H. BERNARD (secretary)	J. H. GRAY, *Prince Edward Island*
A. T. GALT, *Province of Canada* (seated)	J. M. JOHNSON, *New Brunswick*
C. TUPPER, *Nova Scotia*	S. L. TILLEY, *New Brunswick*
E. B. CHANDLER, *New Brunswick*	A. G. ARCHIBALD, *Nova Scotia*
H. L. LANGEVIN, *Province of Canada*	A. A. MACDONALD, *Prince Edward Island*
E. PALMER, *Prince Edward Island*	W. CAMPBELL, *Province of Canada* (seated)
J. H. GRAY, *New Brunswick*	W. MCDOUGALL, *Province of Canada*
R. B. DICKEY, *Nova Scotia*	G. COLES, *Prince Edward Island* (foreground)
G. E. CARTIER, *Province of Canada*	W. H. POPE, *Prince Edward Island*
T. D'A. MCGEE, *Province of Canada*	J. MCCULLY, *Nova Scotia*
W. A. HENRY, *Nova Scotia*	G. BROWN, *Province of Canada*
J. A. MACDONALD, *Province of Canada* (seated)	W. H. LEE (secretary)
	(just visible at extreme right)

Reception of Edward, Prince of Wales, at the Colonial Building, Charlottetown, August 1860

The Maritime delegates were bound to oppose Macdonald's motion. They all expected that Canada would shortly propose a federal assembly based on representation by population. They all realized unhappily that in such an assembly, the members of one Maritime province – even the collective representation of all four of them – would be heavily outnumbered. Inevitably this knowledge gave the federal legislative council a special, a vital, significance in their eyes. It was the one federal institution – apart from the cabinet – in which the preponderance of the Canadas in the central government could possibly be offset. That afternoon the Maritime delegates began a desperate and pro-longed attempt to redress the extreme political imbalance that threatened them, in the one way that seemed to lie open.

At four o'clock when the adjournment came, the vehement discussion was still going on. Next day, Friday, the debate was resumed, and it continued without interruption during the entire session. It was resumed once more on Saturday, with undiminished conviction and with an apparently inexhaustible flow of argument. On Thursday, Tilley and Dickey moved an amendment that Canada West should be given twenty-four members, Canada East twenty-four members, and the Maritimes, among them, thirty-two.[38] Tupper proposed another amendment on Friday;[39] Fisher a third on Saturday;[40] and there were other suggestions, and probably other motions which did not get recorded. The Maritime delegates exhausted their ingenuity in trying to discover a magic formula that would give them the additional places they hungered for, and still satisfy everybody, including their own jealous selves.

They could not do it. At the heart of their case there lay a curious weakness. They desperately wanted – they had convinced themselves they desperately needed – a larger representation in the legislative council; but they could not find a valid political principle upon which this demand could be based. They argued, reasonably enough, that the Canadian plan of equal regional representation in the legislative council would approximate representation by population; and they contended that it was unfair to the smaller and less populous provinces to base the membership in both houses of the federal legislature upon what was essentially the same principle.[41] Yet this equitable argument was not really strong enough. The only effective answer to the principle of regional equality was the counter-principle of provincial equality; and, as everybody knew, this principle was ready to hand in the Constitution of the United States.

At Philadelphia, the small states had tried to defend their interests in very much the same way as the Maritime Provinces were now trying to defend theirs; and they had won the right to equal representation in the American Senate. The precedent that, on the face of it, might have made the Maritime Provinces' case for them was there, before their eyes, readily available. Yet they could not appropriate it wholeheartedly. They could not make it really their own. The one solid foundation for an appeal to such a precedent was provincial sovereignty, and provincial sovereignty was a status which the Maritime Provinces had not sought and could not claim at Quebec. If they had employed the sole valid legal justification for provincial equality in the legislative council they would have used something which historically was not theirs by right. If they had taken it over from the alien history of the United States, they would have appropriated, from a highly suspect source, what the American Civil War had convinced most British Americans was a politically explosive principle. Instinctively, the Maritimers shied away from the perilous doctrine of provincial equality. But they could not give up their struggle for a larger representation in the upper house.

By this time – Saturday, the 15th of October – the conference had been in session a full week. Nearly everybody was feeling depressed and a little alarmed. The weather itself was bad enough to cast a gloom over everything; and the conference, at the moment when it took up the first topic that went beyond mere generalities, had been abruptly and jarringly brought to a complete standstill. 'The admission of Newfoundland into the Conference perplexes the arrangement, as the agreement was, at Charlottetown, to give equality of representation to the Maritime Provinces of Nova Scotia, New Brunswick and Prince Edward Island, with Upper and Lower Canada,' wrote Edward Whelan;[42] and the Montreal *Gazette* referred gravely to a long debate which threatened 'a rupture of the negotiations'.[43] The tired, impatient

George Brown, writing to his wife in the early hours of Saturday morning, admitted that the conference was making very slow progress, but added, with characteristic hopeful optimism, that there was 'no appearance yet of any insurmountable obstacle'.[44] Others, including Whelan, were a good deal more pessimistic. 'Matters do not certainly look very promising for a completion of the deliberations,' he wrote sombrely after the long and unresolved argument of Friday's debate.[45]

It was fortunate that the climax of the crisis came on the last two days of the week. The week-end brought a pause in the hot discussion; and the Canadians, with unwitting or calculated diplomacy, filled a good part of the interval with entertainment. The Canadian cabinet gave a ball in the parliament buildings on Friday night; and on Saturday the Board of Trade of Quebec invited a large company, including all the delegates, to an elaborate dinner in the Russell House in Palace Street.[46] The ball was a much livelier affair than the Governor General's rather formal Drawing Room had been. Obviously the Canadians were trying hard, and spending time and money in elaborate hospitalities; but they were still making mistakes. In the vast crush of the seven hundred people who came to the ball on Friday night, the arrangements – if there were any – for introducing the Maritimers to Quebec society broke down completely. The Maritimers were unanimous in complaining that they had to make their own introductions and find their own partners;[47] and the Misses Gray and Tupper, coming in next day to visit Mercy Coles, who was ill with a sudden attack of influenza and at the last moment had not been able to go to the ball, told the sad story of Canadian neglect; and Mercy gratefully concluded that she 'had not missed much'.[48] Next night, at the Board of Trade dinner, it was distinctly better. The Maritime delegates were given the lion's share of the speech-making; and, facing them, on the walls of the dining-room, were the names of the five provinces, in huge letters, tastefully framed in evergreens.

⇛ V ⇚

B Y THIS TIME it was quite clear to the Canadians that the conference was going to be a much more difficult and protracted affair than they had anticipated. On Saturday, Macdonald moved to increase the hours available for debate. The delegates were to assemble at ten instead of eleven in the morning, and adjourn at two; they were to meet again at half past seven in the evening and, as George Brown expressed it, continue 'as long as we like to sit'.[49] The intervening hours were almost all taken up by meetings of the Canadian cabinet, in which the Coalition ministers tried to plan and prepare for the discussions that were to come. They met that Monday morning, the 17th of October, at nine o'clock; and by the time the conference was about to begin the day's session at ten, they had reached a great decision. They would have to give way, at least a little, in the stubborn controversy over the composition of the legislative council. The rigid symmetry of the Canadian regional scheme, contracted intolerably by the admission of Newfoundland, would simply have to be relaxed. A motion by Tupper, presented the previous Friday, which defined Nova Scotia, New Brunswick, and Prince Edward Island as the third division, with equal representation in the legislative council, and promised Newfoundland 'additional representatives', suggested a way out of the impasse; and the Canadians decided to take it. The compromise solution on which they finally took their stand gave each region twenty-four representatives in the legislative council; divided the third, or Maritime, contingent into three parts, with ten members for Nova Scotia, ten for New Brunswick, and four for Prince Edward Island; and finally granted four members to Newfoundland.[50]

The fact that this solution was Tupper's in origin made it definitely more acceptable to the Maritime delegates. Yet there followed a long, wrangling morning of debate. There were several competing proposals made. At every point there was resistance, chiefly by the Prince Edward Islanders, to the Canadian plan. A. A. Macdonald, an Island legislative councillor, came closer than apparently any other delegate had yet done to asserting the principle of provincial sovereignty according to the

American precedent: 'He considered each Province should have equal representation in the federal upper house, and instanced the different states of the Union, which however diversified in area, were each represented by two Senators in the general government.'[51] It was a brave beginning, solidly based on orthodox American theory; but it trailed away feebly in a demand, not for equal, but for 'better' representation for the smaller provinces. On their part the other smaller provinces gave it little or no support; and by the time the morning session ended the Canadian compromise had been carried, though a large Island minority was irreconcilably opposed to it, and though the Island delegation as a whole may, as A. A. Macdonald later asserted, have voted against the two major resolutions of the morning's debate.[52]

The Canadians had saved their regional scheme – at a price. But, despite this apparent triumph of the larger provinces, there were still many delegates who believed, with A. A. Macdonald, that 'the only safeguard the small Provinces would possess was in the Council'; and the battle over its composition was by no means ended. That night Macdonald moved that the legislative councillors were to be appointed for life by the Crown under the great seal of the central government.[53] This resolution, which abandoned the elective method recently adopted by both Canada and Prince Edward Island, was a return to British North America's constitutional past – a restoration of its fidelity as an 'image' of the British constitution; and to a small minority in the conference it was almost as objectionable as the principle of regional equality had been. Surely appointment by the general government would invalidate the whole conception of the legislative council as the special representative and defendant of the provinces? George Brown's two Reform associates, McDougall and Mowat, the former of whom harked back to the republican principles of the original Clear Grit party, argued in favour of election by the people.[54] Coles and A. A. Macdonald of Prince Edward Island proposed election by the provincial legislatures.[55] But Mowat and McDougall's tiny protest, for which Brown himself had no sympathy, was effectively smothered by overwhelming numbers inside the Canadian cabinet; and Coles and Macdonald could not persuade even the increasingly recalcitrant Island delegation to back them up.

Yet the debate dragged on until midnight. It was not ended until late in the morning of the next day, the 18th of October. Even then the conference was not completely finished with the legislative council. Two more sittings – Tuesday night and Wednesday morning – were given over to a prolonged and highly partisan discussion of the method by which the first councillors were to be appointed. All that remained of Wednesday was now the evening session, beginning at half past seven; and the evening session was perhaps not the best moment at which to introduce a crucially important new topic. But time was getting on. The conference had now been in session for over eight days; and only the first part of one major subject – the structure of the federal legislature – had been settled. The Canadians were inevitably getting a little concerned. They were anxious to press their plan forward as rapidly as possible; and that evening they plunged at once into the composition of the second branch of the federal legislature – the legislative assembly, as it had always been called hitherto.

It was George Brown's great moment – the moment of triumph for which he had waited over ten years. He proposed that Canada East should have sixty-five seats, its existing strength in the Canadian legislature, and the other provinces should have seats in proportion, according either to the estimated population of 1866, or to the population of the censuses of 1861. This, with the censuses of 1861 as a basis, would give Canada West eighty-two seats, Nova Scotia nineteen, New Brunswick fifteen, Newfoundland seven, and Prince Edward Island five.[56] The only new features of this plan were the ingenious device of using the representation of Canada East as a constant base for the allocation of seats to the other provinces, and – a significant sign of the lofty nationalist aims of the Canadians – the substitution of the new and dignified title of 'House of Commons' for the old familiar name of 'Assembly'.

Undoubtedly Brown expected that this at least was one group of resolutions that would be quickly passed. All the delegates were well aware of the fact that representation by population in the lower house was a main feature of the Canadian plan. Nearly all of them assumed that representation by population had been accepted at Charlottetown as an unalterable principle of confederation. All that Brown had done was to apply the principle by using an acceptable formula and working out accurately a few arithmetical exercises. At first the discussion that followed was concerned exclusively with details.[57] Should the conference employ the estimated population of 1866, or fall back upon the indisputable figures of the census of 1861? Was sixty-five the right representation for Canada East? And when should the first decennial redistribution of seats take place? The only alteration in Brown's figures was made after Shea pointed out that Newfoundland's last census had been taken in 1857, and that an allowance ought to be made for the increase of population in the intervening years, and a single member added to the island's representation. The conference agreed that this was only fair. The extra seat was added, giving Newfoundland a representation of eight, and the House of Commons a total membership of 194. Brown's resolutions were then put to the vote and carried.[58]

At this point it was discovered – probably to the genuine surprise of many delegates – that Prince Edward Island had voted against the motion. Apart from a brief comment by Coles, her representatives had not spoken a single word in the debate. They had sat silent, but inwardly seething with a variety of complicated and painful emotions. They were, in fact, more deeply and bitterly divided over the fundamental issues of confederation than any other delegation at the conference. All the other Maritime Provinces, including Newfoundland – though its delegates had not a great deal to say for themselves – approved in general, and often heartily approved, of the Canadian plan. Among the Nova Scotians, Newfoundlanders, and New Brunswickers, numbering fourteen in all, there were only a very few dissentient voices. The Nova Scotian Robert Dickey, under a polite, parliamentary manner, was a fairly persistent, slightly nagging critic of the Canadian scheme. Of the New Brunswickers, Charles Fisher was a somewhat erratic and unpredictable Confederate; and Chandler, the senior member of the conference after Taché, frankly disliked a too-centralized federation.

These independents and critics numbered only a small handful; and even they could not be called Anti-Confederates by conviction. The remaining members of the Maritime contingents were Unionists, some more talkative or more enthusiastic than others, but all supporters in general of the Canadian plan.

The Prince Edward Islanders were very different. Their delegation was divided, not only between Confederates and Anti-Confederates, but also between Conservatives and Liberals, already resuming the game of party politics. The other Maritime delegations, which also included representatives of both government and opposition, tended to adopt a non-partisan attitude to confederation; but George Coles, the Liberal leader on the Island, who evidently hoped to make considerable political capital out of the issue, was not in the least inclined to follow Nova Scotia's or New Brunswick's example. During the debates on the legislative council, he and A. A. Macdonald had formed the original nucleus of Island opposition to union. They were not likely to get much help from Edward Whelan, the third Liberal delegate, for Whelan, a stout, romantic, impressionable Irishman, was rapidly becoming an ardent Confederate; but, on the other hand, Palmer, Attorney General in Gray's cabinet, was showing increasing signs of restiveness as the Canadian plan assumed a concrete form. The other Conservative representatives – Gray, Pope, and Haviland, who were all Confederates – found themselves in a very difficult position. They now realized how completely Prince Edward Island would be swamped in a general parliament on the Canadian model; and they had good reason to fear that, if they accepted the Canadian arrangements without protest, Coles would have the means of ruining them politically as betrayers of the Island's rights. For a variety of reasons, the Islanders were drawing together in opposition. And the vote on the composition of the House of Commons – the second humiliating revelation of Prince Edward's contemptible insignificance in the new national parliament – suddenly roused the whole delegation to a united and passionate protest.

The rules of procedure laid it down that 'after vote put no discussion be allowed'. The Prince Edward Islanders broke the rule. They went on breaking the rule. Nobody paid any attention to it. Everybody was listening, astonished and aghast, while the Islanders indulged in a shocking outburst of pent-up wrath. Haviland began it. 'Prince Edward Island would rather be out of Confederation than consent to this motion,' he declared violently. 'Only five members out of 194 would give the Island no position.'[59] Edward Palmer backed him up strongly, and when Shea of Newfoundland interjected that he understood that the principle of representation by population had already been settled, Palmer turned on him sharply.[60] Nothing, he declared, forcibly, had been *settled* at Charlottetown. Nothing, on such a subject, could have been *settled* at Charlottetown. And why did Shea regard himself as an authority on the matter, when he had not been there?[61] Coles, whose main purpose was apparently to embarrass and annoy his Conservative colleagues, denied Palmer's argument, conceded that population was the agreed basis of representation, and twitted the Premier for not properly instructing his delegates how to speak and vote.[62] George Brown, who was quickly roused to ire on such a subject, denounced Palmer's objection as 'perfectly absurd', and insisted that Rep. by Pop. was well known to everybody at Charlottetown as an essential feature of the proposed federal union.[63] In the end, Gray, the Premier, was compelled to make a statement on the matter. All he could get for the Island, he would, he said unhappily; but he admitted that he had understood representation by population to be the agreed principle.[64]

The shocked conference listened in silence. Then, in some embarrassment, Galt got up to say pacifically that everybody regretted the difficulty which had arisen and that he hoped Prince Edward would reconsider its position. A few minutes later, the meeting broke up.

The delegates pushed back their chairs, hardly daring to look at each other.

CHAPTER SIX

The Design Completed

THE SESSION adjourned at ten o'clock. The night – it was a typical night of that strange Quebec October of 1864 – was mild, soft, and vaporous with repeated rains. People still complained, without much spirit, of the bad weather. They had almost given up hope of really sunny days. But they were also discovering that this curious, rainy, humid autumn had its own peculiar advantages. There had been no repetition of that frightening foretaste of the Quebec winter – the screaming, blinding blizzard that had struck the *Queen Victoria* on the night of the 8th of October, as she laboured up the St. Lawrence towards the Canadian capital. The grass was greener in and about Quebec than it had been at any time during the long drought of the summer.[1] Only a few leaves, parched by the heats of August or killed by an early frost in September, had fallen; and the trees, still richly thick with foliage, gave the autumnal city a false, delicious air of late spring.

That night the Tessiers gave a ball in honour of the Maritime delegates.[2] Ulric Joseph Tessier was a prominent and prosperous Quebec lawyer, who had been made Speaker of the Canadian Legislative Council in 1863. A rich man, with a fine, large house, he and his wife had decided to give a party specially planned to introduce the Maritimers to the French-speaking society of Quebec. The Tessier dance was a more intimate and friendly affair than the state ball had been; and two nights later, the 'Bachelors of Quebec', whose hearts had, of course, been broken by the nine marriageable young ladies from the Maritime Provinces, gave still another ball in honour of the visitors which,

158

though it was held, like the official dance, in the legislative building, was a much less crowded and more informal party.[3]

To the Maritimers, these glimpses of an urbanized, cultivated, and predominantly French-speaking community were strange and fascinating experiences. From the beginning they had thought the French Canadians a hospitable and faultlessly polite people; but now, as they got to know each other better, as they danced together and gossiped awkwardly but gaily in a comic mixture of bad, heavily accented English and deplorable French, the visitors from the east were discovering that their hosts had a variety of attractive and endearing qualities. The French-Canadian women, who at first sight had looked rather stout and hearty, were now found to possess quite as much of that precious mid-Victorian quality 'femininity' as the less robust and more languid beauties of Halifax and Saint John. The crinoline, then billowing out towards its greatest expanse, hardly flattered their stout figures; but the fashionable coiffures and the coquettishly elaborate ornamentation of the season's ball gowns could scarcely have suited them better. Little velvet ribbon caps festooned with tiny ostrich feathers, clusters of curls with a single dark ringlet falling forward coyly over a plump shoulder, tight-fitting bodices sparkling with crystal beads, blooming crinolines lavishly adorned with braid, satin bows, and velvet insertions – all this elaborate prettiness became these short, dimpled, vivacious creatures extremely well. The gorgeous stores of their wardrobes seemed never to be exhausted. 'The same smiling, pretty, chattering French belles were to be seen,' the susceptible, Tupman-like Whelan observed at the Bachelors' Ball, 'only in different attire.'[4] Going to dances, in a series of different but equally ravishing ball-room dresses, was apparently one of the principal functions of their existence. Their constant gaiety was infectious. The fun-loving vitality with which they danced through a long succession of waltzes, polkas, mazurkas, and lancers seemed inexhaustible. When George Coles came back late from the Tessier ball, his clothes were damp with perspiration. 'He says he never had such a time,' his daughter Mercy recorded. 'The French ladies are the very mischief for flying around.'[5]

The French and English gentlemen of Quebec seemed equally

indefatigable dancers, with equally buoyant high spirits. High office under the Crown in Canada, far from requiring its possessors to sit the dances out in dignified repose, apparently inspired them to give their juniors a fine example of party sprightliness. '. . . The cabinet ministers – the leading ones especially – ' marvelled Edward Whelan, 'are the most inveterate dancers I have ever seen; they do not seem to miss a dance during the live-long night.'[6] Cartier, who was always ready to break into a song or dance at the least semblance of an opportunity, was the natural and inspired leader of these ministerial revellers; but Macdonald, though he lacked Cartier's exhibitionist urge and knew he was no singer, could dance with tireless verve into the not-so-small hours of the morning. Even poor, earnest, unwilling George Brown worked hard to give a suitable display of the party spirit; but he found dances 'an insufferable bore', and was only too apt to return to his hotel from a ball or a reception 'weary and worn and with a shocking headache'.[7] He got to know the Maritime matrons – 'Mrs. Archibald is a very nice person,' he informed his wife judicially;[8] but John A. Macdonald went one better – he was getting to know the Maritime girls as well. He had discovered the sad plight of Mercy Coles, whose illness had kept her so long in bed, staring so steadfastly out of the hotel window that she was sure she would remember 'the shape of every shingle on the roof of the house opposite'.[9] 'John A.' – Mercy Coles soon found out his nickname – began making kind inquiries about her state. 'He told Ma', she confided to her diary, 'he could not express how sorry he felt at my being ill.'[10]

On the morning after the Tessier ball, before the conference opened, the Islanders met privately, at Gray's invitation, to consider their stand on the representation question.[11] By this time the delegation was seriously divided; but its members all realized that on this issue it was politically essential to preserve a united front. When the conference reassembled, Gray announced that he and his associates considered the allotment of five members unsatisfactory; and several Island delegates – though some of them privately thought the difference a childishly unimportant one – got up to press for a representation of six.[12] Unfortunately the ground on which they had to base their argument for the solitary additional member was not principle, but pure, rather simple-minded expediency. There were three counties in Prince Edward Island; and, as Gray explained, it was a little difficult to divide five by three. If the Island could only be granted six members, then each of the three counties, with simple but beautiful equality, could be assigned two.

The conference thought this a preposterous request. It was simply absurd to suppose that a trumpery local difficulty – the county boundaries of the smallest of all the provinces – could justify a departure from the fundamental principle of representation by population. The delegates hardened their hearts against the quarrelling and importunate Islanders. 'There is no use in asking the conference to depart from the principle laid down', Galt declared with flat finality.[13] And McCully insisted that the rule of representation by population 'must be rigid and unyielding'.[14] The Upper Canadians, gratified by this ready support from Canada East and the Maritime Provinces, had no great need to rush to the defence of their beloved doctrine; and George Brown, assuming its acceptance, contented himself with pointing out that, if Prince Edward Island were given six members, the representation of all the other provinces would have to be increased proportionally and the result would be an undesirably large house.[15] It was obvious that Prince Edward Island must give way, and the only question was, would she yield generously or resentfully? George Coles, that homespun but agile political manipulator, quickly seized the opportunity of suggesting an antagonistic and threatening attitude. 'The question has been settled,' he said impatiently. 'Let us go on with the business and let Prince Edward Island settle for themselves when the question comes before them.'[16] Obviously he had implied – and his colleagues did not dare to deny the implication – that while the conference might accept the Canadian plan, the legislature and people of the Island would probably reject it.

⇉ II ⇇

With this definitive vote on the constitution of the House of Commons, and with the prolonged and anguished protest of Prince Edward Island that followed it, the Quebec Conference reached and passed a significant stage in its debates. The main bases of the principal federal institution – the legislature – had now been laid, and, with only minor adjustments, in accordance with the Canadian scheme. On the face of things, the Canadians had apparently won nearly complete success; but, below the surface, they were already conscious of partial failure. They felt fairly certain they were winning the mainland colonies – Nova Scotia and New Brunswick; but they were increasingly doubtful and unhappy about the islands. The small Newfoundland delegation, which ominously did not include a single member of the government, was interested and fairly active in the conference, but not very likely to be influential at home. Newfoundland itself was a little-known colony, which up to then had taken no part in the union movement, and its government had explicitly declared that it would not be bound by any decisions taken at Quebec. If the unpredictable Newfoundland joined the union, the Canadians would be lucky. They would be even luckier if Prince Edward Island did not remain sullenly aloof. Defections were possible – even probable; but, though the absence of the two islands would be most unfortunate, it would not, in the view of the Canadians, spoil the grandeur of the union. The islands were dispensable. The mainland provinces were the first essential provinces; and Nova Scotia and New Brunswick, arguing, protesting, but ultimately agreeing, were still accompanying the Canadians in a united body.

Once the vain pleas of Prince Edward Island had been impatiently heard and rejected, John A. Macdonald moved the conference swiftly forward to the next phase of its business. The main lines of the two houses of the federal parliament were determined; but the conference had not yet touched either the constitutions of the local governments or the relationship between the federal and local authorities. Some of its conclusions were virtually foregone conclusions. It was easy enough for the delegates to declare that the executive authority of the federal government was to be 'administered according to the well-understood principles of the British constitution'.[17] British parliamentary government was their fundamental constitutional preference. Responsible government was the vital essence of the parliamentary system. It was absolutely essential that responsible government should be securely established in the federal parliament, which, in the eyes of the delegates, was the heart of the nation they were creating, and the real repository of sovereign power, so far as that could exist in a colony.

The 'local' governments, however, were a different matter. The conference tended to think of them not as continuations of the existing provinces, but as virtually new political entities, greatly inferior to the provincial administrations of the past. The question of their organization had already come up in one of the early sessions, when Fisher and Dickey had unexpectedly moved that the constitutions of both general and local governments should be framed 'on the British model', so far as possible.[18] This, of course, was absolutely unquestioned orthodoxy – so far as the general legislature was concerned; what troubled the delegates was the little word 'local'. Its removal, after a long argument, enabled Fisher's motion, in an amended form, to pass the conference;[19] but it did not solve the problem of the organization of the local bodies of the future. How were the delegates to plan for these strange, nondescript governments, which were about to lose so many of their powers, which would surely function in the future in much the same way as municipalities, but which might yet retain some dim family resemblance to the vanished 'provincial' governments of the past?

The delegates were uncertain; and in their perplexity they fell back on old words and phrases, investing them, at the same time, with a new, but cloudy and imprecise meaning. The chief 'local' executive officer, for example, was to be a lieutenant-governor, as before. Nobody proposed that he be elected locally, a method of selection obviously more consonant with local autonomy and local pride; and nobody seriously opposed Macdonald's motion that he should be appointed by the national government.[20] The declining importance of lieutenant-governors was obviously assumed in advance; it was so widely assumed, in fact, that the sharp-tongued Sir Richard MacDonnell, Lieutenant-Governor of Nova Scotia, thought it necessary to inform some leading delegates that in future it would be beneath the dignity of people like himself to accept an office so essentially municipal in character. 'You shall not make a mayor of *me*, I can tell you,' he informed Macdonald belligerently.[21]

The 'local' legislatures, the conference also agreed, ought to be simple, inexpensive, and unostentatious little affairs. George Brown wanted to go even further: a single-chamber legislature, a few elected officers, no fuss and feathers, and no party politics was his prescription for an acceptably simple and economical little government.[22] But George Cartier objected, protesting, in a characteristic fashion, that the election of officers would introduce 'in our local bodies republican institutions';[23] and the majority of the Maritime speakers, though they showed a good deal of sympathy with Brown's concern for economy and simplicity, agreed with Cartier that the local governments should keep their parliamentary form. In the end, a resolution introduced by Jonathan McCully, permitting each local legislature to decide upon the reconstruction of its own constitution, passed the conference unanimously.[24] But it was significant of the delegates' urge towards simplification that this power was granted 'with a view of reducing the expenses of the local governments'.

Responsible government was to continue, though many delegates were vaguely dissatisfied with it, because it seemed so familiar to British Americans that they could not readily devise an alternative system. It was to continue, but in a very much reduced and simplified form. 'We should diminish the powers of the local governments, but we must not shock too largely the prejudices of the people in that respect,' Tupper reflected.[25] McCully, the author of the successful resolution, put the point more neatly. 'We must', he said 'have miniature responsible governments.'[26] Miniature responsible governments, with diminished powers, authorized to amend their own constitutions 'with a view to reducing the expenses' – where were they likely to end? McCully, who would have much preferred a legislative to a federal union, very probably hoped that they would end in extinction. Macdonald, who had also wanted a legislative union, was certain of it. '. . . If the Confederation goes on,' he wrote later to his friend M. C. Cameron, 'you, if spared the ordinary age of man, will see both local parliaments and governments absorbed in the general power. This is as plain to me as if I saw it accomplished.'[27]

The conference had now been in session ten days. It was Friday, the 21st of October, and the second week of sittings was nearing its end. The optimistic and impatient George Brown, who had been deputed to go to England to acquaint the Colonial Office with the details of the federal scheme, had already changed his sailing date from the 26th of October to the 2nd of November, and was gloomily pondering a further postponement to November the 9th.[28] Only the political structure of Confederation – the federal and local institutions of government – had so far been settled by the delegates, and even here a few tag ends still dangled uncertainly. The second fundamental problem of a federation – the problem of the division of responsibilities and powers between central and local authorities – still confronted the conference. On the one hand was the question of the division of governmental functions, which, despite the majority feeling in favour of a strong federation, might still provoke a dispute between the centralists and the supporters of local rights. On the other hand was the question of the division of debts, assets, taxes, and resources – a money question and hence potentially dangerous – which could only too quickly arouse a sense of injustice and discrimination and might end in a tirade of argument and recrimination.

At ten o'clock on Friday morning, the 21st of October, John A. Macdonald rose to present a long detailed resolution on the powers of the general government. Its fundamental basis was the grant of residuary authority – of all powers not specifically left with the local bodies – to the national parliament. This was the key principle of the Canadian centralized plan; but its crucial importance in the scheme was, to some slight extent, obscured and minimized by the phraseology of Macdonald's motion.[29] The resolution opened with the grant of authority 'to make laws for the peace, welfare, and good government' of the federation – an historic, all-embracing phrase by which the imperial Parliament had in the past conveyed to British colonial legislatures the entire range of their legislative sway. The motion closed with the grant of authority to legislate 'generally, respecting all matters of a general character, not specially and exclusively reserved for the local governments and legislatures'. In between these two comprehensive endowments of power, however, a long list of specific, enumerated, federal functions had been inserted. As at Charlottetown, the Canadians might seem to be proposing both residuary powers and specific powers for the national legislature, at one and the same time.

The debate that followed was temperate and constructive. The conference, in fact, largely agreed with Macdonald; but the unanimity of its support that morning may have been a little more apparent than real. The wording of the resolution may have misled a few delegates as to its basic significance. Yet this was not the real reason for the readiness with which the great majority accepted Macdonald's plan. Their acquiescence had its real origin in their hearty approval of the kind of federation which the Canadians had designed. The great national tasks of the future, the delegates took for granted, should lie with the general legislature; and the general legislature must be equipped with the paramount legislative dominion that would enable it to play its destined role. Residuary authority, they assumed, must be granted to the federation; and the specific enumerated powers, by which the extent and character of the grant were illustrated, were precisely those powers that nineteenth-century British Americans would have regarded without question as overwhelmingly the most important and vital functions of the state. The whole tremendous, engrossing, and costly business of the development of the new country – its territorial expansion, settlement, commercial exploitation, and economic growth – had all been entrusted to the guardianship of the national parliament. The specific details as well as the main lines of the plan were highly acceptable; and the only serious attempt to amend Macdonald's resolution came when Jonathan McCully proposed that 'agriculture' should be deleted from the list of specific federal powers.[30] Not a single provincial delegation – not even that of

Prince Edward Island – voted for his amendment. Even George Coles realized that it would be folly to wrench 'agriculture' away from a federal legislature which, for the next two or three generations, would have the settlement of a quarter of the continent on its hands. 'I think it should be retained for the general government,' Coles declared. 'There should be a Minister of Agriculture in the federal government.'[31] The conference agreed with Coles and the other critics of McCully; and it found an easy compromise in making both agriculture and immigration concurrent powers.

⇥⋙ III ⋘⇤

NEXT DAY, at noon, when the conference opened its final session for that week, Galt got up to present the financial part of the Canadian plan.[32] This, together with the question of the division of powers, was one of the last two important subjects which the delegates had to settle. On the face of it, it looked the more dangerous. The Canadians were well aware of the fact that they faced a horrifying group of existing and potential Maritime bogies about Canadian finance – bogies that would have to be successfully laid in advance if they were to win Maritime confidence. Nova Scotians, New Brunswickers, and Prince Edward Islanders had always professed themselves to be appalled by the monstrous total of Canada's debts. They had already shown fear of the supposedly high level of Canadian customs duties; and, as time was to prove, it would be fairly easy to arouse a suspicion among them that under a federal system their own local revenues would not suffice to maintain the style in which they had been accustomed to live.

Galt was aware of these preconceptions. He was not a statesman or a very able politician, as Taché, Cartier, Macdonald, and Brown might all claim to be; but he possessed, to a larger extent probably than any of his colleagues, sheer cleverness, ingenuity, skill in contrivance and device. He had need of them now. For him, as for most of the other delegates, the general government was the great preponderating fact in the proposed confederation.

The general government would have to carry forward, to its destined continental limits, the great scheme of territorial expansion and material advancement which had been, and would remain, the dominating purpose of colonial British North America. All the burdens, past and future, of national development and consolidation would be piled upon the general government. It would have to have the strength to bear them. It must be granted 'the powers of taxation' without limit or qualification. It must be put in possession of the total assets of British America – of its docks, harbours, steamboats, canals, railways, and other properties – as a partial offset against the total provincial indebtedness which it was to assume. How could these huge transfers be carried out in a fashion that would seem equitable to all? How would the little local governments, freed of their debts but also bereft of most of their accustomed sources of revenue, continue to eke out their rather meagre municipal existence?

Galt had his answers ready. For each of his two main problems – the transfer of British America's capital assets and liabilities on the one hand, and the provision of an adequate current revenue for the local governments on the other – he had found an acceptable device. One was the idea of the annual subsidy, payable by the general to the local governments, which Galt's colleagues endorsed reluctantly as an easy but dangerous way out of their difficulties. The other was the notion of the debt allowance, perhaps the most brilliant of all Galt's inventions, which the Canadian cabinet fondly hoped might silence for ever all this unfortunate talk about Canada's mountainous debt and the crushing burden it would throw upon British American confederation. Both subsidies and debt allowances were to be calculated according to numbers – the unassailable statistical basis of allocation that had already served the Canadians so well in their struggle over the composition of the House of Commons. The annual subsidy, payable to each province, was to be a sum equal to eighty cents per head of population, according to the census of 1861. The debt allowance – the total amount of each province's debt that the general government would assume without charge – was to be computed by multiplying its population in the census of 1861 by twenty-five dollars. Galt had, of course, observed

what was obvious on a little inspection, that the public debts of
the different provinces, which looked so vastly different on the
surface, were relatively, on the basis of population, fairly close
to each other. Thus there was a very satisfactory basic equality;
but there were also discernible inequalities; and Galt saw how
both could be turned to good account in the great Canadian
enterprise of propitiating the Maritime Provinces.

Debt allowances, based on the principle of twenty-five dollars
a head of population, were calculated in round figures and somewhat too generously for New Brunswick. Canada was given
an allowance of $62.5 million, Nova Scotia $8 million, and New
Brunswick $7 million. No specific amounts were determined for
Newfoundland and Prince Edward Island; but it was declared
that they also would be given allowances, based on 'the average
amount of indebtedness per head of the population of Canada,
Nova Scotia, and New Brunswick'. If the actual debt of a province exceeded its allowance – as Canada's did by about $10
million – it would have to pay interest at five per cent on the
excess to the federal government. If, on the other hand, a province had not yet spent up to the limit of its allowance, it could
adopt one of two pleasant options. It could either accept interest
at five per cent on its credit balance from the federal government
or it could lay out the remainder of the total on public works
with the comfortable assurance that the burden of the charge
would fall on other shoulders. Galt, his eyes fixed hopefully towards the east, proposed, in effect, that provincial extravagance
should be fined and provincial economy recompensed. The penalties of his scheme would all fall on Canada; its benefits would
be distributed among the four Maritime Provinces. Nova Scotia
and New Brunswick would enjoy fair balances. Newfoundland
and Prince Edward Island, the two financially innocent provinces which had so far contracted hardly any liabilities at all,
would have their virtue amply rewarded.

It took Galt a long time to expound his resolutions. He had a
retentive and accurate memory for figures, condescended only
occasionally to consult his blue-books for needed statistics, and
gave his explanations and answers with ready fluency. His eloquence and facility were reassuring, disarming; but his scheme

was nothing less than a revolution in the financial history of British America, and it was certain to arouse criticism. Tilley, the only other provincial finance minister at the conference, began the attack; and it was characteristic of Tilley's acute but rather limited approach that he should start, not with the fundamental principles of Galt's scheme, but with one of its most vulnerable details. On the surface, Tilley pointed out, the grant of provincial assets along with the transference of provincial debt looked fair enough; but it was not, for the assets differed. The Maritime Provinces would have to hand over the physical properties of their own provincial railways; but Canada could bring forward nothing but the highly doubtful asset of over $34 million which it had loaned to the independent commercial railway companies, the Grand Trunk, the Northern, and the Great Western, and upon which interest was seriously in arrears. What, Tilley inquired caustically, was the real value of this worthless railway stock?[33] And Tupper, taking his cue from the more experienced New Brunswicker, remarked sententiously: 'It is wrong to assume assets to be of equal value, when they are not so.'[34]

An argument quickly developed.[35] Galt answered Tilley; Brown answered Tilley; Tilley returned to the charge. Tupper, extending the discussion far beyond its original specific subject, began to examine the general financial position which the Maritime Provinces would probably occupy under Galt's proposed system. Everybody was interested. Everybody was obviously eager to speak. A prolonged, time-consuming, acrimonious, and dangerously divisive debate threatened. The conference, faced with the possible abortion of a potential national union, quickly discovered a procedural device that would postpone, and might avoid, the catastrophe. The debate was stopped at five o'clock. The delegates were divided into two committees, one for finance and the other for judicial questions;[36] and that evening the finance committee, reduced to the more manageable proportions of fifteen or sixteen members, resumed the detailed scrutiny of Galt's complicated scheme. It was probably ten o'clock when the committee called a halt to its labours; but for some of the experts the night's work was not ended even yet. It was rumoured later that, long after the other members of the finance committee had found their way back to their rooming-houses or the St. Louis Hotel for the night, Galt and Brown remained closeted with Tilley, Tupper, Pope, and Shea, toiling away over the figures of the financial scheme, and trying to reach some agreement.[37]

⋙ IV ⋘

AT TEN O'CLOCK on Monday morning, the 24th of October, when the session opened and neither of the two committees reported, a small cloud of uncertainty rested, a little ominously, over the conference. In the meantime, another piece of important unfinished business, the problem of the division of powers, was taken up once more. At this point, when probably very few delegates expected it, a real storm of dispute broke, and broke, also, over a matter of fundamental principle. Oliver Mowat began proceedings by rising to move a resolution concerning the powers of the local governments – a resolution that was the obvious counterpart of Macdonald's motion of the previous Friday on the functions of the federation.[38] Mowat barely finished reading the last of the sixteen subjects respecting which the local legislatures could make laws, when E. B. Chandler of New Brunswick was on his feet protesting passionately that the powers of the provinces should not be specified, and that the general government should not be granted residuary authority.

Why had Chandler not spoken before? Why had he waited until Monday to voice a protest that might have been much more appropriately made the previous Friday? The rather confusing Canadian scheme, which enumerated federal, as well as local, subjects of legislation, may have mystified him as well as others. The long list of powers of the general legislature, which Macdonald had read the previous Friday, may have misled him into the belief that residuary authority was to be given, not to the federation, but to the provinces. His protest was belated, but it was an extremely impressive one. He was very far from being a notorious party-minded trouble-maker like George Coles. He was not another Edward Palmer, the lantern-jawed Attorney

General of Prince Edward Island who was already becoming known, according to his own complacent estimate, as the 'malcontent' of the conference. Chandler was a Confederate, but a Confederate with his own distinctive point of view. A well-read man, with a good working knowledge of the American Constitution, he obviously considered that the Quebec Conference should limit itself to the creation of federal institutions and the enumeration of federal powers, and should not otherwise meddle with the local legislatures or their authority. 'You are now proceeding', he thundered to the delegates, 'to destroy the constitutions of the local governments, and to give them less powers than they have had allowed to them from England, and it will make them merely large municipal corporations. This is a vital question, which decides the question between a federal and a legislative union, and it will be fatal to the success of Confederation in the Lower Provinces.'[39]

Chandler's explosive outburst of dissent was more than enough. The conference started off on another long, inconclusive, and vaguely disturbing debate. The argument was still in full career when the busy delegates broke up at two o'clock and divided into the committees on finance and judicial affairs. At half past seven, when the general session was resumed, the debate began again with undiminished vehemence, and it was by no means finished when the conference finally adjourned at eleven o'clock. George Coles moved that 'the local legislatures shall have power to make all laws not given by this Conference to the General Legislature expressly.'[40] He got some support from Dickey and – rather oddly – from Archibald, as well, of course, as from Chandler himself.[41] But many of the delegates remained unpersuaded; the principal Nova Scotians, who believed in federal preponderance as an article of faith, rallied to the defence of the Canadian plan; and the burly Tupper poured long, thunderous salvoes of his heavy artillery at Chandler's exposed position. 'Those who were at Charlottetown', he reminded the conference, 'will remember that it was fully specified there that all the powers not given to the local should be reserved to the federal government. . . . Mr. Chandler says that it gives a legislative instead of a federal union. I think that a benefit. . . . If it were not for the peculiar condition

THE DESIGN COMPLETED «« 173

of Lower Canada, and that the Lower Provinces have not municipal systems such as Upper Canada, I should go in for a legislative union instead of a federal. . . . If Conference limit the powers of the general legislature, I feel that the whole platform is swept away from us.'[42]

This was plain, downright speaking. And Jonathan McCully, Tupper's Liberal colleague, was prepared to go even further in his federalist zeal. He pointed to the provisions of the New Zealand Act of 1852, which empowered the general legislature to supersede all local laws which were repugnant to its own, as an appropriate way out of the British American difficulty.[43] Macdonald, who had been watching the debate with even more anxious interest than usual, realized at once that this was going too far. Within the next twenty-four hours, Mowat, for the Canadians, was to propose that, under the new federal system, the lieutenant-governors should be empowered to reserve local bills for the approval of the general government and the general government given authority to disallow local acts. Macdonald believed whole-heartedly in the subordination of the local to the federal in confederation; but he realized clearly that this could be most satisfactorily achieved, not by some novel and frightening power of annulment imported from New Zealand, but by the traditional methods of reservation and disallowance, which were perfectly familiar to British America. He had to disavow his indiscreetly zealous follower, McCully, though they both shared the same purpose. He brushed the Nova Scotian's suggestion aside as impossible; but it was Chandler, rather than McCully, that he was determined to defeat.

He was desperately serious. Above everything, he wished to secure the grant of residuary powers to the general government. His speech – the second longest that he made during the conference, according to its records – was an appeal of the greatest, most urgent gravity, expressed in emphatic and sweeping words and phrases that were strangely, impressively different from those of his normal debating style. He drove Chandler's arguments and Coles's resolution back to their origin in the American Constitution. Passionately, he reminded the conference that to grant residuary powers to the local legislatures would be to adopt the worst error of the American Constitution, the error upon which all constitutional authorities had expatiated, the error whose awful consequences the great de Tocqueville had foretold. 'Mr. Chandler would give sovereign power to the local legislatures,' he asserted, 'just where the United States failed. . . . We should concentrate the power in the federal government and not adopt the decentralization of the United States.'[44] It was a last great appeal for what he considered the most important general principle of the new constitution.

It succeeded. In the end, no provincial delegation, not even that of Prince Edward Island, voted in favour of Coles's resolution. The worst danger was over. But the long debate seemed, for the moment, to have unsettled the delegates; and even strong federalists began to look back critically at Macdonald's resolution – which the conference had passed unanimously three days before — on the powers of the general legislature. Henry of Nova Scotia, and Johnson and Gray of New Brunswick, all of whom believed in the grant of residuary authority to the federation, warned that the enumeration of specific federal powers would, in Henry's phrase, be 'hampering the case with difficulties'.[45] The rambling, retrospective argument went on so long that, when the conference finally adjourned that night at eleven o'clock, only one specified local power, the right to make laws concerning agriculture – a power that it had already been decided was to be held concurrently by the general legislature – had been approved.

⇒⇒⇒ V ⇐⇐⇐

To THE ANXIOUS Canadian cabinet, and, in particular, to such temperamental and impatient ministers as Galt and Brown, Saturday, the 22nd of October, and Monday, the 24th, must have seemed ominous with the blackest portents. Two solid days had passed in wrangling, inconclusive debate. The solution of the conference's two great remaining problems – the division of powers and the financial settlement – was scarcely closer by so much as a single item. It was not as if the delegates were arguing merely about details; they were arguing – and arguing vigorously, even passionately – over fundamental principles which the Canadians had fondly believed to have been tacitly accepted nearly two months before at the Charlottetown Conference. Obviously, the Canadians had been too confident. They were not yet out of the woods, by any means. They looked forward to Tuesday with mingled hope, uncertainty, and apprehension.

Tuesday, that crucial and dreaded day, finally came. Miraculously, it brought no storm. It brought concord instead. It was as if the delegates had exhausted all their criticisms, reservations, and misgivings in those last two days of debate – as if the prolonged argument had finally brought them to the realization that what they really wanted was a federation on the Canadian model, and that if they did not quickly end the disputes that threatened to make an agreement impossible they might lose it, and for ever. They did not want to lose it. For two weeks they had been struggling in the depths of a blind, tangled jungle of difficulties, through which there was no known road, and from which they sometimes feared there was nothing to do but retreat. The toil and the fun of that fortnight's struggle had brought them close together. They were united – exclusively united – by the one thing they alone had in common – the experience of the past two weeks. Now, through the dark but thinning wood, splashed with a few large golden patches of sunshine, they could dimly see the green shining promise of the land they had come to find. And in a sudden flash of certainty they knew that they must reach it.

When Mowat got up that Tuesday morning to submit his sixteen specified local powers for the second time, the whole attitude of the conference had mysteriously changed. Overnight the Canadian scheme for the division of powers had become acceptable. There were only a few amendments to Mowat's proposals, the most important being D'Arcy McGee's proviso respecting the local control of education – 'saving the rights and privileges which the Protestant or Catholic minority in both Canadas may possess as to their denominational schools at the time when the Constitutional Act goes into operation'.[46] By the time the two-o'clock adjournment came, the delegates had nearly finished their favourable review of local jurisdiction; and it was not until the evening session, when the conference returned once more to federal powers and parliamentary procedures, that Chandler and the other retreating advocates of provincial autonomy were provoked into risking a rear-guard action on the subject of federal controls. Mowat had just proposed — as the Canadians had known in advance he would – that the lieutenant-governors should be empowered to reserve any bill of the local legislatures for the consideration of the general government, and that the general government should be authorized to disallow any local act within a year of its passage.[47]

At this point, the tiny minority of local autonomists turned and struck. John Mercer Johnson, the Attorney General of New Brunswick, with his black, luxuriant beard and curled mustachios, his 'great dash and vigour', and his reputation as a pugnacious champion of popular causes, got up to lodge a protest. The powers of reservation and disallowance were, he complained, 'too great a restriction'.[48] Chandler immediately supported him.[49] By this time Chandler's opposition to the Canadian resolution could have been expected; but Johnson's original intervention was less easily understandable, for Johnson, unlike Chandler, had readily accepted the grant of residuary powers to the general legislature. Still more surprising was John H. Gray's agreement with the view which Chandler and Johnson had expressed.[50] Gray early became one of the strongest and most devoted supporters of confederation in New Brunswick. He had, as time was to show, a special interest in the history and political theory of confederation. And in the previous day's debate on the residuary power he had acutely observed that, in its relations with the future provinces, the federal government would occupy the same position as the imperial government had held before.[51]

This was an epigrammatic and accurate description of the Canadians' main intent. They drew their ideas of federal-provincial relations from the British imperial organization, just as they derived their theories of government and their plans for political institutions from the British parliamentary system. In the Empire in which the delegates had grown up, the imperial government had possessed certain real controls over both colonial executives and colonial legislatures. Colonial governors were appointed by the imperial government. Colonial bills could be reserved and colonial acts disallowed. In the scheme the Canadians had now nearly finished presenting, the federal government was to step into the place which the imperial government had occupied before, exercise its old supervisory authority over the provinces, and wield the traditional controls. Lieutenant-governors would still be appointed, but now by the new federal government. Lieutenant-governors were still to be empowered to reserve local bills. The general government would still enjoy the discretionary power of disallowing local acts.

As every delegate at Quebec was well aware, these powers were drawn directly from the existing law and custom of the British colonial system. Gray was protesting against the logical consequences of his own general principle. Characteristically, the conference refused to endorse his protest; and, when it came to the actual vote, Gray himself may have had sober second thoughts. There was no recorded division on Mowat's motion; but if Johnson, Chandler, and Gray had maintained a united front, they might have forced or persuaded New Brunswick to give a negative vote. Since Peter Mitchell, one of the two additional New Brunswick delegates, had been given permission a few days before to go home on private business, the provincial delegation had numbered six; and the critics of reservation and disallowance could have divided the group equally. Tilley, Fisher, and Steeves may have succeeded in changing their colleagues' minds; or Johnson and Gray – but almost certainly not Chandler – may have felt that an oral protest was sufficient. At all events, Mowat's motion passed, apparently unanimously; and the brief debate had served simply to emphasize the significance of its passage. The powers of reservation and disallowance, like the federal legislature's residuary power on a previous occasion, had been deliberately challenged; and once again that challenge had been completely and emphatically rejected by the conference. The decisive vote of the 25th of October was one more important item in a rapidly accumulating body of evidence which proved that the delegates at Quebec had no intention of establishing a federal system in which, in accordance with twentieth-century abstract theory, the central and provincial legislatures would have co-ordinate sovereignty within their own respective spheres. What the delegates intended was something radically different. They planned a paramount national parliament and government, and subordinate, quasi-municipal local institutions.

So much progress was made in the late evening session of Tuesday, the 25th of October, that next morning at noon, when the conference reconvened, Macdonald was able to present the major recommendations of the judicial committee for what turned out to be a ready approval. The mood of concord lasted into the evening session when Galt proposed a resolution concerning language. He moved 'that in the general legislature and in its proceedings the English and French languages may be both equally employed. And also in the local legislature of Lower Canada and in the federal and local courts of Lower Canada.'[52] This was no declaration of general principle that the British American federation was to be a bilingual, or a bicultural, country. Galt's motion was as severely practical in character as it was strictly limited in extent. It was concerned only with legislative debates, pleadings in court, and the printed proceedings – journals, reports, and debates – of legislative bodies; and it was restricted in its application to the parliament at Ottawa, and the legislature and courts of the future province of Quebec.

All that Galt had proposed was that a concession should be made to the French-speaking minority at Ottawa in return for a similar concession to the English-speaking minority in Lower Canada. Nobody suggested that the legal status of the French language in the national parliament should be extended to the legislatures and courts of any or all of the other provinces – provinces either already existing or yet to be created – of what, it was intended, was to be a truly transcontinental British American federation. The Province of Canada was bilingual only in so far as the debates and records of its legislature and the proceedings of the courts of Canada East were concerned. The French language had no legal or customary standing in the courts of Canada West, nor in the legislatures or courts of any of the Maritime Provinces, including New Brunswick where a minority of the population was French-speaking. In 1858 it was proposed in the New Brunswick Assembly that the record of its debates, which could be carried on only in English, should be translated and published in French; but even this proposal had been rejected on the grounds that such a privilege, if granted to the French, would have to be conceded to other ethnic minorities, with intolerable consequences.[53] The 'cultural dualism' of British America was a notion which the Maritimers as well as the Upper Canadians regarded as completely invalid in their own provinces and which they were prepared to recognize only in central federal institutions, where it was politically essential, and in Canada East, where it had long been established by law and custom.

The great issue of Wednesday was not, however, the question of language, but the anxious problem of finance, which Galt brought up for the second time, late in the session. For days the finance committee had been struggling with the subject. The opening of the conference had been delayed that morning by the committee's final meeting. But even these prolonged and searching discussions had not seriously weakened the bases of Galt's proposals; and the committee's final recommendations, which he presented that night, were a tribute, made perhaps unwillingly, but of necessity, to the wisdom and impartiality of his original scheme.[54] The wording of the resolutions of the previous Saturday was considerably altered for greater precision; but, in substance, the financial proposals were exactly what they had been previously. Tilley, the voluble and determined critic of five days before, had been brought to recognize the statesmanship of Galt's plan. So had Tupper and the Nova Scotians. So had Newfoundland. But Prince Edward Island, sulky, unconvinced, and increasingly dissatisfied, remained; and, partly out of honest conviction and partly, no doubt, as a result of the political blackmail forcibly threatened by Coles and Palmer, the Prince Edward Island delegation decided to oppose a united front to Galt's motion.

W. H. Pope began by explaining at some length how difficult it would be for the Island to exist on the limited revenue which Galt's financial terms would allow her.[55] Coles went one better; he sharpened this general expression of dissatisfaction to a particular point of discontent. He always insisted that at Charlottetown it had been tacitly agreed that £200,000 should be granted to Prince

Edward Island, as the only effective inducement for her entrance into confederation, for the purpose of buying out the rights of her absentee landed proprietors. He was so certain, he told the Island legislature later, that such a grant would be freely made at Quebec that he did not even trouble to reassure himself about the matter; and then when Galt's proposals were first read he discovered, to his amazement and indignation, that the Island's promised due had been completely omitted.[56] He was furious, he claimed, that Prince Edward had been so flagrantly deceived and discriminated against; and he moved that 'a sum equal to the interest of the amount necessary to purchase the said lands' be paid annually to the colony.[57] A. A. Macdonald seconded the resolution in a lengthy speech;[58] and most of the other members of the Island delegation either gave it support or dwelt at length on the general financial difficulties of their province in confederation. But it was all useless. The delegates, believing that Prince Edward Island had already been treated with quite sufficient generosity, remained coldly unresponsive. The conference gave a special annual allowance of $63,000 to New Brunswick for ten years. It offered Newfoundland, in return for its ungranted Crown lands and mineral rights, an annual subsidy of $150,000. But it gave nothing more to Prince Edward Island; and George Brown, who by this time had characteristically lost all patience with his Island friends, told George Coles bluntly that his colony had already been given more money than it would know what to do with![59]

That night the conference sat until midnight. It was the third late night in succession; but by means of these tremendous exertions the weary delegates were now rapidly nearing the end of their work. They were still debating new motions, and still deciding upon others that had been reserved for further consideration; but by this time they had also begun the review of their scheme as a whole, setting out its resolutions in logical order, making terminology uniform, and removing varieties and inconsistencies of style. These readings and rereadings might have seemed, at the start, to be dull and formal work; but for those faithful delegates who followed them through to the end they had a very different and a very powerful effect. For the first time

GEORGE ETIENNE CARTIER
Province of Canada

ALEXANDER TILLOCH GALT
Province of Canada

Legislative Buildings, Quebec

Back row, left to right

G. COLES, *Prince Edward Island*

H. L. LANGEVIN, *Province of Canada*

E. PALMER, *Prince Edward Island*

O. MOWAT, *Province of Canada*

J. M. JOHNSON, *New Brunswick*

A. G. ARCHIBALD, *Nova Scotia*

C. FISHER, *New Brunswick*

J. COCKBURN, *Province of Canada*

J. C. CHAPAIS, *Province of Canada*

W. A. HENRY, *Nova Scotia*

R. B. DICKEY, *Nova Scotia*

A. A. MACDONALD, *Prince Edward Island*

W. H. POPE, *Prince Edward Island*

J. A. SHEA, *Newfoundland*

F. B. T. CARTER, *Newfoundland*

H. BERNARD (secretary)

T. H. HAVILAND, *Prince Edward Island*

The Quebec Conference, October, 1864

Front row, left to right

E. WHELAN, *Prince Edward Island*

A. T. GALT, *Province of Canada*

G. BROWN, *Province of Canada*

J. A. MACDONALD, *Province of Canada*

J. H. GRAY, *Prince Edward Island*

C. TUPPER, *Nova Scotia*

SIR E. P. TACHÉ, *Province of Canada*

S. L. TILLEY, *New Brunswick*

G. E. CARTIER, *Province of Canada*

J. MCCULLY, *Nova Scotia*

E. B. CHANDLER, *New Brunswick*

W. H. STEEVES, *New Brunswick*

J. H. GRAY, *New Brunswick*

GEORGE BROWN
Province of Canada

JOHN ALEXANDER MACDONALD
Province of Canada

in weeks, the design of the new British America stood out clearly as a complete and integrated whole. Up to that moment the conference had fixed its concentrated attention first on one section, then on another. It had been preoccupied, intensely and narrowly, with detail. But now all details were sinking back into their proper places as parts of a coherent whole. The delegates, these not untypical British Americans, had put together a vast, complicated, but integrated structure. It was the product of their inheritance, experience, and statesmanship; and now, as they gazed on its completed totality, they could not help but be impressed. It was a valid expression of British America's collective personality, an aspiring design for its future development. It had balance, symmetry, and unity.

It had something else as well – something that for years to come would be no more than space, enormous dimensions, but that, in the end, might mean greatness. Late that afternoon, the 27th of October, as the last session drew to its close and the tall, narrow room gradually darkened with early autumnal twilight, the little quorum of delegates sitting round the long table caught one last glimpse of the continental proportions of the nation they were trying to create. Some time during the day or late the previous night they had committed the new federal union to the construction of the Intercolonial Railway;[60] and now Montrealers and the Upper Canadians were carefully making certain that what they looked on as the necessary counterpart of the Intercolonial, the political incorporation and the commercial exploitation of the North-West and the Pacific coast, should equally become a main task of the new nation. The resolution Mowat had introduced two days before, providing for the admission of the North West Territories, British Columbia, and Vancouver Island, was passed; and, as one of its last acts, the conference declared that the communications with the North West Territories and the improvements required for the development of its trade with the seaboard were subjects of the highest importance which would be attacked as soon as the finances of the new federation would permit.[61]

⇛ VI ⇚

I T WAS quite dark now, dinner was over, and upstairs, in his room at the St. Louis, Brown was frantically scribbling a brief note to his wife. Many of the delegates had gone already. At four o'clock a large party, chiefly Maritimers, had left in a special train provided by Brydges of the Grand Trunk Railway. But the leaders and some of their principal Unionist followers – Tupper, Henry and McCully, Tilley and Johnson, and a few others – had stuck with the business to the end; and they, together with about half the members of the Canadian cabinet – Cartier, Macdonald, Galt, Brown, and Chapais – were to travel to Montreal by the regular Grand Trunk night train which left Lévis at nine o'clock. It was past eight already, there was not much more than enough time to get across the river to Lévis, and Brown's luggage had already been taken down. At lessening intervals the booming voices of Tupper, McCully, and the rest could be heard from the lobby below, urging him to make haste. He must go, at once; but, before he went, some of his wonder and pride of accomplishment must find expression to Anne. 'All right!!!' he scribbled hurriedly, in triumphant staccato phrases, 'Constitution adopted – a most creditable document – a complete reform of all the abuses and injustices we have complained of!! Is it not wonderful? French Canadianism entirely extinguished!'[62] It was a cry from the heart. In the joy of achievement, the old, incorrigible Brown, the sectarian and sectional leader of Protestant and English-speaking Canada West, had rushed back out of the past with a yell of triumph, though the triumph, in his mind, was over French-Canadian domination, not over French-Canadian culture.

The conference had finished – or nearly finished – its work. Now it was going on holiday. Six weeks before, the Canadians had been presented to Maritime audiences in the tour that followed the Charlottetown Conference. Now a similar triumphal progress – half relaxation for the delegates and half propaganda for confederation – was to introduce the Maritime delegates to the Canadian public. The first stop was to be at Montreal; and the Montrealers had prepared a varied and lavish reception. But it rained that night, as the delegates travelled westward. It was raining the next morning in Montreal; and all day, while the dark clouds thickened unrelentingly and a blustering, piercing wind rose nearly to a gale, the rain came steadily down. 'Never', said the Montreal *Gazette* mournfully, 'was such an auspicious occasion heralded in by such unpropitious weather.'[63] The whole elaborate programme of outdoor entertainment – the steeple-chase, the military review, the fireworks display – had to be given up. Only the ball, the supreme event of the day, was immune to weather; and, by half past eight, long queues of carriages, black and gleaming with rain under the yellow gas lamps, were moving slowly down Craig Street towards the hotel portico. About eight hundred Montrealers were there to greet the delegates and their wives and daughters.[64] They wanted to meet them, dance with them, and talk to them about the conference, and confederation, and the future of British America. And Mercy Coles, now nearly restored to perfect health, had every dance in her card taken.

Late the next morning – the ball had lasted until two o'clock – the conference held its last official session. Cartier presided, for Taché – old and very tired – had stayed behind in Quebec. The proof-sheets of the Quebec Resolutions, which had been printed in Quebec on Friday and brought up to Montreal on the night train, were revised, corrected, and confirmed; and the conference passed the three supplementary Montreal resolutions, in the last of which the Queen was requested 'to determine the rank and name of the Federated Provinces'. Then, after only the briefest of intervals, the luncheon, the *déjeuner*, began its majestic prog-ress through nearly six hours of eating, drinking, and speech-making.[65] At Montreal, and later at Ottawa and Toronto, these deliberate and stately entertainments followed a carefully ar-ranged course. The reply to the toast to the Maritime delegates was shared by representatives from three or all of the Atlantic provinces, who thus had a chance to present themselves to the Canadians, thank their hosts, and enlarge upon the success of the conference, and the glorious future of British North America. At some point, usually towards the close of the proceedings, the chairman would propose the health of the Canadian cabinet; and then a senior minister – Cartier at Montreal – would discuss the conference and confederation in a confidential fashion that grew more expansively detailed as the tour moved westward. A good deal of information about the Quebec scheme – a surprising amount, in fact – had already appeared in the newspapers; but the Canadians seemed to have an insatiable enthusiasm for more news, comment, and opinion about the conference and its work. And – the Maritimers could not help noting this with pride – they greeted the delegates with acclaim and gratitude as the founders of a great new nation.

On Monday, after a day's complete and welcome rest, the visitors were up early and on the road for Ottawa by seven o'clock. By this time it was quite clear that the great storm of Friday had brought the long-expected break in the weather. It was distinctly cool on Monday – cool and dull; and the sun shone for only an hour or two on the breezy deck of the steamer that carried the delegates up the Ottawa River. They were chilled through late that night when they reached the future capital; but the citizens of Ottawa gave them a welcome that would have done credit to a conquering army.[66] And next morning, as they looked upward from the steamer that carried them on a sightseeing trip on the Ottawa River, the new, half-finished legislative buildings, rising spacious and splendid from the masons' hammers, seemed a fitting home for the national parliament they had just created.[67] The contractors gave them a *déjeuner* in the future 'picture gallery', the only large room in the central block that had yet been roofed; and John A. Macdonald was expected to reply at length to the toast to the Canadian ministry.

He was worn out. He had dragged himself thus far on the triumphal western tour; but he felt ill and terribly tired, and he knew he could not possibly give the detailed exposition of the Quebec scheme that he had planned to deliver at Ottawa. When, through the dull ache of his pain and fatigue, he heard the toast to the Canadian administration, he rose, gave his thanks and apologies briefly, and then sat down.[68] For over two months, he had lived under the incessant pressure of work and worry. More, probably, than any other delegate at Quebec, he had guided the conference, explained the Canadian plan, defended its principles, and tried, with all the instinctive arts of his warm, friendly personality, to win the doubtful friends and disarm the potential enemies of confederation. He had even busied himself, during those last difficult days at Quebec, in assiduously cultivating the Coles family, dining with George – that unconvinced and dangerous party tactician – and his wife and daughter, and entertaining them with small talk. 'I went to dinner and John A. sat beside me,' Mercy Coles recorded delightedly on the last night in Quebec. 'What an old humbug he is! He brought my dessert into the drawing room – the conundrum!'[69] Now, as if in return for these last special efforts, he could dimly hear Coles, replying to the toast to the Maritime delegates, announce jocosely that the Quebec scheme was 'a marriage settlement' that would give satisfaction to the entire British American connection![70]

Next morning, Wednesday, the 2nd of November, the delegates' special train resumed its triumphant onward career. There was a lengthy stop at Kingston, where C. J. Brydges, 'the obliging and gentlemanly' general manager of the Grand Trunk Railway, provided a beautiful 'cold collation' with claret and champagne;[71] and, in the midst of these festivities, John A. Macdonald slipped unostentatiously away. A telegram announcing an unexpected civic reception brought the train to a brief halt at Belleville; and at Cobourg, where the Canadian Solicitor-General, James Cockburn, gave the visitors supper, there was another long delay. After this the train picked up speed. It was driving at nearly fifty miles an hour through the darkness on this long last lap of its journey; but even so it did not finally come to rest by the station platform at Toronto until past ten o'clock. Niagara was the terminus of the tour. But Toronto was its climax. All along the way from Quebec the Maritimers had been surprised and moved by the size of the crowds and the warmth of the welcome that greeted them; but the reception at Toronto went beyond anything they had ever hoped for or dreamed of. It was overwhelming.

The crowd was enormous.[72] It overflowed the station platform. It overflowed the station itself and its approaches. York Street, Front Street, and a large part of the Esplanade were thick with people. The delegates, greeted with cheer after cheer, could hardly make their way to the carriages; the carriages could hardly move through the dense crowd that surrounded them. Behind the beleaguered carriages, under a dark sky lit by the coloured cascades of falling rockets and roman candles, came the volunteers, the band of the Queen's Own, the band of the 10th Royals, and three hundred members of the fire brigade, carrying torches. It was only the briefest of journeys between the station and the Queen's Hotel; but more than half an hour had elapsed before the last carriage had unloaded its passengers. The crowd waited. It began to cry 'speech'. And then, a storey above the street, at the west end of the hotel, figures could be seen emerging upon a balcony.

George Brown had realized that the delegates must show themselves. He had led Tupper, Tilley, Gray, and their followers to the balcony.[73] And now the delegates looked down at the crowd below and realized the full force of the enormous demonstration that had greeted them. The long dark expanse of the street was lit by the bright windows of the hotel, the redly waving torches, and the starry showers of fireworks; and they could see the thousands of white, upturned faces, waiting, eager, expectant. It was the culmination of the tour, of the conference, of the whole union movement that had begun – how far away it must have seemed – when the Charlottetown Conference had met for the first time in the Legislative Council chamber in the Prince Edward Island Colonial Building. At Charlottetown and Quebec, the delegates had drafted the constitution of a state; but here, in the masses of cheering people that looked up at the Queen's Hotel, were the faith, the enthusiasm, and the energy that could make the future nation a reality.

The cry for 'speech' became a deafening, irresistible roar. Tupper stepped forward. A great silence slowly descended on the crowd. And he began to speak.

CHAPTER SEVEN

Uncertain Reception

THE DELEGATES were going home. For over a month all their activities – travelling, sightseeing, planning, debating, arguing, and speechifying – had been concerned with confederation. They had given their time and thought so exclusively to a united British America that they might almost have seemed to have forgotten their individual provinces. But at the back of their minds, in some rarely visited but perfectly well-known corner, lay the realization that the making of the Quebec scheme was only the beginning of a fairly long and complicated process, the next stage of which must be carried out at home. The Seventy-two Resolutions would have to be accepted by the various provinces and would then have to be put into statutory form and passed by the imperial Parliament. As the conference's seventieth resolution put it, 'the sanction of the imperial and local parliaments shall be sought for the Union of the Provinces on the principles adopted by the Conference.'

Everybody knew that this would take time. But almost everybody hoped and believed that it would not take a great deal of time. The completion of the federal union in 1865 was something the principal authors of the Quebec scheme took for granted. Monck, writing confidentially to Cardwell, predicted that the provincial legislatures would take early action and that all would be in readiness for legislation by the imperial Parliament at its next session.[1] Shea, the hard-headed Tilley, the robust and sanguine Tupper, all seemed hopeful of quick and easy success.[2] It was true that at the last moment Palmer, Chandler, and a few others had persuaded the conference to make a slight but

significant change in the wording of the seventy-second and last
resolution, which had originally stated that 'the proceedings of
the Conference, when finally revised, shall be signed by the delegates'.[3] The word 'authenticated', which did not imply that the
signatories agreed with the resolutions but simply that they
endorsed them as having actually passed the conference, was
prudently substituted for the more compromising word 'signed'.
Admittedly, there were delegates who did not want to commit
themselves yet; but the friendly remarks made by Coles and
Palmer at the *déjeuners* in Ottawa and Toronto suggested that
even the dissatisfied Islanders had not definitely made up their
minds to oppose. Surely there was every reason to be confident?[4]
The Canadian delegation was the Canadian Coalition cabinet,
with an unbeatable majority in the legislature. Every other delegation save that of Newfoundland had been made up of the
principal political leaders on both sides of politics.

The prospects could hardly have been better. But time was
short. There was a new sense of urgency among the leaders, and
a new and strange precipitancy in the sequence of events. Already, before the tour of the delegates was over, George Brown,
in his long speech at the Toronto *déjeuner*, gave what amounted
to a fairly detailed, semi-official résumé of the Quebec scheme.[5]
By now, the substance of the plan was public property; and what
still remained unknown – the actual wording of the Seventy-two
Resolutions in their entirety – was revealed almost immediately
after the conference had dispersed. The main body of the Maritime delegates left Montreal on their homeward journey on
Sunday, the 6th of November. Two days later, the *Journal de
Québec* published the Quebec Resolutions, minus the amendments and additions that had been passed at Montreal.[6] On
Thursday, the 10th of November, the day after Edward Palmer
had returned to Prince Edward Island, the Charlottetown
Monitor printed the Seventy-two Resolutions in their final form.[7]
In the next few days they were widely published throughout the
provinces. Every British American, if he wanted to, could inform
himself about the Quebec scheme. The delegates had barely
returned home when they were confronted by an electorate that

knew exactly what they had done on their great mission to Quebec.

Of all the delegates at Quebec, the Canadians – the twelve members of the Canadian ministry — had the least reason to feel worried about the popular reaction to the plan – at least so far as their own province was concerned. They expected a few critics; they knew there would be some opposition; but in the political circumstances resulting from the Coalition they felt comfortably certain of the main sources from which the opposition would come, and of the comparatively narrow limits within which it would be confined. In Canada West, a few Conservatives, a few extreme Grits, and a handful of John S. Macdonald Liberals formed an unnatural and heterogeneous group of critics. In Canada East, the *Rouges*, led by Dorion in company with such English-speaking Liberals as Holton and Huntington, would bring to bear a much more organized and united party resistance. Of the two groups, the ill-assorted critics of Canada West were much the less important. They attacked the Quebec scheme for the varied, contradictory reasons of its expense, its divisive character, its despotic centralization, and what some of them took to be its inherent strain of republicanism. Their main criticism was simply that the proposed union was not legislative but federal, and that a federal union was a clumsy, costly, and dangerously explosive system, whose probable fate was horribly exemplified in the American Civil War.

Their second major objection – an objection that both ultra-Tories and extreme Grits could unite to support – was concerned not with the substance of the Quebec plan but with the procedure by which the conference proposed to implement it. They insisted that before any attempt was made to carry out confederation the whole issue should be submitted to the people in a general election.[8] In reply, the Confederates and their newspaper supporters preached constitutional sermons based on British and British American parliamentary practice. A general election on such an issue, they argued, would be nothing more or less than a plebiscite; and a plebiscite was a dreadful republican heresy, French or American in origin, which would violate all the principles of parliamentary government, without the slightest beneficial result.[9] How could you 'appeal to the people' about a constitution drawn up in Seventy-two Resolutions? 'Submission of the complicated details to the country is an obvious absurdity,' Macdonald argued. '. . . If by petitions or public meetings parliament is satisfied that the country do not want the measure, they will refuse to adopt it. If on the other hand, parliament sees that the country is in favour of the federation, there is no use in an appeal to it.'[10]

The sporadic, unorganized, and contradictory criticisms of Canada West did not need to be taken too seriously. The resistance of Canada East was definitely a more formidable matter. Here the *Rouges,* a distinct and organized division of the Reform party, who had recovered from the shock of their abandonment by their western allies, were gathering their resources to resist confederation. In this struggle, the *Rouges'* greatest potential advantage was the vague, pervasive sense of apprehension that ever since June had been felt, not only by *Rouge* supporters, but also by the whole body of French Canadians, including the most docile *Bleus.* From the very beginning, French Canada had been unable to repress the troubled feeling that a federal union, in the making of which that fearful ogre George Brown would play an important part, was likely to be a desperate – a dangerously desperate – remedy for the constitutional ills of Canada. The publication of the Quebec scheme had not completely calmed these terrors. The Seventy-two Resolutions, so laconic in expression, so practical in intent, so utterly devoid of any declaration of theory or statement of principle, did indeed give some comfort to those who hoped that the Canada East of the future would have effective control over its own institutions, laws, and customs. But the Quebec plan was less satisfactory to strict believers in the co-ordinate authority of central and local legislatures; and it could be, and was, read very widely as the project for a highly centralized federation, with a paramount general government, and subordinate, quasi-municipal local administrations. It was this popular, English-speaking interpretation that gave the *Rouges* their chance. On the 7th of November, after Brown had made his explanations at Toronto but before the full text of the

Resolutions had been published, A. A. Dorion rushed into print with a manifesto against the Quebec scheme. 'Ce n'est donc pas une Confédération qui nous est proposée,' he cried, 'mais tout simplement une union législative déguisée sous le nom de Confédération.'[11] A few days later, when it published the Quebec Resolutions, *Le Pays* declared angrily that, in the new constitution, 'le gouvernement général serait tout, les législatures locales rien.'[12]

The moderate and *Bleu* newspapers of Canada East – *Le Canadien, La Minerve, Le Journal de Québec,* and *Le Courrier du Canada* – struggled hard to meet this attack. Of them all, it was Langevin's paper, *Le Courrier du Canada,* that made the best defence. In a series of twenty-one articles, spread out over December 1864 and January 1865, it set out and analysed the Quebec Resolutions with a perceptive, critical commentary.[13] Like its fellow French-language journals, it made no pretence of maintaining that the Quebec plan was an ideal constitution. 'Mais nous disons', declared the *Courrier,* 'que sous les circonstances actuelles, et dans la situation d'infériorité où se trouve nécessairement placé le Bas-Canada, il était impossible à nos ministres bas-Canadiens de mieux sauveguarder nos intérêts les plus chers.'[14] There were fates worse than confederation facing French Canada: a legislative union of the whole of British America; or, infinitely the worst of all, annexation to the United States, 'la plus matérielle, la plus immorale des nations modernes', in which French Canada would promptly be robbed of its autonomy and lose its immortal soul.

It was true that the federal union was more centralized than many French Canadians would have liked to see; but the independent and Conservative press found ways of explaining or justifying this federal preponderance. *Le Canadien,* with an air of plaintively sober resignation, accepted centralization as the inescapable price of security from the United States;[15] *Le Journal de Québec* extolled it as the unifying force upon which a durable and expansive British American nation could be built.[16] *Le Courrier du Canada,* while it did not attempt to evade the centralist provisions of the Quebec plan, concentrated instead upon its more strictly federal features. 'Le premier avantage du projet de la Confédération', *Le Courrier* stated in its first comment on the Quebec Resolutions, 'c'est qu'il met à l'abri de toute atteinte . . . notre religion, nos institutions, et notre nationalité.'[17] The local powers enumerated in the new constitution would help to preserve the institutions and customs in which the essential spirit of French Canada had expressed itself. But, on the other hand, the long list of federal functions ensured that the central legislature could work without limit or restriction to promote the geographical expansion, the economic progress, and the material well-being of the nation as a whole and of all its parts. The Quebec scheme wisely gave 'au gouvernement central une somme de pouvoirs suffisante pour lui permettre de travailler, sans être gêné, au bien-être matériel et à l'agrandissement des différents états de la Confédération, pris collectivement ou séparément'.[18]

⇛ II ⇚

I N BOTH Canada East and Canada West, the newspapers worked hard to give assurance and get support for confederation; but none of them could have any serious doubts about the ultimate success of the Quebec scheme. So far as the Province of Canada was concerned, the first of the two objects set out in the seventieth of the Quebec Resolutions – the 'sanction' of the local parliament – was as good as gained already. The second object – the approval of the British government, and, finally, legislation by the imperial Parliament – remained; but here again Canada was favoured by unique good fortune. Unlike his brother governors in Nova Scotia and New Brunswick, whose dislike of the Quebec scheme was becoming obvious and might be dangerous, Lord Monck had been, from the beginning, a firm believer in confederation. He would, no doubt, have preferred a legislative union, openly acknowledged as such; but he was convinced that the Quebec scheme approximated so closely to his ideal that its popular title, Confederation, was in effect a misnomer.

In the dispatch of the 7th of November, which he sent off with the Seventy-two Resolutions, he had some criticisms of the plan to offer; but they were not many, or, in his opinion, very serious.[19]

He was somewhat dismayed when he discovered that by the forty-fourth resolution, the power of pardon – a prerogative power which in his opinion could be exercised only by a direct representative of the Crown – was to be administered by the Lieutenant-Governors in Council. He preferred, like most of the delegates, to have the legislative councillors appointed rather than elected; but he could not help fearing that a council whose numbers were fixed and whose members were appointed for life could fairly easily run into serious collision with a popularly elected House of Commons. The only enumerated local power that he questioned was the power to legislate respecting 'property and civil rights, excepting those portions thereof assigned to the General Parliament'. And the fact that the conference had empowered the general parliament to render uniform the laws relating to property and civil rights in the English-speaking provinces, though only with the consent of their legislatures, did not completely reassure him.

The submission of the Quebec Resolutions was the most momentous action that Monck had ever taken in his capacity as the channel of communication between the Canadian and British governments. But the Quebec scheme, despite its preponderating importance, was not the only aspect of the ambitious nation-building programme which the Coalition ministry had undertaken. There were two other related problems – the question of Rupert's Land and the North West Territories, and the question of defence – that the Canadian ministers knew only too well they must make some attempt to settle. Obviously the West and defence were closely linked to the formation of the federal union and its subsequent secure expansion across the continent. Indeed, in the minds of W. E. Gladstone and Edward Cardwell, the West, defence, and confederation formed together a threefold unity of positively trinitarian complexity and mystery.[20] It was four months ago since Cardwell had formally asked Canada for its proposals on defence; and Lieutenant-Colonel Jervois had recently presented his second, revised report on the military needs of the province. George Brown had agreed to follow the Seventy-two Resolutions to London, to explain the Quebec scheme to the Colonial Office, and to seek imperial support for confederation. If he was to be well briefed, on a broad front of all outstanding issues, for his encounter with Whitehall, the Canadian ministers would have to make up their minds about the West and defence.

Even this was not all. Three weeks before, something else had occurred that gave emphasis to Cardwell's inquiry and sharpened the Canadian government's concern about it. The *Chesapeake* affair of December 1863 had pointed to the possibility of a desperate Confederacy attempting to use British North America as a base for raids and privateering against the North. In the ten months since then, despite Lee's inspired resistance and the overconfident British American estimate of its significance, the slow erosion of Southern strength had gone steadily on. If ever the North was to be shocked, thrown off balance, or demoralized by sudden attacks from unexpected quarters, it was now; if ever any important change was to be effected in Union leadership and purpose, the approaching presidential election offered a last great chance. Already, in September, a group of Confederates, operating from Windsor, Canada West, had attempted in vain to seize the U.S.S. *Michigan* and to liberate the Southern soldiers imprisoned on Johnson's Island, off Sandusky, in Lake Erie. Then, in the middle of the Quebec conference, came the most notorious and the most nearly successful raid of all.

At three o'clock on the afternoon of the 19th of October, just after the conference at Quebec had finished its debate on the constitution of the local governments, a small band of American Confederate conspirators had held up the town of St. Albans, in Vermont, robbed the banks, destroyed a little property, wounded two citizens, one of them mortally, and escaped across the international boundary, closely pursued by a small force of Vermonters. The raid, with its solitary casualty, caused no more loss of life than had the *Chesapeake* affair; but circumstances gave it an importance that Colonel Braine's venture in privateering had never possessed. While a number of the captors of the *Chesapeake* had been British Americans, the St. Albans raiders were all Kentuckians. They came from, and retreated to, Canada East. They gave reality, in a most frightening fashion, to all the vague rumours of impending Confederate raids that had been circulating through the border states in the tense weeks before the presidential elections. They plunged the border towns into a turmoil of fear and anger that lasted for months.

For a few days the heavens were rent by vast explosions of American rage at Canada. Then, after the erring province had shown signs of a repentant wish to make amends for the enormity of its offence by capturing the raiders and recovering the stolen money, the enormous commotion seemed rapidly to subside. But the St. Albans raid occurred at a time when American anger at British, and British American, conduct during the Civil War had already reached a pitch of dangerous intensity; and the consequences that seemed to flow from the brief little affray of the 19th of October were out of all proportion to its significance. As soon as he heard the news of the raid, General John A. Dix, the fire-eating American commander on the north-eastern frontier, ordered his men to pursue the St. Albans raiders 'into Canada if necessary and destroy them'. This defiance of British-Canadian sovereignty, which was not revoked for nearly two months, was an open invitation to border clashes; and border clashes, which might even yet bring on an Anglo-American war, could hardly have served Confederate designs better. Seward, the American Secretary of State, realized the dangers of Dix's order; but he felt that the security of the northern boundary must be strengthened, and he knew that Congress would be clamouring for safeguards and retaliation against British America. On the 24th of October, only five days after the raid took place, he instructed his ambassador in London to give the six months' notice required for the abrogation of the Convention of 1817, which limited naval armaments on the Great Lakes. 'In conversation both with Mr. Burnley and me,' Lyons, the British minister to Washington, reported to Russell, the Foreign Secretary in England, 'he [Seward] said it would be impossible to resist the pressure which would be put upon the government to abrogate the Reciprocity Treaty also, if these invasions from Canada continued.'[21]

Much, if not all, of this was in the minds of the Canadian ministers when they sat down on November the 10th for the first of a series of cabinet councils which were to decide their western and defence policies.[22] They had just finished framing a constitu-

tion for a transcontinental British America. They were nation-
builders in intention; but by heredity and experience they were
colonials who had not yet completely escaped from the tutelage
and irresponsibility of colonialism. They saw the Hudson's Bay
Company's monopoly in the North-West as a British creation and
a British responsibility that could only be removed at the charge
of the British treasury. In their view, the defence of Canada was
'essentially an imperial question', the main burden of which
must continue to be borne by the imperial government. These
attitudes and arguments, which still had some reason as well as
much tradition to back them, were in the old familiar colonial
manner; but in addition there were clear signs, in the two Minutes of Council which the cabinet adopted on the 11th and 16th
of November, of a novel sense of national purpose and national
obligation. The ministers declared that they were ready to take
up the task of promoting settlement and providing government
in the arable parts of the North-West.[23] At the same time, they
offered to construct the proposed fortifications at Montreal at
Canada's expense, provided that Great Britain would undertake
the defensive works at Quebec and supply the armaments for
both. In addition, the cabinet promised to propose a vote of a
million dollars for the militia in the next session of the legislature.[24]

George Brown left Quebec before the Minute of Council on
defence was finally adopted, though he knew, and approved of,
its general argument.[25] On the 16th of November, in company
with Colonel Jervois, he sailed from New York on the *Persia* for
England. The second stage in the conversion of the Colonial
Office to confederation was about to begin.

»» III ««

BY THE TIME the *Persia* put out from New York harbour, the
first slight but definite responses to the revolutionary Quebec scheme began to appear in the Maritime Provinces. Appropriately enough, they showed themselves in Prince Edward

Island. Prince Edward Island was, in fact, a special case, peculiarly ripe for an early and violent explosion of opinion over the Seventy-two Resolutions. All the other provincial delegations to the conference had gone home fairly firmly united in their approval of confederation on the Quebec model. They all hoped, in the next few weeks, to win a favourable response to the union scheme among their electorates. They desperately wanted to avoid any serious division of public opinion. But the Island delegates had got beyond the point at which these collective purposes of the conference had any real meaning for them. Already they were bitterly at odds among themselves. They had no intention of waiting upon public opinion. And the first result of the Quebec Conference in Prince Edward Island was an open row, not only among the members of the Island delegation, but also — which was far worse – among the members of the Island government itself.

Edward Palmer began it. He may have been jealous and resentful of Gray, who had supplanted him in the premiership a year before. As an old, crusted Tory, notoriously opposed to the slightest political change – not even 'the sweeping progress of mighty events', Whelan declared, could disturb the 'Dead Sea of Palmer's mind' – he may have disliked the Canadian plan from the beginning. He wrote home from Quebec, privately expressing disgust at the proceedings; he took a critical part in a few of the debates; but during the meeting and the tour his attitude to confederation had not been consistently hostile enough to merit the title 'the malcontent of the conference', which he rather complacently applied to himself. On the way home, his hesitations and inhibitions seemed to vanish; and by the time he got back to Prince Edward Island he had definitely made up his mind. On Thursday, the 10th of November, the day after his return, the Quebec Resolutions were published in the *Monitor*, almost certainly with his connivance. And on Friday, so the indignant William Henry Pope learned later, he had been seen publicly haranguing the multitude in the Charlottetown market-place on the iniquities of the Quebec scheme![26] J. H. Gray was convinced that, by the time he got home on the next day, Saturday, a good deal of damage had already been done. He told Tupper later that, on his return, he had found 'the whole community poisoned by Mr. Palmer'.[27]

Poor Gray did his best. He tried to communicate the splendid vision he himself had glimpsed at Charlottetown and Quebec of a great transcontinental northern nation. 'Shall we', he asked rhetorically, 'form part of a nation extending from Halifax to Vancouver, as citizens of which our sons will reach distinction and carve out for themselves fame and fortune?'[28] Unfortunately this dramatic appeal failed completely to excite Charlottetown. 'Will you record your votes among those who are content to vegetate like dormice?' Gray inquired with sarcastic rhetoric.[29] Apparently 'vegetating like dormice' was exactly what the Islanders preferred to do when they were invited to contemplate the thrilling prospect of transcontinental nationhood. Obviously Gray's parliamentary eloquence was not the right way to cope with Palmer; and W. H. Pope, who was a more astute as well as a more pugnacious Unionist than his chief, determined to silence the Attorney General by a direct personal attack. On the 18th of November, he published in *The Islander* a report of the remarks that Palmer had made at the *déjeuner* at Toronto a fortnight before.[30] Palmer had graciously predicted at Toronto that the Island delegates, on returning home, 'will not hesitate to recommend to their people the great union which I hope shortly to see accomplished'.[31] The anti-Confederate Attorney General thus stood accused of the grossest inconsistency and deception.

The results of this abrupt move were highly unfortunate. Palmer was certainly not silenced. He did not even seem to be particularly abashed. With some show of reason, he argued that his consistency should not be judged by 'an unstudied complimentary speech at a *déjeuner* where controversy was neither invited nor expected';[32] and he appealed to his record during the actual debates at Quebec as a proof that he had been throughout a constant critic of confederation. His rejoinder, like Pope's accusation, did serious damage to the union cause. The deep divisions in the ranks of the Conservative government had been exposed beyond hope of concealment and repair; and – what was perhaps even more serious – the acrimonious public dispute among the delegates had been pushed back to the uncertain and debatable ground of what had — and had not – been done and said at the Quebec Conference.[33] Was Palmer really entitled to his self-awarded title of the 'malcontent' of Quebec? Who had worked hardest to persuade the conference to grant the Island a special subsidy for the purchase of the absentee proprietors' rights? Who had struggled most earnestly for that precious additional sixth Island member in the projected 'House of Commons' at Quebec? The vigour and persistence with which the 'rights' of Prince Edward Island had been urged at Quebec became, in short order, the sole test of the political virtue of Island politicians. And, to the amazement and consternation of the Unionists, it immediately became obvious that defence of the 'rights' of the Island meant attack on the 'wrongs' of the Quebec plan.

All this was too much for poor Gray. The tactical move against Palmer's weak flank had been a colossal failure. Consistent or inconsistent, Palmer was now attacking British American federal union with all his power and influence. And opposition to union had invested him with the prestige of a hero, whilst support for confederation had apparently marked Gray with the hideous stigma of treachery. With the exceptions of Whelan's *Examiner* and W. H. Pope's *Islander*, every newspaper on Prince Edward Island was busily denouncing the Quebec scheme; and by the middle of December both Whelan and Pope were admitting that for the present, at least, the cause of confederation was lost. 'We are dead set against union in all shapes and forms,' Whelan wrote to Galt on the 17th of December.[34] And on the same day, alleging that Palmer's Toronto falsehood had brought the people and government of Prince Edward Island into general contempt, Gray resigned his position as premier and his place in the cabinet.[35]

⫸ IV ⫷

LEONARD TILLEY was not very likely to follow poor, desperate Gray's example and commit political suicide. But he had no sooner reached home than he found himself pushed in an unwelcome direction by pressures that were harder than he could have expected. It was not, of course, that he faced the open quarrelling and undisguised disloyalty that had ruined Gray. The New Brunswick delegates were not seriously divided over confederation. Chandler, it was true, had some important theoretical objections to the centralizing Quebec scheme. He had strongly disapproved of the grant to the federal parliament and government of residuary legislative powers and the right to disallow provincial legislation. 'I must not be called to advocate them anywhere,' he told Tilley bluntly.[36] But, as time was to show, Chandler was prepared to give confederation general support in public; and the other delegates were favourable, some of them enthusiastically so. Unfortunately, however, the delegation was not the New Brunswick government. A week after Tilley and the others had returned home, the cabinet met for a long two-day session; and at that meeting, after much discussion, it took the first decisive step towards federal union. It decided to sponsor the Quebec Resolutions as a government measure.[37] The decision was not unanimous; but the only really determined opponent, who later resigned in protest, was G. L. Hatheway, a bulky and uncouth lumberman, whom Gordon described distastefully as 'destitute of principle, as well as of education'.

Unhappily this was not the only decision that Tilley and his colleagues had to take. The fact was that the Tilley government stood in a position of special and extreme difficulty. By law, the term of the New Brunswick legislature would come to an end by June 1865; and thus, within six months, Tilley and his followers would have to face all the hazards of a general election. The Quebec Resolutions required the federal scheme to be submitted to the local legislatures for their sanction; and at the Quebec Conference everybody had been impressed with the urgent need of speed. But could Tilley and his ministers take the huge risk of attempting to push confederation through the last session of the existing parliament? Ought they even seriously to consider doing so? Would it not be constitutionally questionable, even if politically possible, to commit the province to such a revolutionary change in this summary and presumptuous fashion? Surely the quick and complete annihilation of the Tilley government and the Liberal party would follow inevitably upon such an act of political effrontery. 'Every paper in the Province with two exceptions', Tilley wrote later to Galt, 'spoke out strongly against legislating upon the subject previous to a general election.'[38] Most of the members of the existing assembly, a hurried inquiry revealed, could not be counted on to support a union on the Quebec terms.[39] 'All parties', Tilley informed Brown, 'take ground that we should have an election before submitting the question for the decision of parliament.'[40] The weight of all these influences might have overcome Tilley. But it was Gordon who made the pressure irresistible.

That autumn, Gordon was in a highly critical mood. The sorry spectacle of New Brunswick politics and New Brunswick society did not often help to make him amiable; but early in November, when Tilley arrived back from Quebec, his temper was unusually short. He had, he felt, been extremely badly treated. That New Brunswick politicians should underrate his abilities was, of course, to be expected; but that the English governing class, including the Colonial Secretary, Cardwell, should fail to appreciate the true worth of the youngest son of the 4th Earl of Aberdeen seemed almost incredible! And yet the gloomy conclusion that Cardwell had failed to appreciate his merits and claims appeared to be forced on Gordon by accumulating proofs. Only recently, one of the juiciest plums in the colonial service, the governorship of Ceylon, had come up for bestowal. Unaccountably, despite Gordon's evident interest, Cardwell had given the post to another. Still more unaccountably, he had justified the appointment on the ground that his choice was a man of considerable experience. The obvious implication that the colonial service was a 'professional' service, in which promotion was normally earned by proven ability, shocked Gordon deeply.[41] If that were literally true, what would happen to young men 'of independence and social position', such as himself? Would he actually have to wait until he was fifty or sixty for a governorship that was really worthy of the rank and station to which it had pleased God to call him? The whole prospect was disconcerting in the extreme.

Unfortunately, this was not all. The outlook near at hand was equally distressing. That wise and statesmanlike project, the legislative union of the Maritime Provinces, had been sunk beyond hope of salvage; and, in its place, the grandiose but ramshackle enterprise of confederation was riding high in triumph. The conference at Quebec had, in fact, adopted the Canadian federal plan. The New Brunswick delegation had accepted it. Even the Colonial Office – incredibly enough – had seemed ready to approve the scheme in advance, and for reasons that Gordon could not help thinking were the most childish and transparent delusions. Ever since his long talk with Cartier, Galt, and Brown, on the last day of the wanderings of the Charlottetown Conference, Gordon had been convinced that the Canadian plan would not give general government that absolute paramountcy he considered essential. But Cardwell, strangely enough, was apparently not aware of this vital defect. Deluded by Monck, who in turn was no doubt misled by his ministers, Cardwell seemed actually to believe that the Quebec scheme was a legislative union in all but name![42] Gordon was exasperated almost beyond endurance. The fatal confederation movement, spurred on by ignorance, misrepresentation, parochialism, and partisanship, was rushing forward towards its realization in an act of the imperial Parliament!

Was there anything he could do to stop it? Bending his long, lugubrious countenance over the paper, he composed enormous dispatches to the Colonial Office, utterly demolishing the case for British North American federation.[43] But the enlightenment of Cardwell was obviously a long-term and doubtful project; and Gordon began to despair of success. He had almost lost all hope when he suddenly became aware that a wonderful opportunity for action of a very different and much more positive sort had now presented itself. By taking advantage of the rising opposition to the Quebec scheme, he could prevent the passage of confederation in the last session of the expiring New Brunswick legislature. Quickly, he satisfied himself that this time he could play the role of the dominating governor, and dismiss and appoint ministers, with every prospect of success. Then, bluntly, he presented Tilley with an ultimatum. 'Our Governor informed me shortly after my return', Tilley angrily reported to Galt, 'that he would not consent that the measure or address should be submitted to the House for their action until after an election; and that he had ascertained that he could find a ministry who would take the responsibility of advising that course.'⁴⁴ In other words, if Tilley declined to delay, and insisted on presenting the Quebec scheme at once, Gordon would dismiss him and his colleagues and take other advisers. It was as simple as that. Tilley had no option. He would have to yield. And he was both angry and worried for the future. He wrote urgently to George Brown, who, he knew, would soon be seeing the Colonial Secretary, warning him that the three Maritime governors were likely to be hostile to confederation and that, if Cardwell approved the Quebec plan, he must give his subordinates very definite and emphatic orders. 'I am getting no assistance from Mr. Gordon,' he told Brown; 'on the contrary, his course is weakening my hands and embarrassing me.'⁴⁵

In these circumstances, Tilley decided to take the offensive immediately. The special difficulty of his position forced him to realize, more swiftly than most Maritime politicians, that if confederation was to become a reality, an heroic labour of propaganda and conversion lay inescapably ahead of him. His colleagues and fellow delegates – Johnson, Fisher, Mitchell, and Chandler — were veteran politicians who could be counted on to take their fair share of the difficult business of winning the apathetic and suspicious New Brunswickers to the cause of confederation. But from the start Tilley was well aware of the fact that the main burden would fall on himself. As the one New Brunswick politician generally respected throughout the entire province, he carried conviction as no one else possibly could; and, as the senior Member for Saint John City – the city that was the commercial capital of the province and the home of half a dozen of its most widely read newspapers – he was in a position to exert an unusually wide influence. He knew it was absolutely necessary to capture Saint John; and on Thursday evening, the 17th of November, he and his old-time Conservative opponent, John Hamilton Gray, began the assault.⁴⁶

Unfortunately the first meeting was by no means a howling success. The hall of the Mechanics' Institute was packed; but the stolid and silent audience showed interest without the slightest sign of conviction. The Saint John *Morning Freeman*, edited by the fanatical Anti-Confederate, the Irishman Timothy Anglin, pronounced the meeting a failure, 'total, absolute, unmistakable'.[47] The *Morning Telegraph*, which still looked at confederation with a critically impartial air, set the gathering down more temperately as 'singularly devoid of enthusiasm'.[48] Gray and Tilley had not made a particularly good beginning. But it was only a beginning; and the hard streak of tenacity and persistence in Tilley's character left him undaunted. On Monday evening, the 21st, he and Gray spoke again in the town of Carleton; they were back once more at the Mechanics' Institute the following night; and this second effort at persuasion found the crowded Saint John audience much more demonstratively appreciative.[49] Gray, whose easy eloquence was clouded with clichés and pomposities, dealt largely with the constitutional and political aspects of the problem; but Tilley stuck to the single prosaic, material object of proving to the New Brunswickers that they would be financially better off inside confederation than out of it. His powers of logical, lucid explanation, his dexterity and ingenuity with figures, were never seen to better advantage. Tilley, the *Evening Globe* commented admiringly, displayed 'a thorough mastery of his subject'.[50]

He also displayed a becoming readiness to defer to the electorate and to give it plenty of time in which to make up its collective mind. The decision to postpone the submission of the Quebec scheme to the legislature had already been taken at the cabinet meeting a few days before; and Tilley sought to extract every possible advantage from it, committing his government gradually and as if in response to urgent popular demand. At the first Saint John meeting, he rather guardedly promised that the federal constitution would be submitted to the electorate at the polls, 'if there is the least question as to the opinion of the people upon it'.[51] At the Carleton meeting, in response to a pertinacious questioner, he went a good deal further. 'The legislature', he assured the audience, 'would not be asked to pass any resolutions until the people first had an opportunity of voting upon it at the polls.'[52] The *Morning Telegraph* suggested that the assurance was somewhat reluctantly given. 'Mr. Tilley, however,' it concluded with satisfaction, '*did* give the promise.'[53]

Yet, despite Tilley's lucid explanations and conciliatory postponements, it was soon clear that he was not going to carry the province with him without a struggle. By the end of November, Albert J. Smith, a popular 'bully-boy' of the 'Smasher' party, who had resigned his seat in the cabinet the year before in opposition to the government's Intercolonial Railway policy, put himself at the head of the Anti-Confederate movement, and, in a letter to the electors of Westmorland, issued a stentorian appeal for followers.[54] At first Tilley felt surprised and even a little frightened by the unexpected and noisy volume of criticism that met him; but rapidly his cool equanimity reasserted itself. His meetings, he was convinced, were going well. 'We have done wonders in Saint John during the past week,' he told Macdonald proudly after his and Gray's second appearance at the Mechanics' Institute;[55] and by the middle of December he felt still more certain that he and his friends were making progress. 'At first the current was strongly against us,' he wrote to Tupper. 'We have greatly checked, if not fairly turned it, in Saint John.'[56] Beyond Saint John, however, were the 'central counties' which Tilley regarded as his bailiwick, and he planned to visit them on 'a stumping expedition' in the near future.

➤➤➤ V ≪≪≪

IN BOTH Newfoundland and Nova Scotia the public response to the Quebec scheme was more deliberate and tentative than it had been either in Canada or in the other Maritime Provinces. Dorion, in Canada East, had rushed into print with a formal denunciation of the confederation, the day before the full text of the Seventy-two Resolutions was first published; and less than a fortnight after the New Brunswick delegates had reached home, Tilley and Gray, in their first meeting in the Mechanics' Institute, were bravely confronting what was obviously a growing volume of criticism in Saint John. In Newfoundland and Nova Scotia, on the other hand, both Confederates and Anti-Confederates took longer to marshal their forces and to work out and present their considered arguments for and against the union.

There were some very obvious reasons for the delay in Newfoundland. Newfoundland was far away from continental British North America. Schemes of British North American union, either regional or general, which had been familiar subjects of conversation in Canada and the Maritime Provinces for at least a generation, were still strange and doubtful novelties in the sentinel island beyond the Gulf. The response that the merchants and fishermen of St. John's and the outports would make to the Quebec scheme was less predictable than that of any other of the British provinces. It was not until the 1st of December, three weeks after the Quebec Resolutions had been published in Canada, that they appeared in several St. John's newspapers;[57] and only then did the press, politicians, and voters of Newfoundland settle down, for the first time, to a really serious examination and discussion of British American union.

There were well-informed Newfoundlanders who believed, from the start, that the outcome of this first debate would be a fairly ready acceptance of the Quebec scheme. 'We do not apprehend any very serious difficulty in the passage of the scheme in our legislature,' Ambrose Shea wrote hopefully to Galt on December the 15th;[58] and later in the month, when the public discussion had been going on for another fortnight, Lieutenant-Governor Musgrave reported to the Colonial Office that all the information that he had been able to get indicated a favourable view of the federal plan.[59] On the face of it, there were some obvious and very convincing reasons for Musgrave's and Shea's optimism. That suspicious and narrowly parochial local patriotism which was perhaps the strongest political plant in British America had as deep roots in Newfoundland as anywhere; but by now there were a good many Newfoundlanders who were beginning to fear that their province, by itself, could not give its citizens a decent living. The fishery, which was the mainstay of the population, had been seriously depressed ever since the beginning of the 1860s.[60] Destitute and half-starving families were so numerous that they caused a heavy and continuous drain on the provincial treasury. 'Pauperism takes its place among us as a permanent institution,' declared the *Newfoundlander*.[61] It looked as though Newfoundland, as a self-governing colony with all the pretensions and expensive apparatus of representative institutions and responsible government, had just about reached the end of its tether.

Confederation could bring relief from poverty and degradation. British American union would surely be strong enough to carry the heavy burdens that had proved far too much for provincial autonomy. On the surface, there was a strong case in favour of the Quebec scheme; but the merchants of Water Street, St. John's, the most important single group in the community, would not accept it. One of the group's most prominent members, a rich merchant, banker, and landowner named Charles Fox Bennett, who had been a most successful pioneer in the province's mining industry, quickly took the lead of the Anti-Confederate movement. The principal fear which he and his fellow merchants felt was that the proposed federal parliament was very likely to copy the high Canadian tariff. As Shea pointed out, it was only too easy to excite the multitude with the prospect of higher taxation and higher prices; but the high cost of living and the inadequacy of provincial revenues under confederation were not the only bugbears the resourceful Bennett conjured up to terrify his clients, the fisher-folk. In a series of letters which appeared in the *Newfoundlander* early in December, he drew an affecting and mournful picture of the Newfoundland legislature of the future, robbed of its legislative independence, its fiscal autonomy, and all its principal sources of revenue, and reduced to the level of an insignificant municipal corporation.[62]

The geographical isolation and the total unfamiliarity of the very idea of British American federation, which had delayed discussion in Newfoundland, could obviously have no effect in Nova Scotia. Nova Scotia knew all about unions, regional and national. She was as quickly and as fully informed about what was going on in the world as any other province in British America; and she had a long tradition of reasoned and able political discussion. As soon as the delegates had returned and the Quebec Resolutions were published, her politically-minded citizens set to work on a careful examination of the Quebec scheme. They talked about it and wrote about it, but at first in a characteristic Nova Scotian fashion, deliberate, reflective, decorous. The discussion started out on a very lofty plane of political theory. It took some time to change; but change it did, in the end, from a discussion to a debate, from a debate to a hot argument, and finally from an argument to a violent controversy.

At first the principal criticism that the Anti-Confederate newspapers in Halifax brought against the Quebec scheme was simply that it was a federal rather than a legislative union. McCully had been quite right in his statement on the opening day of the Quebec Conference. Articulate public opinion in Nova Scotia, as in English-speaking Canada East and much of Canada West, definitely did favour the strength and unity of legislative union. Why, asked the Halifax *Citizen*, in tones of outraged British constitutional orthodoxy, had the Quebec Conference abandoned the security of a single sovereign parliament for the hazards of the ill-omened American system?[63] For a while, Tupper's *British Colonist* and the other Confederate newspapers were kept very busy explaining that the proposed constitution was really a legislative union in an almost transparent federal disguise. The local governments, the *Colonist* declared emphatically, making the same point that had been so often made at Quebec, 'will not be legislatures in the sense in which we have been used to understand that term. . . . Nova Scotia, for instance, will be a large municipality under the central government; but just as clearly a municipality as the City of Halifax now is under our Provincial Government.'[64]

The sturdy and hopeful Tupper was not easily alarmed; but by the time December came he was beginning to feel a little uneasy. At first, the Halifax press came out strongly in favour of union; but it soon became clear that a great majority of the provincial newspapers would be firmly Anti-Confederate. Archibald and McCully, the Liberal leaders, showed no sign of wavering in their support; but Tupper could not help wondering whether, in this matter, either the Conservative or the Liberal rank and file would be likely to follow its leaders with docility. The Lieutenant-Governor, MacDonnell, was, he knew, highly critical of the Quebec scheme. MacDonnell had, in fact, returned from Quebec with what he described to the sympathetic Gordon as 'a very strong disgust' for the work of the conference in general and for its arrangements for local government in particular.[65] He was overjoyed to discover that on the subject of 'the deterioration of the local administration' under the Quebec plan, he and Gordon spoke in almost identically gloomy tones.[66] They were also using much the same threatening language to their ministers about a possible use of the royal prerogative of dissolution. 'If left to myself to act as may be most consistent with my ideas of right and wrong,' MacDonnell wrote righteously to Gordon, 'I shall certainly not allow the question to be carried through the existing legislature, which was elected without reference to the question.'[67]

The Nova Scotian ministers, MacDonnell added, were 'quite prepared' to have him insist upon a dissolution. It was a strange way of describing the painful feelings which the Premier of the province must have felt when he first heard of this dreadful possibility. And the news that Tilley had promised New Brunswick an appeal to the people only deepened his alarm. What if MacDonnell should be moved to imitate the example of the fellow Lieutenant-Governor whose opinions he so obviously shared? Tupper wrote anxiously to Tilley, hoping – in vain – that he might deny the rumour that he had promised an election.[68] He told Macdonald in Canada that 'the precedent is a bad one';[69] and he obviously feared that the mounting pressure of public opinion would force him to make the same pledge himself. For a whole month after his return from Quebec, he had made no open attempt to win popular approval; but now, though he dreaded the results of a public meeting, he decided that it was absolutely necessary to hold one. 'The current sets here quite as strongly against Confederation as with you,' he informed Tilley realistically.[70] At the first meeting, which was to be held in Temperance Hall on the 9th of December, he frankly expected 'a stormy time'.

It did not come – yet. Henry, the Attorney General, who was to have begun the speech-making that Friday night, was ill and could not be present; but McCully, Tupper, and Archibald made up an impressive non-partisan trio, each member of which seemed to be at the top of his form. 'Never did McCully, Archibald or

Tupper speak before with the ability or eloquence displayed at the great meeting,' the *Acadian Recorder* reported;[71] and Tupper, writing to John A. Macdonald, felt justified in describing the affair as 'a great success'.[72] The huge audience was seriously attentive. There was 'scarcely a rustle in the hall'.[73] And the speakers, clinging to the lofty plane of constitutional argument, concentrated their attention on proving that a strongly centralized federation was quite as good as a legislative union. Yet, though the first Temperance Hall meeting gave no sign of serious change, the opposition had been growing in strength and pugnacity, and its arguments were taking on a new and more popular character. Ten days later, at the adjourned meeting to which both sides had agreed, the row which Tupper had been expecting finally broke out.[74] The Anti-Confederate speakers wanted to monopolize the whole meeting. The Confederates insisted that they had expected a debate, and would agree to nothing else. Within an hour, the meeting had broken up in disorder and recrimination.

Very quickly, however, the Anti-Confederates gained their point. On the 23rd of December, in Temperance Hall, again crowded to capacity, their leaders – Andrew Uniacke, William Stairs, William Annand, and others – had their say, uninterrupted and unanswered.[75] A fortnight before, Jonathan McCully had compared those who had 'money made' and opposed confederation with those who hoped to be 'money making' and supported it.[76] The requisition for the meeting on the 23rd, which had been presented to the mayor, was signed by a very impressive contingent of 'money made' men. The platform that night was adorned with rows of solidly respectable, comfortably rich merchants and bank directors. There were numerous other solidly respectable and comfortably rich merchants and bank directors applauding delightfully in the audience. And it was William Stairs, Halifax's veteran financier, the seventy-five-year-old president of the Union Bank, who made by far the best speech of the evening and sounded most clearly its hard materialistic keynote. Stairs had nothing to say about constitutions, either legislative or federal. He apparently could hardly have cared less about British American union, or British American security, or

British American expansion. What interested him was the contrast between the Nova Scotian and Canadian tariffs and the discrepancy between the revenues Nova Scotia would give up under confederation and the subsidy she would receive in return. With columns of statistics and an impressive series of tables, Stairs calculated that under the Canadian tariff the population of Nova Scotia would have paid an additional tax of $1.42 per head on the consumption of 1863.[77] He also tried to prove the shocking conclusion that, on the basis of Galt's financial system, Nova Scotia would surrender revenues amounting to $4.02 per head in return for a subsidy of eighty cents.

Nova Scotians had been roused slowly from the normal, sober moderation of their politics to a realization of the infinitely debatable importance of confederation. By the end of the year, with two more argumentative meetings on the 30th and 31st of December, the vehement debate was reaching a discordant crescendo.

⋙ VI ⋘

GEORGE BROWN's mission to London had seemed important to the Canadian ministers when they had decided upon it early in the autumn; but now, as the year drew to a close, the object of the mission – the conversion of the Colonial Office to confederation – began to look like a vital and urgent necessity, not only to the Canadians, but to British Americans everywhere. British approval of the Quebec scheme would strengthen colonial convictions and remove colonial doubts. British approval would intimidate and disarm opponents of confederation, including, above all in importance, those strategically placed and potent adversaries, the lieutenant-governors of the Maritime Provinces. Tilley had relied on the imperial government to curb that aggressive Anti-Confederate, Arthur Gordon. Tupper's most optimistic hope was that he might be able to carry confederation in his province, 'if properly sustained by the British Government'. 'Will you let me know', he wrote anxiously to Macdonald, 'what you hear from the British government?'[78]

Imperial support was necessary for the achievement of British American federation. Imperial support was equally necessary for the maintenance of British American security. And in the last half of December, Canadians and Maritimers were realizing just how terribly vulnerable that security could suddenly become, and as a result of their own sins of omission and commission. On the 13th of December, the long-drawn-out preliminary hearing of the St. Albans raiders ended, to the amazement and consternation of everybody, in the discharge of the prisoners. The testy, self-important Magistrate Coursol – 'this wretched prig of a police magistrate', Macdonald called him – who was plainly out of his depth in the complexities of the affair, decided suddenly that, as a result of a technical defect in the Canadian extradition laws, his court had no jurisdiction in the case. He swept aside the incredulous protests of the Crown counsel and the lawyers representing the United States. 'Not a word more on this matter,' he ordered peremptorily when John Rose ventured to question the wisdom of his judgment.[79] The raiders walked out of the court-room free men; and although the bank in which the stolen St. Albans money was deposited had closed for the day a half-hour before Coursol ended the hearing, the entire sum, $84,000, was quietly handed out through a side door to a waiting Confederate agent.[80]

Once again, the sky over North America was split by the thunder and lightning of American anger. American newspapers yelled loudly for total non-intercourse, or counter-raids, or full-scale war. American editors reflected pleasurably on the high state of military fitness with which they could carry out any – or all – of these punitive measures. American generals, high executives, and Congressmen issued orders and passed resolutions that expressed the moral indignation of the Republic with almost equal pugnacity. As soon as he heard the news of the discharge of the prisoners, the indomitable General Dix issued a new directive to his troops, confirming his previous order to pursue any other raiders into Canada if necessary and adding the truculent injunction that if caught they were under no circumstances to be surrendered to the Canadian authorities but must be brought back to the United States for trial by martial law.[81] On the 17th of December, President Lincoln revoked Dix's provocative

New Parliament Buildings, Ottawa, 1865

Left to right

HECTOR LOUIS LANGEVIN
Province of Canada

WILLIAM MCDOUGALL
Province of Canada

THOMAS D'ARCY MCGEE
Province of Canada

Left to right

CHARLES FISHER
New Brunswick

FREDERIC BOWKER TERRINGTON CARTER
Newfoundland

J. AMBROSE SHEA
Newfoundland

SIR CHARLES HASTINGS DOYLE
General Officer Commanding,
Nova Scotia

SIR WILLIAM FENWICK WILLIAMS
Lieutenant-Governor of Nova Scotia

LORD MONCK AND HOUSEHOLD, *Rideau Hall, Ottawa, 1866*

commands; but on the same day another executive order from Washington required passports from all British Americans wishing to visit the United States. As soon as Congress had assembled that autumn, it began to take the now unpopular Reciprocity Treaty into serious consideration; and, by a strangely appropriate coincidence, the House of Representatives voted for the abrogation of the Treaty on the very day that the discharged St. Albans raiders took the train from Montreal with the stolen money in their pockets. All this, together with the six months' notice to terminate the Rush-Bagot agreement, which had been made public by President Lincoln in his opening message to Congress, assumed the ominous appearance of a crisis such as had not been seen since the *Trent* incident in the autumn of 1861.

The Canadians were badly alarmed. Most of them believed, with John A. Macdonald, that Coursol's decision had been an 'unhappy and mistaken' one.[82] Most of them were ready to do what they could to make amends for the past and to prevent a recurrence of the offence in future. A number of the St. Albans raiders were rounded up again; restitution was offered for the stolen money. The government called out the volunteers for service at strategic points along the border; and, on the night of the 27th of December, a crowd of curious and excited Torontonians came down to the Union Station to greet the arrival of six companies of Volunteers – nearly 400 men in all – who had come in a huge train of fourteen carriages and were on their way to Windsor.[83] The muster of troops for border patrol was matched by the creation of the first counter-espionage service, 'a detective and preventive police force for the purpose of watching and patrolling the whole frontier', with Gilbert McMicken in charge of the Canada West division and Edward Ermatinger in charge of that of Canada East. Finally, in a further effort to strengthen the agents of the law in their pursuit of offenders such as the St. Albans raiders, the Attorney General's Department began work on the draft of a neutrality bill, which was to be passed in the next session of the legislature as the Alien Act.

On their part, the Americans knew that there were good reasons for responding, at least slightly, to these frantic efforts at appeasement. They realized that, if war with England should break out, the southern Confederacy, at the eleventh hour, would almost certainly gain its independence. The State Department let it be known at the British Ministry that the American cabinet appreciated 'Lord Monck's extremely energetic and conciliatory policy'.[84] The portentous displeasure of the Republic had apparently been slightly relaxed; but, in fact, most of the serious American threats and retributive actions had neither been withdrawn nor countermanded. The 'all clear' could definitely not be sounded yet. The Canadians had looked at the fierce eyes and felt the hot breath of danger so closely that they were not likely to recover from the experience for some time to come.

They were unhappily aware of the fact that the St. Albans raid had once again raised the whole question of British American defence – and in an acute and strangely novel fashion. The bottom had at least been partly knocked out of the old Canadian contention that if war came to British America it would come for imperial, not colonial reasons, and that its cost, in consequence, ought to be mainly borne by the imperial government. Obviously, the St. Albans raid was a 'colonial' reason, and this fact might have important effects in both Great Britain and British America. In British America, the crisis called, many people believed, for a more energetic effort at colonial self-defence, and as a result strengthened the cause of confederation on the familiar ground that union was strength. But neither union nor improved collective self-defence could alter the plain truth that British North America depended for its survival upon British diplomatic and military protection. Would the St. Albans raid, which might still involve the United Kingdom in a war for which Canada had provided the occasion, have a bad or a good effect upon the unfinished Anglo-Canadian negotiations on defence? Would it give aid and comfort to those anti-imperialists and Little-Englanders who were anxious to cut British overseas responsibilities to a fragment and were even prepared to break the tie of obligation completely and leave the colonies to shift for themselves?

⋙ VII ⋘

O N FRIDAY NIGHT, the 2nd of December, when George Brown reached London – he had spent the first week of his overseas visit with his wife and relatives in Edinburgh – the discharge of the St. Albans raiders was still ten days away. The news of the crisis that followed Coursol's 'abominable conduct' would take another ten days to arrive in England; and at the moment the great new intelligence about British North America was the full text of the Quebec Resolutions, which had reached England at the end of the third week in November. The British newspapers gave the Quebec scheme a flattering amount of space. They had watched the whole union movement – from the formation of the Coalition government through the Charlottetown and Quebec conferences – with a condescending but cordial interest; and they greeted the Resolutions with positive enthusiasm. 'No project of modern times rivals in boldness and vastness the proposed union of the British dominions upon the American continent,' the *Daily Telegraph* exclaimed excitedly, and perhaps with some ironic exaggeration. 'The wildest dreams of universal conquest – the aspirations of an Alexander or a Bonaparte – scarcely attained to such enormous dimensions.'[85] Extravagance such as this was rare; but the other newspapers seemed impressed and even respectful; and there were only a few notes, in this chorus of approval, that might have slightly disturbed the hypersensitive British Americans. The whole London press stressed the close and satisfactory connection between confederation and improved British American self-sufficiency and self-defence. It seemed instinctively to regard the union of the future as very nearly a nation in its own right. The present status of the federation, *The Times* observed, 'will be only a state of transition, marking the passage of British America from colonial tutelage to national independence.'[86]

The London newspapers reflected fairly faithfully the views of the British governing class, of the British government, and, in particular, of the Colonial Secretary, Cardwell. They were not new or hastily formed views. The St. Albans raid had not been a factor of any importance in the process by which the Colonial

Secretary reached his decision on the Quebec scheme. Long before the St. Albans raid occurred, and longer still before the news of it reached him, Cardwell had been convinced, by Monck's private letters, that the federal plan the Canadian ministers were proposing would be a very acceptable plan indeed for his colleagues and himself. As early as the 1st of October, ten days before the Quebec Conference assembled, he was already confident, as a result of Monck's assurances, that the Canadians wished 'a strong central legislature, with subordinate municipal institutions'.[87] When the Quebec Resolutions, the ultimate test of his confidence, arrived, he did not feel disappointed or believe that he had been misled.

This did not mean, of course, that Cardwell and his permanent advisers, the senior staff of the Colonial Office, were entirely satisfied with the Quebec scheme. They were not. Like Brown, Macdonald, Galt, Tupper, and so many others, Cardwell would have preferred the centralized strength of a legislative union. But he knew enough of British America to realize that this was politically impossible; and, like the others again, he recognized that the introduction of the 'federal principle', in small, carefully measured quantities, was a concession that had to be made to the French Canadians. The basic problem of the union was, therefore, that of transferring the minimal essential powers to the 'local' authorities without weakening, in any important way, the paramountcy of the central government. As Sir Frederic Rogers, the Permanent Under-Secretary of the Colonial Office, put it, 'the great difficulty is to arrange for a real union of the five provinces . . . on terms which shall make the central or federal legislation really dominant, so as to make one body politic of the whole, and yet to provide security to the French Canadians that this dominancy would not be used to swamp their religion and habits'.[88] Cardwell and Rogers would probably have preferred to protect French-Canadian interests by special guarantees within a legislative union; but the Quebec Conference had decided to confide special local interests to local governments, and to treat all local governments alike. The amendment of its own Civil Code was obviously an important special interest for Canada East; and so 'property and civil rights' had been made a 'local' subject, though with the provision that the laws relating to property and civil rights in the English-speaking, common-law provinces could, with the approval of the provincial legislatures concerned, be rendered uniform by the general parliament. This complicated arrangement, Rogers pointed out, 'renders the affair rather wanting in neatness and scientific character'.[89] Or, as Cardwell put it more diplomatically in his dispatch, a few of the Quebec Resolutions appeared to be 'less consistent than might, perhaps, have been desired with the simplicity and unity of the system'.[90]

These irregularities and inconsistencies were, however, apparently inevitable; and Cardwell recognized that they would have to be accepted. By the time George Brown reached London on Saturday, the 3rd of December, the crucial dispatch to Monck, warmly approving of the Quebec scheme, was nearly ready for the Colonial Secretary's signature; and, late in the afternoon, Brown spent a happy two and a half hours with him, going over the text together. It was not all praise, of course. Apart from the vague reflection on the inconsistencies in the division of powers, there were two main criticisms of the scheme. Like Monck, whose strictures he was obviously copying, Cardwell preferred to have the prerogative of pardon left with the Governor General, the 'direct' representative of the Crown; and he expressed a mild concern lest the legislative council, with its fixed numbers and life membership, might run foul of the elected assembly.[91] They were not very serious criticisms; and, as Cardwell explained to Brown, the government had decided to put them in mainly 'to save themselves in the House of Commons in the event of attack'.[92] The dispatch, apart from these minor qualifications, was almost all that Brown, or the Canadian Coalition, or the unionists throughout British America could have hoped for. 'Nothing could be more laudatory,' Brown rapturously told his wife. 'It outdoes anything that ever went to any British colony – praises our statesmanship, discretion, loyalty, and so on.'[93]

Brown's main object had been attained. But he stayed in London until the 20th of December trying to make some progress with the two other charges of his mission: Canadian defence, and the Hudson's Bay Company's territories. He struggled to convince the British government that Canada was serious about these matters in a way she had not been before; but Cardwell and his colleagues wanted to postpone a final settlement of the defence issue until the New Year; and Canada, despite her earnest interest in western expansion, was still not willing to come down to the practical politics of buying up the Hudson's Bay Company rights in Rupert's Land. No final decisions about defence or Rupert's Land would be reached this time, it was clear; but Brown put the Canadian case in his usual forceful fashion; and, at the same time, he took advantage of the occasion to explain the Quebec scheme to Lord Palmerston and other cabinet ministers besides the Colonial Secretary, in the hope of getting the strongest and best-informed support for confederation. When Tilley's letter arrived, with its ominous news of Gordon's hostility, Brown marched down at once to the Colonial Office, and, since Cardwell happened to be away, took up the matter with Sir Frederic Rogers, and received from him a most reassuring reply. 'He laughed and pooh-poohed it as coolly as you could imagine,' Brown reported to Tilley, '– said they understood all that sort of thing – but the dispatch going out on Saturday would settle it completely and if not Mr. Cardwell would not hesitate to see that the cordial aid of all the Governors was given to the scheme.'[94]

The unanimity of British opinion was most impressive and most flattering. 'Our scheme has given prodigious satisfaction here,' Brown informed Macdonald. 'The Ministry, the Conservatives, and the Manchester men are all delighted with it – and everything Canadian has gone up in public estimation immensely.'[95] Everything Canadian – Brown included – was treated with a new respect. Everywhere people made him feel that he was the bearer of immensely important and gratifyingly welcome news. Rogers, in a letter to his daughter, referred to him as 'the Canadian Prime Minister'; and if he used this title in conversation, Brown made no recorded attempt to correct him.[96] He met all the cabinet ministers in town. His company was sought, his advice was asked. He was showered with invitations to all kinds of entertainments. From the start, the British governing class treated him seriously and ceremoniously, almost as if he were the ambassador of a foreign sovereign state – a young, but independent and self-sufficient sovereign state, with a glorious future before it. By degrees he began to realize that this was the way in which the British liked to regard him – that this, in fact, was the way in which the British government would have preferred him formally to have presented himself. 'I am much concerned to observe . . . ,' he told Macdonald, 'and I write it to you as a thing that must seriously be considered by all men taking a lead hereafter in Canadian public matters, that there is a manifest desire in almost every quarter that ere long the British American colonies should shift for themselves and in some quarters evident regret that we did not declare at once for independence.'[97]

CHAPTER EIGHT

The Hard Check

B Y THE END of the year, the prospects for confederation had mysteriously but definitely changed. Six weeks before, the Quebec delegates, their work finished and their triumphal tour over, had been scattering to their homes, full of elation and hope. Now, after the troubled fortunes of November and December, they scarcely knew what to think. Cardwell's laudatory dispatch of the 3rd of December, which had been published everywhere, had certainly encouraged the Unionists, and, so MacDonnell thought, weakened the cries for an appeal to the people.[1] The threatening gestures and menacing shouts of the United States had given a new, sharp point to the old argument that real strength lay in union. There were encouraging as well as dismaying signs. But, though the Quebec scheme seemed safe enough in Canada, it had met strong opposition in Newfoundland and Nova Scotia. A violent quarrel in Prince Edward Island had stopped all progress towards union; and in New Brunswick Tilley had been forced, by both public and secret pressure, to postpone ratification and put the Seventy-two Resolutions to the test of an election. Already the speedy confederation time-table, drawn up so confidently at Quebec, had been altered. The future looked confused, contradictory, uncertain.

Then, with the New Year, it began to clarify. But what emerged from the confusion was simply the increasing likelihood of delay and the possibility of defeat. In Prince Edward Island, the dispute inside the government rushed to its conclusion through a rapid sequence of charges, counter-charges, resignations, unexpected appointments, and repeated cabinet crises. Gray's withdrawal from the Executive Council was, in effect, an admission that the attack on Palmer's consistency and veracity had failed. The Attorney General ought to have been satisfied with his apparently successful vindication and his obviously growing popularity; but he was not. He angrily determined to take the offensive in his turn; and, making in his rage far too confident use of a very faulty memory, he charged that both Gray and W. H. Pope had failed to back him up in his struggle on October the 19th for a sixth Island member in the federal House of Commons, and that they both had thus basely betrayed the real interests of Prince Edward Island.[2]

Unfortunately for Palmer, the results of this offensive move, like the consequences of Pope's original attack on the Attorney General, were very mixed. Gray, now out of office but by no means silenced, wrote at once to the papers pointing out the awkward fact that Pope had not been present at the debate in the conference on the representation question on October the 19th.[3] Pope, a more deliberate and careful controversialist, bided his time for a while. He asked and received permission from the Executive Council to prepare an answer to Palmer's assertions; and on the 6th of January, in full cabinet, he overwhelmed Palmer with a comprehensive and crushing rejoinder.[4] He repeated and amplified his original accusation that the Attorney General had lied in his speech at the Toronto *déjeuner*. He proved that in important respects Palmer had falsified the record of the Island delegation's attempt to gain an additional member in the Commons. He showed that for the past few weeks the so-called 'malcontent of the Conference' had been steadily garbling the truth, in order simply to satisfy his private spites and to advance his political interests.

The next day, Palmer resigned. The remaining members of the Council, who had watched unmoved when Gray had left them a fortnight before, now reversed their stand and invited their ex-chief to return to the cabinet and occupy his old position as premier. On the surface, it might have seemed that the cause of confederation was again in the ascendant and that the Confederate Colonel might yet lead his province into union. But Gray was not tempted by this seeming opportunity. He probably realized that it was impossible for him, or for any other man, to persuade Prince Edward Island to accept the Quebec scheme at that time. He may have suspected that his colleagues' invitation to return to office was prompted not so much by a high regard for himself and his views as by a stubborn determination to keep the Conservative party in office. In any event he declined to come back; and, in still another sudden and surprising move, J. C. Pope, who had also resigned executive office in protest against Palmer's accusations, rejoined the Conservative cabinet and took over its leadership.[5]

This rapid reversal marked the end of serious Confederate hopes. William Henry Pope was an ardent Unionist; but his younger brother, James Colledge Pope, was rapidly becoming a strong Anti-Confederate; and he had now become premier of a government whose uniting bond was its Conservatism and not its views on confederation. The two places left vacant by the resignations of Gray and Palmer were filled up by the appointment of Kenneth Henderson, who was opposed to union, and T. H. Haviland, who had been a delegate to the Quebec Conference and was a firm Confederate. The unionist element in the cabinet, though represented as before by two members, was perceptibly weaker than it had been during Gray's premiership; and the government, under its new Anti-Confederate leader, maintained an attitude of carefully passive neutrality to federal union.[6]

By the 9th of January, the prolonged struggle in the Island cabinet was over and Governor Dundas was briefly recording the results for the benefit of the Colonial Office. On the very next day, the centre of interest in the battle between the Confederates and their antagonists shifted suddenly from Charlottetown to Halifax. The Halifax *Morning Chronicle* for the 10th of January carried a brief announcement which, in the eyes of all politically interested Haligonians, was full of sinister meaning for confederation. Up to that point, the Halifax press, with the exception of two tri-weeklies, the *Sun* and the *Citizen,* had solidly supported the Quebec scheme; and in this chorus of approval the voice of the *Morning Chronicle* was among the heartiest and the most influential. It was the town's one daily newspaper, Liberal in politics, and edited for the last seven years by that prominent Liberal politician Jonathan McCully. McCully had gone to Quebec with Tupper, had returned home a convinced Unionist, and ever since then had continued to preach confederation with evangelistic zeal in the columns of the *Chronicle*. Now it was clear he would do so no longer. 'The editorial management of the *Morning Chronicle* will be changed after the issue of this number,' ran the brief announcement in the issue of January the 10th. 'The proprietor re-assumes control of the paper, which will reflect his own opinions and those which he believes the country ought to and will ultimately sustain.'[7]

The proprietor and now effective editor – though his son Charles managed the business side of the enterprise – was William Annand. Annand was a Liberal. He sat in the Assembly for Halifax County and had held office in the recent Liberal government under Joseph Howe. During the autumn, when the Charlottetown and Quebec conferences were being held, he had been in England; and when he returned to Halifax, he found his editor, McCully, back in triumph from the great doings at Quebec, a flaming convert to confederation. Annand, like most of his rich merchant friends in the city, was instinctively and immediately hostile to the Quebec plan; but there was another influence, more revered and powerful than the agreement of his fellow merchants of Water Street, that urged him forward against McCully and confederation. For long years he had been a political follower and intimate friend of Joseph Howe; he had edited Howe's speeches and public letters. Howe, of course, had not publicly declared his opposition to confederation. As Imperial Fisheries Commissioner under the Reciprocity Treaty, he had been reasonably circumspect during Halifax's frenzied argument over the Quebec scheme. He had been present on the platform at some of the Temperance Hall meetings; but he had taken no part in the debates; and he insisted later that when Annand had come to him, seeking his advice on the dismissal of McCully, he had declined to commit himself to a definite opinion. But a week before Annand's final break with his editor, Tupper was convinced that the real force back of the Anti-

Confederate movement in Nova Scotia was his old antagonist, Joseph Howe.[8] And once Annand had made up his mind, Howe readily joined him in planning the vigorous offensive against confederation that the *Chronicle* was about to launch.

A few weeks before, on the 13th of December, Howe had turned sixty. The best of his life was gone. He was entering the last tired and disillusioned decade of a career that had never been quite what he had hoped it might be. He was conscious of great powers, of abilities that had not been, and could not be, completely realized within the narrow limit of his own province. He yearned passionately, persistently, with the irrepressible hope of high ambition, for an imperial career. In 1863, after the general election, he had given up the premiership – the highest office save that of lieutenant-governor that he could attain in his own province – and had retired from provincial politics. Now, if ever, was the moment at which the imperial government might reward his public services. And he had been given – what? He had been given the commissionership of fisheries at a salary of £750, a post that conferred little prestige, brought no real financial comfort, and imposed no more responsibilities than would have readily been borne by an industrious clerk.

It was this almost menial duty that had prevented him from accepting Tupper's invitation to go to the Charlottetown Conference. He had pleaded the needs of the public service, and sailed away on a routine tour of the drear Labrador coast.[9] On his return he had discovered to his astonishment and chagrin that Tupper and his own two subordinates, Archibald and McCully, had been helping to redraw the map of British North America. So many of his own hopes and plans for his province and himself had never materialized; but in only two months Tupper, whose chief political assets were a brassy, confident voice and a bullying manner, had gone from Charlottetown to Quebec and had inseparably identified himself with a vast, ambitious plan for the political reorganization of British America. In two months the nebulous dream of a great transcontinental northern nation had taken the firm shape of a concrete, detailed design. In another month, the Colonial Office, which had never seemed particularly impressed either by Howe's abilities or by his great imperial projects, had unaccountably given its cordial approval to the plan of his despised rival.

Howe did not like the plan. It was true that he had spoken often enough, in his easy, hearty fashion, of British American union and expansion. Less than six months before, he had told D'Arcy McGee's band of touring Canadians that he was glad 'to think the day was rapidly approaching when the Provinces would be united'.[10] But a great continental federal union was not the federation that was closest to his heart. The son of a Loyalist sea captain, his thoughts went nostalgically, yearningly back to the old Empire, the first British Empire, the world-wide maritime Empire of ships and commerce and coastal colonies. He dreamed of a great imperial parliament at Westminster, in which all the self-governing colonies, including Nova Scotia, would have their representatives.[11] He longed for a truly imperial public service – a service that would be open, not only to the governing class of Great Britain, but also to distinguished colonials who had proved their ability and devotion in any and every part of the Empire.

In fact, his position in history was a tragic one. A liberal imperial federationist, he looked backward into the past, or forward towards some not entirely sympathetic future. But the world around him was alien. He had been born out of his time. Even Whigs like Russell and Palmerston would have thought him comically old-fashioned. Hard-eyed, cost-accounting Liberals like Cardwell and Gladstone would have regarded his imperial dreams as stupid and dangerous. There was not the slightest chance that the Empire for which he hoped could ever come into existence during his lifetime. There was not now the faintest possibility that he would ever occupy that distinguished imperial post to which he believed his great gifts entitled him, and for which he had longed, schemed, and cadged through humiliating and frustrating years. Tired, disappointed, unfulfilled, troubled by a haunting sense of lost causes and unused abilities, he had to look on enviously while others exactly matched the measure with the moment. The future was not for Joseph Howe and imperial reorganization. The future was for Charles Tupper and the Quebec scheme.

This was the final intolerable injury. It was not only that the scheme was wrong, nor that it was inimical to Nova Scotia's whole character and destiny. It was worse even than that. The scheme was not his. He had not had any part in it whatever. It was Tupper's. If he accepted it now, belatedly, he would have to come in after Tupper, if not also after Archibald and McCully. 'I will not play second fiddle to that damned Tupper,' he said – or somebody said he said.[12] It was a credible outburst of a spirit tormented by disappointed ambitions and injured pride. He would not accept the Quebec scheme. He would show Great Britain and British America that it was he, not Tupper, who represented Nova Scotia's true spirit and stood for Nova Scotia's real interests. He would defeat confederation.

Rapidly, inevitably, Howe became involved in Annand's plans. The crisis in the *Chronicle* office moved towards its climax. Earlier, after his return from Europe, Annand had warned Mc-Cully not to commit the paper, and the Liberal party, any more deeply to the cause of union.[13] But by this time the ardent editor was scarcely amenable to discipline. He did, it was true, take care to report the Anti-Confederate speeches at the Temperance Hall meetings just as fully and faithfully as those in favour of union; and he was easily able to refute Annand's ridiculously unfair charge that for two months he had employed the privilege of flaunting his own views before the readers of the *Chronicle*, 'to the exclusion of everything that was, or might be, said on the other side'.[14] He had given good news coverage to the arguments of the Anti-Confederates. But news coverage was not what Annand was interested in. He was interested in editorial policy. He wanted to use the *Chronicle*'s leading articles to forward the opposition to confederation; and he dismissed McCully.

The very next day, the 11th of January, the first of what was to be a long series of articles attacking confederation appeared on the editorial page of the *Morning Chronicle* under the heading, 'The Botheration Scheme'.[15] The articles were unsigned; but anybody who knew anything much about Nova Scotia journalism and politics could tell from their easy, conversational debating style that the author was probably Joseph Howe. Howe was an extremely able journalist and pamphleteer; but, despite the greatness of the theme and his own passionate convictions about it, he curiously failed to achieve his talented best. 'Botheration' was apparently intended as a disrespectful pun on the word 'confederation'. It was a feeble enough pun; and the articles themselves did not rise much above the level of their lame title. Howe was, of course, quite incapable of taking part in the arithmetical conflict – 'with columns of figures dashing themselves against one another in the shock of battle' – into which, so Tupper complained, the argument over confederation had degenerated.[16] Instead, he set off on a devious ramble through history, returning with a rather ill-assorted and unconvincing collection of lessons and cautionary tales, some of which seemed beside the point, others likely to prove the reverse of what they were intended to do, and still others oddly at variance with the known views of their author. The champion of Great Britain and a united Empire was to be seen denouncing the Quebec scheme on the ground that union with England had proved disastrous to both Scotland and Ireland.[17] The advocate of parliamentary institutions and responsible government now saw fit to pen a glowing eulogy to the federal constitution of the United States, at a moment when the American Civil War was nearing the end of its fourth year.[18] The defendant of colonial autonomy and self-government gravely proposed that the imperial Parliament should solve the problem of defence by imposing a general tax on the whole Empire – a right the imperial Parliament had itself solemnly renounced over eighty years before.[19]

Yet the twelve 'Botheration Scheme' articles, which ran from the 11th of January to the 2nd of March, did what only Howe could have done with such magical effectiveness. They roused Nova Scotia's local patriotism against the Quebec scheme. They focused Nova Scotia's Anti-Confederate crusade on the demand for an appeal to the people. On January the 15th, four days after the first article appeared, Governor MacDonnell reported to Governor Gordon, with a certain malicious satisfaction, that the *Chronicle* had gone over to the enemy, and that the chances of success for confederation were already diminishing.[20]

⇾⇾ II ⇽⇽

AT FREDERICTON, Arthur Gordon had, during the last four weeks, been passing through a grievously agitating series of emotional disturbances. Cardwell's private letters had, of course, given him advance notice that the Colonial Office, despite all his good advice and solemn warnings, had perversely determined to follow a course of incomprehension and error. Now, with Cardwell's public dispatch of the 3rd of December, this blind infatuation with the federal union of British North America had reached its incredible conclusion in the solemn approval of the Quebec scheme. Up to this point, confederation had been a subject of confidential debate among the servants of the Colonial Office. Now it had suddenly become the public policy of the United Kingdom; and, so far as it was possible for them to do so, all the officers of the colonial service must try to carry it out.

How could he bring himself to make the attempt? And what effect would his unwilling efforts have upon his governorship, his reputation, and his career? It was this aspect of the new policy, and not the results of its success or failure for New Brunswick or British North America, that most profoundly troubled Gordon. His first thought – and the frequent conclusion of his long hours of painful speculation on the subject – was to resign. His resignation, he told Cardwell, would remove a governor whose heart was not in the new policy, and leave room for another who would carry it out with the zeal of conviction. 'I can do what I am bid,' he argued, 'but you may wish it done more heartily. I cannot "talk up" Confederation which an enthusiastic advocate of it might do.'[21] In such moods, when his position seemed false and embarrassing, Gordon had no difficulty in making up his mind; but almost immediately his first firm resolution was weakened by unhappy afterthoughts. He could not help but fear that his resignation might close the door on further, more agreeable employment in the colonial service. Would he ever see that enchanted tropical Crown colony of his dreams? He didn't like the idea of becoming an 'utterly idle man'. And – oddly enough – he discovered that he really wanted another summer vacation in the deep woods of New Brunswick! At last, on the 2nd of January, he sent in his resignation – or rather, his two resignations, one short and one long, either of which Cardwell could use, according to taste.[22] Before the day was out, he cancelled both.[23] A fortnight later, he wrote again to the Colonial Secretary, authorizing him to do what he 'thought fit' about his offer to resign.[24]

In the meantime, until Cardwell made up his mind, Gordon would have to remain in Fredericton and promote the Quebec scheme as best he could. He had very little doubt of its success in New Brunswick. In New Brunswick, he knew, politics were supremely easy. All that was required was to buy up a newspaper or two and a handful of votes in the legislature and the thing was done![25] Tilley, rather strangely, never realized that the business was quite so simple. Within ten days of his return from Quebec, the Premier had sensed that it would need an earnest effort throughout the entire province to meet the hard current of Anti-Confederate feeling. The 'stumping expedition through the central counties' that he had planned for the late autumn had had to be postponed in order to give him time to fight the hard battle in Saint John to a favourable finish; but early in the New Year, when the Christmas season was barely over, he set out on the first of his tours of the interior. With Charles Fisher, he addressed a public meeting at Fredericton on the 5th of January.[26] A few days later he and Chandler spoke to a gathering at Sackville.[27] He appeared with the local member, Steadman, before a large audience at Moncton on the 12th of January, and again on the following day at Shediac.[28]

The tour marked a distinct change in Tilley's technique of persuasion. The St. Albans affair and the pugnacious outburst of threatening rage which it aroused in the Republic forced British Americans to think about defence in a serious fashion which they had forgotten since the *Trent* crisis, and gave to Maritime as well as Canadian Unionists a new and supposedly compelling argument for confederation. 'This is no time for trifling,' the *British Colonist* cried shrilly. 'The tide of war is rolling towards us. Already its surf and spray are on our shores. Who can tell how soon the crimson flood may follow? . . . What do men mean, talking about cents per head of taxation, when the question is, shall we be free and secure, or shall the horrors of the Shenandoah be repeated among us?'[29] Tilley had certainly talked a great deal about 'cents per head of taxation', and he now began to vary these arithmetical arguments with more general political calculations of peace and security. At Fredericton and Sackville, he argued that confederation would have equally beneficial effects in both the United Kingdom and the American republic. It would prove to Great Britain that British America deserved military assistance because she was willing to bear her fair share of the burden of defence. It would prove to the United States that British America valued her separate political existence on the continent and was determined to maintain it, together with her connection with the United Kingdom. 'To reject this scheme [the Quebec scheme] now', Tilley told his Sackville audience, 'would be a direct invitation to American agression.'[30]

In the meantime, although Tilley had agreed to put the issue of confederation to the electorate, he and his colleagues had not yet decided upon the time of the general election. By law, the existing legislature would expire in the spring of 1865; but, within the few months remaining for political manoeuvring, there were two possible alternatives. Either a final session of parliament, beginning in February, could be held; or the House could be dissolved at once and the province go to a general election immediately. Tilley's cabinet, though possibly with a small minority of dissent, preferred the choice of a final winter session; and Tilley agreed with them that delay would be best. He was only too well aware that Albert Smith was winning a rapidly growing army of followers to his side. The Confederates would certainly have to meet and defeat a resistance far more formidable than they had yet encountered. Tilley was convinced that he needed time for a thorough campaign of propaganda and persuasion – time to take the issue to the scattered settlements of thinly populated New Brunswick, time to eradicate the ingrained prejudices of parochialism and ignorance.[31]

But time was what he was not going to get. And it was Gordon who compelled him to forgo it. Cardwell, of course, was also eager for action – action on confederation. As soon as he realized that there might be delay at Fredericton, he wrote in some alarm to Gordon that he wanted 'the voice of New Brunswick' on the Quebec scheme to be heard next session.[32] But, before he received this positive order, Gordon had himself made up his mind to a blunt move that would compel a decision. On the 4th of January, the New Brunswick cabinet held a meeting to consider the future, but did not change its policy of delay; and on the same day G. L. Hatheway resigned his position on the Executive Council. The united front of Tilley's ministry had been openly broken; and this, Gordon perceived, gave him once more an opportunity for viceregal intervention. His first successful effort to bend Tilley to his will must have been an exhilarating experience. It had whetted his appetite for more.

Council had agreed to meet again on the 19th of January. Tilley employed the interval in carrying out his daring raid on Moncton, Sackville, and Shediac – the fortresses of Albert J. Smith's kingdom of Westmorland. But when he got back, Gordon was ready for him. He presented Tilley with a second ultimatum: either the Premier must agree to an immediate dissolution or the Lieutenant-Governor would feel it necessary to record his dissenting opinion in the minutes of the Executive Council.[33] The meaning of this threat was obvious enough to Tilley. Gordon was again prepared to seek new advisers who would implement his policy of an immediate appeal to the people; and, with the evidence of Hatheway's resignation before him, he believed he could find such advisers readily enough.

Moreover, as Tilley recognized, the Lieutenant-Governor had a case that even Confederates would have to admit was plausible, if not entirely convincing. At Quebec, the delegates had assumed that the federal plan would be laid before each provincial legislature at its next session. Canada and Nova Scotia were apparently ready for action. If the New Brunswick legislature held a final session without reaching a decision on the Quebec plan, the other provinces would be disappointed and excusably annoyed, and legislation by the imperial Parliament during the year would be impossible. Even if Tilley were prepared to accept the odium of upsetting the whole agreed-upon time-table, how could he be certain that he would be able to keep confederation out of the Assembly's debates? What was to prevent the opposition from itself bringing the issue – 'the one question with which alone all men's minds must be chiefly occupied', the Governor reminded him – before the legislature?[34] If the government failed to submit the Quebec plan for approval, surely the opposition could be expected to try the obvious device of censuring it for its failure.

For the second time, Tilley's hand had been successfully forced. He knew that he must give way. There was a warm discussion on Thursday, the 19th of January, 1865, when the Council met, but in the end the ministers recommended an immediate dissolution;[35] and next Monday morning, the 23rd of January, the newspapers were full of the approaching general election. 'The great test question in the election will be Confederation,' commented the Saint John *Morning News*, which was stoutly Unionist in its sympathies.[36] 'Confederation or no Confederation,' declared the *Morning Freeman*, which was Anti-Confederate with equal conviction, 'that should be the one and only question which will be settled at this election.'[37]

⋙ III ⋘

I T W A S deep winter now. The memory of the long, dry summer, of the mild, rainy, deceptively spring-like autumn had been buried deep under gleaming expanses of snow. For most British Americans, this was the year's most certain period of relaxation. It brought outdoor sports and evening parties – skating, sleighing, tobogganing, dances, concerts, lectures, and theatricals. It meant time for festivities. It also meant time for politics. The winter meeting of the legislature had become a fairly well-established tradition in all the provinces; but this year the little provincial parliaments faced a session and a problem that was likely to change their accustomed existence drastically and for ever. As the members prepared to return once more to their local Province House or Colonial Building, many of them must have wondered whether things political would ever be remotely the same again. 'I hope most sincerely it is the last *Canadian* parliament that will ever assemble,' Monck wrote from Quebec to his son Henry. 'I trust next year we shall have the Parliament of the Union.'[38]

It was the hope with which they had all left Quebec – the hope that they were still cherishing, a few of them rather desperately. And Canada was expected to make the first successful move towards the desired objective. The Canadian legislature, where strong and reliable support for confederation was known to exist in advance, was to meet and pass the Quebec Resolutions by thumping majorities; and then the other provinces, urged on by this inspiring example, were to follow in what it was hoped would be a triumphant procession. The Newfoundland legislature was scheduled to assemble on the 27th of January, the Nova Scotian on the 9th of February. Prince Edward Island had begged to be placed last. Dundas, the Lieutenant-Governor, had argued that if the Island were permitted to bring up the rear the influence of the Confederates at Charlottetown might possibly be strengthened, if only for the reason that the province would likely not relish the prospect of being left completely outside a general union.[39] He had urged that the Prince Edward Island opening be delayed until the 28th of February, and Cardwell and Monck had agreed.

On Thursday, the 19th of January, Monck was driven down to the parliament buildings in a fine four-horse sleigh.[40] The long perspectives of Quebec, the Lévis heights, the river valley curving slowly around the Island of Orleans, the Beauport flats rising deliberately towards the distant ridges of the Laurentians, lay spread out in an immense and varied expanse of pale or brilliant white, heavily accented by blue-black patches of hardwood trees and conifers, and splashed with purple shadows. Winter – the severest for some time – had once again given a hard emphasis to the primitive austerity of Quebec's long, sweeping lines and angular masses; and the 'ice bridge', as it was called, between the Lower Town and Lévis was unbroken and thicker than it had been for several years. The 'scenes of gayety and festivity' that the 'chattering French belles' had assured the impressionable Edward Whelan were so characteristic of Quebec in winter-time now followed each other rapidly, both indoors and out. On sunny days, the solid expanse of ice that had stilled the river was thick with people and lively with movement. Sleighs, carts, pedestrians crowded the tracks that crossed in every direction from shore to shore. Skaters thronged the numerous smooth green sheets of ice that had been carefully cleared of snow. Little wooden houses, with gaily-coloured fluttering flags, helped to strengthen the impression that the river in winter-time had become a suburb of Quebec.[41]

Inside, in the Legislative Council chamber, Monck was reading the Speech from the Throne. The room was crowded. The parliamentarians and their ladies had turned out in force; the galleries were packed. Monck read the speech with gravity and deliberation; his audience listened in profound silence and with the greatest possible interest.[42] It was an historic moment. A sense of the significance of the occasion, an awareness of the approach of a definitive event in the parliamentary history of British America, hung in the air almost palpably. The room was still; but the silent audience was deeply moved, and there were spectators who believed that it might have burst into applause if the well-known decorum of such occasions had not inhibited such an outburst. In silence, Monck moved serenely on to his conclusion; and what was expected to be the last session of the last parliament of the Province of Canada had begun.

Canada had led the way to the future with a hopeful fanfare of trumpets; but unfortunately one province, New Brunswick, had already left the procession. On the 19th of January, the very day in which Monck was reading his speech to the thrilled and expectant Canadians, Tilley's cabinet made its decision, and New Brunswick set out on a most distracting diversion of its own. Up to then, the Maritime Provinces had been waiting to see what the Canadian legislature would do. Now they were waiting to see how the New Brunswick electorate would vote. Unquestionably the prospect of the general election strengthened the Anti-Confederate forces everywhere. It imposed caution and delay on the Unionists. It seemed to justify the Anti-Unionists' demand for an appeal to the people. If the electorate of one province was given the opportunity of accepting or rejecting confederation at the polls, why should the others be denied the same privilege?

And even if a provincial government decided to go ahead according to plan and to submit the Quebec scheme to the legislature during the winter session, it could hardly dare – without the gravest risk of defeat for itself and others – to open a debate on confederation before the contest was settled in New Brunswick.

These fears and inhibitions could be quickly seen at work in Newfoundland, though the Lieutenant-Governor, Anthony Musgrave, made a gallant attempt to defy them. In his Speech from the Throne he declared confidently that confederation was a matter of 'the deepest interest to the whole community', and predicted that the 'future beneficial consequences' of union would not escape the inquiry of the House.[43] Brave words! But, for the mass of Newfoundland politicians, they failed to carry conviction. In the debate on the Address, the assemblymen dwelt, in horrified tones, on Canada's monstrous debt, denied that confederation would bring any advantages to Newfoundland, and piously hoped that 'the interests of the people would not be compromised' until there had been a general election.[44] At the close of the first day's debate, when Glen asked peremptorily whether the government intended to force the Quebec scheme through the House in the present session, the Premier, Hugh W. Hoyles, decided that he must move cautiously back in retreat. 'The government never forced any matter through the House,' he declared virtuously. 'The question would be submitted to the House, and it would be for the honourable members to decide what course should be adopted. The government were prepared to acquiesce in the decision of the House.'[45]

It was not a good beginning. Already New Brunswick had suddenly dropped out of the parade, and now Newfoundland was lagging irresolutely in the rear. The future was depressingly uncertain; but Canada was committed to the Quebec scheme beyond qualification or rejection, and there was nothing to do now but to go forward without pause and with all possible confidence. On Friday, the 3rd of February, Sir Etienne Taché, white-haired, dignified, and urbane, moved the adoption of the Seventy-two Resolutions in the Canadian Legislative Council; and on the following Monday Macdonald got up to open the debate in the Assembly. It was not, so far at least as manner was concerned, one of Macdonald's better speeches. He had been ill, had returned late to Quebec for the session, was still under doctor's orders, and had by no means recovered his health or spirits.[46] His voice, always rather high-pitched and lacking in volume, did not carry effectively; and George Brown, never one to think the best of his colleagues, was frankly disappointed. 'It was a very poor speech for such an occasion in my humble opinion,' he wrote to his wife. 'There was not one new idea in it. He simply went over the details of the scheme and said very little indeed in commendation or to urge its adoption. However, to those who heard the thing explained for the first time it no doubt appeared an able exposition.'[47] It was a detailed analysis of the principles of the new constitution rather than an inspiring glorification of the future of a transcontinental British America that Macdonald attempted to give that evening. His speech was to remain, for future generations, a main source for the understanding of the purposes and principles of the Fathers of Confederation.[48]

Next afternoon and evening, Cartier, 'screeching at the height of his lungs', discoursed at length on his favourite topic of the infinite superiority of the 'monarchical principle', as exemplified in England, over the 'rule of the mob', so deplorably exhibited in the United States.[49] Brown, who had been seated third, between Cartier and Galt, in the front ministerial row – 'quietly laid up at last', the Conservative *Spectator* commented satirically, 'between the two greatest corruptionists in the country' – was to have spoken next;[50] but Brown did not feel that he was ready, and Galt, a colleague whom he was already beginning to regard doubtfully and with faint stirrings of jealousy, amiably agreed to take his place.[51] Speaking in the fluent and lucid fashion which always gained him attention, Galt followed immediately after Cartier, finished on the same night, and left the whole of the next to Brown. Brown certainly took full advantage of the time so generously given. His speech lasted from eight o'clock to half-past twelve; and whatever his predecessors may have lacked in energy and vigour of utterance Brown, 'in his own bold, rough style', fully made up.[52] Finally, on the fourth night, D'Arcy McGee, the first speaker in the debate to make the House laugh repeatedly, finished the government's presentation of the case for confederation.

The debate was then adjourned for a week. It was obvious that the ministry had divided the various aspects of the union plan among the five government speakers, 'so that the speeches of all the Ministers grouped together may form one united, entire argument in defence of the scheme of intercolonial union'.[53] Macdonald had emphasized constitutional law, Galt finance. Brown had defended the scheme as an Upper Canadian triumph, and Cartier and McGee had tried to show how it would serve the varied and complicated interests of Canada East. Brown found it fairly easy to demonstrate that the old grievances of Canada West – an inadequate parliamentary representation, an unfairly large part of the financial burden, and an inability to control its own local affairs – had all been satisfactorily remedied in the Quebec scheme. But the task that Cartier, Galt, and McGee faced was more complex. They had to show that confederation would equally safeguard the interests and promote the welfare of two quite different minorities – the French-speaking minority in the nation as a whole and the English-speaking minority in Canada East. Cultural affairs – religion, education, distinctive institutions, where local differences were obvious – had been transferred, they emphasized, to the local governments; economic and social matters – those 'large questions of general interest', as Cartier put it, 'in which the differences of race or religion had no place' – had been reserved for the national parliament. Galt reassured the English speaking Lower Canadians by dwelling upon the fact that, in the proposed constitution, all commercial and financial matters would be as completely under the control of the central government as they would have been in a legislative union.[54]

⋙ IV ⋘

ON THE 9th of February, the very day on which D'Arcy McGee had closed the government case for confederation in Canada, the Nova Scotian legislature began its winter session in Halifax. The contrast between the two legislatures in their approach to the Quebec scheme could hardly have been more striking. In place of Monck's thorough and gravely appreciative review of the movement for federal union, the references to confederation in MacDonnell's Speech from the Throne were detached and non-committal. All too accurately they reflected Charles Tupper's inhibitions and embarrassments. Normally a confident, bold, and combative man, Tupper had suddenly found himself, to his astonished discomfiture, in a strange and utterly uncongenial position. He had been put, dexterously and unmistakably, upon the defensive. The public support upon which he had counted confidently had in the last few weeks died mysteriously away. Archibald and McCully had, he acknowledged, stood by him 'like trumps';[55] and McCully, thrust out of the editorial chair of the *Morning Chronicle*, had bought up the *Morning Journal*, renamed it *The Unionist*, and continued his advocacy of confederation with undiminished zeal.[56] But Archibald and McCully, who brought very few Liberals with them, yet in effect prevented Tupper from making confederation a Conservative measure, seemed to be almost as much a source of weakness as of strength. At the moment, the strength of popular acclaim was apparently all on the side of the Anti-Confederates. Everybody was reading Howe's 'Botheration Letters'. Everybody seemed to be vociferously demanding an appeal to the people on the issue of confederation. The approaching general election in New Brunswick, which granted what Tupper knew he did not dare concede, intensified the difficulties of his situation.

There was, however, one compensating circumstance. Lieutenant-Governor MacDonnell was not nearly such a constant trial to Tupper as Lieutenant-Governor Gordon was to poor, harassed Tilley. It was true, of course, that MacDonnell disliked the Quebec scheme almost as strongly as Gordon, and for much the same reasons. The continuance of the local governments – little nests of parochialism, pettiness, and jobbery – under an insufficiently strong and insufficiently centralized general government was for him also a vital defect of the federal plan. But MacDonnell's circumstances differed in one enormously important particular from those of Gordon; and this difference perceptibly weakened his opposition to the Quebec scheme. Gordon, as he himself pointedly reminded Cardwell, was a gentleman of 'independence and social position'. MacDonnell obviously was not. MacDonnell was a professional civil servant, who depended upon his salary for a living, was accustomed to obey orders, and could not indulge in the heroics of resignation. It was only when the Colonial Office had not yet reached a decision, as he reminded Gordon, that 'we may do a bit of statesmanship on our own account'. Well, the Colonial Office had definitely reached a decision about confederation now, as Cardwell's dispatches clearly revealed; and any really constructive gubernatorial 'statesmanship' was out of the question. Besides, though MacDonnell disapproved of the Quebec plan on principle, he could not help desiring its success for personal reasons. He disliked Nova Scotia intensely. With all the ardour with which Gordon longed for the bliss of some politically docile tropical island, he yearned for those lost paradises the Australian colonies, where he could cultivate a group of socially desirable civil servants, fresh out from English public schools, and where a governor's initiative was still treated with becoming deference. MacDonnell did not dare to resign; but he ardently hoped to be transferred. He came to the sardonic conclusion that confederation was probably the the surest way of speeding 'my departure from this unlucky "cul de sac" in which I have got pouched'.[57]

In these circumstances, the Lieutenant-Governor and his Premier were likely to agree readily on tactics. Both MacDonnell and Tupper, for widely different reasons, wanted the success of confederation; but they both realized that the business of getting the acceptance of the provincial legislature could only be undertaken with the greatest circumspection. Delay and caution, which had seemed wise even earlier, had now, with the announcement of the dissolution in New Brunswick, become absolutely necessary. The Speech from the Throne was prudently undemanding; the government let it be known to its followers that confederation was not to be regarded as a 'ministerial matter'. Then, when every care had been taken not to provoke trouble, and the legislature safely occupied with less dangerous problems, the Nova Scotian ministers sat back and nervously waited, hoping with painful fixity that the New Brunswick election would end in Tilley's triumph, and that, in the meantime, the Anti-Confederates would not maliciously raise the issue of confederation at Halifax.

Tupper had sought safety in keeping quiet and doing nothing. But to do nothing about confederation in the winter of 1865 was in itself a significant deed of omission; and, together with the New Brunswick dissolution – a definite if negative action of importance – it was bound to have a discouraging effect upon the other Maritime Provinces. The obstinate Island needed no discouragement, of course; but Newfoundland, which stood hesitating in doubt, ignorance, and suspicion, was peculiarly susceptible to outside influences. Newfoundland's legislature was due to expire in 1865. It was very much in New Brunswick's situation; and it was only natural for the Newfoundland government to decide that the wisest course would be to follow New Brunswick's example and to postpone the perilous subject of confederation until after the general election. This was the unheroic proposal that Premier Hoyles made on the 20th of February when he moved the Assembly into committee of the whole upon the Quebec scheme.

Like many other prominent Newfoundlanders on both sides of politics, he was personally favourable to confederation. In a long opening speech, he supported it strongly on the ground that autonomous responsible government had not worked well in poverty-stricken Newfoundland and that the island would be much better off under a strong national British American government. He had thought at first, he admitted, that it would be highly unfortunate for Newfoundland to postpone consideration of the scheme while others accepted it, and then to 'have to knock at the door, twelve or eighteen months after the Confederacy was organized, asking for what we were now entitled to accept'. It *would* have been highly unfortunate, he might have added; but now it was extremely unlikely to occur. Obviously other provinces were delaying their decisions. Among the Newfoundland people as well as in the Newfoundland legislature, the desire for delay seemed unanimous. Hoyles had given up his first resolutions submitting the Quebec scheme to the legislature for acceptance or rejection. Instead he now proposed that the whole issue of confederation should simply be shelved until after the next election.[58]

By the 28th of February, when the Prince Edward Island legislature began its winter session, the triumphant forward march of the Quebec scheme had been stopped dead throughout the Maritime Provinces. New Brunswick threatened to turn this standstill into a rout. Prince Edward Island nearly realized New Brunswick's threat in advance, and during the first few days of the session. In the Island, as in Newfoundland and Nova Scotia, Cardwell's firm demand that the Quebec scheme be submitted to the legislature was honoured simply by the inclusion of an unprovocative passage in the Speech from the Throne and the promise to table the relevant papers. But, under responsible government, both the Speech and the Address in Reply were properly to be regarded as the responsibility of the existing government; and the Maritime ministries, by the slightest mention of confederation in their governors' speeches, were running the risk of trouble as soon as the debate on the Address began. Hoyles had avoided it by promising a debate and declaring that the subject was an open question. Tupper had so far escaped disaster by a statesmanlike silence and a masterly inactivity. J. C. Pope and his colleagues in Prince Edward Island obviously hoped and believed that they would be able to do the same.

But luck – vigorously twisted by that incorrigibly persistent party politician, George Coles – was against them. Coles did what the opposition could have done in either of the other provinces, what Tupper had never ceased to dread might happen in Nova Scotia. He attacked the Pope government on the ground of its indecisive stand on the Quebec scheme. The sudden emergence of a new and apparently strong Anti-Confederate party in New Brunswick – a party composed both of former Liberals and former Conservatives – may have inspired Coles. He may have come to the conclusion that his best political prospects for the future lay in a party formed on the single principle of opposition to confederation. His amendment censured the government for the recent appointment of T. H. Haviland, 'a red-hot Unionist', to the Executive Council.[59] His speech was an implied appeal to men of all parties to unite in opposition to confederation. And the House, including at least one prominent Conservative, showed some inclination to respond. At once J. C. Pope moved in resolutely to prevent disaster. He declared – he was the third Maritime premier to make such a declaration – that the Island government was not flying in the face of public opinion, since no definite action would be taken on confederation until the question had been submitted to the people at the polls.[60] Tilley and Hoyles had made the same promise. But Pope went one better. He formally announced that his government was opposed to the Quebec plan. After that it was obvious that Coles's strategic move had failed. Unfortunately, it was equally obvious that confederation had also.

On January the 19th, Canada had started off at the head of what it was hoped would be a cheering Unionist procession. Six weeks later the procession had been almost entirely dissolved. New Brunswick had suddenly bolted from the ranks. Newfoundland and Nova Scotia were lagging equivocally far in the rear, and Prince Edward Island had mutinously refused to move an inch. Canada had lost her followers. But, whatever happened elsewhere, she could not immediately abandon her stand or change her policy; and she plunged ahead down the set course. On the 16th of February, when the debate was resumed, A. A. Dorion attacked the Quebec scheme as a legislative union in all but name, a union which its principal authors fully intended and expected would become formally legislative in short order, and which would result infallibly in the subjection and assimilation of the French-speaking minority.[61] Joly followed him on the 20th of February. Langevin spoke. Rose spoke. Christopher Dunkin, the independent Conservative from Brome, in a long speech sparkling with wit and irony, picked the Quebec scheme apart into a heap of ill-assorted and contradictory pieces.

The debate settled down into the long, unhurrying, tireless stride of a marathon. Days went by. Weeks went by. The Province of Canada did not ordinarily publish its legislative debates; but it had been decided early that an official record of the debate on confederation should be kept; and the importance of this exception was still further emphasized when the Ministers, in a laudable effort to impress everybody with the gravity of the occasion, gave the House a most unfortunate example of verbosity. As a result, every member wanted to be on the record, and every member was convinced that the only way he could do justice to himself, as well as to the subject, was by talking at enormous length. The opposition leaders, whose only hope now was delay and postponement, quickly took in the situation and changed their tactics to suit it.[62] 'Holton, Dorion, Cameron, Wallbridge, Scatcherd and a very few others', Brown told his wife, 'are talking night after night against time, so that they may circulate in Lower Canada petitions against the scheme. They are sending emissaries through the French counties, frightening the people with bug-bears that their language and religion are to be swept away and Lower Canada placed completely under the heel of Upper Canada.'[63]

The debate droned on. At times it looked as if it would go on for ever. But the shock that was to bring it to a close was even then impending.

≫≫ V ≪≪

FEBRUARY CAME to an end. The cold deepened. Warmed by fires and stoves, or muffled in furs, scarves, comforters, and mittens, British North America waited. It waited for the results of the New Brunswick election, which was now immediately at hand; but not for these results alone. The New Brunswick election, however fascinating and worrying, was not the only contest that held British America's anxious scrutiny. Far to the south that other conflict which for nearly four years had never ceased to trouble British America now seemed, at last, through the confusion of report and rumour, to be approaching some kind of obscure conclusion. On Christmas Eve, General William Tecumseh Sherman had telegraphed triumphantly to President Lincoln, offering the captured city of Savannah as a Christmas gift to the Union. He had cut a wide swath of desolation through Georgia, the granary of the South; and now he started north towards Richmond, through the little tier of seaboard states that was all that was left of the Confederacy. Early in February, the final peace negotiations ended in utter failure at Hampton Roads; and people knew now for certain that the decision would be by battle, and that – incredibly enough, after all these years of war – it might come in the approaching campaign. During the autumn and early winter, influential British American newspapers had kept on insisting that the Confederacy had 'no vulnerable spot for a mortal wound', that Sherman's operations did not amount to more than 'cutting water with a knife', and that 'the exhaustion of the South is an utter delusion'.[64] Now these complacent assurances died sullenly away. All that could be uttered was a prayer for a miracle, a frightened, hopeless hope that somehow the South might live.

In both Great Britain and British North America, fear of the future reached its climax in mid-winter 1865. The consciousness of American military might haunted the British cabinet ministers who sat down on the 19th and 20th of January to come to a decision about the defences of Canada. They were very acutely aware of the 'hostile spirit towards England which pervades all classes in the Federal States'. As Palmerston told the Queen, they could not easily dismiss 'the probability that whenever the Civil War in America shall be ended, the Northern States will make demands upon England which cannot be complied with, and will either make war with England or make inroads into Your Majesty's North American possessions which would lead to war'.[65] Gladstone – as 'troublesome and wrong-headed' as he invariably was on matters of defence – attacked the proposed initial appropriation for the fortifications of Quebec with tiresome verbosity and, at the same time, urged a reduction in the strength of the navy.[66] He was, of course, overborne in the cabinet. The two old Whig leaders, Palmerston and Russell, were determined to carry out the scheme that had taken shape the previous autumn. But, though Gladstone could not prevent the specific commitment for Quebec, he and his school of thought did exert a profound influence upon the imperial attitude to British America in this hour of its greatest potential danger.

The dispatch, containing the British answer to the Canadian defence proposals, which Cardwell sent off to Monck on the 21st

of January, was apparently written in a mood of Olympian detachment from the perilous circumstances of the winter of 1865.[67]
It was rather like the reply of a rich, self-satisfied, tight-fisted
uncle to the pleas of a remote and extremely irresponsible young
nephew who has been trying to set himself up in business by
touching his aged relative for a loan. The promise to make a
beginning that year on the Quebec fortifications was the only
positive item in Cardwell's avuncular lecture; and the proposed
appropriation of £50,000, though it had been virtually settled,
was not disclosed. A series of bleak negatives made up the rest
of the dispatch. The Colonial Secretary flatly declined to say what
help, if any, the United Kingdom would give Canada in the event
of war with the United States. He shrugged off the request for
an imperial guarantee in aid of the loan that Canada would
have to raise in order to carry out her part of the bargain – the
construction of the fortifications at Montreal. Finally, he agreed
very readily, with an almost suspiciously cheerful alacrity, that
the whole negotiation of the defence agreement should be postponed until after confederation – bluntly reminding the Canadians, at the same time, that this postponement did not imply
assent to any of their proposals.

This highly disappointing dispatch, which reached Canada
early in February at the same time as the news of the Hampton
Roads negotiations, was bad enough. But there was worse to
follow. When the imperial Parliament met, the Palmerston government tabled the second Jervois report, in explanation and
justification of the £50,000 which it intended to put into the
estimates for Quebec. In another fortnight, the report was being
widely reprinted in Canada; and the pitiless candour of its revelations of weakness produced, as John A. Macdonald put it, a
'panic' in the western part of the province.[68] In England, Jervois's
survey was so closely related to a matter of deepest national concern that it offered an obvious and attractive opportunity for
party exploitation in Parliament; and barely two weeks of the
session had gone by when Lyveden rose in the House of Lords
to accuse the ministry of the 'official indiscretion' of laying bare,
for all the English-speaking world to see, the 'utterly defenceless
state of Canada'.[69] Lord Derby and other Tory lords hastened

patriotically to take up the scandalous tale. They denounced the publication of the report and the government's neglect of Canadian defences, emphasized the danger of Canada's exposure to the imperialistic pressure of the United States, and ridiculed the appropriation of £50,000 – which De Grey, the Minister for War, revealed was all the ministry had in mind – as 'so trumpery as to assume the character of a farce'.[70]

If Lyveden and his friends expected these charges to result in anything more than a brief skirmish, they were quickly undeceived. The government spokesmen were not in the slightest degree intimidated. Fortified by public approval, they remained completely unabashed. The London newspapers, commenting upon the debate, seemed to feel that the ministry had reached an almost perfect solution of the problem. *The Times*, in tones of mingled condescension and annoyance, observed that Canada was 'vulnerable all over' and that Canadian loyalty was a source of both 'pride and embarrassment' to Great Britain.[71] It thought that the ambitious Jervois plan required very cautious scrutiny and that the government in proposing the appropriation of £50,000 had already gone quite far enough.

'The wretched debate in the House of Lords', as Macdonald called it later, took place on the 20th of February. As communications were then, in the last year before the laying of the transatlantic cable, it took about a fortnight for news to come from England to Canada. The report of the debate in the Lords would probably arrive towards the end of the first week in March. In all likelihood it would follow hard on the heels of the results of the New Brunswick election.

⇛ VI ⇚

IN THE MEANTIME, the crucial, decisive struggle in New Brunswick was rushing towards its conclusion. Tilley was under no illusions as to the desperate nature of the conflict in which he was engaged. From the beginning, as soon as he had done the deed of dissolution, he had begun to suspect that he had made a terrible mistake in yielding to the Lieutenant-

Governor's insistent pressure. He could not really believe that there was time enough in which to bring the intricate issue of confederation before his fellow colonists with any hope of success. Inwardly he was sceptical and pessimistic; but to the province at large he showed only his usual easy composure and his characteristically undemonstrative but persistent courage. A small man physically, a reasoning, unaggressive speaker, with nothing of Tupper's 'bow-wow' manner and stentorian voice, Tilley yet seemed perfectly ready to take on the most intimidating opponents. Earlier, during the autumn, he had issued a challenge to Timothy Warren Anglin, the editor of the *Morning Freeman*, a paper that wielded a formidable influence with Irish Roman Catholics throughout the province. Tilley challenged him to a public debate on confederation in the Mechanics' Institute Hall in Saint John.[72] Anglin found it prudent to decline. He was quite ready to keep a constant fusillade against the Quebec scheme in the columns of the *Morning Freeman*, firing half-truths, insinuations, and falsehoods about in all directions. But he quailed at the thought of meeting Tilley on the platform.

Albert J. Smith was no braver. The Smasher 'bully-boy', the 'lion of Westmorland', was a hardened professional with an out-thrust jaw, quantities of hair and side-whiskers, a hot temper, and an air of pugnacious determination. The Smasher party's most notorious demagogue, who had broken with his colleagues a year before as a result of his opposition to large railway expenditures, Smith contrived to combine a stock of cautiously conservative views on finance with the popular methods of violent radicalism. He took over the leadership of the New Brunswick Anti-Confederates in the manner of a crude, unlettered, and slightly disreputable Joseph Howe. On the last day of January, in reprisal for Tilley's raid into 'fortress Westmorland', he invaded Saint John and addressed a packed and wildly enthusiastic crowd in the Mechanics' Institute. For over two hours he spoke; but the moment he had finished, Tilley walked coolly on to the platform and challenged him to a debate.[73] Anglin's bully-boys and *claqueurs*, sitting in purposeful rows, hissed and shouted the Premier down. As soon as Smith had succeeded in re-establishing order, Tilley boldly taunted the audience by asking whether it was afraid of discussion. He told Smith that he was ready to meet him on the same platform two nights hence. And, when Smith regretfully explained that previous engagements made it impossible for him to be present on this occasion, Tilley promised the crowd that he would come himself in any case to expose his opponent's fallacies.[74]

Unfortunately, Tilley did not stand alone. If he and not his government had been on trial, he would have had an easier ordeal to face. 'Wherever he goes,' the *Morning Telegraph* exclaimed, 'his reception is a perfect ovation, and when he speaks on the great question now before the public, the delighted multitudes are constrained to shout "Great is Confederation and Tilley is its prophet".'[75] He may have been the prophet of the new order, but he could not be the redeemer of his government's sinful past. The Smashers, who, with one brief interval at the beginning of their ascendancy, had been in power for ten years, had always been distinguished for mediocrity rather than talent. During a decade, their government had by degrees taken on the stale smell of extreme old age as well as the unsavoury odour of corruption. Tilley had to drag behind him the disrepute of his commonplace colleagues and the disillusionment of a bored electorate.

He had another and still heavier burden – the dead, unyielding weight of provincial loyalty, provincial distrust, and provincial inertia. Everywhere throughout the province there were copius deposits of a peculiarly hard and resistant parochialism; and Albert J. Smith, with his popular mixture of hidebound views and demagogic methods, was an expert at mining them. He paid even less attention than did Howe to the details of the Quebec scheme. Instead he concentrated upon such broad general themes as the faithlessness of the spendthrift and turbulent Canadians, the low, self-interested, place-seeking motives of the delegates at the Quebec Conference, and the certain exploitation and impoverishment of New Brunswick in the service of western Canadian expansion.[76] His speeches were largely formless, highly repetitive, and torrentially eloquent. He specialized in moral indignation, lofty patriotism, broad satire, and heavy-handed irony. With his bushy side-whiskers waving defiantly like a medieval panache, he became the paladin of New Brunswick's provincial personality and independence.

The economic significance of the election closely resembled the political. It was a battle over the orientation and direction of the provincial economy. To the north, New Brunswick faced Canada. To the south-west, it looked towards the New England states. In terms of railway transport, which was the age's pre-eminent form of communication, the province's northerly association with Canada was appropriately symbolized by the Intercolonial Railway. Its westerly connection with the New England states was represented, equally fittingly, by Western Extension, the extension of the existing provincial railway, the so-called 'European and North American', to the international boundary. These two projects were not, of course, direct competitors, or mutually exclusive alternatives; but the pressure of the south-western part of the province in general and of the city of Saint John in particular had, as early as the winter of 1864, given Western Extension an apparently distinct advantage over the Intercolonial in popular favour.

Tilley had been obliged to recognize the force of this regional pressure; but he had tried to satisfy it in a general measure designed hopefully to please all sections of the province. By a statute of last session, the 'Facility Bill', popularly known as the 'Lobster Act', New Brunswick had offered generous aid to a company or companies that would contract to extend the European and North American in several specified directions, including the United States border.[77] Since then, a year of complete inaction had gone by. It began to seem highly unlikely that any commercial company would ever come forward to build Western Extension with the subsidies of the 'Facility Bill'; and a clamour arose that the project should be immediately undertaken as a provincial work.[78] This popular uproar gave Albert Smith his chance; and with cynical effrontery he took it. Always, in the past, he had regarded expensive railway projects with old-fashioned suspicion. He had resigned from the government in protest against the heavy financial commitments of the Intercolonial. But now, unblushingly, he presented himself to the cheering public as a warm advocate of railways in general, and a special enthusiast for Western Extension.[79]

Tilley struggled, but with great difficulty, to overcome the incredible advantage that Smith had captured. He found it hard to dispute Smith's new-found popularity as champion of Western Extension, and equally hard to acquire a comparable prestige as the author of the Intercolonial. Vainly he tried to remind the voters that his government had already provided subsidies for Western Extension, and that, in consequence, Western Extension was not a real issue in the election. Vainly he tried to prove that the great new fact in railway transport was the certain prospect of the Intercolonial, as a virtually free gift of confederation. Undoubtedly the Intercolonial was Tilley's biggest potential asset; but it was very doubtful whether he could convert it, at what he thought was its true value, into the hard political cash of votes. The north-shore route, already partly surveyed and favoured by both Nova Scotia and Canada, would almost certainly be chosen for the railway; but Saint John City, which was dominant in commerce, and the St. John River valley, which was heavily represented in the legislature, obstinately refused to be convinced that they would derive any particular benefit from so remote a line. Poor Tilley could go as far as to declare that he personally was in favour of the central or St. John valley route; but obviously he could not promise that it would be adopted.[80] Only in the north-eastern part of the province could the Intercolonial Railway be counted upon to win votes.

And, for a dreadful interval early in the campaign, it looked as if even this advantage was imperilled. At Quebec, in the opening skirmish of the confederation debate, Macdonald was betrayed into making a too precise, professionally legal explanation which had instant and violent repercussions in the New Brunswick election. Luther Holton had been badgering him about the sixty-eighth Quebec resolution, which concerned the Intercolonial Railway; and Macdonald remarked that the Intercolonial guarantee could not be 'a portion of the constitution'.[81] Smith and his followers exploited this unfortunate statement to the full.[82] Here, they exclaimed triumphantly, was a plain intimation that the Quebec guarantee was worthless and that the Canadians were getting ready to commit a second great act of betrayal. Tilley and the Confederates were aghast.[83] And the worried Macdonald replied by telegraph to Tilley's frantic appeal for reassurance. He explained that, in his view, the Intercolonial guarantee, though not properly a part of the federal constitution, was one of the fundamental conditions on which it rested, and would therefore be inserted in the imperial act.[84] The terrified Unionists were reassured, though shaken. They fairly effectively silenced their opponents. But the damage could not all be repaired.

Tilley failed to make as much as he had hoped of the Intercolonial. He also failed completely to win over the Irish and French Roman Catholics to confederation. The Acadians, who wanted to protect their special individuality against French-speaking as well as English-speaking Canadians, trembled at the thought of being submerged in a larger political community; and the Irish Roman Catholics, who formed the largest coherent ethnic and religious group in the province, were frightened of the preponderating influence which they expected Protestant Canada West would have in the federation. Bishop Sweeney of Saint John frankly advised his flock to vote against the Quebec scheme.[85] That unsubdued ex-rebel, Anglin, whose influence over New Brunswick Roman Catholics was almost as powerful and extensive as that of the Bishop himself, flung the full force of his abusive and mendacious journalism against confederation. The Irish, spurred on by these varied encouragements, broke up Confederate meetings and shouted down Confederate speakers.

Tilley, realizing more clearly every day the frightful insufficiency of time at his disposal, was dryly non-committal about his prospects.[86] Even Gordon, who had confidently predicted an easy victory at the moment when he had precipitated the election, was now falling back upon more cautious prophecies.[87] The contest began on the last day of February; but in New Brunswick, as in the other British American provinces, general elections were spread over two or three weeks. The first returns, if they went strongly and fairly uniformly one way, were apt to have a most persuasive effect upon the voters in the later elections; and it was Tilley's misfortune that the five constituencies that went first to the polls were hostile. From the beginning it was a rout. On the 28th of February, Kent County, which was the first to vote, returned two Anti-Confederates. York voted against confederation on the 2nd of March; St. John County followed its example on the 3rd; and Saint John City and Westmorland County repeated the same results on the 4th.[88] When night fell that Saturday, Tilley and his two fellow delegates to Quebec, Gray and Fisher, had all lost their seats; and Albert Smith had been returned, at the head of the polls, in Westmorland. 'The government is practically overthrown,' Gordon informed the Colonial Office coolly, as if he were reporting a slight change in the weather, 'and the scheme of union virtually defeated.'[89]

CHAPTER NINE

Appeal to Caesar

THIS IS NOT merely a misfortune to New Brunswick,'
declared the Halifax *British Colonist* solemnly in commenting upon the results of the general election, 'it is
a British North American calamity.'[1] To the Unionists throughout the provinces this sombre conclusion was simply the flat statement of an obvious fact. New Brunswick was essential to confederation in a way that was peculiarly her own. Newfoundland
could be spared. The union could certainly get along for a while
without Prince Edward Island. But the three mainland provinces would have to join any British American federation that
was worthy of the name; and without New Brunswick, which
was the link between Canada and Nova Scotia, there could really
be no union at all. Tilley's defeat had, in effect, brought the
whole union movement to a complete – if temporary – stop. The
Ides of March, moralized the Halifax *Citizen*, had seen Caesar
stabbed by patriot daggers in the Senate. The Ides of March of
1864, bringing the returns from the remaining New Brunswick
constituencies, would witness the death-throes of the Tilley government. 'Thanks to the noble action of New Brunswick,' the
Citizen announced gratefully, 'Confederation will soon be as
dead as Julius Caesar.'[2]

The New Brunswick general election upset all plans and
disconcerted all British American politicians. But for the members of the Canadian Coalition it had a special and a much more
sinister significance. In the Maritime Provinces, the defeat of
the Quebec scheme did not necessarily compel the various governments to reconsider their basic policies or to decide upon

253

some positive, new course of action. They could each relapse back into the placid and deliberate continuity of provincial politics from which they had been so dramatically lifted by the Charlottetown and Quebec conferences. But this door of easy return into the past was very firmly closed to Canada. In Canada, the new Coalition government was pledged not to continue the old political life, but to end it for ever, by the application of the 'federal principle', either to British North America as a whole, or – failing that – to the Province of Canada alone. In the light of the defeat in New Brunswick, what did the Coalition propose to do now? Would it – could it – fall back upon the second alternative, the federal union of Canada? Or would it continue to press for a British North American confederation? And, if the latter, by what means did it hope to bring this about?

The first of the bad news from New Brunswick reached Quebec on Saturday, the 4th of March. Over the week-end there were persistent rumours that the catastrophe at Fredericton would force the Canadian government to abandon confederation. It was even hinted that the Coalition itself might break up in despair. The cabinet realized that, in order to disarm the opposition and re-establish confidence among its own followers, an announcement of future policy must be made at once; and, as soon as the House opened on Monday, Macdonald rose to make what was evidently a carefully prepared statement.[3] His tone was confident and purposeful. The ministers, he told the House very firmly, regarded the New Brunswick election, not as a reason for any reconsideration or postponement of their declared programme, but rather as an incentive to 'prompt and vigorous action' in carrying it out. Up to the moment of this unfortunate reverse, he reminded his listeners, the confederation movement in British North America had been an unbroken triumphal progress. And, in the light of the known facts, this was no evasion of the truth. The news of Newfoundland's postponement of the question had not yet arrived; the final outcome in Nova Scotia and Prince Edward Island was still uncertain; and there remained the solid facts of the agreement at Quebec, the support of a large group of representative British Americans on both sides of politics, and the hearty approval of the British government. In these circumstances it was essential, Macdonald argued, that the Canadian legislature should pass the Quebec Resolutions without alteration and as quickly as possible. Acceptance by Canada would offset rejection in New Brunswick, provide a good example to the other provinces, and help to convince Great Britain that confederation would yet make British North America a source of strength rather than of embarrassment. The Coalition government intended, Macdonald announced, to seek an early decision – yes or no – on the Quebec scheme. It would then wind up the business of the session as quickly as possible, prorogue parliament, and send a governmental mission to England to confer with the United Kingdom government on confederation and two intimately related topics – defence and commercial relations with the United States.

This was positive enough: but next day a still more decisive move was made. On Monday, Macdonald had simply announced that the government proposed to bring the confederation debate to a close 'with all convenient speed'.[4] But within the next twenty-four hours there arrived at Quebec the apparently garbled report of the debate in the House of Lords on Canadian defence. The mere possibility that this terrifyingly small appropriation of £30,000 or £50,000 – the reports varied – was all the British government intended to spend on the fortifications of Quebec in the crucial year, 1865, was more than enough to deepen the Canadian government's sense of alarm and to quicken its urgent wish for action. How and why had this astonishing sum been decided upon? Macdonald and his colleagues thought they knew very well the stage that the still unfinished defence negotiations with Great Britain had reached. Cardwell had promised that his government would undertake its part of the defence scheme – the fortifications at Quebec – that year. But no definite sum for the first appropriation had yet been fixed, and the Canadian government took the view that all such details were still subject to discussion between both parties.

'The figures', Macdonald told the House with as much assurance as he could muster, 'are apparently a mistake for £300,000.'[5] Obviously the Canadian legislature and the Canadian people must be reassured; but if the imperial government had gone so far in its planning as the debate in the Lords seemed to indicate, and if it was reaching conclusions as deplorable as the dispatch implied, then it was absolutely essential that Canadian delegates, vigorously representing Canadian interests, should be in London as soon as possible. Tilley's defeat in New Brunswick had inspired the idea of the mission to London. The report of the debate in the House of Lords made it an enterprise of even greater urgency. If the confederation debate must be ended 'with all convenient speed', then the government must take steps to bring this about; and moving the previous question, which precluded any further amendments to the main motion, was the one method then available. 'I move, sir,' said Macdonald to the Speaker, 'that the main question be now put.'[6]

In fact, it was not put until three days later. In the meantime, the opposition made its last desperate efforts to induce the Assembly to postpone its decision. On the 8th of March, the day after Macdonald had made his announcement, J. B. E. Dorion presented the petitions against the Quebec scheme that had been so industriously circulated in Canada East during the previous few weeks. Unfortunately, the fine, impressive effect of these protests was somewhat marred when Cartier got up to read a 'gentil petit document' – a letter from Dorion to a French-Canadian mayor – which revealed 'la manière ingénieuse' by which the opposition had tried to swell the list of signatures. 'Ayez la complaisance', J. B. E. Dorion had begged the mayor, 'de faire signer le plus tôt possible ci-incluses par les hommes, les femmes et les enfants.'[7] This revelation cheered the bored and impatient government side and discomfited the opposition. 'Honourable gentlemen were fairly caught,' Macdonald remarked cheerfully, 'and felt hurt at it, like the man in the play who said he didn't mind lying for a friend, but it hurt his conscience to be found out.'[8]

Then, at last, it was all over. At half past four on Saturday morning, the 11th of March, while a blinding blizzard raged outside, the Assembly passed Macdonald's original motion, accepting the Quebec Resolutions without amendment, by a majority of 91 to 33.[9] On Monday the formal Address to the Queen, expressing this decision, was adopted; and next day the

whole Assembly, preceded by a band and accompanied by a
guard of honour, marched up in 'full fig', as George Brown
expressed it – to lay the Address before the Governor General.[10]
Canada had accepted confederation. Canada had decided to send
a special mission to England in the hope of saving confederation
from the total shipwreck that New Brunswick threatened. The
mission was crucial to success. But what members of the government were to compose it? And what chances did it really have of
success?

⋙ II ⋘

THE FIRST THOUGHTS that the results of the general election
inspired in Arthur Gordon were naturally concerned with
himself. At that moment his principal object was his own transference to a more salubrious climate, a more gentlemanly company of subordinates, and a sphere of greater political 'usefulness' for himself. He had resigned, withdrawn his resignation,
and resubmitted it for Cardwell's consideration and action; but
Cardwell, alleging that he could not understand why Gordon
wanted to resign and that he saw no public reason for it, had
decided, with characteristic caution, not to act 'hastily' in the
matter.[11] Confederation, if it had been carried through, would
have ended these hesitations and indecisions and transferred
Gordon to the bliss of a Crown colony, by the simple method of
abolishing the office of lieutenant-governor as an imperial appointment in British America. Confederation would have made
Gordon's mind up for him; but confederation, accelerating hopefully in its onward course, had run straight into the road-block
of the general election. 'It destroys all chance of a speedy natural
termination of my government,' Gordon reflected gloomily,
'. . . and it brings into power as leader of the new government the
only man in the Province [Smith] who has chosen to consider
himself my personal enemy.'[12]
It was a shattering experience – even for one of Gordon's
superlative self-confidence. Failure, and the public discredit that
inevitably accompanied it, was something no civil servant – even

a Gordon – could contemplate lightly. He knew very well that – though undeniably 'a gentleman of independence and social position' – he could not really consider the idea of giving up his career in the colonial service. He realized only too clearly that the Colonial Office had backed the Quebec scheme for British America, that the Quebec scheme had been overwhelmingly defeated in New Brunswick, and that he himself, as Lieutenant-Governor, was deeply and inescapably involved in its failure. Yet the complete miscarriage of the strategy of the immediate general election, which he had done so much to inspire, left him depressed and curiously silent. He seemed bankrupt of the confident hopes, the busy plans, and the bold political manoeuvres that had been so characteristic of him in the past. Once again flight appeared the only possible way out of his intolerable situation. 'If you offer me Hong Kong,' he told Cardwell fervently, 'I shall certainly accept it.'[18] In the meantime, he simply waited upon events; and in the end a conclusive event – the resignation of Tilley's familiar government – forced him to take action.

It gave him, in fact, what he liked most – another opportunity for discretionary viceregal intervention. The Anti-Confederate movement was an odd mixture of Conservatives and disaffected Smashers; and the fact that it had not yet produced any officially recognized leader allowed the Lieutenant-Governor a fair range of choice. In the end, he invited Robert Duncan Wilmot, a Conservative, and Albert J. Smith, a renegade Smasher, to accept office as joint premiers. Smith, the 'lion of Westmorland', had certainly done the lion's share of the fighting – and the execution – during the campaign; and it might have seemed only fair that the man who, by his own heroic exertions, had thrust himself head and shoulders above the general mêlée should be given a leader's reward. But Gordon did not see it this way, and not simply because Smith was his sworn personal enemy.

Wilmot and Smith, who stood on opposite sides of the familiar party fence, would together give to the Anti-Confederate movement an air of truly provincial scope and unity. They represented non-partisan resistance; but they represented something else as well – something that Gordon regarded as equally important. They stood for two quite different critical approaches to the Quebec scheme, two contrasted attitudes to British North American union. Smith was a provincialist who, if there had to be a union, preferred a weak, decentralized federation, and believed that the Quebec scheme threatened the identity and autonomy of his province. Wilmot was a Unionist who, like so many other Canadians and Maritimers, strongly favoured a British American legislative union and disliked the Quebec scheme because of its introduction of the dangerous federal principle. The two men, Gordon pointed out to Cardwell, 'may be considered to represent the two different sections of which the Anti-Confederate party is composed'.[14]

It looked like an extremely strong government. Its following of thirty members in a legislative assembly of forty-one seemed to ensure a long lease of power for Smith and Wilmot, and permanent defeat for the Quebec scheme.[15] Yet, despite the overwhelming Anti-Confederate victory that had brought it into being, the Smith-Wilmot government had about it from the beginning a curiously impermanent and indecisive air. For one thing, the Confederates, who ought to have been reduced to hopeless despair by the catastrophe that had overtaken them, never really lost their faith in the future. Even before the last returns were in, the laconic, realistic, non-committal Tilley predicted that within fifteen months the people of New Brunswick would change their views about confederation.[16] 'Our defeat is only temporary,' J. H. Gray wrote earnestly to George Brown, begging him not to let these transitory reverses in the Maritime Provinces induce the Canadians to make the appalling mistake of abandoning the Quebec scheme.[17]

There were some good reasons for these confident hopes. The Anti-Confederates had won nearly three times as many seats as the Unionists; but they were very far from holding a correspondingly large share of the popular vote. The New Brunswick constituencies were multi-member ridings, which made accurate statistical comparisons difficult. But this did not prevent the newspapers on both sides from attempting an estimate; and the *Morning Telegraph*, basing its calculation in the main on the total number of votes cast for the leading Confederate and Anti-Confederate in each constituency, produced a result that gave the Unionists 15,492 votes and their opponents 15,947.[18] The resulting feeble Anti-Confederate majority of 455 infuriated the *Morning Freeman*. Its editor, Timothy Anglin, adopting the simple method of adding all the votes cast for all the Unionist and Anti-Unionist candidates in each constituency, arrived at the much more satisfactory figure of 27,509 votes for confederation and 46,268 against.[19]

This, of course, was only the beginning of a long debate. The Confederate newspapers ridiculed Anglin's ingenious method of counting each voter four, three, or two times, in accordance with the number of members in each constituency; the Anti-Unionist editors replied in kind, and the argument went on. But nothing that Anglin and his friends could say could get around the painful fact that in such important ridings as Queen's, Saint John City, and St. John County the results had been uncomfortably close.[20] So close were they, in fact, that Smith did not venture to assign portfolios to several important members from these marginal constituencies. As ministers of the Crown they would have to seek re-election, and re-election in these doubtful counties was anything but certain. Wilmot, the joint premier, who had won a seat in St. John County, remained without a portfolio. So did Anglin, who had done so much to win the Irish Catholic vote for the Anti-Confederate side.

'It is thought', Joseph Hickson, chief accountant of the Grand Trunk Railway, wrote from Halifax, 'that six months will see a change, as the number of votes cast throughout the Province for and against the scheme was very nearly equal.'[21] This comforting rumour, backed by the statistical evidence of the *Morning Telegraph*'s table, travelled far and wide. It reached the Canadian ministers at Quebec, where reassuring letters from New Brunswickers like Gray and Fisher had also been arriving. Monck quickly heard the good news, passed it on to Cardwell, and Cardwell in turn reported it to Gordon.[22] Gordon was anything but pleased. With highly offended dignity, he instantly assumed that the kind of news about New Brunswick that the Colonial Office preferred to receive was contained in 'hearsay reports' from Canada rather than in his own well-informed and judicious analyses, made on the spot.[23] The *Telegraph*'s estimate of the

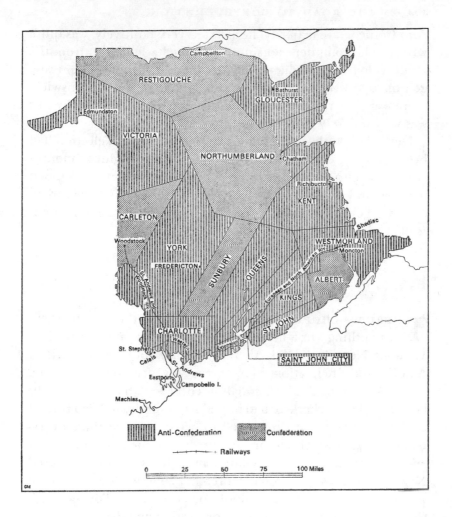

New Brunswick – General Election 1865

Counties were multi-member constituencies – two, three, or four members in each. Voters usually voted the whole 'ticket', and the counties went one way or the other as a whole. But in 1865 Northumberland elected three Confederates and one Anti-Confederate. Hence the division of shading within Northumberland (artificial, for the whole county was the constituency).

Anti-Confederate majority, he asserted very positively, was quite wrong. The compiler had simply dropped a final zero from the total! As for the Canadian ministers' ignorantly impertinent suggestion that a reaction had already set in in New Brunswick, there were several important reasons – he listed them – why this was very unlikely to be true.

Nevertheless, the notion that the New Brunswick election had been a very 'close run thing', and that a year or eighteen months might conceivably see a complete reversal of fortune, continued to grow and spread. It was very odd. The election seemed so decisive. Yet a good many people felt instinctively that it had not really settled anything.

»» III ««

THERE WAS HOPE for the future; but for the present there was nothing but a helpless feeling of defeat and frustration. Without New Brunswick, there obviously could be no British American confederation. The great advance towards union, which Monck had led off so confidently less than two months before, had been checked, had halted irresolutely, and had turned back in a retreat that threatened to become a total rout. Everybody had been watching for the outcome of the first and crucial engagement; and everybody knew now that the rashly exposed New Brunswick division had suffered a complete defeat. There was no longer any reason for doubt or uncertainty. For the Anti-Confederates there was no need for caution and delay. Any provincial government that opposed confederation could now publicly avow its beliefs with complete impunity, and in total disregard of the views and injunctions of Her Majesty's ministers in London. Any provincial government that favoured confederation but had not declared itself could henceforth avoid disaster only by the most adroit political manoeuvres.

On Monday, the 6th of March, the very day on which Macdonald was publicly announcing the Canadian government's positive answer to the catastrophe in New Brunswick, Premier

Hoyles's motion, postponing the issue of confederation until after the next general election, passed the Newfoundland Assembly. In Prince Edward Island, Coles had already taught the government a sharp lesson on the danger of delay and evasiveness about confederation; and J. C. Pope and his colleagues were perfectly well aware that if they wanted to stay in power, they would have to come out firmly and definitely against the Quebec scheme. On Friday, the 24th of March, the Island Assembly was moved into committee to consider the papers on confederation; and J. C. Pope was about to rise to define the government's policy on the issue, when his brother, W. H. Pope, nimbly forestalled him.[24] Adroit and pertinacious in adversity, the elder Pope was eager to gain a small initial tactical advantage, even though he knew the main battle was certain to go against him. He successfully 'jumped the gun' on his brother, the Premier; and, while John Colledge could do nothing but sink back in his chair, his mouth opening and shutting in impotent silence, the suave and imperturbable William Henry was reading a series of eight resolutions, highly favourable to British American federal union. As soon as this was done, and J. C. Pope had slightly recovered from the first shock of surprise, he got to his feet, interrupted his brother's speech, mildly reprimanded him for being out of order, and emphatically declared that his resolutions did not express the views of the government.[25] Later, when W. H. Pope's speech was finished, the Premier rose again and, in a series of five rival resolutions, presented the government's firm and uncompromising position.[26]

For a solid week, from Friday the 24th to Friday the 31st of March, nineteen different assemblymen debated the two sets of resolutions. The little knot of Confederate speakers – W. H. Pope, J. H. Gray, who seconded the resolutions, and T. H. Haviland – all praised the wisdom of the Quebec scheme and expatiated on the benefits it would bring to Prince Edward Island; but just as Tilley, in the second phase of his campaign of education, had stressed the argument of defence, so Pope and his fellow Unionists saw in confederation and the maintenance of monarchical institutions the best possible protection against danger from the United States. The emphasis on the defence argument was so heavy, and the underlying appeal to the loyalty of Prince Edward Island so strong, that a good many Anti-Confederate speakers felt a rather embarrassing compulsion to answer it. If confederation ever became the only means of preserving British America's separateness and her imperial connection, then confederation, with all its dreadful disadvantages, would of course have to be accepted.

But, insisted the Anti-Unionists with unshakable conviction, no such crisis had yet arrived. 'I look upon this talk about the Mother Country casting us off from her apron strings,' said George Coles contemptuously, 'and this shaking of the Stars and Stripes in our face, as only stories intended to frighten the timid.'[27] The Prince Edward Islanders were certainly not timid. The Confederates, it soon became quite clear, could never succeed in 'making their flesh creep'. Resting comfortably in their colonial assumption of security, the Island assemblymen kept on talking about the really serious defects of the Quebec scheme – Prince Edward Island's pitiful representation in the House of Commons, the humiliating degradation of the well-loved legislature at Charlottetown, the dismal prospect of higher national taxation and declining provincial revenues, and finally, the fatal omission of any scheme for the liquidation of the property rights of the Island's absentee landlords.

Yet, though the debate continued for eight solid nights of argument, it was really, at bottom, a sham battle. The real question of the moment was between confederation and no confederation; and this was not the issue at Charlottetown in the last week of March 1865. The alternatives that faced the Prince Edward Island legislature were, on the one hand, indefinite postponement of all consideration of the Quebec scheme, and its total rejection on the other. The most that the senior Pope had dared to propose was that the Island should put off its decision until the larger provinces had agreed upon the terms of union and that then the question should be submitted to the people at the polls. He hoped merely for delay until the situation had clarified, and people had had time for second thoughts. His brother demanded the immediate and total rejection of a plan which, he insisted, 'would prove politically, commercially and financially disastrous to the rights and interests' of the Island people.[28] On the last day of March, at a late hour, the Premier's resolutions were carried in the Assembly by a vote of 23 to 5.[29] On the Monday following, after a brief, half-hearted debate, a similar motion passed the Legislative Council unanimously.[30] And on the same day, the 3rd of April, having prorogued the Island legislature, Lieutenant-Governor Dundas dispatched the glad tidings of its rejection of the Quebec scheme to Edward Cardwell.[31]

Newfoundland had postponed consideration of the Quebec plan. New Brunswick had just elected a government that was hostile to it. And Prince Edward Island had rejected it utterly. Of the four Atlantic provinces that Canada and the Colonial Office had hoped to cajole into confederation, Nova Scotia alone remained; and Nova Scotia, the most important of the four, had still to declare itself. Tupper, fearful of the disastrous results of any premature action on his part, had purposely delayed consideration of the Quebec Resolutions in the hope that Tilley would win the New Brunswick general election; and now that Tilley had been defeated and Anti-Confederate feeling was spreading through the Maritime Provinces like an epidemic, he knew very well that the last chance of getting the Quebec scheme through the present session of the Nova Scotian legislature was gone. He would have been glad enough to push this dangerous subject unostentatiously aside – to drop this extremely hot potato for an indefinite period; but he was perfectly certain that, if he did, the opposition would never let it lie there, slowly congealing. Tupper, in fact, faced exactly the same difficulty that would have confronted Tilley if he had held a final session of the New Brunswick legislature without submitting the Quebec scheme to it. Any obvious reluctance on Tupper's part to risk a test vote on confederation would be even more likely now, after Tilley's defeat, to inspire the opposition to press the subject forward. Delay and silence were no longer good enough. Delay and silence might be fatal. 'I found', Tupper admitted to Macdonald, 'that all my ingenuity would be required to avert the passage of a hostile resolution.'[32]

How could it be averted? Obviously, government would have

to give a positive lead in some definite direction. It would have
to divert attention from the perilous topic of confederation; it
must persuade the legislature to wander off down a side-track
which might turn out in the end to be a cul-de-sac, but could not
look like one to begin with. Surely the answer was obvious?
Where could one find a better, more diverting alternative than
the abandoned scheme of Maritime union, that unexceptionable
project which so many Nova Scotians had vaguely advocated in
the past and which so many Anti-Confederates now professed to
find infinitely preferable to the hated confederation? Possibly,
MacDonnell suggested the plan first. He liked to prove that he
could take the initiative, in the fine Australian manner, even in
a deplorably democratic British American colony such as Nova
Scotia; and, since the Quebec scheme had collapsed and no fresh
instructions had as yet been received from the Colonial Office,
he thought it might be possible to indulge in 'a little statesmanship on our own account'. On the 7th of March, when the news
of the first electoral defeats in New Brunswick had barely reached
Halifax, he wrote to Gordon, suggesting that a revival of Maritime union might be the best way of saving 'something out of
the wreck'.[33]

While MacDonnell approached this project with some of the
real interest of conviction, Tupper regarded it mainly from the
point of view of political expediency. He was even more concerned than MacDonnell to save 'something out of the wreck',
though he had his own government as well as the Quebec plan
in mind; and the more he looked at the idea of a revival of
Maritime union, the more he thought it might serve both purposes surprisingly well. Maritime union would disarm the Anti-
Confederates and please the Canadians who had always declared
that they preferred the Atlantic provinces to join confederation
as one government. Maritime union might even win over some
critics of the Quebec scheme on the ground that a united Acadia
would be much better able than a feeble group of separate
colonies to stand beside Canada East and Canada West on something like equal terms.[34] Finally – and this was a matter not of
marginal advantage but of political survival – a return to Maritime union was probably the only way in which Tupper could

avert a frontal attack on confederation and the downfall of his government. On the 10th of April, after two months' embarrassing silence on the subject, he rose in the Assembly to propose a renewal of the negotiations for Maritime union, since, for a time at least, the federal union of all British America had become impracticable.[35]

The long succession of speeches that followed – it lasted nearly a fortnight – was even more obviously a mock contest than the argument in the Prince Edward Island Assembly had been. In Charlottetown, W. H. Pope had at least dared to propose that the Quebec scheme should be reconsidered some time in the future. In Halifax everybody assumed in advance that the revival of Maritime union would never come to anything. The debate, ostensibly about a legislative union, was in fact concerned almost exclusively with confederation. Tupper's resolution, MacDonnell informed Gordon with cheerfully cynical candour, 'is not being debated in this legislature, as it is only used as a peg whereon the different speakers hang up and ventilate their several opinions on the larger question of a general federation'.[36] 'The opening speech of the Provincial Secretary', he continued, referring, with not much exaggeration, to Tupper's effort, 'occupies six columns of a newspaper, and does not contain two sentences on the question of a union of the Maritime Provinces.'[37]

An air of unreality, of insincerity, invested the whole elaborate performance. Everybody knew that Prince Edward Island, determinedly exclusive in its parochialism, would summarily reject a new proposal for a legislative union. In New Brunswick, the Anti-Confederates had shown not the slightest sign of interest in the subject during the last election. MacDonnell, who early in March had proposed reconsideration of the old project with what amounted almost to positive enthusiasm, came to realize by the end of the month that nothing very much would follow the passage of Tupper's resolution.[38] And on the 21st of April, when the dragging, meaningless debate finally creaked to a halt, Tupper himself admitted that he was far less hopeful than he had been a year before that his resolution would lead to any constructive action whatever.[39]

Six months earlier, the delegates to the Quebec Conference had promised to submit the Quebec Resolutions to their respective legislatures during the winter months. In one fashion or another, this pledge had been discharged. It had been carried out in New Brunswick where the Resolutions had been submitted, not to the legislature, but to the people. It had been tacitly honoured even in Nova Scotia where the scheme had been presented under the painfully imperfect disguise of a resolution on Maritime union. Canada alone had ratified the Resolutions with conviction and without amendment. New Brunswick had ejected its authors and apologists from power. Prince Edward Island had hurled out the scheme itself, as if it had been a highly offensive piece of refuse. Newfoundland and Nova Scotia had deliberately shelved it – had pushed it back, apparently, to the end of a very deep cupboard.

It looked, certainly, as if it were dead and done with for good.

⇉ IV ⇇

THE DEFEAT of the Confederates in New Brunswick – the first of this gloomy sequence of rejections and postponements – had inspired the Canadian mission to England. The dismal bulletins from the other provinces, which kept arriving at intervals during the next few weeks, simply confirmed the urgent necessity of the mission. The last powerful card the Canadian government could play in a losing game was British support. British influence was the only remaining influence that could exert any significant pressure on the recalcitrant Maritime Provinces. Without British diplomatic assistance there could be no renewal of the Reciprocity Treaty; and without British military aid there would be no solid basis for an effective system of Canadian defence. It was all true. The mission to England was the last hope. Was it, unhappily, a forlorn hope as well?

Most of the senior ministers did not want to go to London. For nearly twelve months now they had been struggling to carry out their great plan of British American reorganization – and with completely negative results. Collectively they knew that a last effort must be made; but individually each cherished the private conviction that he had done enough. Of the four seniors, Macdonald, Cartier, Brown, and Galt, only Galt was at first apparently prepared to undertake the journey; but Brown, with an impulsive and temperamental man's instinctive distrust of an equally impulsive and temperamental colleague, was very firmly convinced that Galt was 'not to be trusted alone'.[40] Cartier was reluctant to go. Brown himself, who had travelled on a solitary mission to London only four months before, naturally considered that he had already done his stint. His colleagues and his Grit followers in the Assembly had, he told his wife, made a 'dead set' on him to go; but he had 'decidedly refused'.[41]

John A. Macdonald, the effective leader of the government under Taché, was another obvious choice for the mission; but at first he insisted just as positively as Brown that he would not go. He had been repeatedly ill during the winter; and the fact that some of his fellow parliamentarians, including George Brown, always assumed that he was drunk on these occasions did not make his illnesses any easier to bear. Brown, who was not notably sympathetic with any of his new colleagues and rarely charitable to Macdonald, had a ready explanation for his old rival's absences from the House. 'John A. is on the spree,' or 'John A. has been tipsy since Friday,' he would inform his wife with cheerful and conclusive brevity.[42] Sometimes he was wrong, and once he went so far as to admit it. 'I did an injustice to John A.,' he wrote to Anne. 'He has been really ill.'[43] He was really ill again at the end of the session, just as he had been at the beginning; and, in this state of almost chronic ill health, it was natural enough for him to go back unhappily to the unprofitable disorder of his neglected legal practice. His colleagues – Cartier the corporation lawyer, Galt the railway contractor, and Brown the newspaper proprietor – were all rich men in comparison with him. And once again he reached the old conclusion to which he had returned so often in the past few years, that he must get out of the hopeless mess of Canadian politics and build himself a competence before it was too late.

Yet something would have to be done, and done immediately, about the mission to England. Everybody realized this; and by the 21st of March, only three days after the prorogation, all the ministers, with the exception of Macdonald, were back again at Quebec.[44] The cabinet discussions, which began that Tuesday and lasted until Friday, the 24th, were the gravest that Brown could remember in the brief but eventful history of the Coalition. The membership of the delegation – still undecided – would have to be settled; but beyond the mere matter of personnel was the far more important question of the purpose of the mission; and beyond that again, formidable and terrifying, lay the awful problem of what course was to be taken if the purpose could not be achieved. A vague sense of impending failure hung in the air. Brown, usually so optimistic, had hardly a hope that the mission would succeed.[45] Lord Monck, he suspected, was equally pessimistic.[46] And behind the reasons with which each minister sought to justify his reluctance to go there lay, probably, in careful concealment, a foreboding of inevitable defeat. Surely Canada was asking too much! She was asking Great Britain to help her in carrying out confederation against the united and stubborn opposition of the Maritime Provinces. She was asking the United Kingdom to lend her aid in establishing an elaborate and costly defence system at the very moment when British America lay at the mercy of a truculent United States.

Was it possible for the United Kingdom to comply with these requests? How could she persuade or compel a group of recalcitrant colonies, all of which had been granted responsible government, to accept a federal plan that they seemed unanimously to abominate? How could she conciliate an aroused and bellicose American republic, or, if appeasement proved impossible, what chance would she have of defending vulnerable British America from the onslaught of one of the greatest armies in human history? Could she accomplish these miracles? Would she even be willing to *try* to accomplish these miracles? The anti-colonial feeling in England – the curious mixture of boredom, embarrassment, and exasperation with which most of the English governing class looked at the old settlement colonies – had been growing stronger even before the recent crisis in relations with the United States. But now the fear that Canada might help to involve Great Britain in a calamitous war with the great republic had put a new and powerful argument in the hands of that influential group that urged the abandonment of England's costly and dangerous colonial responsibilities. The anti-colonial faction might prevent the negotiation of a really effective joint defence programme. It might even stop the offer of imperial help in the completion of confederation on the ground that in the circumstances of the moment such aid would be simply another dangerous colonial entanglement.

In such a contingency, what was Canada to do? If imperial aid was denied, Canadian defence was hopeless. But if confederation proved impossible, the Canadian government could not simply throw up its hands in despair. The Coalition was committed irrevocably to the task of ending the sectional difficulties of Canada by the introduction of 'the federal principle'. If the mission to England proved a failure, and English injunctions or persuasions failed to weaken the resistance of the Maritime Provinces, then the first of the Coalition's two alternative policies – British North American confederation – would have reached a dead end. If that happened beyond all doubt and question, was not the Coalition bound to proceed immediately with the second of its two declared alternatives – the federation of Canada East and Canada West? George Brown believed so, very firmly. From the beginning he had preferred Canadian federation to British North American confederation. And he now insisted that his colleagues confirm their commitment to the smaller project, adding to the agreement of the 22nd of June, 1864, a new and more precise time-table in place of that which the events in the Maritime Provinces had invalidated.

The Conservative ministers, French-speaking and English-speaking, looked doubtfully at this proposal. They hesitated, demurred, and argued. It was not simply that they liked British American confederation better than Canadian federation; in addition, some of them – particularly the French-Canadian ministers – vaguely doubted and distrusted Canadian federation. Union with Canada West alone, without even the possibility of a counterpoise, in a small federal parliament based on George Brown's hated Rep. by Pop., was a doubtful future which Canada East hardly dared to face. The French Canadians, Edward

Whelan had reported from Quebec after a long talk with Sir Etienne Taché, 'would rather lean upon the Maritime Provinces for aid and sympathy, and reciprocate with them in the same way, than trust to Upper Canada. . . .'[47] The hope of this additional security was something that Cartier and his French-speaking colleagues were obstinately reluctant to give up. They wished, along with Macdonald, Galt, and the other British American expansionists in the cabinet, to cling to confederation as long as a glimmer of hope remained. The original agreement of the 22nd of June was enough – if not more than enough – for them. They saw no reason to confirm it and to make it more rigid with a quicker and more precise time-table.

But Brown was adamant. Obsessively intent upon his original and prime object – the liberation of Canada West – he demanded a new commitment to Canadian federation and a definite and not too distant date for its implementation. On Thursday, the 23rd of March, the conflict in the cabinet reached its climax.[48] Twice during that acrimonious six hours of argument Brown was on the point of resigning. His colleagues, faced with this unshakable determination, realized that a break-up of the Coalition was unthinkable and that there was nothing to do but give way. A face-saving compromise settled the dispute over the personnel of the mission to London. The four senior ministers – Macdonald, Cartier, Brown, and Galt – all formally agreed to form part of the delegation; but Brown and Macdonald, who had refused so positively and frequently to go, were each permitted to nominate a substitute, if suitable substitutes could be found. There was little latitude in this obvious and doubtful attempt to save appearances; and there was no freedom of movement at all inside the rigid new definition of policy that Brown had imposed upon his colleagues. It was agreed that the Coalition should attempt to remove the objections of the Maritime Provinces and should 'earnestly strive' for the adoption of confederation. But if sufficient progress to ensure the completion of the larger union had not been made by the opening of the session of 1866, then the Coalition would present to parliament, 'and press with all the influence of government', a measure for the federal union of the two Canadas alone.[49]

It was all settled. The terminal date was 1866. If the legislature met in January as it had done this year, that meant that only nine months were left. If confederation could not overcome all the obstacles in its way in nine months, it must be dropped. Nine months in which the decision in New Brunswick would have to be reversed, and the reluctant consent of the four Maritime Provinces secured! Nine months in which the troubled relations between Great Britain and the United States might end in war – a war that would sweep away in ruin all hopes of a united and transcontinental British America before they even approached their realization! Nothing was certain or secure. Everything depended upon a set of circumstances and a sequence of events which, in the main, were fortuitous, unpredictable, and utterly beyond British American control.

As the cabinet broke up on the 26th of March, and the ministers hurried home for a brief rest before departure for England, they scanned the troubled horizon for signs of hope. On the 8th of March, the United States had revoked the obnoxious passport order; and at the same time Seward, the American Secretary of State, had withdrawn the notice terminating the Rush-Bagot agreement limiting armaments on the Great Lakes. These, surely, were promising indications; but, strangely enough, the imperial Parliament and the London press, far from being reassured, remained in a highly nervous and excitable state on the subject of Anglo-American relations all during March and early April. Any news about British American federation, any reference to Canadian defence, seemed enough to provoke members of Parliament into long, serious debates, and newspaper editors into copious editorial reflections.

On the 23rd of March – the very day on which the cabinet crisis at Quebec reached its climax – the Marquess of Hartington introduced the army estimates, and G. W. P. Bentinck moved in amendment that the £50,000 for the defences of Quebec be deleted.[50] This proposal was pretty thoroughly stamped on by a vote of 40 ayes to 275 noes;[51] and it was comforting for Canadians to read later that Palmerston, in his sturdy, downright fashion, had declared: 'Sir, this is not a Canadian question – it is not a local question – it is an imperial question. It is the question

which affects the position and character, the honour, the interests, and the duties of this great country.'⁵² The £50,000 – yet
how pitiful, derisory a sum that was! – was through in safety; but
Robert Lowe, that vitriolic essence of anti-colonialism, had
argued that Great Britain should make no attempt whatever to
defend Canada by land; and this appalling suggestion seemed
actually to be taken seriously by a section of the London press.
The *Morning Post* and the *Daily Telegraph* considered that
Parliament had done the only possible thing for Canada;⁵³ but
The Times and the *Daily News* agreed with Lowe that Canada
was an untenable battlefield which British troops had better
abandon in time and that the only effective contribution that
England could make would be through naval attacks on the
American Atlantic ports.⁵⁴ Jeeringly *The Times* and the *News*
compared Palmerston's 'point of honour' with the miserable
£50,000 appropriation. All that Parliament would get, *The
Times* felt sure, was 'a cheap reputation for magnanimity'.⁵⁵
'This is the approved way', the *News* observed cynically, 'of
gently letting the colonists down.'⁵⁶

In early April, while the London papers were still arguing
about Canadian defences, the heroic resistance of the Confederacy suddenly collapsed. In British North America, the
hope of the survival of the South had been slowly ebbing during
the late winter; but up until nearly the end a considerable section of British American opinion had refused to believe that
the South would not ultimately win its independence. 'Points
here and there may be brought under Federal rule,' the Montreal
Gazette observed as late as January the 20th, 1865, 'but the real
subjugation and conquest of the South seem to be almost as
distant as ever.'⁵⁷ Richmond, the capital of the Confederacy, was
finally abandoned on the 3rd of April; but, as the *British Colonist*
had noted far back in November, 'the nearest approach to a vital
spot in Southern strength is Lee himself'.⁵⁸ And it was Robert
Edward Lee's surrender of the Army of Northern Virginia on the
9th of April that marked the real downfall of the South. Now, in
the end, the sacrifices of a devoted civilian population, the military genius of a score of great captains, the matchless fighting
qualities of an army of ill-equipped but light-hearted and gallant

soldiers had all been crushed to pieces under the slow, ponderous, lurching leviathan of Federal wealth and power. Now all hope of that salutary balance of strength on the North American continent which, British American commentators realized, a Southern victory would have established was gone for ever.[59] The transcontinental nation that Canada hoped to create would have to stand for all time in the deep, permanent shadow of the colossus to the south.

The long-awaited, long-dreaded moment, which many believed would be the moment of British America's greatest peril, had arrived. Lee's surrender confirmed the desperate need of a solid Anglo-Canadian agreement on defence; and it settled the one not completely decided point about the mission to England – its personnel. Even after accepting his formal commitment to join the delegation, George Brown had fully intended to find a substitute and had kept reiterating his determination to stay at home.[60] But this intention, like so many other personal preferences during these crowded years, had to yield in the end to the unrelenting pressure of events. The tragedy at Appomattox made up Macdonald's mind – if, indeed, he had not already decided that he must go to London; and on the 11th of April, only a day after the news of Lee's surrender had been published throughout British America, he wrote to Brown reminding him that all sections of the Coalition cabinet ought to be represented in the mission to England and hoping that they would sail together from New York. 'The surrender of Lee and close of the war bring matters to a crisis between England and Canada,' Macdonald argued. 'Either the United States, flushed with success, with their armies full of fight and their fleet in prime condition, will at once put the pistol to England's breast and demand satisfaction for the *Alabama* and *Florida* affairs, or, we may look for peace for a series of years. Should the first contingency arise, it will be sudden and speedy and no time is to be lost in putting on our armour of defence. Should peaceful counsels prevail, we should settle now the gradual and systematic growth of a defensive system, to be carried on steadily until we find ourselves strong enough.'[61]

Brown yielded. The Coalition government would send the

most impressive delegation that had ever crossed the ocean from Canada to England. The four senior ministers would all undertake the mission, Galt and Cartier departing first.

❯❯❯ V ❮❮❮

THE MORNING PAPERS carried the news of the surrender of the Army of Northern Virginia the day Cartier and Galt set out together from Montreal. The Cunard steamer *Asia*, which they boarded at Boston, was scheduled to stop at Halifax; and the Nova Scotian Confederates, joined by Tilley, who came over specially for the occasion, prepared a great reception for the Canadian ministers at Temperance Hall. It was past midnight before the *Asia* docked at the Cunard wharf; but bands and torch-bearers were at hand to escort the visitors' carriages through the dark streets; and at Temperance Hall a huge crowd had been patiently filling in a three-hour wait by listening to a succession of local Confederates, including Tilley, who, the *Citizen* reported, 'like Mark Tapley did his best to appear jolly' under the trying circumstances of his recent defeat.[62] Then the procession – 'hardly longer than a first class funeral' cortège – arrived at the Hall, the Mayor read an address of welcome, and Galt and Cartier, 'a vociferous, spasmodic little gentleman', replied.[63]

The Nova Scotian Unionists intended their demonstrations to show that the Confederate movement was still very vigorously alive in the Maritime Provinces and that the Canadian delegation to England was off on an important mission which was likely to have an unspecified but profound effect upon future events in British America.[64] Privately the Anti-Confederates were inclined to suspect that this latter assumption might be true, and that, in any case, the Canadian delegation to England was a dark conspiracy against the rights and liberties of the Maritime people. But publicly it was their obvious duty to pour quantities of contempt and ridicule on the overflow meeting in Temperance Hall. 'The demonstration', wrote the *Citizen*'s reporter, managing with difficulty to contain his grief, 'was the funeral of Confederation. . . . One long white transparency looked so like a coffin that we began to feel sorry that we hadn't come in our black clothes. The coffin was white – for Confederation died young. It had the name of the deceased very handsomely printed on it. . . .'[65]

When, late in April, Cartier and Galt reached London, English public opinion on British North America was not in a uniformly sympathetic and uncritical phase. The gloomy news about confederation, which kept arriving in puzzling and irritating batches with every ship that sailed from Halifax, prompted impatient questions in Parliament and exasperated editorials in the newspapers. *The Times*, it was true, affected a serenely impartial detachment on the subject of confederation. 'The question is so entirely the affair of the colonists themselves', it explained loftily, 'that we shall not greatly disturb ourselves whichever way they decide it.'[66] Unfortunately, this Olympian tone was hard to maintain in the face of the New Brunswickers' 'perverse determination' to 'reject so peremptorily a proposal we think desirable'.[67] Equally annoying was the complacent assumption, held apparently by Islanders and Nova Scotians as well as by New Brunswickers, that Great Britain, even if she abandoned Canada, would be obliged to hang on to the Maritime Provinces in order to keep her naval base in North Atlantic waters.[68] Finally – and most exasperating of all – was the impertinently ungrateful reception which Canada had given to the news of the £50,000 appropriation for Quebec! Galt had spoken of it with disdain. Macdonald had actually ventured to suggest that there had been a mistake and the figure must be £300,000 or £500,000.[69] *The Times* argued angrily that Canada expected more than England could or should give;[70] and the *News* suggested that England should 'hold her hand' in the defence negotiations until the success of confederation was assured.[71]

English anti-colonialism, however, was not news to Galt and Cartier and they had not come to England to read the newspapers. Their business was with the British government; and on the 26th and 27th of April they had their first two long interviews with the Colonial Secretary. It was the first time the Canadians had met the man who was playing such an important role in the crisis in their affairs; and Cardwell left them impressed, if not exactly enthusiastic. A well-built, distinguished-looking man with clean-cut, regular features framed in fluffy side-whiskers, he might have seemed the very pattern of a nineteenth-century public servant – highly intelligent, prudent, thorough, efficient, and devoted. His long oval face, with its firm chin and high-bridged roman nose, suggested calm authority and careful deliberation. His eyes were thoughtful, scrutinizing, appraising. The urbane smile with which he greeted Cartier and Galt was definitely provisional. He listened with attentive interest to all they had to say; and, as he listened, far beneath his blandly civil exterior he was conscious of a slight sense of shock. Cartier, to be sure, produced no surprises. He simply asked that the British government should use its full influence with the Maritime Provinces in favour of confederation and he frankly suggested that if progress were to be made the Colonial Office would do well to find more suitable substitutes for those two notorious Anti-Confederates, Gordon and MacDonnell.

All this was to be expected. It was Galt who provided the shock. The Canadians had travelled a long way since they had drafted that prying and peevishly exculpatory Minute of Council of the previous November; and everything that had happened, from the damp squib of the £50,000 appropriation to the violent impact of the news of Lee's surrender, had hurried them along on their way. The Jervois plan, with which they had been solely concerned before, was a long-range plan for a system of fortifications. They had got beyond that now. What was needed, they felt convinced, was a programme both more comprehensive and more immediate. In the final week of the session, the Canadian legislature had carried a special, additional appropriation of a million dollars – four times the amount of the British vote of £50,000 – 'for the permanent defence of the country'; and this sum was intended as an indication both of the gravity of the situation, as the Canadians conceived it, and of the magnitude of the remedy they thought essential.

Briskly, in his usual fluent, expert fashion, Galt proceeded to propose that, in addition to the measures recommended in the Jervois report, the imperial forces in Canada should be largely increased, and a very considerable body of Canadian militia equipped and trained.[73] Canada, he announced, intended to go ahead with the building of the Intercolonial Railway and the improvement of the Canadian canals, for defensive as well as commercial purposes; and the Coalition government believed that munition factories should be established on Canadian soil. When the astounded Cardwell asked him for an estimate of the cost of this enormous programme, Galt, who was never inclined to soften the dramatic impact of his effects, replied blandly that exclusive of canals and railways the whole expenditure would probably run to something between eight and ten million pounds sterling.[74]

At an early hour on Monday, the 1st of May, four days after these preliminary encounters, Brown and Macdonald arrived to join their colleagues.[75] The four Canadians occupied a set of rooms at the Westminster Palace Hotel, a long, narrow, wedge-shaped building that stood at the junction of Victoria and Tothill streets and overlooked Westminster Abbey, St. Margaret's, and the Houses of Parliament beyond. They had a spacious sitting-room in common and four rather small bedrooms; but if, as George Brown thought, their quarters in the hotel were only fairly comfortable, London in spring-time gave them a welcome that could hardly have been more gratifying. The English spring – fickle but more gracious than the reluctant, niggardly spring of Quebec – smiled capriciously upon them; and the reception of Westminster and Whitehall was a sustained parade of flattering courtesies.

The Canadians were taking their mission seriously; but so, very obviously, were the British. The appointment of a special committee of the cabinet to carry on the negotiations with the delegation – a committee which included Gladstone, the Chancellor of the Exchequer, and De Grey, the Minister for War – was one prominent indication of the concern the Imperial government felt for her largest and most dangerously vulnerable North American colony. The polite attentions and civilities – so familiar to foreign diplomats and so strangely new to colonial delegates – which were showered upon the four Canadians in London implied fairly obviously that, for once in a way, their visit was actually being regarded as important.[76] They were presented at Court, entertained by the Prince of Wales, invited by

Whig and Tory hostesses to enormous receptions and at-homes, and wined and dined by cabinet ministers, titled personages, and livery companies. This parade of civilities amused Macdonald, hugely delighted Cartier, bored Brown, and roused doubts and misgivings in that hypersensitive and suspicious colonial, Galt. 'I do not quite like the very marked attention we have received,' he told his wife doubtfully. 'They have treated us too much as ambassadors and on an equality, and I think it bodes no good, however flattering it may be.'[77]

The other ministers may not have shared Galt's suspicions; but they soon began to realize that their lavish reception in London implied no cordial acceptance of their military plans. The magnitude of Galt's original proposals had appalled Cardwell. 'I hope', he wrote to Palmerston, reporting his preliminary interview with Galt and Cartier, 'that when we meet for the transaction of business they may not press their impossible demands.'[78] The professional soldiers were the only people who gave the Canadians much support; and the Memorandum of the Imperial Defence Committee, presented on the 17th of May, confirmed Jervois's belief in the defensibility of the Province, and went far to endorse the enlargement of his plan that the Canadians now proposed.[79] But the special committee of the cabinet and the cabinet itself were a very different matter. The shaky government, Brown admitted, had 'a very narrow ledge to stand on' in Parliament.[80] It was frightened of the House of Commons, of general anti-colonial sentiment, of what the Americans might think of the Canadian proposals, and of the effect which the whole business might have in the next general election.[81] The British ministers, moreover, were, as the Canadians quickly realized, at odds with each other. The cautious Whigs wanted to get ahead with the modest, half-agreed-upon programme of fortifications.[82] Gladstone, Palmerston suspected, hoped by a minutely detailed examination to prove the impossibility of the larger, more ambitious project that the Defence Committee had sketched, and thus perhaps to frustrate the entire negotiations.[83]

It was upon the Defence Committee's favourable report that the Canadians based their final variation of Galt's first bold proposals. They offered to construct the fortifications west of

Quebec, to deepen the provincial canals, and to spend up to a million dollars annually in training the Canadian militia, provided the British government would guarantee the loans necessary to finance these undertakings and, in addition, provide an adequate force of gunboats for the defence of Lake Ontario.[84] In this plan, speed was of the essence. The Canadians believed that, now the American Civil War was over, their great danger would come soon or, probably, not at all. They wanted the British government to obtain parliamentary authority for the financial guarantee in the present session, so that the construction of the works could be begun at once. They wanted also to be able to inform their own legislature, before it was asked to sanction the fortifications scheme, that the imperial government had promised to provide an adequate naval force for Lake Ontario.

But if the urge of the Canadians was for speed, the bias of the British — and particularly of Gladstone and his friends — was equally strongly towards delay. 'I frankly own my entire inability to comprehend the feverish impatience of the deputation,'[85] Gladstone wrote to Cardwell. But Canadian impatience was not the only Canadian characteristic that lay beyond Gladstone's comprehension. He did not understand, and made no attempt to understand, the fundamental political ideas and purposes of the Canadian people. He distrusted their devotion to the imperial connection and their belief that their best future lay within the British Empire. Before the British government committed itself to the defence programme, he argued, the Canadian legislature, or, better still, the legislature of united British America, must solemnly declare its belief in the continuance of the imperial connection;[86] and the best practical proof of this moral commitment would be the immediate authorization of the fortification plan in advance of the imperial guarantee. This condition, which was, of course, the exact opposite of that which the Canadians had laid down, became the prerequisite to which the British ministers clung immovably. They would make no promise about the gunboats, and they refused to validate the guarantee before the Canadian legislature had authorized the building of the fortifications. 'The ministry', Brown declared angrily, when the negotiations had reached their penultimate stage, 'have behaved

in the most miserable, shuffling fashion you can imagine. . . .
Their whole effort is to find some mode of getting quit of us
without a row.'[87] 'It is very grievous', Galt wrote sombrely to his
wife, 'to see half a continent slipping away from the grasp of
England with scarcely an effort to hold it.'[88]

In the end, the whole defence plan, with the exception of the
works at Quebec, to which the imperial Parliament had already
committed itself, was postponed until after confederation. This
highly inconclusive conclusion was perhaps the most startling
but not the only result of a month and a half of continuous discussions. Canada – thereby reassuring the sceptical Gladstone –
pledged itself to devote its whole resources 'to the maintenance
of her connection with the mother country'; and Great Britain,
in return, acknowledged 'the reciprocal obligation of defending
every portion of the Empire with all the resources at its command'.[89] There was to be imperial help, also, for the completion
of confederation and for the renewal of the Reciprocity Treaty,
and even the promise of a guarantee for a loan to enable Canada
to buy up the rights of the Hudson's Bay Company – rights which
she had at last sensibly agreed to acknowledge. George Brown,
who bounded with characteristic rapidity from the black depths
of angry despair to the hopeful heights of satisfaction, extolled
the final settlement as a Canadian diplomatic triumph. 'So we
will be able to return with flying colours,' he wrote happily to
his wife.[90]

What, in fact, had they accomplished? The negotiations, failing of their main purpose, had left behind a curious, unresolved
complex of risks and promises. Unfortunately for the Canadians,
the risks were mainly on the one side of the ocean and the
promises on the other. Great Britain, safe beyond the Atlantic,
was protected from any direct damage that the Americans could
attempt by the world's greatest navy. Canada, defenceless and at
the moment virtually indefensible, lay at the mercy of an angry
nation which had suddenly shown itself to be one of the most
powerful military states of the nineteenth century. Canada would
have to rely upon the willingness of the Americans to settle their
outstanding disputes with Great Britain and British America by
peaceful means. Canada would have to put its trust in the ability

of the British to overcome the resistance to confederation, though how this was to be done in an age when responsible government practically precluded coercion was something nobody was very ready to explain. There was no certainty of nationhood, and no security against invasion. The future was nearly as dark as it had been before.

CHAPTER TEN

Imminence of Failure

THE PRAYERS FOR 'Thy Servant Arthur' with which pious New Brunswick clergymen had been importuning the deity for so long had now at last been answered. Lieutenant-Governor Gordon had, as a result of the general election, been granted an Executive Council several of whose members, if not exactly gentlemen – this, perhaps, was scarcely possible in New Brunswick – were at least 'gentlemanlike'. Unfortunately, one of their leaders, Albert J. Smith, a man of 'considerable obstinacy', narrow views, and violent temper, was the Governor's self-declared enemy, who had not only quarrelled with him over matters of public policy, but had also found a way to humiliate him over the delicate subject of his salary.[1] Smith was highly objectionable on personal grounds, and there could be no doubt that he was not nearly so able as Tilley. But a hard vein of what Gordon comforted himself by thinking was 'honesty of purpose and resolution' ran through his character;[2] and, best of all, he was accompanied, as a result of the bizarre combination of forces that had fought the Quebec scheme in the general election, by a little group of that fast-decaying order, the New Brunswick 'patricians'.

It was a fairly competent and extremely genteel ministry.[3] Among its members were the other joint leader, the 'honest and able' R. D. Wilmot; J. C. Allen, the new Attorney General, an educated and very generally respected lawyer; W. H. Odell, who had inherited broad estates and might almost, by a stretch of the imagination, be classed as 'landed gentry'; and Bliss Botsford, who, though not particularly notable for either intelligence or

284

energy, was at least a gentleman by birth and education. Unhappily, most of the other members of the new council were distinguished by that lack of education, ability, and principle which, Gordon regretfully considered, was so characteristic of New Brunswick politics. But the little group of patricians nearly redeemed their disreputable colleagues. In delighted astonishment, the Lieutenant-Governor realized that the election had given him a 'gentlemen's government'. 'It is probable', he wrote sardonically to Cardwell, 'that the government will fall under the imputation of being too much a "gentlemen's government".'⁴ He was already wondering doubtfully how long it would last.

A great many other people were wondering exactly the same thing. The eyes of the whole of British America were fixed upon Smith, Wilmot, and their colleagues in a gaze of concentrated, undeviating, and anxious scrutiny. Obviously the fortunes of confederation were closely and inextricably bound up with the success or failure of the Smith-Wilmot government. The balance of forces, tilted ominously against the Quebec scheme, had not yet fallen conclusively to the other side. Canada had accepted the Seventy-two Resolutions without amendment; Prince Edward Island had rejected them without qualification. In Nova Scotia, where the government, by a small, dexterous manoeuvre, had only recently escaped disaster, Tupper lay waiting, gasping with both relief and apprehension and scarcely daring to move. In Newfoundland, Hoyles had retired and his government had been replaced by a coalition formed by F. B. T. Carter and Ambrose Shea, the two delegates to the Quebec Conference, who were now pondering whether they could commit their united Conservative and Reform following to confederation as a government measure.

For all these waiting, watching, undecided people, what happened in New Brunswick in the immediate future was of crucial importance. It was not enough for Smith and Wilmot to wrest power from Tilley; it was equally essential for them to hold on to it until the time necessary to ruin confederation had elapsed. If the Anti-Confederates could manage to retain office in Fredericton for eighteen months or more, they might succeed not only in compelling Tupper and the Newfoundlanders to drop confederation but also in forcing the Canadians to take up their alternative project of the federation of the two Canadas. George Brown had agreed to wait until the session of 1866; but if by that time all real hopes of confederation had vanished, the Canadian Coalition was committed, by repeated and precise pledges, to abandoning the larger for the smaller federation, and thus perhaps to delaying British American union for another generation at least.

If the Smith-Wilmot government could last, the Anti-Confederates would probably win. But could the Smith-Wilmot government last? Despite the massive support of its thirty members in the Assembly, the new Executive Council was weakened by serious divisions within itself – divisions that expressed a certain fundamental contradiction in its position. To their followers in the legislature and to the electorate, the new ministers appeared as the champions of New Brunswick's separate and self-sufficient identity. Yet, in fact, they had not fought against British American union in principle, but only against the Quebec scheme. Wilmot preferred a legislative union, or at least a much more centralized federation. Allen definitely wanted a British American legislative union. Smith professed himself a Unionist in principle, though he thought the Quebec scheme a very bad bargain for New Brunswick. Even Timothy Anglin, the most passionately parochial of them all, had once admitted, at the dinner given to D'Arcy McGee's touring Canadians, that in the end British North American union would probably be the only alternative to annexation to the United States.[5]

The line separating these alleged Anti-Confederates from Tilley's followers was thin and wavering. Yet it was as the defenders of a vehement and assertive provincialism that they had won the election. Their popularity was deserved only in so far as they had defeated the Quebec scheme; and this was a justification that was likely to seem quite insufficient in the long run. Resistance to the Seventy-two Resolutions by itself was purely negative. It was a denial of confederation, but not a satisfactory answer to it. At the heart of the Anti-Confederate movement in New Brunswick was a gnawing and insatiable need for a positive alternative to confederation – an affirmative policy that would express the province's distinctive character and promote its independent interests in ways very different from that of the Quebec scheme. It was a tall order. And the new ministers had not been long established at Fredericton before they began to realize that it was going to be very hard to fill.

Maritime union, for example, would definitely not do. The struggle against the Quebec scheme had certainly not awakened any great new wave of enthusiasm for the lost cause of a united Acadia. Gordon might still prefer it secretly to confederation; but he made no attempt to revive it; and the Smith-Wilmot government looked at the project with even more indifference than the Tilley ministry had done eighteen months before. The initiative for the apparent renewal of Maritime union in 1865 had come from Nova Scotia, largely for tactical reasons; and when the Colonial Office became aware of these strange, equivocal doings at Halifax, it informed MacDonnell quickly and firmly that it was interested in confederation and nothing else, and that all efforts to revive the smaller union must be frowned upon.[6] Even this imperial prohibition did not arouse New Brunswick to take up Maritime union as an act of rebellion. In a tepidly non-committal speech, A. J. Smith moved a resolution empowering the government to appoint delegates to confer with the Nova Scotians on the subject; and in the brief, unenthusiastic debate that followed there was a good deal of talk, as there had been in Prince Edward Island the year before, about acceptance as a mere matter of courtesy to Nova Scotia. Certainly, acceptance of the resolution was all that Nova Scotia wanted now. At one point, when it was rumoured that New Brunswick actually proposed to nominate delegates, MacDonnell and Tupper hurried over to Fredericton in great alarm to assure the New Brunswickers that, even if Colonial Office instructions permitted it, Nova Scotia would not move a step further in this dangerous business.[8] Maritime union, having been very briefly exhumed, was at once reburied, deeper than ever.

There was no hope of an alternative here. But Western Extension, the one positive policy which the Anti-Confederates had urged in the recent election, looked much more promising. Western Extension was, in fact, an alternative that revealed perspectives widely different from those of confederation. It implied reliance on transport and commercial connections with the American republic rather than with British North America. It meant the orientation of New Brunswick away from the St. Lawrence valley and towards the New England States. Obviously this was a daringly positive programme; but obviously also it had serious implications and might involve grave financial risks; and the Anti-Confederates, once they were safely in power, approached the enterprise in a very gingerly fashion. A paragraph was placed in the Speech from the Throne, promising reconsideration of the whole subject and regretting that, in the meantime, existing legislation precluded an immediate attack on the project.[9] The existing legislation was, of course, Tilley's measure of the previous year, the Railway Facility Act, which offered government subsidies to commercial companies that would extend the European and North American in a variety of different directions, including towards the American border. 'Albert J.', that cautious financier, explained to the Assembly that the government felt it must honour Tilley's legislation for a while at least in order to give capitalists a chance to take advantage of the government's offer.[10]

This may have been an astute move financially. But to many people it seemed strangely unlike the 'lion of Westmorland' and the heroic campaign he had waged for New Brunswick's independent economic growth. A number of Smith's followers in the Saint John region were bitterly disappointed by the tame announcement in the Speech from the Throne; and one of Smith's colleagues in the Executive Council, Timothy Anglin, was seriously disturbed. For some time, Anglin had been convinced that no bona fide New Brunswick capitalists would be strong enough by themselves to build Western Extension;[11] and during the election campaign he had gone so far as to declare that he would proceed with it immediately as a government work.[12] Now, in considerable embarrassment, he was obliged to support the ministry in the debate on the Address.[13] But if he was temporarily reconciled to delay, there were other Anti-Confederates who were not.

One of the most determined and prominent of these was John

W. Cudlip, member for St. John County, who had led the struggle for Western Extension in the previous year. Cudlip waited until nearly the end of the session; and then, early in June, he moved that the government should 'forthwith proceed with the construction of the Railroad from Saint John westward towards the American frontier, as a government work. . . .'[14] An important qualification to this apparently forthright declaration of purpose provided that if any commercial company was prepared 'without delay' to take advantage of the Railway Facility Act of the previous year it was not to be prevented from doing so by the new resolution. This face-saving proviso permitted the government to accept the Cudlip motion; and though two North Shore Executive Councillors voted against it, it passed by twenty-five votes to thirteen.[15] An alternative and easy way out of the problem still lay open, theoretically. But despite this, the Smith-Wilmot government had committed itself, more deeply than before, to Western Extension as a major governmental enterprise.

-»» II ««-

THE COLONIAL OFFICE had promised 'strong help to carry Confederation'. And Cartier had plainly intimated that one of the best ways of giving it would be to transfer those two unsympathetic lieutenant-governors, Gordon and MacDonnell, to other posts in the service and replace them by suitable substitutes. It was a delicate operation, of course, but one that the Colonial Office could surely carry out easily, in the circumstances. Confederation had not abolished MacDonnell's distasteful job for him. He found the role of governor in British America 'disagreeable to the last degree';[16] and he would no doubt jump at the chance of being extricated from his dark, unlucky cul-de-sac in Halifax. Gordon, though he was a temperamental young man who submitted and cancelled letters of resignation with dizzying speed, would surely be equally ready to welcome the offer of a good post elsewhere. Best of all, a new colonial position, one that seemed almost ideally suited to Gordon's requirements, had suddenly become available. It was Hong Kong, not an objectionable 'colonial democracy', but a submissive Crown colony, with entirely suitable social amenities and a pleasant salary of £5,000 a year. At the end of April Cardwell wrote to Gordon officially offering him Hong Kong, and obviously assuming that he would accept it.[17]

Unfortunately, by the time this agreeable invitation arrived, Gordon's views about himself and his future had entered a new phase. At first he was simply annoyed that the Colonial Office had so signally failed to understand and appreciate his heroic efforts in the cause of confederation. By degrees he became aware of the fact that he was suspected of having done a good deal less than he could or ought to have done, in a situation that was judged to be much more favourable than he knew it to be.[18] Finally he realized that he was dragging behind him not only a record of failure but also an imputation of ill-will, hostility, even obstruction, in a matter that the Colonial Office believed to be of the highest importance. If he accepted a transfer at this peculiarly significant moment, might it not be regarded as a tacit admission of guilt? Would the fact of the recent Anglo-Canadian talks in London encourage Englishmen to assume that his new appointment was, in fact, a recall, successfully demanded by those insolent colonials, the Canadian ministers?[19] The mere thought was insupportably humiliating.

Another circumstance may have strengthened Gordon's hesitation about Hong Kong. He was in the delicious throes of an even more personal agitation. His engagement to Rachel, the daughter of Sir John Shaw-Lefevre, had just been announced. Sir John was a Whig. His son George John, Rachel's brother, was a Gladstonian Liberal who believed in the entire separation of the defence and foreign policies of Great Britain and Canada as the ideally perfect solution of a most vexatious imperial problem. On every score, political and personal, the projected union of Rachel Emily and Arthur could hardly have been more suitable; and Cardwell, who knew the Lefevres well, hastened to write to Gordon, declaring how fully he could 'appreciate the prospect of happiness before you'.[20] Rachel would certainly comfort and delight Arthur Gordon's future life; but, on the other hand, she would also complicate it. Could he begin married life with an admitted failure in New Brunswick? Would not his bride find the climate at Fredericton more healthful than at Hong Kong? It was all very puzzling. 'I infer', Cardwell wrote rather resignedly, 'that you are coming home and that it is your wish if possible to return to New Brunswick with your bride.'[21]

Cardwell had been foiled. The Canadians, with some help from Rachel, had spoiled the projected transfer of the more difficult of the two Anti-Confederate governors. Hong Kong, of course, was still available, and Cardwell promptly offered it to MacDonnell who, with faint regrets for that lost Atlantis, Australia, promptly accepted.[22] But the problem of Gordon was another matter. Gordon was the youngest son of the Earl of Aberdeen, whose memory Gladstone venerated to the point of idolatry; and Cardwell recognized that if Gordon decided to stay in Fredericton, he would just have to be left there. Not left alone, or uninstructed, however. The congratulations that he sent Gordon on his engagement simply supplied an inadequate sugar-coating for the large and powerful dose of administrative medicine which the Colonial Secretary then proceeded to administer. 'You must perceive', he told Gordon flatly, 'that in your high position your personal sentiments cannot have been a matter of small moment; and, if you suppose the world in general have not been aware of these sentiments, you are entirely mistaken. It is as well known here that the Lieutenant Governors of Nova Scotia and New Brunswick are adverse to Confederation, as it is that their names are Gordon and MacDonnell; and though I have never heard any suggestion fall from anyone that they have not loyally obeyed their instructions since they received them, it is felt that all the weight of their personal convictions has been thrown . . . into the opposing scale.'[23]

This was very plain speaking indeed. Gordon was furious. He was now more strongly convinced than ever that his malevolent enemies, the Canadians – probably including Governor General Monck – had been talking slanderously about him in Downing Street, and that Cardwell – convinced by these malicious charges – had offered him Hong Kong with the simple intention of getting him out of New Brunswick. Indignantly he wrote to Monck;

and Monck's answer was not likely to mollify him greatly.[24] He brooded darkly. He felt unappreciated, injured, and aggrieved.[25] Hardly knowing whether to remain in New Brunswick or to ask again for another appointment or to resign from the colonial service altogether, he relapsed into a profound sulk.

≫ III ≪

CARDWELL HAD DEALT, though not finally or very effectively, with personalities. He now passed on to the business of exerting a more general pressure on the Maritime Provinces. It was not an easy task to fulfil his promise of 'strong help to carry Confederation'. There were not many arguments in favour of the Quebec scheme that Great Britain could urge as peculiarly her own. There were even fewer sanctions she could impose, or penalties she could exact, if the Maritime Provinces stubbornly refused to follow her advice.

In Prince Edward Island, the salary of the lieutenant-governor had long been paid out of the imperial treasury, and Cardwell could, and did, warn the Island government that this practice would be stopped in short order if union did not take place.[26] But Dundas's salary was a lonely survival of an earlier colonial paternalism which Cardwell would probably have wanted to reform, confederation or no confederation. The fact was that the only major contribution which Great Britain still made to British America was the military defence she provided. In the past, miserly and irresponsible colonial governments, anxious to reduce the costs of their militia and police, had sought to use imperial troops simply to maintain order; and when, in the summer of 1865, the Tenant Union in Prince Edward Island started a violent protest against the payment of rents and the Island government called in two companies of British soldiers from Halifax to suppress the commotion, Cardwell promptly informed Dundas that keeping order was a colonial, not an imperial, obligation and the colony would have to pay for the cost of the operation.[27] But opportunities such as this for exerting a little pressure were rare. If the Maritime Provinces refused to unite with Canada, Great Britain could scarcely neglect imperial defence as a means of retaliation. Even if her own prestige had alone been at stake, she could not conceivably begin a wholesale withdrawal of troops from British America at a time when her relations with the United States were so tense.

Yet, if defence did not provide the imperial government with a material sanction, it at least gave her a position of great moral authority. She could urge confederation much more earnestly than she had done as yet, and with all the persuasive force of a recognized guardian and protector. The dispatch Cardwell had sent Monck on the 3rd of December, 1864, had expressed a benevolent though not entirely uncritical approval of the Quebec scheme; but it did not clearly indicate that the British government thought the plan a highly desirable one and was ready to give it enthusiastic and vigorous support. These deficiencies the dispatch of the 24th of June to New Brunswick amply repaired. Confederation, the dispatch asserted, was, in 'the strong and deliberate opinion' of the British government, 'an object much to be desired'. Confederation would have a variety of advantages for the northern provinces, but above all it would enable them to plan more effectively for their joint defence; and their defence was a subject in which the British government, because of its responsibilities, was deeply concerned. The colonies, Cardwell declared, 'must recognize a right and even acknowledge an obligation incumbent on the Home Government to urge with earnestness and just authority the measures which they consider to be most expedient on the part of the colonies with a view to their own defence'.[28]

It was an admonition, an injunction, a reproof – a public reproof, for it was circularized to all the Maritime Provinces. To the two most refractory governments, Prince Edward Island and New Brunswick, it appeared as an obvious attempt at moral coercion. They hardened their hearts. Prince Edward Island made no protest at the time, though it had a good deal to say later on; but the response of New Brunswick was immediate and defiant. Already Smith and his colleagues had shown a prickly sensitivity to criticism from outside and a pugnacious readiness to set ignorant critics straight about the true state of affairs in the province. On the 20th of May, that busy Anti-Confederate, J. H. Cudlip, proposed in the Assembly that a special delegation should be sent to London to acquaint the British government with the strength of the opposition to confederation.[29] By the time the dispatch of the 24th of June arrived, the two delegates, Smith and Allen, had already departed. The agreeable task of composing a rejoinder was left to Anglin and Wilmot.

There may have been a third principal author. Anglin, not a very credible witness, later insisted that another person – no less a person, in fact, than Lieutenant-Governor Gordon – had taken a part in the drafting of the reply;[30] and something of the argument as well as the irritated tone of the Governor's private letter of the 5th of June to Cardwell found an echo in the caustic and assertive Minute of Council of the 12th of July. In it, the cabinet expressed a lofty surprise that the British government should be so ignorant of the true state of opinion in New Brunswick as to imagine that the province would quickly change its views of the Quebec scheme. The Colonial Secretary was right in thinking, the Minute rather patronizingly conceded, that the wishes of Great Britain would be received with great respect in New Brunswick; but Cardwell was reminded that the great principle of British imperial rule was that, with reference to their own local affairs, colonies should act precisely as they thought best in their own interests. 'To confer on this Province a right of self-government', declared the authors of the Minute, working themselves up into a high state of moral indignation, 'would have been a mockery if, in consequence of its claim to deference as a protector, the wish of the Mother country was in all cases to be followed whenever expressed. . . .'[31]

In the meantime, in pursuit of the same object – the education of the British cabinet on the subject of confederation – the two New Brunswick delegates, Smith and Allen, had reached London.[32] They were not the only politically-minded Maritimers who paid visits, official or unofficial, to the imperial capital that summer. Tupper and Henry had arrived from Nova Scotia and were staying in the same hotel as the New Brunswickers. Tupper, like MacDonnell, had been mystified and annoyed by Cardwell's summary rejection of Maritime union and by his apparent inability to appreciate the clever manoeuvre by which the Nova Scotian government had avoided a hostile vote against the Quebec scheme. He and his colleagues had considered an explanatory mission to the Colonial Office earlier in the spring; but they had postponed their visit on the well-grounded suspicion that if they went at the same time as the Canadians, they would probably be regarded as aiding and abetting a sinister conspiracy against Nova Scotia.[33]

Tupper and Henry did not arrive until after the Canadians had left, and they came ostensibly seeking that invariable object of British American politicians – more capital for railway construction. The little procession of official colonial emissaries now ended; but two other visitors – William Annand and Leonard Tilley – were also busy in London with confidential explorations during the summer. Annand, who, while Joseph Howe continued as Imperial Fisheries Commissioner, remained the public leader of the Nova Scotia Anti-Confederates, was anxious, if he could, to pry a little deeper in to the purposes of the Colonial Office.[34] Tilley 'gave out' that Cardwell had called him over for private talks; and Gordon evidently considered it desirable to protect himself against anything that Tilley might say. His former Premier, he informed Cardwell, was a nice man, but an inveterate liar; 'even the certainty of speedy detection', he wrote helpfully to the Colonial Secretary, 'will not prevent him from telling any lie which may appear to serve the purpose of the moment.'[35]

All of them – Nova Scotians and New Brunswickers, official delegates and unofficial visitors – saw Cardwell. Cardwell was affable and reasonable. He was ready to talk and to listen. The British government, he told them all, was ready to consider amendments to the Seventy-two Resolutions. In the matter of the details of the plan, he was quite prepared to be accommodating; but on the necessity for British American union he was adamant. He told Smith and Allen that the British government was strongly in favour of the union of the northern colonies.[36] He frankly informed Annand that the United Kingdom would do everything, short of actual coercion, to push confederation through.[37] These earnest declarations had a profound effect upon Annand and Smith. They were both Unionists, in principle; and they were now faced with the fact that the British government was determined, if possible, to carry out a British American federation, in the immediate future, on lines comparable with those of the Quebec plan. Even this was not all. Smith was also forced to realize that New Brunswick's only possible alternative programme to confederation was already running into serious difficulties. He and Allen had tried to borrow money in London for the building of Western Extension as a government work. And they had failed.

Cardwell's attempt to give 'strong help to carry Confederation' had probably been more effective than he himself was inclined to believe. Up until the summer of 1865, Anti-Confederates could argue plausibly that the attitude of the imperial government to confederation was one of permissive approval only; but the dispatch of the 24th of June, which showed unmistakably how earnest and determined Great Britain was in its advocacy of union, put the whole matter in a completely different light. Many New Brunswickers were strongly moved by the dispatch of the 24th of June. Many were outraged by the argumentative and insolent tone of the notorious Minute of Council of the 12th of July. And – perhaps most important of all – Cardwell's pleasant but firm declarations in his office in Downing Street had deeply impressed his important Maritime visitors that summer. The Colonial Secretary himself doubted that his arguments had had much effect upon Smith. But he had been forthright with Annand; and at Tupper's anguished request he had made an attempt to get at the potent personality that stood, undisclosed but threatening, in Annand's rear. He wrote to Russell, reporting Tupper's remarks, 'that if Mr. Howe could be sent for to come here, *on business connected with the Reciprocity Treaty*, he might easily be converted into a supporter of Confederation.'[38] In a few days, the Foreign Secretary did exactly what he had been requested to do. 'I have to instruct you', he wrote to Howe, 'to come to England at your earliest convenience, on business connected with the Reciprocity Treaty.'[39]

It remained to be seen whether Howe could be 'easily converted into a supporter of Confederation'.

≫≫ IV ≪≪

BY THE END of the first week in July, all the Canadian ministers were back in Canada. Macdonald had returned with an
Oxford D.C.L., Brown with chandeliers, plate, and glassware for
his new house, Galt with a sadly reduced opinion of the quality
of English statesmanship, and Cartier with the delighted recol-
lection of over two months of virtually uninterrupted dining
out.[40] They had spent a very long time in England; but, apart
from personal trophies, purchases, and memories, what had they
brought home? The only solid result of ten long weeks of
diplomacy was the exchange of unqualified pledges of mutual
assistance in case of war; and the anti-colonial London newspapers, which were certain in due course to be quoted in the
colonies, set themselves immediately to depreciate the value of
these promises as much as they could. *The Times* was gratified
to learn that the British government seemed to feel that as few
obligations as possible should be incurred;[41] and the *News* rejoiced that the 'vague assurances' that had been exchanged 'do not
amount to much'.[42] It was impossible for the Canadians to claim a
diplomatic triumph. Neither they nor the British had committed
themselves to do anything immediate or positive. Canadian
policy had become a policy of postponement and waiting, sustained by hope and disturbed by recurrent fits of apprehension
and despair. There might be war – or there might not. The
Maritime Provinces, exhorted by the Colonial Office, might
change their minds about confederation. Or they might not. In
the meantime, the Coalition government marked time in a spirit-
less fashion.

Into this depressed state of enforced inactivity, the news of
Sir Etienne Taché's death broke like an alarm. Taché, who
was seventy but feeble beyond his years, had gone neither to
Charlottetown nor to London; but he was the premier of the
ministry, as well as its kindly old doyen; and, as the ministers rode
back from the funeral that hot, dusty August evening to Quebec,
they all realized that the Coalition government was confronted,
not by any of the anticipated external obstacles or dangers, but
by a crisis within itself. The meeting of the legislature – called

for the 8th of August – was only five days away. Somebody must be appointed to succeed Taché as first minister at once. But who was it to be? Monck faced what was probably one of the worst crises of his entire governor-generalship. And in his painful difficulty he decided to fall back on what seemed to him, as a practical politician, the least objectionable basis of selection – seniority.[43] Macdonald, as head of the Canada West division in the ministry and as leader of the government in the Assembly, was the second in command after Taché. And, as Taché was now gone, he should be asked to take over the leadership. Monck invited Macdonald to come out to Spencer Wood for breakfast on the morning of the 3rd of August. He asked him to take Taché's vacant post; and Macdonald accepted the commission.[44]

This was only the beginning. The unhappy Monck had now to face the second and far more formidable interview of that August morning – the interview with Brown. He had the best of reasons for dreading the approaching encounter. The prospect of a repetition of the prolonged and difficult negotiations of June 1864 was frightening to contemplate; and when, only a little later, he and Brown met, the Governor General was obviously embarrassed, and apprehensive. He expected trouble, and trouble quickly came. Brown rejected both his principle of selection and the choice based upon it. The Governor General, Brown informed his interlocutor coldly, 'had committed a grave error'.[45] Instead of choosing Macdonald, he should have selected 'some member of the Legislative Council of good personal position and moderate views' under whom 'the three active party chiefs' – Macdonald, Cartier, and himself – could have continued in the Coalition on a plane of perfect equality and 'without injury to party interests'.[46] Monck, who during this extended and vehement lecture had grown steadily more distressed and alarmed, refused to accept Brown's resignation, broke down completely, and begged him to see Macdonald, in the hope that if the case for a neutral first minister were presented to him as Brown had just put it, Macdonald would probably accept.

Brown instantly deepened the gravity of the crisis by insisting that if there were to be any further negotiations they must be carried on in frigidly formal terms. He would see Macdonald, but

only officially, and only after he had consulted his two Grit colleagues, Howland and McDougall. When, later in that eventful
day, he and Macdonald did finally meet, they met as old, inveterate antagonists, who had retraced the recent course of their
relationship back to the point at which it had stood on the 17th
of June, 1864, when the negotiations for the Coalition had
begun. This time they hardly made an attempt to understand
each other. To the earnest Brown, all Macdonald's ingratiating
efforts at persuasion seemed, as Brown contemptuously put it,
mere 'coaxing and wheedling'.[47] To the diplomatic Macdonald,
Brown must have appeared at times like a self-righteous peda-
gogue or an evangelical clergyman in a peculiarly elevated state
of moral indignation. On the one hand Macdonald argued that
the only result of Taché's death was that the other senior members of the government had moved up one place – that he, as
second in command, had taken Taché's position as first minister,
and that Cartier had assumed Taché's leadership of the Canada
East division of the ministry and was now therefore second in
command. On the other hand, Brown insisted that the Coalition
had been 'a coalition of three political parties, each represented
by an active party leader' – Macdonald, Cartier, and himself –
united under one chief, who no longer possessed strong party
feelings or personal ambitions and could therefore inspire confidence in all three divisions of the government.[48]

Historically, Brown's basic constitutional assumptions were
quite invalid. Taché may have been old, inactive, and a member
of the Legislative Council rather than of the Assembly (he had
also been a member of the Legislative Council in 1856 when the
first Taché-Macdonald government had been formed). But there
was not the slightest uncertainty about his political record or his
political allegiance. He was a Conservative and had been a Conservative since the Liberal-Conservative union of 1854. In 1864,
when the negotiations for the Coalition took place, he had been
the first minister in a defeated but still existing Conservative
government, with Macdonald as his associate in the dual premiership. It was with the representatives of this government, and not
with Macdonald and Cartier as separate party leaders, that Brown
had carried on the negotiations in June of 1864. All the pledges

that the Conservatives gave were given in the name of the government; and the final promise, to place three seats in the cabinet at Brown's disposal, was made, as it could only have properly been made, by Taché and Macdonald as joint leaders.[49] Macdonald's right of seniority was based, not on the irrelevant circumstance that he had been an executive councillor and a premier before either Brown or Cartier, but upon the extremely pertinent fact that he was joint leader and second in command of the government which negotiated the Coalition.

Historically and constitutionally, Brown's case was weak. Politically, it was far from negligible. Its strength lay in the thirty-odd Western Reformers that he had brought to the support of the Coalition, in the important contribution he had made to its work, and in the prominent part he had played in all its activities. He kept on saying, very repetitiously, that he had no personal ambitions; but the fact that the premiership had possibly few attractions for him did not lessen in the slightest degree his grim determination to prevent his old rival from getting it. His own personal feelings – the hypersensitive feelings of a proud and imperious man – were deeply engaged in the issue; but though they were powerful enough to prove conclusive in themselves, they were not the only compulsions that made it impossible for him to accept Macdonald as premier. His pride was not alone at stake. The place of his followers in the House and the standing of the Reform party in Canada West were also considerations of the utmost importance. Brown came to the quick and sure conclusion that both would be seriously damaged by an apparently passive acceptance of Macdonald's undisguised leadership.[50]

Macdonald, confronted by this immovable resistance, began to beat an increasingly rapid retreat. At first he suggested Cartier as a possibly more acceptable alternative than himself as leader. Brown, who was willing to continue the oral negotiations only if his own conception of the Coalition were accepted as their basis, chose to consider this as a proposal for a completely new government and demanded that the offer be submitted formally, in writing. He then obviously had to consult his colleagues, Howland and McDougall; and he and they decided that they could not possibly accept Cartier's leadership without seeking the approval of their 'political friends'. The correspondence, which had descended to a depth of frigid formality approximately level with that adopted by two highly belligerent nations on the eve of a declaration of war, now reached dead end in a demand that could not be conceded because it could not possibly be carried out in time. It was Friday, the 4th of August, and on Tuesday, the 8th, parliament was to open. If the Coalition was to face the legislature intact, there was no opportunity of sounding out the scattered company of Reform members; and, with the excuse of this impossibility, the Conservative leaders yielded to Brown's demand. An undistinguished senior member, and former Speaker of the Legislative Council, Sir Narcisse Belleau, was finally persuaded, after a good deal of earnest solicitation, to accept the purely titular leadership of the great triumvirs. Brown, though he protested sourly that his Reform colleagues would not themselves have selected Sir Narcisse, agreed to 'offer no objection' to his appointment.[51]

The crisis was over. But it had been a deeply disturbing event in the history of the Coalition and it was full of significance for the future. In his long and agitated interview with the Governor General on the 3rd of August, Brown had declared that the Reformers 'had sacrificed a great deal already but they could not go on always sacrificing, that the other party must not have the victory at every turn'.[52] If, in fact, the first year of the Coalition had been an unbroken record of Reform sacrifices and surrenders, Brown had certainly revenged himself against the shameful past. This time he had made no sacrifices. He had won a complete and unqualified victory. In June 1864 his potential authority – as one of three Reform ministers in a Coalition of twelve– had been uncertain. Now it was formally defined and acknowledged, and exactly as he wanted it to be. The man who had had only three days' experience as a minister of the Crown, whose Reform associates had rejected his policies, and who had been compelled to stand on the side-lines for years while others took over the leadership of his party, had now thrust himself into a position of equality with those veterans Cartier and Macdonald. With swift, forceful strides, he was making his way towards a position of dominant importance in the Coalition. Five months before, in the tempestuous cabinet arguments of March, he had compelled his colleagues to agree to his rigid interpretation of the government's policy. Now, with equally complete success, he had forced them to accept his conception of its structure.

He went further. The juicy fruit of his triumph was squeezed to the very last drop. Up to this point, the March agreement on policy had remained a cabinet secret. Now, as the final trophy of Brown's victory, it was made public and in consequence was fixed even more unalterably as a government commitment. In his letter to Macdonald accepting Sir Narcisse Belleau as first minister, Brown set out, with clarity and precision, the agreement that the completion of confederation could not be delayed later than the opening of the parliamentary session of 1866.[53] This letter was read aloud, as part of the ministerial bargain, to both houses of the legislature; and if any doubt existed as to the strictness with which the government would be held, by a new and inflexible time-table, to constitutional reform through the federal union of the two Canadas alone, Brown himself, in his speech on the 9th of August, very effectively removed it. 'We held', he told the House emphatically, 'that time was the essence of the contract, and I wish the house distinctly to understand that all the members of the government were fully alive to the importance of the bargain being carried out so far as regards time.'[54]

In this satisfied announcement, the full measure of Brown's victory was revealed. He had ensured the success of his own plan, at the risk of the total failure of that of his colleagues. All that he had sacrificed in the negotiations of June 1864 had now been triumphantly recovered. He had not wanted confederation – the federal union of the whole of British North America – for its own sake. His original and still his primary object was 'justice to Upper Canada' – the reform of the Canadian constitution. In June 1864 he had fought hard but in vain to have the federation of the two Canadas given first place in the programme of the Coalition. Now he had contrived to put it in an equally prominent and impregnable position. The federation of the Canadas had become a certainty, timed to a fixed date. Confederation – the union of British North America – had been lowered to the level of a pious hope or a highly improbable piece of good fortune. If the prospects for confederation were not good at the time when preparations for the session of 1866 became necessary, then confederation would have to be dropped and a plan for the federation of the two Canadas substituted for it. For the Confederates, it was a darkly uncertain outlook. The chances for British American union had been bad four months before when George Brown had first driven his hard bargain. They were even worse now. In the meantime, Cardwell, upon whose efforts so much reliance had been placed, had tried, and tried in vain, to win over the recalcitrant New Brunswickers and Prince Edward Islanders. Obviously a long and difficult campaign of manoeuvre and battle lay ahead. Would there be time for it now? Even if the next session were postponed as long as possible, until the early summer of 1866, that would still leave only about eight months in which the decision in New Brunswick could be reversed. How could such a miracle be accomplished in that time?

»»» V «««

LATE IN JUNE, after a long conversation with that fiery patriot General Dix, Monck had written happily to Gordon, informing him of the General's reassuring estimate that 200,000 Union soldiers would be disbanded by the 4th of July.[55] The colossal and terrifying Federal army, nearly a million men in size, was being mustered out into civilian life with all the speed that unmilitary democracies would henceforth find necessary. The fear, which had for years been haunting Queen Victoria's subjects on both sides of the Atlantic, that as soon as the Union armies had finished the conquest of the Confederacy they would march north to wreak vengeance on British America, was being rapidly laid to rest. But if British Americans no longer dreaded an immediate invasion, as they had done in the winter of 1865, they were as yet very far from being reassured about the ultimate intentions of either the American government or the American people.

Politicians and newspapers in the Republic had been busily making a mountainous grievance out of the exploits of the *Alabama* and the *Florida* – cruisers built in British shipyards and acquired by the Confederate government which had inflicted substantial losses on Union shipping during the war. On the 17th of March, the United States had given the year's notice necessary to terminate the Reciprocity Treaty. There was an enormous accumulation of resentment against Great Britain and British America stored up in the Republic. It might yet find satisfaction in diplomatic pressure or military aggression. In the meantime, while the nation began its recovery from the war and the politicians drew up their elaborate indictment against the criminally 'unneutral' British, the pent-up, angry feelings discovered another, unofficial – and perhaps for that very reason, more satisfactory – form of expression: the Fenian movement.

The object of the Fenian brotherhood was to free Ireland from British 'subjugation'. The original and still orthodox strategy for the attainment of this end was, of course, to foment rebellion in Ireland. But fomenting rebellion in Ireland was a difficult, dangerous, and obviously long-term business; and, in the six months after the Civil War, the leaders of one militant branch of the American Fenian movement began to argue that an indirect, circuitous approach was far better than a direct attack, and that the quickest way to Irish freedom was the conquest of British North America. Nothing could have been more characteristically 'Irish' in the broadest, most farcical meaning of the word than the conception and execution of this great enterprise. With one or two significant exceptions, the leaders of the Fenian movement against British America were a crew of grandiloquent clowns and vainglorious incompetents. Their plans, frequently changed, widely circulated, and executed with chaotic inefficiency, were probably better known to the Canadian border police than they were to the Fenians themselves. The soldiers of their 'armies', who drilled and paraded ostentatiously in northern American towns and, on a few abortive occasions, actually attempted invasions of British North America, behaved mostly like a crowd of seedy theatrical extras, hired by the hour for some battle scene in a play or a film. In its British American aspect, the Fenian movement was mainly low burlesque. Mainly, but not entirely. There was also in it a small but real element of peril.

The peril had its explanation in the fact that the Fenian movement drew strength from certain historic American traditions as well as from the prevailing mood of post-war America. The Roman Catholic Irish, who had been emigrating to the United States in very large numbers ever since the troubles of the 1840s, had now become a recognized and important factor in American politics. They were flattered and cajoled by American politicians, partly because they formed such a clearly distinct and powerful group and partly because their aspirations were so closely attuned to certain permanent American sentiments. The Fenian movement – the chief political manifestation of the Roman Catholic Irish – represented not only the traditional anti-British feeling of the Republic, roused to fever pitch by the war, but also the historic American urge towards Manifest Destiny through the annexation of British America. There was very little likelihood that the Fenians would get much support from their compatriots north of the border. Apart from small groups in cities such as Toronto and Montreal, the Roman Catholic Irish of British America, who had benefited so largely from their denominational schools, were strongly loyal. The danger of a real response to a Fenian invasion in Canada or New Brunswick was very slight. The real danger of the movement was that some Fenian raid or border skirmish might seriously involve the two governments and ultimately take on the gigantic and terrible proportions of a war with the United States.

If that ever happened, the collapse of the great fortifications plan might prove fatal. But, in the meantime, so long as the Fenians alone were concerned, the Canadian government could rely with some assurance on Gilbert McMicken's counter-espionage service, the Volunteers, and, in the case of a more serious crisis, on the remaining British regulars. In July, when the cabinet met for the first time after the London mission, it took up the second grave American threat – the now almost certain abrogation of the Reciprocity Treaty. Eight months had yet to elapse, however, before the year's notice terminated; and the Canadian Coalition, like all the other British American governments, hoped fondly that in the meantime the Americans might be persuaded to change their minds, and either continue the treaty or agree to some acceptable substitute. At the cabinet meeting on the 15th of July, Galt, the Minister of Finance, produced a set of proposals for the renewal of the treaty and suggested that he should go down to Washington at once to begin tentative negotiations. As soon as he had finished, Brown vehemently disputed his proposals; and one of those clashes of assertive personality which had threatened the Coalition from the beginning broke out explosively.[56]

Brown and Galt were far too much alike for the peace and comfort of themselves and their colleagues. Each had a great deal of pride, some vanity, and a stubborn independence of mind; and both were sensitive, temperamental, and moody men. Unfortunately, their respective spheres of interest in public and private life were dangerously close together. They were enterprisers on a considerable scale, who had both achieved marked success in the commercial life of the province and were equally interested in its economic and financial problems. If Galt lacked something of Brown's strong moral force of character, he was fully his rival's equal in general, all-round ability; and in addition he possessed a sheer cleverness, a creative ingenuity, which Brown conspicuously lacked. Throughout the Maritime Provinces as well as Canada, Galt enjoyed the reputation of a veritable financial wizard. In the Coalition cabinet, his position, as Minister of Finance, was very strong. But Brown looked on both his prestige and his pervasive influence with doubt and distrust, sharpened by jealousy. He had no confidence in Galt as a solitary emissary to Washington. An impulsive man himself, alternately over-optimistic and unduly depressed, he regarded Galt as impatient, rash, and headstrong. He insisted, in the stern cabinet battle on July the 15th, that another minister must accompany him to Washington on the business of the Reciprocity Treaty, and that the efforts of the two diplomats must be strictly limited to tentative exploratory approaches. Galt was a prickly person, impatient of criticism or direction; but he was not as vehement or aggressive as his intransigent rival, and in the end he yielded.

He and W. P. Howland, the Reformer who had taken Oliver Mowat's place in the cabinet, went off to Washington together. They returned in time for the adjourned session of the legislature in August with the news that there seemed to be at least a faint hope for the renewal of the treaty.

In the meantime, while the Canadians were starting investigations on their own account, Nova Scotia had successfully insisted upon a general British American approach to the renewal of the treaty. It was an old Nova Scotian grievance that their province had not been consulted in the negotiation of the original treaty in 1854; and when Tupper and Henry were in London in July, they reminded Cardwell of this slight and urged that on the present occasion there should be a common understanding among the provinces and joint negotiations in Washington. Cardwell and Russell approved; and the result was the Confederate Council on Commercial Treaties, which met in Quebec on the 15th of September.[57] In comparison with its famous predecessor, the Quebec Conference of October 1864, the Confederate Council was a small affair with only half a dozen delegates: Galt and Brown from Canada, J. W. Ritchie from Nova Scotia, R. D. Wilmot from New Brunswick, J. C. Pope from Prince Edward Island, and Ambrose Shea from Newfoundland.

Yet the little meeting had a considerable and – in some ways – unexpected significance. Its resolutions, which were to be presented to the British government for its guidance in the negotiation of imperial treaties, were generalities in form, but they were important generalities. The delegates declared that British America was prepared to continue the existing Reciprocity Treaty or to negotiate a modification of it, and they urged that their council, or a committee of its members, should consult with the British minister in Washington on negotiations with the American Secretary of State. If all efforts failed and the treaty unfortunately lapsed, it was agreed that all the provinces should co-operate cordially in a common commercial policy for the benefit of British America as a whole. And in the meantime, as an initial and joint attempt to diversify the provinces' external commerce, the delegates suggested that trade missions should be sent to the West Indies and South America.⁵⁸

Three of the Maritime delegates – Ritchie, Pope, and Wilmot – had not been members of the Quebec Conference the year before. Ritchie, Solicitor General in Tupper's cabinet, was a Unionist, but the other two – J. C. Pope, the new Premier of Prince Edward Island, and R. D. Wilmot, the joint leader (with Smith) of the new New Brunswick government – were strong Anti-Confederates. The three days of discussion at Quebec, the tour of Canada West that followed, the visit at the comfortable, well-appointed house of George Brown, that dynamic and compelling advocate of confederation, had no known effect on Ritchie's opinions, and certainly did not weaken Pope's invincible resistance to union with Canada. But Wilmot, the other Anti-Confederate, experienced a notable change of outlook. Two things happened to him during his Canadian visit; and together they drastically altered his point of view. Like many another Maritimer who made the long journey to Canada and saw the division between English-speaking and French-speaking Canadians, Wilmot came to the conclusion that a legislative union of British North America was impracticable.⁵⁹ Like many another realistic British American, he was also nearly convinced that the Reciprocity Treaty was doomed and the provinces would have to find or create new markets. Five separate colonial governments with five different tariffs could never do this satisfactorily by themselves. They would have to co-operate. Union was the only effective kind of co-operation. And the only possible union for British North America was federal.⁶⁰

When Wilmot set out on his journey home, he had virtually become a Unionist.⁶¹

→»» VI «←

YET, DESPITE all the plans and conferences and negotiations, a profound feeling of gloom and frustration settled down upon the Confederates in the late summer and early autumn of 1865. So much effort had been expended; so little seemed to have been accomplished. The great Canadian mission had gone to

England in the spring to enlist the support of the British government. The British government had done its best to win over the obstinate Maritime Provinces to the Quebec scheme. The British North American provinces had met together in a first attempt to plan a co-operative commercial policy in the light of the probable ending of reciprocity. Months of struggle on all fronts – struggle that was apparently vain. The whole defence programme had been postponed. The fate of the Reciprocity Treaty and the hope of new markets were quite uncertain. And no open breach had yet been made in the Anti-Confederate defences in New Brunswick.

'My present information about the prospect of Confederation', Cardwell wrote to Russell on the 15th of August, 'is not very favourable.'[62] He must have felt that he had done everything possible to reverse the apparently invincible trend of events. No more earnest exhortations than his dispatches to New Brunswick could have been penned. He had worked hard to persuade Annand, Allen, and Smith – the Maritime visitors to England in the summer of 1865 – that confederation was necessary and that the United Kingdom was thoroughly in earnest in supporting it. But he could not really believe that he had had much success; and when September came and there were no visible signs of a change of heart in the Maritime Provinces, the attitude of the Palmerston cabinet towards British North America began to harden with impatience and exasperation. Gladstone, that dedicated advocate of 'Home Rule' for small countries, protested indignantly against the absurdity of New Brunswick's daring to differ from the express wishes of the Mother Country.[63] 'I incline to the opinion', Russell wrote to Cardwell, 'that in order to preserve our British North American Provinces they must be united, and that some coercion will be necessary.'[64]

The slow attrition of events had equally serious consequences for the Coalition government in Canada. The delays, the postponements, and the frustrations all bore heavily upon the ministers and their programme; and under this pressure the latent divisions in the cabinet threatened to become open breaks. The dispute over the Washington mission had exposed the suspicious and jealous competition between Brown and Galt. The grim battle waged after Taché's death had brought into the open the still more serious rivalries between the three senior ministers, Brown, Macdonald, and Cartier. Brown, imposing his views of both precedence and policy upon his colleagues, had emerged the victor from that encounter; and everything that had happened since the opening of the adjourned session in August had seemed to emphasize his increasing political pre-eminence. His greatest rival was his old enemy, John A. Macdonald; and Macdonald, troubled by financial worries and ill for long periods during both the winter and summer sessions of parliament, had almost seemed at times to be under an eclipse.[65]

Brown was taking his place. In the Assembly, he frequently acted, with assured competence, as government spokesman; out-side, in the parliamentary society of the capital, he was gradually assuming the public appearance of a prime minister. During the summer session of 1865, he had leased Bishop Mountain's large, suitably episcopal residence, with its 'capital' dining-room, drawing-room, and 'lots of bedrooms';[66] and Anne Brown came down to Quebec to 'do the honours of the session' in a stately and expansive fashion that very few, if any, wives of English-speaking ministers had ever before attempted. Leonard Tilley stayed at the palace when he visited Quebec for a few days early in September;[67] and when the Maritime delegates to the Confederate Council – Ritchie, Wilmot, Pope, and Shea – travelled to Toronto on their inevitable tour of Canada West, it was Brown who hospitably put them up at Oak Lodge, his comfortably spacious house on Wellington Street which glittered now with the silver, glassware, and chandeliers he had bought in London.[68] To Maritime visitors, Canadian assemblymen, and London journalists and civil servants, he was becoming – had perhaps become – the key figure in the ministry. Rich, masterful, brimming with vitality, instinct with an imperious urge to command, he had made his forceful way to place and power.

It was not until the end of September, when the year was three-quarters over, that Macdonald seemed to turn and confront his rival. The occasion was symbolic. The removal of the government from Quebec to Ottawa had at last got under way; and Craig and Vallière, the contractors for the job, were in the first stages of transporting vast masses of books, papers, records, equipment, and furniture by river and railway to the new capital.[69] That autumn both Macdonald and Cartier – it was a characteristic gesture on their part – paid visits to the little lumber town on the banks of the Ottawa, which was so soon to be invaded by an army of uprooted civil servants, searching for rooms and flats and houses.[70] Macdonald, who was the first to come, seemed a very different man from the tired invalid of much of 1865 and the worried, undecided politician of 1862-3. His old form had come back so completely that it might never have left him. He was jaunty, jocular, complimentary. But he did more than flatter and amuse. He issued challenges. He made confident prophecies.

Confederation, he told the citizens of Ottawa, was 'a fixed fact' and he himself was now determined to stay in politics until the whole great transcontinental union had become an accomplished reality. Public life, he reminded them frankly, had always been an unprofitable career in Canada, and was becoming a purpose-less one. He had tried hard, on more than one occasion, to get out of it. 'Well, gentlemen,' he went on, 'they would not let me go when I wanted, and now I won't. I won't go unless I am compelled, and because I have an object in view worthy of any statesman's ambition.' The 'mere struggle for office' – the fight between the 'out's' and 'in's' – had become unsupportably weari-some; '. . . but now' – and his voice lifted in conviction – 'I have something worth fighting for and that is the junction of Her Majesty's subjects in all British America as one great nation.' Canada would soon become the 'owner' of the great North-West. The first stage of confederation – the union of Canada with the Maritime Provinces – would be realized 'before another year has passed'. 'You may read in the papers', he continued in a tone of calm and convincing assurance, 'about obstructions in one colony or another, but I do not speak incautiously, or without the book, when I say that the union of all the Provinces is a fixed fact.'[71]

A fortnight later there came a curious rejoinder. On the 27th of September, Macdonald had emphasized the certainty of con-federation. By the middle of October, the *Globe*, George Brown's newspaper, was affirming the essential importance of the alternative to confederation, the federal union of the two Canadas. It was a by-election in North Wentworth, made necessary by the death of the sitting member, the Reformer William Notman, that provided the occasion for this virtual repudiation of Macdonald's assurances. North Wentworth was by no means the first seat to fall vacant in Canada West since the Coalition had been formed. Eight by-elections had already been held; and with three exceptions – the re-election of the new Reform Ministers, Brown, Mowat, and Howland, all by acclamation – these seven contests had been vigorous party battles, very much in the old pre-Coalition tradition. All the candidates – with the possible exception of M. C. Cameron in North Ontario – had declared their belief in confederation and their support of the Coalition government; but all had equally obtained party nomination or sought party votes in the traditional fashion. Even if the ministers had tried to suppress the ingrained partisanship of the constituencies, they would have been quite unable to do so. And, in fact, all of them – and perhaps particularly Brown, who feared to be caught, like so many earlier Reform leaders, in Macdonald's tentacles – were determined to defend the autonomy and guard the future of their respective parties.

It was not particularly surprising, therefore, that the Conservatives of North Wentworth nominated Alexander Brown for Notman's vacant seat, and that the Hamilton *Spectator* came out supporting Brown's candidature.[72] But the *Globe* instantly showed extreme displeasure. It professed to find Alexander Brown's nomination a shocking novelty which all right-thinking supporters of the Coalition ought to repudiate instantly. In the issue of the 29th of September, it contended that, at the time of the forming of the Coalition, the Conservative and Reform ministers had made an agreement about elections; and 'that (so far as the parties to the compact could secure it) the counties held by the Liberal and Conservative parties respectively should continue to be so held during the short space necessary to accomplish the purpose of the Coalition'.[73] Alexander Brown was a Conservative who was trying to capture a traditionally Reform seat. He was flagrantly breaking the compact. He must be disavowed and the Liberal candidate, James McMonies, elected in his place.

The Hamilton *Spectator* was not impressed by this thunderous revelation from Olympus. It flatly declined to believe that such a sweeping agreement existed. Even if an improbable compact of that kind had been made, it had certainly not been honoured. It had been grossly violated, the *Spectator* asserted, by the Liberals and their newspapers, particularly the *Globe* itself, which had ardently supported the Reform candidates in both the Niagara and Peterborough by-elections, though both were traditionally Conservative seats.[74] To these charges, the *Globe* replied in kind;[75] and for a while the two newspapers argued happily over the character and significance of the by-elections of the past fifteen months. Then the *Spectator* moved on to a supposedly higher, but much more doubtful, argument.[76] It deplored the *Globe*'s attempt to raise a party fight in North Wentworth on the ground that party divisions had now become virtually meaningless. The old issues and the old animosities had been settled and reconciled in the Coalition and its programme. Why revive them? Why had McMonies, the Liberal candidate, come out to oppose Brown, when both stood essentially upon the same platform?

If the editors of the *Globe* saw in advance where the appropriate rejoinder to this might end, the spectacle did not give them pause for an instant. The sanctimonious non-party attitude of the *Spectator*, they retorted angrily, was all a silly pretence. It was no time for the Reformers to be taking off their armour and dismantling their strongholds. Of course there were issues between Liberal and Conservatives that were not yet settled. There was, for example, the still undecided question of the local constitutions of Canada East and Canada West in the federal system of the future.[77] Even more important, there was the central ambiguity in the very programme of the Coalition government, the basic uncertainty as to which of the two alternatives – British American confederation or the federation of the Canadas – would ultimately be carried out.[78] The declared policy of the government was to introduce a measure for the federation of the Canadas in the session of 1866, if confederation had proved impossible to secure by that time. Brown, the Conservative candidate in North Wentworth, and the *Spectator*, his newspaper supporter, were, the *Globe* charged angrily, silent or evasive about this second, fundamental part of the Coalition's policy.[79] But to the Reformers it was just as vitally important as the first. Their prime object was constitutional reform in Canada – 'justice for Canada West' through Rep. by Pop. 'If Confederation will bring them [these reforms] in a few months, all will be well; but, if not, then we get reform without waiting indefinitely for the accession of the Lower Provinces.'[80]

In a week, the North Wentworth affair was the sensation of the Canadas. None of the previous by-elections – not even the contest in North Ontario – had aroused a tithe of its interest and excitement. The journalistic battle which the *Globe* and the *Spectator* had begun was quickly extended throughout the press, both English and French, of a large part of the province. The Conservative and independent papers poured ridicule on the idea of a cabinet compact that could, or should, bind the constituencies; and when the debate moved on to the programme of the Coalition, they met the *Globe*'s insistence on the smaller, provincial federation with all kinds of reservations, qualifications, and objections. The time had not yet come, the *Spectator* asserted, for the discussion of the smaller scheme; it was defeatist and unpatriotic at this stage even to hint at an alternative to confederation; and even if, in the end, confederation did calamitously fail, there were surely far better solutions for the problem of the Canadas than federal union.[81] *La Minerve* of Montreal called it 'la désunion';[82] it was a scheme, the Toronto *Leader* observed, inspired by nothing but 'narrow prejudices and contracted views'.[83] 'La Confédération', declared *La Minerve*, 'faisait de nous un grand peuple; la désunion des Canadas diminue au contraire notre sphère d'action, rétrécit l'horizon de notre influence.'[84] There were Reformers, it hinted, who were so exclusively devoted to the interests of Upper Canada that they were prepared to sacrifice everything for it. The federation of the Canadas, *Le Canadien* insisted, was simply a pleasant euphemism for the hated Rep. by Pop.[85] 'Nous n'avons jamais, pour notre part,' it declared flatly, 'adhéré, même par notre silence, à la seconde partie du programme du coalition.'[86]

The issue was now fairly joined. George Brown's *Globe* had insisted that the second alternative in the Coalition's programme had the same binding force as it had had in June 1864. A good many people believed that so much had happened, and the confederation movement had progressed so far since then, that the two parts of the policy could no longer be regarded as having anything like equal authority. George Brown had imposed his evaluation on the cabinet in March 1865. In August, he had revealed his triumph to the legislature; and now his newspaper was publicly carrying the issue, as a party battle, into the constituencies. 'The difference between them [the Conservative ministers] and their colleague', observed the *Leader* virtuously, 'is that they have too much self-respect to interfere directly in a contest where both candidates are supporters of the government.'[87] 'If party lines are to be drawn in any case while the Coalition lasts,' McDougall, Brown's Reform associate, wrote to Macdonald, 'it ought to be done without any member of the government showing his hand.'[88] He begged Macdonald to be prudent and forbearing, to tolerate 'these splurges of G.B.'. But in the end Macdonald, pestered by Conservative inquiries about the truth of the alleged compact, was goaded beyond endurance. 'No such agreement was made,' he telegraphed defiantly. 'Run your Warden [Alexander Brown] at all hazards, and if you like tell them he is *my* candidate.'[89]

Two days later, McMonies was elected by a majority of fourteen votes.[90] Up until the North Wentworth election, the one great indisputable fact favouring confederation had been the union of the Canadian people and their government. Now even that concord had been publicly broken.

CHAPTER ELEVEN

The Calculated Risk

O N THE 28TH OF OCTOBER – the day that McMonies won the North Wentworth by-election – in the midst of a torrential downpour, Gordon and his bride arrived at Saint John.[1] Over two months before, when he had left New Brunswick for England, it had been generally assumed that he was very unlikely to come back. 'My return to this Province', he had remarked darkly at his farewell levee in Fredericton, 'is subject to contingencies, some of a private, others of a public nature.'[2] New Brunswickers were left to make what they could of this peculiarly obscure utterance, and most of them came to the conclusion that their Governor was not going to return. In fact, Gordon had simply not made up his mind. At times it seemed to him both foolish and degrading to attempt any longer to carry out policies so wilfully and dangerously mistaken as those that the Palmerston and Russell governments were pursuing in British North America. When he reached London late in August he was still wondering whether, if the post was still open, it might be better for him after all to go to Hong Kong.[3] And a fortnight after his marriage to Rachel Shaw-Lefevre, which took place on the 20th of September, he still felt a last lingering doubt about returning to Fredericton on the terms Cardwell had laid down.[4]

Then he decided. He would go back to New Brunswick. He would, in spite of all difficulties, put through confederation. He would make an unexpected but triumphant success of his first colonial appointment. He had never lacked self-confidence; and, in his new mood of vigorous purpose and determination, he was even prepared to accept the severe – the really humiliating – condition that the Colonial Secretary had imposed on his return. For by this time Cardwell was extremely weary of the endless shilly-shallying of his temperamental and opinionated subordinate. The British government was just as firmly determined as ever to carry confederation if possible; and Cardwell had made up his mind that this incorrigible lieutenant-governor should not be permitted to go back to his province until he had solemnly pledged himself to carry out orders with enthusiasm, conviction, and energy. Gordon complied. The oral promises he made to Cardwell in a single, highly unpleasant interview at the Colonial Office were formally repeated in writing.[5] 'I am prepared', he wrote, copying the Colonial Secretary's words with legal exactitude, 'to do my utmost to promote the wishes of Her Majesty's government and to act in furtherance of the public pledges they have given.'[6] On the transatlantic voyage, he repeated his assurances: 'It is not my nature to do things by halves,' he declared.[7] It was an ominous remark. Six months later Cardwell may have remembered it. He certainly had cause to do so.

He was barely back in Fredericton when he began to lay plans and make moves. At Halifax, at the end of the Atlantic voyage, he had warned Cardwell that for the first little while he might have to act 'slowly and with caution'. But it was scarcely in his nature to act 'slowly and with caution';[8] and besides he discovered, as soon as he began to examine provincial affairs, that important circumstances were beginning to favour the cause he had solemnly sworn to advance. The Smith government's programme of provincial economic development was running into serious difficulties; and – what was perhaps even more serious – the Smith government was itself increasingly divided by jealousies, resentments, and disagreements over policy. As Gordon had noticed from the start, the ministry was composed of two groups: the New Brunswick isolationists, such as Smith and Anglin, who thought the Quebec scheme threatened provincial autonomy, and the British American Unionists, such as Wilmot and Allen, who believed that the federalism of the Quebec plan would result in national disunion. Both groups, for different reasons, were now visibly weakening in their respective shares of the joint resistance. The probable failure of Western Extension was alienating Anglin. The logic of British American politics was converting Wilmot to confederation.

Even this was not all. Another problem, the distribution of patronage, which had always been a highly controversial matter in the province, emerged in an acute form that autumn. For several reasons the Smith-Wilmot government found it very difficult to handle. The mortality rate in the judiciary was certainly high; the incidence of claims and ambitions among the politicians was equally wide and embracing. Two members of the government – Allen and Wilmot – had accepted office on an avowedly temporary basis in the confident expectation of places to come. Allen looked forward to a judgeship. Wilmot had his eye on the pleasant sinecure of the auditor-generalship for himself and the splendid office of chief justice of the province for his cousin, Lemuel Allen Wilmot. Some appointments were certainly unavoidable; but making them was dangerous in two ways. It inevitably disappointed certain ambitions; and, if the lucky appointees were ministers, it left awkward gaps in the cabinet. New ministers would have to go back to their constituencies for re-election; and the Smith-Wilmot government, conscious of the first chill breath of unpopularity, regarded by-elections with frank dismay.

But there was no way of avoiding them. Allen had already been made a judge; and his departure left behind a peculiarly perplexing problem. As ill luck would have it, it necessitated two elections, one to fill Allen's place in the Assembly, and one to put the approval of the electorate on his successor in the office of attorney general. It was rumoured that A. R. Wetmore, member for Saint John City, had expected to be given the post; but in the general election, Wetmore had beaten Tilley by a scant 133 votes; and the frightened government had to tell him bluntly that it did not dare to 'open' a Saint John City seat again.[9] In the end, Smith was compelled to take the post of attorney general himself; and Westmorland, which was looked upon as a safe constituency, lived up to expectations by returning the Anti-Confederate leader easily in an October by-election. But York, where Allen had held his seat, unfortunately remained. And

York was a very different affair. It was a chancy, tricky, unpredictable county, and the ample majorities the Anti-Confederates had rolled up in March gave no real assurance for the future.

For weeks, for months, the Confederates watched the slowly ripening fruit of opportunity in York County with glistening eyes. Charles Fisher was their candidate, and Fisher, though he had been badly beaten in March, was a formidable contender. His career in New Brunswick politics had been prominent, tempestuous, and, at times, extremely unsavoury, even by provincial standards. 'I am not ignorant', the Duke of Newcastle, Cardwell's predecessor, had once coldly observed, 'that Mr. Fisher is one of the worst public men in the British North American Provinces. . . .'[10] Fisher's indiscretions were indeed notorious; but he had paid for the worst of them by resigning office over four years before; and his appointment as one of the additional New Brunswick delegates to the Quebec Conference was an indication that his old friends, the Smashers, were learning forgiveness. Now, obviously, they looked upon him fondly as their ideal champion for the crucial combat in York. 'I am quite certain Fisher can be returned under any circumstances,' Tilley reported to Macdonald, prudently adding, his eye on the long Canadian purses, 'with an expenditure of eight or ten thousand dollars.'[11] Fisher was a former premier, a long-time member for York County, a veteran politician, who knew every trick of the trade.

There were few that he did not put to strenuous use during the campaign. He was suitably generous in promises, advocating Western Extension, with branches running in every conceivable direction, and at the same time supporting the Intercolonial Railway which, he declared with the utmost conviction, was certain to run by the St. John River route. The special, local needs and interests of York County in general and Fredericton in particular were certainly not forgotten;[12] but the main object of Fisher's strategy was to convince the electorate that this was not an ordinary election, a debate over small local issues, but an extraordinary and fateful contest, full of tremendous significance for the future. The grand old province of New Brunswick, 'the home of the Loyalists', was confronted, Fisher vehemently proclaimed, by the frightful menace of Fenianism; and this

menace was incarnate in Timothy Warren Anglin, the scheming, dangerous, still fundamentally disloyal ex-rebel, who was
the real dictator of the Anti-Confederate government. Anglin,
Fisher announced with patriotic conviction, was the avowed
enemy of worthy Orangemen, of pious Protestants, of faithful
British subjects, of devoted United Empire Loyalists, of the sons
and grandsons of the York volunteers, Queen's Rangers, and
other heroes of the American Revolutionary war.[13] Dramatically
Fisher appealed to all of these to 'maintain British rule' and to
'hurl this government from power'.

Indignantly the Anti-Confederate newspapers protested that
Fisher was raising totally irrelevant and distracting issues.[14]
Earnestly they warned the voters not to divert their attention
from the central point in dispute; 'let not the electors be deceived,' the *Globe* exhorted. 'The real issue is between Confederation and Anti-Confederation.'[15] Fisher willingly agreed
that union was 'the great discussion of the day'; but he picked his
way through the inviting traps and pitfalls of this dangerous
subject with sure-footed dexterity. He was, he freely admitted,
in favour of British American union. He had thought the Quebec
scheme 'the best compromise that could be effected at the time'
and 'highly advantageous to New Brunswick'.[16] But the Quebec
scheme had been pressed too soon upon the public; and the
public had rejected it. Before a second attempt at federal union
could be made, 'it would be absolutely necessary to have another
dissolution and consequent appeal to the whole people'.[17] He,
Fisher, was seeking election in order to ensure that no nefarious
second attempt would be made until the people had spoken.
And – it was the crowning effrontery of his campaign – he
announced that the Smith government was even then conspiring
to impose 'some arrangement for a union of the Provinces' without a popular appeal![18]

It was too much for poor John Pickard, the Anti-Confederate
candidate. Bewildered, baffled, attacked from all sides, he was
outclassed in such a combat. On the 6th of November, Charles
Fisher won the York by-election by a majority of 709 votes.[19]

⋙ II ≪

THE MOST IMPORTANT CONTEST, in its results, that ever occurred in British America . . .' – so Jonathan McCully described the York by-election in the Halifax *Unionist*.[20] The announcement of Fisher's victory, however ambiguous its meaning, certainly produced an immediate, widespread, and profound sensation. For the Confederates, it was an unqualified and unquestionable triumph, all the more joyfully acclaimed because it was almost the first event of the year that looked in the least worthy of celebration. Determinedly, but in vain, the Anti-Confederates set themselves to belittle its significance. The Saint John *Evening Globe* reminded its readers that Fisher had firmly declared that he would oppose any union scheme presented in the existing parliament.[21] The Halifax *Citizen* reasoned ingeniously that Fisher's success could only be regarded as the greatest defeat that Confederation had yet sustained, since it proved that only converted ex-Confederates, apostates to their former faith, could satisfy the New Brunswick electorate![22]

Yet this disparagement never quite succeeded in discrediting the York election as a Unionist success. The Anti-Confederate newspapers had repeatedly declared that Confederation was the issue in the campaign; and, despite heroic efforts, they could not erase the meaning they had attributed to it. In his speech of thanks after the result had been announced, Fisher pointedly recalled the fact that he had openly affirmed his belief in union and his 'adherence to the principles of Confederation'.[23] To the Confederates his victory inevitably appeared as the first longed-for sign of a reaction, the first indication of that 'sober second thought' which would eventually take the whole of British America into Confederation; 'we congratulate loyal men and true all over British America – ay, and elsewhere –', the *Unionist* enthused warmly, 'that the second thought is proving itself to be the better thought in all the Provinces.'[24]

No group looked forward to the York by-election with more eager interest or welcomed the result with greater relief than the Canadian cabinet. It met on the 7th of November in Montreal – a half-way house on the move from Quebec to Ottawa. Fisher had won his victory the day before; and if it had not been for the good news that was circulating so briskly in Montreal that morning, the ministers must have met in a mood of angry tension. Inevitably, the memory of the North Wentworth by-election lay like a painful burden on their minds. Brown's 'splurges' in the *Globe*, his open intervention in the primitive party politics of the constituencies, and Macdonald's final blunt response to repeated provocations were not yet even a fortnight in the past. The stresses inside the cabinet, revealed and intensified by the North Wentworth disclosures, were probably strong enough at that moment to break the Coalition apart. 'John A', Brown reported to his wife, was 'evidently expecting a blow-up'.[25]

But the blow-up did not come. The York by-election prevented it. York postponed and therefore frustrated the dangerous, possibly fatal consequences of North Wentworth. York gave renewed and real hope for the success of confederation. For the first time in months, confederation became again a cause to fight for; and, as everybody knew only too well, there was now very little time in which to fight. The triumph in New Brunswick was a call to action in Canada; and in this mood the Coalition gave a ready response to a special invitation that had just arrived from Fredericton. Lieutenant-Governor Gordon had requested a visit from a representative of the Canadian government, in order to concert policy. Of course, the invitation must be accepted; and, of course, George Brown was the man to go. Brown, who had seemed at moments to put Canadian federation before confederation, was the most appropriate person to prove Canadian sincerity in the cause of British American union. Readily Brown accepted the mission. He would go at once. For him constitutional reform in Canada was the great ultimate goal of the Coalition. He had just proved to his own satisfaction, in the hard-fought by-election in North Wentworth, that Canada West shared this conviction; and his triumph over all the forces of Conservatism disposed him to be generous. British American union was one way, if not the only way, of winning constitutional reform; he had already put a lot of earnest effort into the struggle for British American union; and if, as the York by-election seemed to suggest, there was still a chance of its realization, then he was willing to give his best help once again to the cause. With a hearty generosity that was just as much a part of his nature as its fierce intransigence, he threw himself into this new endeavour to reunite and strengthen the forces working for confederation.

Next morning, Wednesday, the 8th of November, he spent an hour before Council in shopping for furs for 'baby'. That night he was standing on the Grand Trunk Railway station platform waiting impatiently for the train to Portland;[26] and by Friday evening, the Portland steamer brought him up the coast to Saint John. When he reached the Waverley Hotel, he found a letter from Lieutenant-Governor Gordon, confirming his invitation to visit Government House in Fredericton;[27] and that night R. D. Wilmot called on him. Next day he and Wilmot took the train to Moncton for a talk with the 'lion of Westmorland', Albert Smith;[28] and afterwards Brown busied himself with arrangements for bringing Tilley, New Brunswick's prophet of confederation, and Wilmot, its latest important convert, together.[29] 'Things look well here,' he summed up realistically to his wife, 'but there is much difficulty – such intense jealousy.'[30] Yet despite the rivalries and difficulties, the crumbling of the solid Anti-Confederate resistance was plainly to be seen. 'Even the present ministry of New Brunswick, formed as it was to defeat Confederation, would take it up now,' he told Anne confidently, 'if they could have the face to make such a change.'[31]

The next part of the mission was even more exacting. Early on Monday morning he started out in an open carriage to make the long journey up the St. John valley to Fredericton. It was eight o'clock, the cold November night had fallen, and the huge, robust frame of the editor of the *Globe* was chilled through when at last he reached the capital. The Gordons were hospitably waiting for him, dinner was ready; and after the exertions of the last few days he was glad enough to settle down for a rest in the comfort of Government House.[32] Here, over a year before, at the end of the perambulatory Charlottetown Conference, the sponsors of confederation had met the champion of Maritime union in personal combat; and now it began to look as if that combat would end in the complete victory of the Canadian plan. The big, tall Scotch-Canadian, with the long legs, the large feet, and the broad Lowland Scots accent, who relaxed expansively before Gordon's study fire on that chilly November night, had triumphed over the sensitive and imperious host who sat beside him.

A year before, in one of his large, sweeping, condemnatory gestures, Gordon had dismissed the editor of the *Globe* as 'the most dangerous and most unscrupulous demagogue in British North America'.[33] Even now, despite his pledges for confederation, he could not summon up 'a good opinion' of George Brown. But at intervals during his guest's two-day visit they confidentially discussed the strategy of promoting confederation in New Brunswick; and, in Gordon's own words, they got on 'capitally' together. In the rapidly changing interplay of personalities and circumstances, it was impossible to plot a single, undeviating course of action; but Brown and Gordon could – and did – decide upon alternatives and arrange a possible sequence of manoeuvres. 'We confidently settled the whole course of operations to be pursued here,' Gordon informed Cardwell airily, 'and found ourselves almost perfectly agreed.'[34]

The first stage of Brown's Maritime mission was accomplished. Late Saturday night, the 18th of November, he reached Halifax. The situation in Nova Scotia differed, but in a not easily definable fashion, from that of New Brunswick. In Nova Scotia, confederation had neither suffered so complete a defeat, nor shown such obvious signs of recovery, as it had in New Brunswick. Yet Nova Scotians, just as they might have a vague presentiment about a change in the weather, were vaguely conscious of a slight shift in the fortunes of the struggle for union. In the fortnight before Brown's arrival in Halifax, they might have perceived two signs, faintly suggestive at least of a Confederate revival. The first and more obvious was the coming of the new Lieutenant-Governor, Sir William Fenwick Williams. The second, much less obvious but significant nevertheless, was the appearance, on the 15th of November, in the *Morning Chronicle*, of a strange leading article on the subject of 'The Union of the Colonies'.

Sir William Fenwick Williams was a very recent arrival. He

had been sworn in at Halifax on the 8th of November, the very day on which Brown had left Montreal for his Maritime tour. Williams was a native of Nova Scotia who had started out, as had John Hamilton Gray of Prince Edward Island, to make a career for himself in the British Army. He had begun earlier, stayed longer, and gone further than Gray. A British commissioner with the Turkish army in 1854, he had played an important part in the Crimean War, had won fame and a baronetcy for his bold though unsuccessful defence of Kars in Turkish Armenia, and for the last six years had been Officer Commanding the Imperial Forces in British North America. At sixty-five, Williams was a stout old veteran with a fine military presence, a hearty manner, a few firm soldier-like convictions, and a blunt, downright approach to matters political. His abrupt, explosive, military ways – he wrote letters as if he were barking orders – served to conceal what became quite evident later on, that he kept in reserve a large fund of caution and a strong relish for defensive manoeuvre. But, from the beginning, there was not the slightest doubt about the reasons for his appointment to Halifax or the part that he was about to play in Nova Scotian politics.

He was just as openly in favour of confederation as Mac-Donnell had been covertly opposed to it. As it happened, he had met MacDonnell when he was on leave in London in the summer of 1865 and had taken an instant and intense dislike to him. He derisively called him 'Governor McPotato', thought him 'the most transparent and impudent humbug' that he had ever seen in his life, and told Gordon that, even at the Cardwells' dinner-table, he could hardly keep his 'fangs out of him'.[35] While MacDonnell had looked at the Quebec scheme from the point of view of an experienced colonial administrator, Williams, like every other soldier concerned, accepted it eagerly as the best means of bringing uniformity, cohesion, and strength to British North American defence. Cardwell had picked him to go to Nova Scotia and put confederation through by every means in his power. He intended to do exactly that. He was quite prepared to have the purpose of his mission clearly understood by everybody of the slightest consequence in the province. He was determined to play the part of an affable and conciliatory, but firm and persuasive leader.

A response, hesitant, uncertain, but growing in conviction, was waiting for him. And when he had only been a week in the province and before his personal influence could have had much effect, a striking evidence of it appeared. Ever since the ejection of Jonathan McCully from the editorial chair, the *Morning Chronicle* had never ceased to denounce confederation; but on the 15th of November it printed a leading article on 'The Union of the Colonies' with a message strangely different from that of innumerable previous editorials on the same subject.[36] The British government, the *Chronicle* admitted on this occasion, favoured British American union; but it was equally obvious that the Quebec scheme was unfair to the Maritime Provinces. In these circumstances, a new 'convention' or conference, in which all opinions as well as all provinces must be fairly represented, should be called to consider the collective future of British North America.

This, from a paper whose proprietor was the leader of the Nova Scotian Anti-Confederates, was a highly significant suggestion. The government papers greeted it with polite interest, a good deal of surprise, and a measure of scepticism. The *British Colonist* pointed out that what the *Chronicle* proposed for deciding the future of British North America was exactly the method that had already been tried in the Charlottetown and Quebec conferences.[37] If, however, the *Chronicle*'s actual proposal was viewed with a good deal of misgiving, the change of heart that must have prompted it was welcomed, if rather complacently; and the reasons that lay behind this altered opinion became the subject of a good deal of curious speculation. The *British Colonist* argued that it was the York by-election that had 'wrought this marvellous change' in the sentiments of the *Chronicle*'s proprietor, William Annand.[38] The *Unionist* aired the rumour that Annand's opposition to confederation had been weakening ever since the Colonial Secretary had told him, during the summer, that the imperial government had determined to go ahead with the union project and that he might just as well give up his resistance to it.[39]

It was exactly at this point that George Brown arrived in Halifax. His visit could hardly have been better timed. Annand had just revealed a new face in the *Chronicle*, and now, if ever, was the moment to approach him. Joseph Howe, it was true, wielded a potentially greater influence with his countrymen; but Howe had not yet returned to Nova Scotia, and, in any case, so long as he kept his official position as fisheries commissioner, it was quite impossible for him to take a prominent part in the Anti-Confederate movement. Annand was the man to see – Annand and Annand's associates and followers, including one William Miller, another Anti-Confederate member of the Assembly, who had also been visited by 'sober second thoughts' about confederation. Miller and Annand were key people who together might weaken the force, or even change the direction, of the Anti-Confederate opposition. As soon as Brown reached Halifax and had a preliminary talk with Tupper, the decisive move was made. Annand and Miller were invited to meet Brown at Tupper's house.

Miller could not come, but Annand accepted the invitation.[40] The fact that he went to Tupper's house that night and talked at length with Brown was another illustration, as striking as the *Chronicle*'s editorial of the 15th of November, that a strange and fundamental change had come over the Anti-Confederate opposition in Nova Scotia. Brown worked his hardest to take advantage of it. He urged Annand to accept confederation as the only politically possible form of British American union. He reminded him forcibly that the chance of making a real union was strictly limited in time. The annual session of the Canadian legislature could hardly be delayed longer than the spring or early summer of 1866; and if by that time the prospects for confederation were not obviously promising, the Coalition was pledged to give it up, to substitute a plan for the federal union of the Canadas alone, and to press that measure forward 'with all the influence of government'. Such a regional reorganization might exhaust the reforming zeal of the Canadians, leave the Maritime

Provinces in their accustomed isolation, and postpone union for a generation. But if Annand could only bring himself to accept the Quebec scheme in principle, a different and splendid prospect would open up, not only for British North America in general, but also for its noblest political expression, the Liberal party, and for the Liberal party's ablest leaders, including William Annand.

'I was reminded by Mr. Brown', Annand explained later, 'that I belonged to the old Liberal party, of which he had been for very many years the leader in Canada. I was approached by him in this way: "I have always sworn by the *Chronicle* and the *Nova Scotian*. We are all Liberals. They are in the ascendancy in Canada; they will also be in the ascendancy in Nova Scotia. Come up to Canada, and the Liberals will rule." '[41] Brown had come east to exploit the success of the York by-election and to reunite the forces favouring confederation throughout British America. He had done all this; but he had done it with careful attention to that other major interest, the fortunes of the Liberal party. Macdonald had made a party compact with Tupper at Quebec; Brown was intent upon making a party compact with Annand in Halifax. For nine months, through the March disputes about policy, the summer crisis over Taché's death, the North Wentworth by-election, and the mission to the Maritime Provinces, he had been playing his sectional and party game with unswerving and ceaseless diligence. He had ensured that, even if confederation failed, 'justice' would infallibly be done to Canada West. He had tried hard to make equally certain that, if confederation succeeded, its future would be dominated and its policies controlled by a united British American Liberal party.

⇛ III ⇚

ON THE 28TH OF NOVEMBER Brown left Nova Scotia for home. He had visited Saint John, Fredericton, and Halifax; but apparently he had never even considered going to Charlottetown or St. John's, Newfoundland. So far as Prince Edward Island was concerned, this total neglect was readily understandable. Ever since the conclusive legislative debates of the previous spring, not the slightest tremor of doubt or regret had disturbed the complacent inertia of the Island's resistance to confederation. Prince Edward Island, everybody assumed, would have to be written off for the moment. But Brown's disregard of Newfoundland was less easily explicable, for in Newfoundland a contest of sorts was going on, and going on, moreover, at the very time when he was rushing about on his Maritime mission. On the 6th of November, the day of the York by-election, and two days before he left Montreal for the east, nomination meetings were being held in a number of the constituencies in preparation for the Newfoundland general election.[42] And this was the general election which Hugh Hoyles had promised eight months before would decide the fate of confederation.

In fact it decided nothing. Despite all the circumstances that seemed to favour its success, confederation was not even made an issue in the election. Ambrose Shea and F. B. T. Carter had united to form a coalition government – much the strongest government, Governor Musgrave considered, since the introduction of responsible government into Newfoundland.[43] Premier Carter and his chief associate were both veterans of the Quebec Conference and ardent Unionists; and among the able members of their coalition ministry, there was a majority of convinced Confederates. But not even the combination of ministerial conviction and strong parliamentary support was enough to dispel Carter's and Shea's fears.[44] In the end they could not bring themselves to make confederation the avowed policy of the coalition. Confederation was not a general issue in the campaign, though it played a part, of greater or lesser importance, in many of the individual contests. In a number of constituencies, candidates stood bravely on their own record as Confederates; but unhappily they were outnumbered by other candidates who promised that they would 'renounce the advocacy of a measure' disliked by their constituents or who boasted proudly that they had taken 'every opportunity to denounce the scheme as ruinous to the best interests of the country'.[45] The *Newfoundlander*, which took comfort from the fact that most of the avowed Unionists had been returned, conceded that they would be in a slight minority in the Assembly.[46] Other newspapers gave still lower estimates of their strength; and Governor Musgrave regretfully predicted that the new Assembly would not consent to union on the Quebec terms.[47]

The Prince Edward Islanders and Newfoundlanders were not essential to confederation; but without New Brunswick confederation could not be. The whole future of British American union depended, as it had depended ever since the election of the previous March, upon a reversal of political fortunes in New Brunswick; and the chances of such a reversal, at least at the beginning, depended upon Arthur Hamilton Gordon and his relations with a small group of New Brunswick politicians, of whom A. J. Smith, R. D. Wilmot, Leonard Tilley, and Peter Mitchell, of the Legislative Council, were the chief. Gordon was pledged to carry confederation by every means in his power. His pride, his honour, his whole future career were all bound up in the achievement of success. He was determined to test confederation in the present House, or, if that failed, in a new House, after a second general election. His hopes – and, as usual, they were confident hopes – were based upon the obviously growing unpopularity of the Smith-Wilmot government, on Wilmot's conversion to confederation, Anglin's alienation from his colleagues, and Smith's unsettled and changing views about British American union. As Gordon saw it, he had two major alternatives. If Smith, the most prominent and popular man in the ministry, could be persuaded to go the length of accepting confederation in principle, then he and his colleagues could be entrusted with the task of sponsoring union resolutions in the present House. If, on the other hand, despite all his wavering, hesitant approaches to the Unionist faith, Smith remained obdurate to the end, a new government would unhappily become necessary, and, in all likelihood, some of the present ministers would join with other Confederates in or outside the legislature.

The key to the whole complex puzzle was Smith. He must either be won over or got rid of. And getting rid of him would involve a forceful change of government from which even Gordon shrank. A dangerous cabinet crisis seemed unavoidable. But was it? For a few light-hearted days, Gordon indulged the blissful hope that it was not. Robert Parker, who only a few weeks before had succeeded Sir James Carter as chief justice of the province, was now himself mortally ill; and Gordon, who was now quite ready to exploit the political value of patronage with a daring freedom that would have made seasoned New Brunswick politicians blink, had conceived the brilliant notion of making Albert J. Smith Judge Parker's successor. If Smith could only be lifted to the bench as chief justice, he would be removed instantly, completely, and for ever from all part and influence in New Brunswick politics. And the dwindling and dispirited Anti-Confederate forces of the province would have lost the one leader who could rally them.

On the 17th of November, the day after Brown left Fredericton, Gordon had a crucial interview with his Premier. By every means in his power, he strove to persuade him to accept the office of chief justice; and in the end the reluctant, undecided Smith seemed ready to consent. Gordon was convinced that, if Parker had been dead at that moment, Smith could have been sworn in on the spot as his successor.[48] But unfortunately Parker was still alive. If ever there was a suitable time for the Almighty to show his favour to His Servant Arthur by some special act of Providence, it was then. But the divine countenance remained hidden, or directed elsewhere, and Robert Parker was not immediately snatched to his reward. He enjoyed the dignity of his new office for an extremely short time; but, short though it was, it was just a little too long for the designs of Lieutenant-Governor Gordon. On the 17th of November, Gordon had virtually won Smith's consent; but Parker did not die until November the 28th, and during those fateful eleven days, Smith went away, conferred with his Anti-Confederate friends, and was loaded with reproaches for even considering their abandonment. When at length the dead Parker's position could be offered to him, he declined it.[49]

The swift, easy passage through which Gordon had hoped to escape from his perplexities remained obstinately closed. But the normal courses of provincial politics were still open to him; and, as the days shortened in Fredericton and the fearful winter closed relentlessly in once more, he thought he could see his way more clearly into the future. Anglin, that adamant provincialist, was obviously nearing the limit of his disgust and disappointment with the dispirited government of which he was a member. His main positive interest in public affairs was Western Extension; and, ever since the Smith government took office, the history of Western Extension had been a dismal record of deception and frustration. Despite all the fighting words of the last session, the government, faced with declining revenues and heavily depreciated provincial bonds, had not been able to borrow on the London market. It could not build Western Extension as a government work; and in the end it fell back lamely upon private enterprise, in the shape of an American firm – an arrangement which, to the disgusted Anglin, was not even a second-best alternative. He had always been suspicious of American companies, which, he insisted, had not the slightest intention of taking any risks themselves and would simply ride along on the money which they could manage to extract from the provincial treasury.[50] In cabinet meetings he expressed utter disbelief in the good faith of the American firm and in its ability to carry out the building of the railway.[51]

That autumn, with almost theatrical swiftness and completeness, his gloomy prophecies were realized. On the 8th of November, two days after Fisher won the York by-election, the first sod in the construction of Western Extension was officially turned, to the accompaniment of hopeful speeches by both Tilley and Smith.[52] It was a cold, wintry, dreary day, heavily overcast, and snow fell thickly on the forlorn little group of black-coated figures that huddled together protectively while the reluctant sod was wrenched with difficulty from the half-frozen earth. A small company of workmen attended to give a show of reality to these optimistic proceedings; but like theatrical extras, they were evidently hired for only a short engagement. For a few days they laboured; then they were laid off. Nothing more happened. It looked as if the company was finished. At any rate, Anglin was. Without any further delay, he submitted his resignation; and, as Gordon pointed out to the Colonial Secretary, this removed 'the most determined isolationist' from the cabinet.[53]

But Anglin was not its only disappointed and dissatisfied member. From the beginning, R. D. Wilmot, the joint leader and second in command, had been an equally unhappy and restive minister. Jealous perhaps of Smith, disagreeing with him over some of the original ministerial appointments, criticizing the Quebec scheme for reasons almost diametrically opposed to those of his colleagues, Wilmot was an uncomfortable man who had been contemplating and threatening resignation almost from the beginning of the ministry.[54] He had hoped that, as soon as the first session was over, he would inherit the agreeable sinecure of the auditor-generalship; but the legislature, in the most unkind fashion, reduced the salary of this post by $400, and Wilmot brooded angrily over this piece of spiteful ingratitude. His visit to Canada in September had convinced him that federalism was the only practical method of uniting British America; but when he returned to New Brunswick, he found the minds of many of his colleagues obstinately closed against this enlightenment from the west.[55] Finally, as the offensive culmination to a long list of affronts, came the appointment of the new chief justice, the successor to poor Robert Parker. Lemuel Allen Wilmot, Robert Duncan's cousin, was the senior surviving judge on the bench; and Robert was convinced that he had a firm, indisputable claim to the succession. But Lemuel Allen, either because of his present belief in confederation, or some past failure in the struggle for responsible government, was deliberately passed over. The government made William J. Ritchie the new chief justice; and R. D. Wilmot felt more intensely aggrieved than ever.

It was in this conflicting tangle of disagreements, resentments, and jealousies that Gordon saw the promise of success. The dispatch of the 24th of June had ordered him to bring the subject of confederation before the legislature at its next session and to express the imperial government's 'strong and deliberate' preference for a British American union. He had solemnly promised Cardwell to carry out his instructions with energy and conviction; and he realized that once again the hesitations and divisions of his cabinet gave him the opportunity of fulfilling his promise to the letter. Twice before he had taken advantage of his Council's weakness to impose his own preferred solution; and now, for the third time, these embarrassed and quarrelling New Brunswick politicians had provided him with the means of getting his own way, with every prospect of success. His plan, like all great plans, was beautiful in its simplicity.[56] He would simply insist that in the Speech from the Throne with which he opened the next session of the legislature, there must be included a paragraph recommending British American union to the consideration of the members and expressing the hope that it might be successfully accomplished. If Smith and his friends were prepared to accept responsibility for such a statement and to carry out the policy it foreshadowed, well and good. If not, he would simply seek new advisers. He had not the slightest doubt that he could find them – some, like Wilmot, inside the present government, others, like Peter Mitchell, outside it. A new combination of Confederates of both parties was a real possibility; but possibly also it would not be necessary to go this far. A long conversation that Gordon had with Smith in the late autumn left the Governor still hoping that his Premier might himself finally agree to sponsor union. If that solution were possible, Gordon infinitely preferred it. In those circumstances, the passage of union resolutions through the House would not 'wear the character of a party triumph', and could be carried through without a cabinet crisis or the turmoil and expense of an election.

Within a month of his return, Gordon had recovered his superb self-confidence. 'I am convinced', he wrote Cardwell, 'I can make (or buy) a union majority in the legislature' – possibly, he thought, in the present Assembly; if not, with virtual certainty in the next.[57]

⇾⟫ IV ⟪⇽

O N THE 12TH OF DECEMBER – not ten days after Gordon had written his hopeful dispatch to Cardwell – the Canadian cabinet assembled in Ottawa. By now the move from Quebec to the new capital was complete. Ottawa, with fewer than 20,000 inhabitants, was a raw frontier town; and the political importance which had suddenly been conferred upon it seemed not so much to elevate it as to complicate and perplex its character with startling incongruities. The great river, the shaggy forest to the north, the lonely, sombre blue sweep of the Laurentian Plateau at the horizon, formed an odd, primitive setting for the focus of national law and order. The rough operations of the lumber trade – the stacks of boards, the piles of sawdust, the rafts and slabs that choked the river – were like a rude affront to the traditional grandeur of the new structures that crowned Parliament Hill. The Parliament Buildings, spacious and ornate in their grandiose Victorian Gothic, looked down condescendingly upon the rather slatternly rows of humble clapboarded cottages that straggled along the sides of the wide streets of Lower Town. Even Parliament Hill had a primordial look about it. The huge blocks of unused stone and the piles of builder's rubbish that cluttered the forecourt were like the detritus of some moraine of the ice age.

Ottawa was not only simple and rude in character; it was also a northerly town with a harsh climate. When the ministers arrived in December, they found the streams about the capital fast frozen and horses drawing sleighs across the Ottawa. Two days later, snow began falling heavily from a leaden, windy sky. The wondrous steam-heating system which warmed the huge rooms and the echoing, cavernous corridors of the new buildings was disconcertingly capricious; and beyond Parliament Hill, the hotels and houses of the real Ottawa seemed primitive and comfortless places. George Brown thought his hotel a very poor affair, with a decidedly 'indifferent' table.[58] Fresh from the cosy amenities of Oak Lodge in Toronto, he told his wife Anne very firmly that she must not even think of coming down with him to Ottawa until they could get a house of their own. Macdonald had already leased a modest house, one of a terrace at the corner of Daly and Cumberland streets, where he, Galt, Brydges of the Grand Trunk Railway, and Macdonald's future brother-in-law, Hewitt Bernard, were to live at intervals for the next few years.[59]

The Christmas season was near, and the ministers hoped to get away from the capital by Saturday, the 16th of December. But it was not to be. 'We have so many disputed points to argue out and settle,' Brown told his wife ominously on Saturday.[60] In fact, there was only one major point at issue – the renewal of the Reciprocity Treaty; and once again, Galt and Brown, those two assertive and hypersensitive rivals, were the principals involved. In November, at the invitation of David Wells, the Chairman of the United States Revenue Commission, Galt had gone down to New York to discuss the terms of a new trade agreement between the two countries. He had gone, of course, on the authority of Council, and actually at Brown's own suggestion; but Brown, with his fixed conviction of Galt's imprudence and pliability as an ambassador, had assumed that the Finance Minister would limit his visit to talks with the Revenue Commissioners in New York.[61] Galt had not done so. On Wells's advice he had gone on to Washington. He had seen Sir Frederick Bruce, the British Minister, and with his sanction had had long discussions with McCulloch, the Secretary of the Treasury, Seward, the Secretary of State, and J. S. Morrill, the principal author of the war-time American tariff of 1861.[62]

But in Brown's scandalized eyes even this was not the sum of Galt's enormities. The Finance Minister had gone much further. He had naïvely and tamely accepted the American officials' assertion that a renewal of the Reciprocity Treaty was out of the question. It was true, of course, that this had been their unvarying opinion; they had all insisted that any new trade agreement must be carried out, not by treaty, but by the concurrent or reciprocal legislation of British North America on the one hand and the United States on the other. In the end Galt had been forced to accept their contention; but he had not done so without protest. He had criticized the efficacy of concurrent legislation by the various parliaments concerned. He had pointed out that some parts of the Reciprocity Treaty – the sections relating to the inshore fisheries and the navigation of the St. Lawrence – could be dealt with only by treaty, and he had argued that legislation by Congress and the legislatures of five separate British American provinces would be a difficult and ticklish procedure.[63] The Americans swept these objections aside brusquely. The fisheries, they declared, were not a matter of great importance, and they were not very much interested in the trade of the Maritime Provinces.

To Galt it seemed that an impasse had been reached. Either

some concessions must be made, or all hope of a trade agreement with the United States was ended. Canada might have to agree to the doubtful method of concurrent legislation; and she might have to accept some of the financial demands that the United States was making as a result of the burden of its huge war-time debt. The heavy customs or excise duties that the Republic had imposed on whisky, tea, tobacco, and sugar were being systematically evaded, the Americans charged, by large-scale smuggling from Canada; but, if Canada were willing to equalize – or, as they put it, 'assimilate' – its duties on these taxable articles with those of the United States, then smuggling would cease to pay and the treasury would profit. Galt listened sympathetically to these suggestions, and, stressing the fact that his mission was purely unofficial and exploratory and that he was making no definite proposals, he indicated that Canada would be willing to consider the 'assimilation' of the duties on a few articles of key importance. As for the scope of the trade agreement, some manufactures, he suggested, as well as natural products could be included in the free list or admitted at low rates of duty. The navigation of the Great Lakes and the St. Lawrence might be placed 'on a footing of perfect equality' and the coasting trade of both nations opened to the ships of either.[64]

Brown listened to Galt's fluent, confident report of his proceedings with mounting consternation and disapproval. Forcefully and at length, he disputed the Minister of Finance's request for a Minute of Council that would confirm his negotiations and authorize him to continue along the same lines. Galt, he charged angrily, had showered the Americans in advance with 'every concession we had in our power to make'. Despite the commitments made to the Maritime Provinces at the time of the Confederate Council on Trade, he had taken it upon himself to settle the basis of a new trade agreement 'without one word of communication with any of the sister colonies'. He had supinely accepted the iniquitous principle of 'reciprocal legislation', condemning the Canadian people to the ignoble role of 'dangling from year to year' upon the caprice of the American Congress and 'looking to Washington instead of Ottawa as the controller of their commerce and prosperity'.[65]

Under this sustained and concentrated fusillade, Galt and his supporters retreated a little. The offending Minute of Council was drastically revised. The new version omitted the detailed terms for which Galt had sought approval, emphasized the difficulties in the way of concurrent legislation, and authorized co-operation with the Maritime Provinces.[66] A second member of Council was to assist the Minister of Finance in his future negotiations, in order apparently to control the rashness of which Brown complained. But it was Howland whom Galt nominated as his associate; and, although Howland, at Brown's own suggestion, had accompanied Galt on his first pilgrimage to Washington, Brown now chose to regard his nomination as 'a direct personal affront' to himself.[67] He was willing, he declared, to accept 'the snub'; he would not reject Galt's draft because of it. But the fatal defect of the proposed Minute of Council – its implied acceptance of the idea of reciprocal or concurrent legislation – remained. Brown would not endorse it. And as soon as the long wrangling debate had ended in the passage of Galt's draft, he got up and walked out of the room.

Howland, who thought the issue Brown had raised 'a question of very little importance', followed his old leader back to his lodgings and begged him to reconsider his course.[68] Campbell and Cartier called on him next day at the Russell Hotel in the hope of persuading him to change his mind. It was all useless. He would not withdraw his resignation. He was convinced that 'a very great blunder has been committed in a matter involving the most important interests of our country'.[69] It was a disagreement over policy, but also – and perhaps more importantly – it was a clash between temperamentally incompatible personalities. Brown's jealousy of Galt, his rivalry with Macdonald, his imperious urge towards domination, his impatient distaste for the compromises and frustrations of political life, the irrepressible longing which he always felt for his far more satisfactory existence as publisher, landed proprietor, husband and father – all these played their part in the crucial decision of December the 19th. It was the whole Brown – the Brown who acted both on impulse and principle – who had determined to resign.

If that resignation had been submitted four months before,

at the time of the Taché crisis, it would almost certainly have broken up the Coalition and ruined the hopes of union; but now it had no such disastrous consequences. In August, the dispute had raged over the composition and leadership of the government; the issue in December was a trade agreement which, Brown freely admitted, was much less important than confederation. 'In conclusion', he wrote to Cartier, 'let me say that if you stick to the compact that you made with me when Sir Narcisse came into the government – my being out of the government will not change my course in the slightest, and that you will have my best aid in carrying out the constitutional changes we were then pledged to.'[70] In this pointed reminder of the agreement that, even if confederation failed, 'justice' must be done to Canada West, there was a steely hint of Brown's inflexible devotion to his sectional cause; and, as Cartier and the others were well aware, the Canadian parliament would have to meet within the next six months. If the miracle in New Brunswick did not happen within that time, Brown would certainly insist on the smaller federation. Even if the Unionists regained power in Fredericton, and confederation seemed assured, he might feel perfectly free to attack the Coalition on other grounds than its union policy; and if he thus openly returned to the opposition, he might, if the issue seemed big enough, take the bulk of the western Reformers with him, break up the Coalition, and frustrate confederation before it could be realized. On the surface, this did not seem a very probable danger. Brown had told his wife that he and his colleagues were not parting in anger;[71] the *Globe* repeated these assurances; and, even more important, the solidarity of the Coalition did not seem in the least unsettled by his resignation. Howland remained in the government, and McDougall, who was then away on a trade mission to the West Indies, followed his example. A meeting of the reform members, which Howland called at Guelph, pledged continued Reform support for the ministry; and Fergusson Blair took Brown's place as the third Grit minister in the Coalition.[72]

Yet, despite all these assurances, the ultimate meaning of Brown's resignation remained disturbingly ambiguous. A perceptible tremor had disturbed the precarious stability of Confederate hopes. Confederation, a new issue in the political stock market, was apt to fluctuate widely under the slightest influence; and with the news of George Brown's resignation, it dropped a few points. Unfortunately, this was not the first sign of weakness that it had shown during December. The news of the Newfoundland general election, which by now was known generally throughout British America, had had a depressing effect; and the brilliant triumph of the Confederates in the York by-election in New Brunswick was now partly obscured by their dismal defeat in the Lunenburg by-election in Nova Scotia. Lieutenant-Governor Williams, who thought the contest in Lunenburg a crucial one, looked forward to it with apprehension. A new dispatch from Cardwell, with a new exhortation to loyal Nova Scotians to support confederation, would, he hoped, work wonders with the electorate.[73] But it turned out differently. The Lunenburg voters perversely rejected the Colonial Secretary's good advice. 'Well done electors of Lunenburg!' cried the *Morning Chronicle* jubilantly. 'Who will say, after this, that there is any large party in this Province favourable to Confederation?'[74]

⫸ V ⫷

IF NO 'LARGE PARTY favourable to confederation' existed, what hope was there now of that rival programme upon which A. J. Smith and other Maritime Anti-Confederates had staked their fortunes? The Western Extension project had ignominiously collapsed. The prospects for a renewal of the Reciprocity Treaty could hardly have looked grimmer; and early in January the British American governments prepared for the final encounter in Washington with official hope but with hardly any real conviction.

The Reciprocity negotiations had already caused one ministerial resignation in Canada; they now helped to precipitate a second in New Brunswick. Nova Scotia appointed W. A. Henry and New Brunswick A. J. Smith as their representatives at the Washington talks. Neither delegate had been a member of the

Confederate Council on Trade at Quebec; and Smith's appointment had been made when R. D. Wilmot was absent from Council, on a sick-bed. Wilmot, when he learnt the news from a newspaper, was furious.[75] This, he felt indignantly, was the intolerable climax of the long list of slights, discourtesies, and injuries he and his family had suffered at the hands of his own government. It was Wilmot, not Smith, who had gone to the Confederate Council at Quebec. Wilmot, not Smith, ought to have been authorized to go to Washington. The appointment of Smith, he told Gordon angrily, was 'such an act of discourtesy and want of confidence' as to clinch his determination to leave the government. Already, on January the 4th, he had sent in his resignation, stressing his new inclination to confederation.[76] He now confirmed it.

To Gordon, critically scrutinizing, sensitively weighing every factor favourable to confederation, this abrupt move on Wilmot's part came as a distinct embarrassment. The fairly simple, straightforward scheme he had devised for forcing the issue was now complicated by Wilmot's premature resignation. The Lieutenant-Governor had planned to insist upon the insertion, in the Speech from the Throne, of a paragraph strongly advocating union. If his present Council was prepared as a whole to accept responsibility for such a paragraph, and to act upon it, that, of course, would be the easiest way out. But if not, and if the cabinet divided, then its Confederate division, along with some Unionist members of the former Council, would be asked to form a government to carry confederation. The plan was simple, with a clean-cut choice of alternatives; but it largely depended for its success upon Wilmot as the leader of the Confederate sympathizers in the ministry. Wilmot's determination to resign did not, of course, destroy his usefulness to the Lieutenant-Governor; but if his resignation were accepted now, it would abruptly precipitate the ministerial crisis upon which Gordon counted.[77] Wilmot, along with Smith, was joint premier of the province; and his withdrawal from the ministry could be used as a justification for its dismissal and the formation of a new government. Was such a brusque, drastic viceregal intervention necessary or desirable? Or had he better wait until the drafting of the Speech from the

Throne provided an unforced and natural occasion for a ministerial break-up?

Long and carefully, he studied the alternatives. Some delay at least was essential. He postponed his reply to Wilmot for a few days; and then, when Smith was safely on his way to Washington, he wrote saying that Wilmot's letter raised important issues which he must discuss with the President of the Council and that therefore he could not accept or refuse the proffered resignation until Smith's return.[78] Really, he told himself grimly, he could scarcely dismiss a ministry when one of its principals was out of the country! And besides, though every day did not noticeably add to the popularity of confederation, it at least increased the unpopularity of the Smith government. Nothing, certainly, could be done until Smith was back in Fredericton. But then a sudden move was possible, and might be desirable. And it was best to be prepared. With a nonchalant disregard for the constitutional niceties of responsible government, he talked the whole business over confidentially with such prominent members of the late government as Peter Mitchell and Leonard Tilley.[79] Wilmot and Mitchell, he made certain, were prepared to form a Confederate government, with the warm support of Tilley, who was still without a seat in the Assembly. Strengthened by these assurances, he prepared for action. 'We are on the eve of a crisis here,' Tilley wrote hopefully to Macdonald.[80]

Over in Halifax, and almost as anxiously, Sir William Fenwick Williams, the new Lieutenant-Governor of Nova Scotia, was also peering into the future. Outwardly, to the Haligonians who visited Government House, he seemed a bluff, hearty, affable old warrior, with a manner that suggested brusque impatience and impetuous action; but within, the tug of a highly developed caution kept him in due restraint. As he watched provincial affairs with a curious but critical interest, he could detect a few more unmistakable signs of growing favour for confederation. One of the most important of these was the appearance, in that fanatical Anti-Confederate newspaper, the *Morning Chronicle*, of still another leading article on British American union. In it, the editor argued that the collective future of British America was a matter of urgency, that if the provinces wished to preserve an identity separate from that of the United States, they must seriously reconsider their relations, and that the only way to do this was by a new 'convention' under the sanction of the Crown.[81] It was true that a few days later, in a further editorial, the *Chronicle* pronounced the Quebec scheme 'virtually dead', and insisted that 'the work must be commenced *de novo*';[82] but despite these reservations it was plain that the Anti-Confederates in Nova Scotia, like those in New Brunswick, were dropping their isolationist, separatist notions and accepting the principle of British American union. The Confederate newspapers, the *Unionist* and the *British Colonist*, greeted these signs of repentance with what the *Unionist* described as 'a cheerful, hearty amen'.[83] Williams himself was pleased but not completely reassured. He was by no means out of the woods yet. The legislature, he was sure, would still require 'gentle handling'. 'High-sounding phrases' about confederation in the Speech from the Throne would, he felt, be distinctly out of place.[84]

In Nova Scotia, as well as in New Brunswick, the opening of the legislature would have to be delayed until the return of the delegates from Washington. The fate of the Reciprocity Treaty was a vital matter for both provinces. It was almost certain to have a serious effect, one way or the other, upon the fortunes of confederation; and everybody awaited the results of the negotiations with curious interest. Unfortunately, the concern shared by both Maritimers and Canadians found not the slightest echo south of the international boundary. A fortnight's perfunctory discussions in Washington were enough to expose the hollow futility of the great dispute between Alexander Galt and George Brown. Brown had contended that a new treaty was possible. Galt had argued that the dubious method of reciprocal legislation would probably have to be accepted. Both were wrong, but Brown much more ludicrously so than his rival. There was, in fact, not the slightest chance that the United States would negotiate a liberal trade agreement with British North America, either by treaty or by any other method. The Republic, its political nationalism intensified by war and its economic nationalism hardened by debt, could hardly have cared less about trade with the northern provinces. It was not interested in lowering customs duties; it was interested solely in collecting revenue. Brown divined the truth, though he was too angry to notice its implications for his vain hope of a treaty. All the Americans wanted, he told Monck bitterly, was an arrangement by which they could 'have our aid in collecting their revenues – the one sole thing they are now bent on'.[85]

The end was inevitable and it came quickly. The negotiation of a new treaty was not given a moment's consideration. The American government washed its hands of the whole business immediately. All it would do was to introduce the British Americans to the members of the Committee of Ways and Means of the House of Representatives – a committee of which the formidable Morrill was chairman; and from the beginning the only hope left to the Maritimers and Canadians was that something of the treaty might be saved by legislation. For a few days, Morrill monopolized the desultory discussion, scoring debating points, depreciating British American productions, glorifying the advantages of the American market, and making pleasant little jokes about the annexation of the northern provinces to the United States.[86] When he had had enough of this one-sided sparring, he produced a short list of what the United States expected and was prepared to concede by way of concurrent legislation. Only four articles – rags, firewood, unground gypsum or plaster, and unfinished grindstones or millstones – were included in the free list; and all the other natural products, which had entered the Republic untaxed under the Reciprocity Treaty, were now subject to stiff or prohibitive duties. Galt said wearily that there was such a difference in their views that prolonged discussion would only waste time for both of them. Henry urbanely invited the Americans to pay a visit to Nova Scotia. And then, after a little chat, it was all over.

The hope of a good trade agreement, like the hope for Western Extension, had been dashed, and apparently for good. The bottom had been knocked out of Smith's plan for closer railway and commercial connections with the United States; and, as the news of the failure of the negotiations at Washington sped across the province, the *New Brunswick Reporter* reflected complacently how grossly the Anti-Confederates had been deceived in their belief in a possible 'offset' to confederation.[87] Smith was expected back in Fredericton on February the 13th; and the day before, Gordon wrote another of his long confidential dispatches to the Colonial Secretary.[88] He was not so sure now as he had been about the future. What was he to do? The Canadians, whose time was inexorably running out, were pressing him for action. Should he force a decision now? Could he persuade Smith to sponsor union?

CHAPTER TWELVE

The Last Chance

A YEAR BEFORE, in the winter of 1865, Canada had started out at the head of what it was hoped would be a procession of five British American provinces, all bound towards the ratification of the Quebec scheme. What an enormous change a single year had brought! Now there was no certainty that even the smallest Unionist parade could be formed. The original objective – the passage of the Seventy-two Resolutions – had been tacitly abandoned in the Maritime Provinces, and the Confederates there had been forced to define their purpose in much more general terms. Even the sequence of the parliamentary openings was significantly altered. Canada, the leader in 1865, was certain to delay as long as possible in the hope of the long-promised reversal in New Brunswick. Prince Edward Island, which had brought up the rear on the previous occasion, was likely to be late again; but its place in the queue hardly mattered, for most people expected it to repeat, with emphasis, its objection to union of any kind. Nova Scotia and New Brunswick both had had to postpone their openings slightly, as a result of the Reciprocity negotiations. And so it was that Newfoundland, a remote and highly unlikely candidate for union, found itself at the head of the legislative procession of 1866.

Apart from Prince Edward Island, a more inappropriate and uninspiring leader could hardly have been selected. The general election of the autumn of 1865, which was supposed to settle the issue of confederation in Newfoundland, had in fact settled nothing. All that the Confederates could hope to do, Musgrave

346

reported, was to guard against an adverse vote, to prevent the legislature from committing itself on the question of union before it got some encouragement in the right direction from the other Atlantic provinces.[1] Obviously Newfoundland should have taken its place at the end, not the beginning, of the parade; and on the 30th of January, when the Lieutenant-Governor opened the legislature, the uncertainty and indecision of the Carter government became painfully apparent. In his Speech from the Throne, Musgrave hopefully advanced the cautious thesis that the abstract advantages of union were incontestable and the question of equitable terms alone in doubt;[2] but even this prudently academic proposition was roughly handled. Two proposed rejoinders to the paragraph on union – rejoinders which would have meant the rejection or indefinite postponement of confederation – were defeated on the initiative of government; but the Address that finally passed the House was scarcely more encouraging. It admitted the advantages of union, but stressed the differences of opinion about terms, and ended by declaring that the Assembly could not attempt to reconcile these differences now.[3]

Newfoundland was a very improbable follower of union; she was an impossible leader. The two mainland colonies, Nova Scotia and New Brunswick, were the only two Maritime Provinces that were at all likely now to decide in favour of confederation. And – what was equally important – the sessions about to open were the last sessions in which they could declare for union with any hope of its realization in the near future. Further delay was quite impossible; two apparently unalterable circumstances prevented it. The first of these was the time limit that the Canadian Coalition had imposed on its struggle for British American union; the second, as yet not much appreciated outside Nova Scotia, was the approaching end of the Nova Scotian legislature. The existing Assembly, which had been elected in the spring of 1863, had the usual four years to run; and, if confederation was not achieved in the meantime, a dissolution and a general election were inevitable in May of 1867.[4] A fourth and final session of parliament in the winter of 1867 was, of course, quite possible; but it would be just as difficult and dangerous for Tupper to attempt to push confederation through then as it would have been for Tilley to do so in the winter of 1865. No, there was no possible escape from the clutch of these circumstances. This was the last chance.

Gordon at Fredericton and Williams at Halifax were both aware of the fact. Cardwell's instructions required them to submit the union scheme to their respective parliaments in the coming session; and they both realized that within the next few months, a decision one way or the another was inevitable. Their goals were the same; but the courses by which they sought to approach them differed significantly. Gordon had everything to gain and Williams much to lose by a political crisis. A change of government and a general election might very well ruin confederation in Nova Scotia; but they would almost certainly improve its chances in New Brunswick. The resignations of Wilmot and Anglin, the failure of Reciprocity and Western Extension, Smith's changing opinions about union, and the growing discredit and unpopularity of the Smith-Wilmot government all strengthened Gordon's hand. On his side also were his youth, his superb confidence in himself, and his fixed determination to fulfil his promise to Cardwell, to retrieve his damaged reputation in the colonial service. Williams was a much older and more cautious man. The circumstances in Nova Scotia, which seemed to show a slight improvement in the prospects for confederation, suggested delay rather than action. Privately he and his advisers decided that the impetuous Gordon should take the lead and that the Lieutenant-Governor of Nova Scotia should follow discreetly after.

Gordon was eager to begin. The issue had now been postponed long enough; and if he were ever to make use of Wilmot's suspended resignation, he must do so soon. On the 15th of February, the day after Smith's return to Fredericton, he tackled his Premier firmly; and there began a long discussion – a discussion which, with intervals, lasted three days and involved most of the other members of the Executive Council.[5] Gordon put his proposal to Smith in the form he had already determined upon. He told him that the approaching opening of parliament, now set for the 8th of March, made it necessary that he should have a 'distinct' understanding with his advisers, without delay. Then he presented his alternatives. Would the present ministry accept responsibility for a union policy, or would it not? If Smith and his colleagues were willing to include a paragraph favouring union in the Speech from the Throne, then Wilmot's resignation could be accepted. If, on the other hand, they declined this choice, Wilmot's resignation would have to be refused and Wilmot himself would be invited, along with others, to take part in a new government which would sponsor the union scheme.[6]

It was an ultimatum – peremptory and uncompromising. And Gordon made only one modification of its bluntness: a union policy, he indicated, need not necessarily be the Quebec scheme in its entirety. He confidently believed, he told his Premier, that if the Quebec Resolutions were accepted as a basis, the imperial government would no doubt be willing to consider amendments in detail. As Gordon knew very well, the Canadian legislature had adopted the Quebec scheme without changing a single word, and the Colonial Office was supporting it with increasing emphasis and fervour. But the British government had by no means closed the door on all possibility of change; and he felt free to discuss with Smith the changes the latter would consider satisfactory. Their understanding of these conversations differed, as time was to show; but they agreed on two important points. Like the Prince Edward Islanders at Quebec, Smith disliked both representation by population as a basis for the House of Commons and 'regional' representation as the guiding principle in the composition of the legislative council. But Gordon apparently succeeded in persuading him that the Canadians would never give up Rep. by Pop.; and finally Smith seems to have agreed to concede this point if, in compensation, New Brunswick were given a larger representation in the legislative council.[7]

At last, after prolonged consultations with his colleagues, Smith came back with a portentous announcement. He would agree to the Lieutenant-Governor's proposal. He would accept responsibility for a paragraph on union in the Speech from the Throne. The principle of union was no longer in doubt; what troubled him apparently was not the end but the means. The real difficulty – and Gordon admitted it was acute – lay in the problem of finding a method of making such a drastic change of policy without incurring charges of inconsistency, deception, or even betrayal. Finally, it was agreed that the whole matter should be referred to a joint committee of the two houses of the legislature, 'with an understanding that it should report in favour of a measure of union'.[8] Gordon insisted that the committee must be regarded as purely *pro forma* – a mere face-saving device for the government. Smith replied that he could hardly bind the committee in advance; but he assured the Governor that in accepting the paragraph in the Speech from the Throne, his purpose was to carry out the policy of union.

The bargain was not yet concluded, however. Both parties felt the need of further reassurance about the strange compact they were making. Gordon wanted to talk the arrangement over with Monck in Canada. Smith knew he had to make certain of the support of the Anti-Confederate members in the Assembly. His colleagues in the government had given their consent; but whether or not his supporters in the House and his friends in the constituencies would follow him so readily was another and a much more difficult question. He had to make sure; and he left Fredericton at once, with the idea of consulting as many members as he could in and about Saint John and in his own county of Westmorland.[9] Less than a week later, Gordon departed for Montreal.

His departure coincided with the opening of the legislature at Halifax. For a gallant old soldier, the 'hero of Kars', it was a remarkably tame, not to say timorous, opening. Tupper and the Nova Scotian cabinet had confidently expected that New Brunswick would move first; and Williams was highly disconcerted to find himself out in front, conspicuously leading the van. He had already warned Gordon that he did not intend to use any 'high sounding phrases' about confederation in his Speech from the Throne. In the end he decided to take even more stringent precautions; he would simply not make any mention of confederation at all in his Speech! A last-moment appeal, made by Gordon just before he left the province for Montreal, failed to change his mind;[10] and on the 22nd of February, when he opened parliament at Halifax, he kept a complete silence on the most important issue of the day – the issue which, everybody expected, must be decided one way or another within the next few months.[11]

Gordon was angry, Monck shocked. Gordon complained bitterly to Cardwell that Williams's silence had 'seriously added to my embarrassment';[12] and Monck gravely reminded Williams that Smith and Company in New Brunswick might very reasonably complain that they had been forced to accept a paragraph on confederation on the orders of the Colonial Secretary, when the government of Nova Scotia had disobeyed the same instructions with complete impunity.[13] Williams was somewhat abashed, but unconvinced and unrepentant. Only quite recently Cardwell had agreed with him that, so far as he could judge the matter accurately, New Brunswick 'should move first'.[14] And, as he informed Gordon bluntly, he was simply obeying orders. He reminded Cardwell that a majority in the Assembly was still hostile to confederation. He told him he was convinced that if he had brought the subject up at the very beginning of the legislature, his government would have suffered a defeat before Gordon and Smith could have made a start on their campaign.[15] 'It is evident', he wrote stoutly to Cardwell, 'that the *initiative* rests in the hands of Mr. Gordon, and indeed I am instructed by you to follow his lead.'[16]

Gordon was willing enough to take the initiative; but he wanted to talk the whole problem over with the Governor General before he finally closed with Smith. Advice was all that Monck could possibly give him. When the news of Gordon's intended visit arrived in Canada, he had hurriedly replied 'no' by telegraph. He had followed this up with a letter candidly informing Gordon that if his purpose in coming north-west was to get Canadian consent to some modifications of the Quebec scheme, his mission was certain to have no results.[17] The only remaining hope of change, he reminded the Lieutenant-Governor, lay in the final judgment of the imperial government. He could not strengthen Gordon's position, or increase his bargaining power; but as between Smith and some other government leader or leaders, there was no doubt where his preference lay. If at all possible, he reasoned, the incalculable risks of a change of government and a general election must be avoided.

He much preferred to see union carried in New Brunswick through the 'agency', as he put it, of the present government.[18]

With all this Gordon was more and more inclined to agree. His decision was based partly on the same politic reasons that had convinced Monck, and partly on preferences and inclinations that lay deep in his intense and emotional personality. He felt increasingly that he could trust his present ministers. His self-confidence, as always, was almost boundless. He rated his influence with his cabinet very high. He had liked most of its members from the beginning; and the very fact that they had opposed the hated Quebec scheme, and opposed it – some of them – for reasons exactly the same as his own, inclined him in their favour. He had enjoyed working with them more than with any other group of ministers since he had come to the province; and, strangest of all, his former emphatic dislike of Smith, the man he had once acknowledged as his greatest enemy in the province, had mysteriously vanished. He now thought him honest and agreeably amenable to persuasion. He believed he could control him. He did not know – or he forgot – that Smith could be both stubborn and devious.

When Gordon and Smith met again in Fredericton on the 3rd of March, they had both made up their minds.[19] Gordon knew now, better than ever, that he could not commit the Canadian Coalition to changes in the Quebec scheme; but he agreed – and no doubt sincerely, for he had strong views about the important part that the British government could and should play in the making of British American union – that amendments could be suggested and submitted to the arbitrament of the imperial cabinet and Parliament. Smith on his part reported that the Anti-Confederate party seemed ready to approve the strange new course he proposed to follow. There was a slight struggle over the wording of the paragraph on union in the Speech; and the tenacity with which Smith fought to avoid any definite commitment on the part of his government must have left Gordon with a slight feeling of uneasiness.[20] But there was no turning back now; and on the 8th of March, in the low, clapboarded, white-painted Provincial Building in Fredericton, the Lieutenant-Governor read the decisive words: 'and I am further directed to express to you the strong and deliberate opinion of Her Majesty's government, that it is an object much to be desired, that all the British North American colonies should agree to unite in one government.'[21]

⋙ II ⋘

LESS THAN A FORTNIGHT LATER came the 17th of March, a day much marked in Canada and New Brunswick as a result of the great Irish immigration of the mid-century. It would be even more particularly marked this year, for by an odd chance the Reciprocity Treaty was to come to an end on the 17th. British Americans looked forward to the day with some gloom and anxiety for that very reason; but not for that reason alone. St. Patrick's Day, 1866, might, it was rumoured, bring a much more terribly appropriate disaster. On that day, the Fenians might launch an invasion, or invasions, of British North America.

During the winter of 1865-6, the Fenian agitation in the United States reached its frenzied climax. John O'Mahony, the original but deposed 'Head-Centre' of the 'Brotherhood' called a 'convention' of his followers in January. In February, William R. Roberts, the successful usurper, assembled his faction in a second, grandiloquently competing 'convention'. O'Mahony, a conservative strategist, still believed in the original plan of fomenting rebellion in Ireland; but his vigorous lieutenant, B. D. Killian, favoured a flank attack on British power in North America; and Roberts and his second in command, W. R. Sweeny, had from the beginning preached the great new gospel of northern invasion and conquest. Both factions were thus gnashing their teeth fiercely at British America; and throughout the winter they kept up their frantic competition for prestige and support. They sought to excel each other in threats, boasts, defiances, and every other possible evidence of vast plans, overwhelming strength, and reckless bravery. Much, but not all, of this was verbal bombast; and as the 17th of March drew closer, the British American intelligence of Fenian movements grew more alarming. On the 12th, Gordon wrote to Cardwell that the rumours of a Fenian raid were growing in 'strength and consistency'.[22] On the same day, McMicken, the western chief of the Canadian intelligence, dispatched an even more urgent message to Macdonald. 'Information just received', he telegraphed, 'very positive for general move on the frontier on or about 17th.'[23]

On March the 7th, the Canadian government had called up 10,000 volunteers. This mobilization, which aroused a popular response even greater than that of the troop movements of December 1864, and recalled the patriotic enthusiasms of the *Trent* crisis, produced an immense sensation throughout British America. Ten days later, on St. Patrick's Day itself, Nova Scotia summoned its militia for duty. In New Brunswick, Gordon had been happily busy all winter organizing the defences of the province. 'New Brunswick is, as you know,' he wrote later to a friend, 'a very democratic country, but it was amusing to see how in such a crisis all power and control naturally fell into one's hands.'[24] If military control could be said to have 'fallen naturally' into Gordon's hands, he certainly grasped and held it there with jealous and monopolizing tenacity. Accompanied only by his favourite aide-de-camp, he travelled by sleigh over hundreds of miles of snowy country roads, visiting frontier towns and communities, reassuring local authorities, speaking at mass meetings, organizing home guards and companies of volunteers. When March arrived, these amateur soldiers had developed a fine martial spirit and acquired at least a semblance of training; but by that time the growing danger seemed to demand more general preparations. On the 16th of March, in a special message to the Assembly, the Lieutenant-Governor announced the calling up of part of the militia; and Smith, Fisher, and Anglin joined in declaring that the House would act as one man in strengthening the hands of government for the defence of the province.[25]

Ever since the autumn, the Fenian menace had been Charles Fisher's specialty. He had used it with shameless excess in the York by-election; and when the session opened he still considered it the most effective weapon with which to attack Smith's Anti-Confederate government. What other public issue was available? He could hardly try to outdo the Speech from the Throne by urging the immediate adoption of confederation, when he had publicly sworn during the York by-election that he would not do so until after another general election. He could scarcely put himself in the outrageously equivocal position of attacking the Premier as a Unionist, though he and the other Confederates were already a little fearful that Smith might run away with the leadership of their cause. He could jeer at ministerial inconsistencies and ask Smith tauntingly where he stood now. But that was as far as he could go. No, it would have to be the Fenians. And so, when he got up to propose his amendment to the Address, it was on the fourth paragraph – the paragraph that dealt with the Fenians – that he moved his want-of-confidence motion.[26]

The prolonged debate that followed, like most debates on the Address in reply to the Speech from the Throne, ransacked the remotest corners of provincial affairs. The focus of attack was Fenianism; but unquestionably the main subject of argument was British American union. Fisher established the theme of inconsistency and deception; loudly he sounded the tone of inquisition and challenge. Every possible criticism was hurled into his prolonged indictment of the government; but it was his insistent rasping questions – what did the paragraph on union mean? when and why had the ministry changed its mind? – that arrested attention and provoked response.[27] In short order a single ambiguous sentence in the Speech from the Throne became the cause or pretext of speculations, insinuations, charges, and counter-charges. At the beginning of the session, the government papers had complacently observed that, despite all the rumours of viceregal pressure on Smith and his colleagues, the paragraph on union had turned out to be a very tame and innocuous affair.[28] But it soon became clear that a good many people, including a number of former Anti-Confederate members of the Assembly, did not see it in this pleasant light at all.

DesBrisay, of Kent, began the defections. He told the House that when he had read the paragraph on union, he felt completely 'absolved from any tie to the government'.[29] Gilbert, who came from Smith's own county of Westmorland, and Wetmore, who had headed the poll for the Anti-Confederates in Saint John City, both attacked the ministry for the evasions and inconsistencies of its union policy. Wilmot, who explained at length the reasons for his conversion to confederation, predicted that the notorious paragraph must surely foreshadow the submission of some new plan, the Smith plan, of union;[30] and the newspapers were already speculating jocosely about the nature of the 'Dorchester scheme' (Smith came from Dorchester) as contrasted with the Quebec scheme of confederation.[31] Gordon assured Cardwell that the ministers were losing Anti-Confederates without gaining Confederates by their ambiguous course.[32] Including Fisher and Wilmot, the Unionist strength in the Assembly had been increased by at least half a dozen members; and the original hopeless disparity was gone.

Smith felt himself beset as he had never been before. He behaved like a man whose political career was at stake. He was constantly interrupting other speakers, constantly on his feet, attacking his adversaries and desperately trying to maintain the offensive. His wide, plump, jowly face, with its sprouting side whiskers, was aflame with the righteous indignation of a wronged and injured tribune of the people. A hardened professional in the game of bluffing, abuse, and demagoguery that normally made up much of New Brunswick politics, he knew every conceivable dodge and ploy; but this time they seemed mysteriously ineffective. He kept on valiantly asserting that 'he was just as strongly opposed to the Quebec scheme as ever'.[33] When DesBrisay mockingly asked him on what side he was now, he could only reply that he was 'against the Quebec scheme'.[34] At the very end of his enormous reply to Fisher, he did admit that he would 'go' for any plan of union 'that would promote the interests of our people'.[35] But beyond this he could not be budged. The very nature of the opposition attack – its emphasis on the inconsistencies of his union policy – stiffened his resistance.

Day after day, the debate on Fisher's want-of-confidence motion went on. And, as long as it continued, Smith could very reasonably claim that the time had not yet come for a frank announcement of his change of policy. The House, he insisted, must confirm its confidence in him before he made a move; he must not suffer the stigma of appearing to yield under pressure.[36] It was a plausible excuse; but with every day that passed the

Premier's long-delayed announcement became progressively more difficult to make. For him the only way of defending his integrity against Confederate jeers was to fall back upon his old Anti-Confederate stand. Little by little, he was becoming the prisoner – perhaps unwilling, perhaps only too willing – of his own defence. And day after day before crowded galleries – applauding, hissing, but unrebuked – the debate went on.

New Brunswick had not 'moved' first. New Brunswick was not moving at all. And it was in Nova Scotia, where a few weeks before Williams had been anxiously waiting for Gordon to take the lead, that the first real advance came. Williams had promised that he would repair the glaring omission of opening day and, in a special message, request the legislature to take up the subject of confederation;[37] but he had done nothing as yet. And then, without warning, there came a sudden move that looked at first like a severe retribution for his failure. On the 7th of March, the day before the opening in Fredericton, William Annand got up to ask the dangerous question that Tupper had been dreading for two sessions. What, he asked, were the prospects for confederation?[38] What was the government policy on union? Tupper blustered a bit in his best 'bow-wow' manner, insisted that confederation was not a party measure, and talked about the futility of action in Nova Scotia while an Anti-Confederate government still remained solidly established in New Brunswick.[39] But this did not satisfy Annand. He wanted an answer. And finally Attorney General Henry replied flatly that 'the government had no policy on the subject . . .'.[40]

Annand had won his great chance. If he had still been a convinced Anti-Confederate and if he had been sure of the support of a majority in the House, he might have exploited the confessed weakness and evasion of the Tupper government with devastating effect. But he did nothing of the kind. He seemed reluctant to take advantage of his opportunity; and his unwillingness was significant both of the change in his own opinions and of the altered attitudes of the members of the Assembly. Like Smith in New Brunswick, he was firmly opposed to the Quebec scheme; but, also like Smith, he began to realize that some kind of British North American union was probably necessary and might be unavoidable. He became convinced also that these assumptions were rapidly gaining a strong hold on the minds of his countrymen. Nova Scotia was drifting, half-heartedly, irresolutely, without really knowing where it was going, into the Quebec scheme. It must be stopped. And the only way to stop it was by calling a new 'convention', in which the critics of confederation would be well represented and in which he and others could 'make the best possible bargain under the circumstances' for Nova Scotia.[41]

Williams, listening attentively to the slightest murmur in the Province Building, was quickly aware of the troubled alteration in the Anti-Confederate mind. His own affable propaganda, the persuasions of the British government, the growing menace of Fenianism, the end of the Reciprocity Treaty and the resulting problem of the protection of the fisheries: all these potent influences on public opinion had obviously been doing their effective work. The union paragraph in the Speech from the Throne at Fredericton – a paragraph that seemed to imply a totally new approach to confederation – was a clinching argument for many. 'Since the members have assembled here', Williams wrote triumphantly to Gordon on the 12th of March, *'a very great change* has taken place in their manner of viewing the question of confederation.'[42] Earlier he had been more than willing to wait for Gordon's initiative. Now he was impatient for action. He kept trying to stir Gordon up. But suddenly Monck prodded him. 'Could you not venture', the Governor General telegraphed, 'to go on without waiting for Gordon?'[43] Williams stared at the telegram. Why not indeed?

⋙ III ⋘

IF DISENGAGED AFTER BREAKFAST, any time after ten, I should be glad to see you for a few moments.'[44] On the morning of the 13th of March, the day after Williams had received Monck's telegram, Annand went off to Government House with this invitation in his pocket. The Lieutenant-Governor was his usual hearty, affable, straightforward self that morning. He had a simple proposition to make. He proposed that Annand should rise in the Assembly and move a resolution authorizing the appointment of delegates to take part in a new 'convention' or conference, to be held in London under the supervision of the imperial government, with the object of framing 'a measure of union' that would 'effectively guarantee the rights' of all the provinces.[45]

Annand was interested. This was apparently his own idea of a 'convention' – or something very like it. Would he ever get a better compromise? He felt certain, as he told Smith a few days later, that there was 'a growing feeling among members in favour of union of some sort';[46] and he strongly suspected that 'a proposition for a new convention from our side of the House would be eagerly seized on by some of the government supporters'.[47] In effect, what the Governor was apparently inviting him to do was to take a leading part in a new and important movement which seemed almost certain of success. It was an invitation that flattered Annand's rather wounded self-esteem, for only a few weeks earlier, at their first caucus of the session, the Liberals had rejected his proposal to depose Archibald for his complicity in the Quebec scheme. Annand may not have wanted the leadership himself; but he looked forward with satisfaction to the prospect of playing a large role in the remaking of the Quebec scheme. 'I made the advance to Annand,' Williams reported to Gordon, 'and he has now a chance of *playing a great part* and moving in an *extended theatre. . . .*'[48]

Yet, in spite of the lure of 'an extended theatre' in London, Annand hesitated. He wanted to talk the proposal over with Smith. He had already been in communication with the New Brunswick Premier; and his aim was to maintain a close association between the Anti-Confederates of both provinces, to give each other support, and, if possible, to act in unison.[49] A conference with Smith was absolutely essential, he felt, before he committed himself to this new and radical departure. Williams and Tupper were all agreement. On the 19th of March, the Governor telegraphed Gordon that Annand was about to leave for Fredericton; but before the day was out Gordon replied briefly but conclusively that it would not be advisable for Annand to come.[50] Annand himself wrote at length to Smith on the following day;[51] but Smith proved no more eager than Gordon had been for talks about possible future conventions. His stubborn reluctance was strengthening. He believed now that he could beat Fisher's want-of-confidence motion by five or six votes. In comparison with the majority of twenty which he had won in the election of 1865, it was a pitifully small number. But it was still enough. He could get through in safety, he felt, without further compromises or concessions. And this he was now determined to do.

Annand had been rebuffed. He backed away uncertainly. And then a week later, on the 27th of March, Howe came back from Washington. For Annand and for the Anti-Confederate movement, Howe's return at this particular moment was decisive. During the previous autumn, when he was in London, he had told Cardwell that he did not want to go back to Nova Scotian politics, but preferred to give his time to literature and any 'suitable employment' that the imperial government might offer him. Two days after his arrival in Halifax he was back again at the old embarrassingly familiar task of offering his services to the Colonial or the Foreign Office.[52] Once again Cardwell told him that neither he nor Clarendon had anything to suggest.[53] But this time Howe did not wait for the answer. A week in Halifax was enough to make him fling all prudent counsels and sensible plans for the future to the winds. He called to pay his respects to the Lieutenant-Governor; and the Lieutenant-Governor told him with a jovial smile that he was 'getting along famously' with confederation.[54] He learnt that his friend and disciple Annand, utterly forgetting the Anti-Confederate demand for an appeal to the people, was apparently about to support the idea of a new conference with the prospect of imperial legislation in the near future. All this had been done without him, in complete forgetfulness of him, in utter indifference to his views! He was outraged. His every instinct urged him to arrest this unconvinced but accelerating drift towards provincial extinction. 'I had to determine my own course,' he wrote to Cardwell rather pompously, 'and at once decided that as a man of honour it was my duty to enter my protest and give my countrymen my reasons. . . .'[55] Annand, unhappy, uncertain, with 'no idea or will of his own' – so one of his colleagues charged – was only too willing to listen to the master's 'reasons'. And, as Howe said grimly, 'there was an end to intrigue and editorials' on union.[56]

Annand dropped out; but the movement of opinion towards union, of which his editorials in the *Chronicle* had been such a striking indication, steadily continued. His last-minute reversal could not stop it; neither could the potent influence of his master, Howe. If he had declined the Lieutenant-Governor's invitation, there were others who were willing to accept it; and among these was the former Anti-Confederate William Miller, Liberal member for Richmond in Cape Breton, who had been Annand's confidant in the union discussions and 'intrigues' of the past few months. On Tuesday, the 3rd of April, Miller got up to make the proposal that Annand had been seriously considering making three weeks before. 'William Miller made William Annand's motion,' it was satirically said later.[57] In effect Miller announced that, if the government would propose a new conference on union in London, under the 'arbitrament' of the imperial government, he would support the resolution. His justification for his change was that within a single year circumstances had altered drastically and very unfavourably for Nova Scotia as well as all the other northern colonies. 'Sir,' he declared solemnly, 'the Provinces of British North America are in no ordinary period of their history – and that man is heedless to the signs of the times . . . who exhibits indifference to, or affects to disregard danger in, the present state of public affairs on this continent.'[58]

'Miller, the violent Anti Quebec scheme,' Williams telegraphed to Monck and Gordon, 'moves the resolution for Confederate union to be framed by Act of imperial Parliament assisted by delegates. . . . Annand dead against measure.'[59] It was quite true. Annand, sternly instructed by Howe, had retreated to the orthodox Anti-Confederate contention that any discussions in London must be preceded by another conference in British America and an appeal to the people of the provinces. Miller, he insinuated, had been swayed by malign secret influences. 'I can imagine them,' he declared darkly.[60] He could indeed imagine them very vividly, for he had virtually yielded to them himself. His long, indignant harangues were answered by Tupper in his usual trenchant fashion. Tupper complimented Miller on his patriotic proposal; but he did not immediately take it up. Confederation, he explained again, was not and never had been a party question. The government could not properly adopt Miller's proposal before consultation with the Confederates in the opposition.[61] This bland excuse gave Tupper a little time; but it was impossible for him to delay much longer. Parliament had nearly finished the business of the session. Friday, the 6th of April, was a slack day. Nervously he drafted a resolution on union. And then, when he and his harassed colleagues had almost ceased to hope, the crisis in New Brunswick broke.

⇶ IV ⇷

EVER SINCE WEDNESDAY, the 4th of April, the day after William Miller had made his famous proposal in Halifax, affairs in Fredericton had been rapidly approaching a decisive clash. On that day the Legislative Council of New Brunswick took up the question of confederation for the second time that session.[62] A substantial majority of Unionists dominated the Council; and it had already amended, in a fashion much more definitely favourable to confederation, the paragraph on union in the government Address in Reply to the Speech from the Throne.[63] But the Councillors were not yet finished with the Governor's speech on the subject of confederation; and they now proceeded to give their approval, not simply to union in general, but to a particular kind of union. On the 4th of April A. E. Botsford introduced two new resolutions which affirmed that a British American confederation based on the Quebec scheme was an object much to be desired and that the Council would support any measure designed to carry it into effect.[64] Two days later these resolutions were passed by a vote of twelve to five.[65] The Councillors, in fact, had gone much further than either William Miller or Charles Tupper had any thought of going. Like the Canadian parliament, the Legislative Council of New Brunswick had endorsed the Quebec scheme. It was the only legislative body in the Maritime Provinces that ever did so.

Gordon probably knew of the resolutions in advance. He certainly realized, the moment they were passed, that his hour of deliverance was at hand. He could act now – and successfully. He must act now, or his last chance was gone. Smith, he felt certain, had accepted the agreement about union simply in order to escape the pressing danger of dismissal. He had perhaps not deliberately decided, from the beginning, to break his promise; but he had very soon found good reasons – the obstruction of the opposition, the doubtful support of his own friends – for not carrying it out. The declaration of his new union policy had been repeatedly postponed; the joint committee on union which he had promised had never been established. His statements in the House were either unfriendly or evasive; and his smooth explanations of these temporizing statements began to look increasingly disingenuous. Gordon was sick of what might be either vacillation or duplicity. He was also getting desperate. He knew that he must either get his present ministers to announce a union policy immediately or find others who were prepared to do it. 'I felt', he wrote, 'that the opportunities of doing this with propriety and effect were rapidly escaping me.'[66]

No, they would escape him no longer. The Legislative Council's union resolutions gave him a last good chance. The resolutions, embodied in a formal address to the Queen, were certain to be presented to him for transmission to Her Majesty; and he would be obliged to give the Legislative Council a formal reply. The reply, a final test of the sincerity of his premier's professed union sympathies, would be the effective means of forcing the issue with him. If Smith agreed to an answer that expressed satisfaction with the stand taken by the Legislative Council, all would be well; but if he demurred, or if he declined to advise anything but a neutral or a non-committal reply, it would prove conclusively that he had no intention whatever of honouring his promises. In that case Gordon would be amply justified in confronting his premier with the ultimatum that he had tried to lay down in February – the ultimatum that Smith had evaded with such easy dexterity. This time there would be no evasion.

Smith could either accept responsibility for a reply that would be favourable, though couched in very general terms, or he could resign.

On the morning of Saturday, the 7th of April, at about eleven o'clock, Smith called at Government House, and he and Gordon discussed, among other matters, the address of the Legislative Council on union. Smith gave it as his opinion that the Lieutenant-Governor, in reply, should simply offer to transmit the address to the Queen.[67] Gordon pointed out that this advice was another deplorable example of the embarrassments that resulted from Smith's stubborn reluctance to avow his union policy; and he added that when the address was presented to him, he would probably have to express approval.[68] When, a few minutes later, the two men parted, Smith apparently was not aware that the Legislative Council might ask for an audience that very day. Gordon himself may not have had any clear idea of when the presentation would take place; but Smith had not gone long when, at about twelve o'clock, a committee of the Legislative Council arrived and asked for an interview. In a flash Gordon made his decision. He would receive the Address that afternoon. His reason, or his excuse, was that he wished to include it in Monday's mail to England; but in any case the time hardly mattered, for he had already determined upon his reply. He appointed three o'clock for the presentation. And he asked A. E. Botsford, a member of the committee, to take a note down to Smith, requesting an immediate interview.

Strangely enough, it was after half past two before Smith received the message. He went out to Government House and the Lieutenant-Governor showed him his proposed reply. It was a moderate unprovocative answer, which made no mention of the Council's defiant adoption of the controversial Quebec Resolutions and simply approved its desire that 'all British North America should unite in one community under one strong and efficient government'. Smith strongly objected to it nevertheless. Even more strongly he complained that the Governor had not consulted with his Executive Council before framing it. This, of course, was precisely what Gordon had tried and failed to do; and now apparently it was too late. The Legislative Councillors had arrived at Government House and it was now nearly three o'clock. Gordon suggested that Smith should drive down to the Provincial Building to consult his colleagues. Smith declined. The Governor then proposed that one of the carriages that had brought the Legislative Councillors should be sent back to Fredericton to fetch the ministers out to Government House. Smith vetoed this second suggestion, on the same grounds as he had the first, that the want-of-confidence debate was going on and that the ministers could not possibly leave the House.[69] Gordon went out of the room for a few minutes to find out whether it might still be possible to postpone the reception of the Address for a few hours, but he discovered that the Councillors had already been waiting some time, and he came to the conclusion that any further delay would be a 'gross discourtesy' to them.[70] Smith, vigorously condemning the action of the Legislative Council and repeatedly complaining of the 'unfair and ungenerous' treatment he had received from the Lieutenant-Governor, refused to make any attempt to consult with his colleagues. It was a complete deadlock. Smith left Government House. Gordon walked into his reception room and faced the Councillors. 'I rejoice to believe', he declared, 'that the avowal of your desire that all British America should unite in one community under one strong and efficient government, cannot but tend to hasten the accomplishment of this great measure.'[71]

⋙ V ⋘

THE SMITH GOVERNMENT took its time deciding what to do. The crisis had occurred on Saturday. The cabinet did not hand in its collective resignation until Tuesday; and another two days passed before the Lieutenant-Governor accepted it. In the meantime a brisk but voluminous correspondence was going on between Gordon and his ministers. Each side was busily preparing its case for public consumption. And, while the province waited and speculated, the government papers were already sounding the first appropriate notes of indignant protest. The Saint John *Evening Globe* charged that the Lieutenant-Governor had 'taken the business of the country into his own hands'.[72] The great question that must now be settled, it declared, was 'whether the Lieutenant-Governor or the House of Assembly is to control the government of New Brunswick'.[73] The murmur of rumour and speculation was incessant; but as yet nothing had been officially revealed. Wednesday and Thursday went by with only the briefest sessions in the Assembly.

In the meantime, in Nova Scotia, Tupper decided to act. The break-through in New Brunswick had apparently not come in the simple, uncomplicated, uncontroversial fashion for which he had hoped. Like Confederates throughout British America, he was mystified and a little dismayed by what had happened in Fredericton over the week-end. But the prolonged stalemate had at last been ended; and now he could escape from the painful and embarrassing inaction of the past weeks. If ever he were to accept Miller's proffered invitation, this was the moment. He could propose a conference on union in London with the confident hope that a new Confederate government in Fredericton would have at least a fighting chance of carrying a similar resolution in the near future. On Tuesday, the 10th, immediately after the House opened at three o'clock, he got up to move that the government be authorized 'to appoint delegates to arrange with the imperial government a scheme of union which will effectually ensure just provision for the rights and interests of this Province . . .'.[74]

The debate on Tupper's motion lasted, with one short interval, for the better part of a week. Gradually it revealed the growing strength of the union forces; almost immediately it exposed the equivocal vacillations and wrangling disagreements of the Anti-Confederates. There were insinuations, charges, denials, and rejoinders on all sides. Annand began these damaging revelations on Friday, the 13th of April, when, after a day's delay which he himself had insisted on, he led off the attack on Tupper's resolutions. By the time he was half way through his speech, he was flinging accusations freely in all directions. Tupper, he declared furiously, was a deceiver, a betrayer of his country – a traitor; George Brown, he revealed, had tried, on his recent visit to Halifax, to bribe him with offers of money, place, and preferment.[75] Miller disputed this simple interpretation of Brown's interview with Annand; and Brown himself, appealed to overnight by Tupper, telegraphed back that Annand's statement was a 'villainous falsehood'.[76] On Saturday, after Tupper had read Brown's telegram to the accompaniment of cheers from the galleries, Annand attempted rather lamely to prove that he had not really meant bribery with money. He and Miller got into a violent dispute over the truth of this disclaimer; and the argument trailed away in a desultory exchange of abuse and recriminations.[77]

That night, when the House adjourned, the end was not yet in sight. And it was not the debate but the Fenian scare that first reached its climax. Weeks before, in a dispatch to Cardwell, Gordon had predicted that St. Andrews, Campobello Island, and the other small islands at the entrance of Passamaquoddy Bay were some of the likeliest places for Fenian attacks;[78] and now the event was to prove him correct. During the first week in April groups of Fenians, armed with revolvers and 'bowie knives', began crowding into the towns along the north-eastern coast of Maine from Machias to Calais. Several hundred of them, headed by the intrepid 'General' Bernard Doran Killian, assembled at the chief rendezvous, Eastport, which looked out over Campobello Island. Killian promptly rented a hall for the inevitable Fenian 'convention'; but this time he had other things than oratory in mind. He was chartering schooners, buying powder, eagerly awaiting a shipment of arms. And late on the night of Saturday, April the 14th, a small party of his followers slipped across to Indian Island, close to Campobello, flourished their revolvers in the face of the terrified customs officer, and compelled him to surrender the British flag.[79]

Gordon called out the provincial militia for service and appealed to Nova Scotia for aid. Halifax was the British North Atlantic naval base and the military headquarters for the Maritime region; and it threw itself at once into active preparations. On Sunday morning, General Doyle and Admiral Sir James Hope began to mount a small but formidable preventive force; and for the next few days Halifax was in the grip of the wildest excitement. On Sunday the most dramatic rumours sped through

the city. There were supposed to be three to four thousand
Fenians in Eastport, ready to descend upon New Brunswick.
On Monday morning, April the 16th, several batteries of Royal
Artillery, with field-pieces and ammunition wagons, embarked
for Saint John. H.M.S. *Duncan*, with eighty-one guns, was Sir
James Hope's flagship; and it sailed on Tuesday with over 700
officers and men of the 17th East Yorkshire Regiment of British
regulars under General Doyle's command.[80]

It was in the midst of this purposeful agitation that the debate
on union moved rapidly towards its end. And as the guns
rumbled on board the men-of-war and the troops swung down
the crowded streets to the harbour, the reality of British protection and the wisdom of British exhortations came home
to Haligonians with painful acuteness. The House sat late on
Monday night; but at eleven o'clock on Tuesday morning, the
17th of April, the debate was resumed, and Stewart Campbell
moved in amendment for an appeal to the people in a general
election.[81] Hour after hour, without interruption, the argument
went on. At midnight, when the House was plainly wearied after
more than twelve hours of talk, a handful of opposition members
pressed insistently for the adjournment. But Tupper, impatient,
determined, unmoved by the Liberals' playing for time, threatened the previous question, and the debate went wearily on.
Finally, at half past two in the morning, Campbell's amendment
was negatived, and Tupper's main motion passed by thirty-one
to nineteen.[82] Parties were split over the issue, as indeed they had
been ever since the Quebec Conference; but the four Conservatives who voted against Tupper's resolution were outnumbered
by the five Liberals who voted for it.

The motion that was carried while the city slept became at
once a favourite theme of the outraged Anti-Confederate press.
The supporters of Tupper's resolution were pictured skulking
home like malefactors to their dens through the deserted streets.
The passage of the resolution was a black crime, a deed of darkness, done like robbery and murder in the dead hours of the
night. 'It was a most significant circumstance', gloomily reflected
the Halifax *Citizen*, 'that Nova Scotia was wrapt in sleep – that
few in the country were awake when these political destroyers

struck at the heart of our constitution and left it dead at their feet. . . .'[83] 'The agony is over,' mourned the *Chronicle*. 'Confederation has been carried in the Assembly and the rights and privileges we so dearly prize have been basely betrayed by a majority of the representatives of the people.'[84]

It was this last circumstance – the substantial Unionist majority – that particularly exasperated the Anti-Confederates and helped to inspire both their horrified tones and their accusations of 'influence' and treachery. Even the Legislative Council, about whose support Williams had been extremely doubtful a few months before, passed the resolution by thirteen votes to five.[85] How was the size of these majorities to be explained, inquired the *Chronicle* indignantly? Its proprietor, William Annand, who had nearly made William Miller's motion and who had openly acknowledged the wisdom and the probable necessity of union, might very appropriately have answered his own question. The truth was that the great majority of the Anti-Confederates saw union as the inevitable destiny of a surviving British America. A long and compelling chain of circumstances – the end of the American Civil War, the post-war Republic's mounting hostility to Great Britain and her American provinces, the abrogation of the Reciprocity Treaty, and the rise of the Fenian movement – had all helped to compel the conviction that union was not only desirable for the future, but also necessary in the present, and that the Quebec scheme might be modified, under imperial supervision, to meet their objections and suit their needs.

⋙ VI ⋘

ON THE EVENING of the 12th of April, Gordon accepted the resignation of the Smith government; and next day – an unlucky Friday the 13th, the future victim of whose bad omens still remained unknown – Smith announced the fact in the Assembly. He read in full the memoranda that he and his colleagues had been exchanging with Gordon for the past few days, adding a copious critical commentary of his own.[86] Once again

he sought his own justification in the time-honoured New Brunswick fashion of attacking the Lieutenant-Governor. He drew an
affecting comparison between the Representative of the Crown,
a gentleman of 'noble blood' and 'titled lineage', and himself,
'one of the people', 'of humble origin', who yet had rights and
would use them to defend the rights of others. 'Responsible
government they had had,' he told the House solemnly, 'but now
it lay bleeding before the people of this Province.'[87]

The next day, Saturday, a new government, with R. D. Wilmot
and Peter Mitchell as principals, took office;[88] and in the Legislative Council Mitchell began a long, detailed rejoinder to
Smith's defence of the previous day.[89] His speech, not yet complete when the adjournment came, was resumed on Monday,
April the 16th; but in the meantime the new government had
come to the conclusion that it must immediately prorogue.
There was not the slightest chance that Smith would consent to
a lengthy adjournment during which the new ministers might go
back to their constituencies for re-election. On Friday night,
George Otty, one of the Anti-Confederate members in the
Assembly, had given notice that on Tuesday next he would move
resolutions opposing those just passed by the Legislative Council.[90] Smith and his followers were certain to launch a major
attack on the vulnerable new government at the very first opportunity.

There was only one way out. As soon as the Assembly met,
the Speaker gave notice that the Governor was going to prorogue
the legislature that day; but Smith seized the last hours of the
dying session to present Otty's resolutions, which rejected union,
denounced the unconstitutional action of the Legislative Council, and demanded the Governor's recall.[91] Yelling the familiar
hunting-call of New Brunswick politics, 'the Governor cry',
Smith was off in swift pursuit of his old quarry. And all the while,
in the Legislative Council Mitchell was systematically destroying
what remained of the pursuer's reputation for honesty and good
faith. Mitchell's censorious refrain 'Mr. Smith cannot deny . . .
Mr. Smith cannot deny . . .', repeated over and over again, in a
long cumulative series of charges, was like a Wagnerian leit-
motiv, solemn, threatening, rising deliberately to its crescendo.[92]

A prorogation was inevitable. But could a dissolution be avoided? The Canadians, who were impatiently waiting for a union resolution similar to Nova Scotia's, hoped earnestly that it could. Gordon himself, more than a week after the formation of his new government, was still considering doubtfully whether it might be possible to get approval in the existing legislature. He hoped; but, as he and his new advisers realized, the chances of defeat in the Assembly – which would mean a dissolution in any case – were perilously likely. Smith had certainly lost a substantial part of his following; but on the day after the prorogation, twenty-two members of the Assembly, including the Premier, signed a petition to the Queen, protesting against the conduct of the Council and the Lieutenant-Governor.[93] The Confederates had come close to doubling their numbers; but they could not yet control the Assembly. 'I do not think we can now carry it in this House,' Tilley told Macdonald realistically the day after the prorogation, 'and a general election appears inevitable. . . .'[94]

On the 9th of May, Gordon dissolved the twentieth parliament of New Brunswick, with writs for a general election, returnable on the 20th of June. The final test– the last possible chance – was at hand. Everything depended upon the events of the next few weeks. The second general election in New Brunswick would decide the fate of confederation. It might well determine the future of British North America, at least for a generation, and probably for ever. In the other Maritime Provinces, the issue of union either was dead or lived mainly in expectation of success in New Brunswick. Nova Scotia, though it had agreed to attend a new and final conference in London, could hardly unite with Canada across the barrier of a separate New Brunswick; and in the two island provinces, confederation had once again been either postponed or rejected during the winter and spring. In Newfoundland, Lieutenant-Governor Musgrave's well-meant efforts to keep the subject of union alive despite its obviously hostile reception in the debate on the Speech from the Throne had simply provoked an even more determined resistance from the Assembly. Resolutions decisively rejecting confederation were defeated under government pressure; but the Premier,

Carter, was able to stop the debate only by moving himself that it was not 'expedient' to attempt to reach a decision at the present time.[95] As for Prince Edward Island, it had gone beyond mere delays and postponements. It would have nothing whatever to do with confederation, and during May both its Assembly and Legislative Council rejected union once again in terms of the utmost finality and conclusiveness.[96]

No, the only hope lay in New Brunswick; and in New Brunswick the decisive engagement was imminent. But it was not the engagement that Wilmot, Tilley, Mitchell and the other Confederates had intended and expected to fight. It was no longer simply a battle between union and nationalism on the one hand and provincialism and colonialism on the other; it was also a struggle – at least as far as Smith and his followers could make it – between responsible government and the prerogatives of the Crown. By his imperious haste on the afternoon of April the 7th, by his failure to consult his ministry as a whole before replying to the Legislative Council, Gordon had put himself technically in the wrong; and now, reclaiming the stellar part in New Brunswick's familiar and well-loved constitutional melodrama, Smith charged that the Lieutenant-Governor's conduct was 'subversive of the rights and liberties of the people'.[97] 'The opposition are raising heaven and earth . . . ,' Tilley informed Macdonald worriedly, 'Smith and his friends now attempt to keep Confederation out of sight, and make it a constitutional test, and you know how the masses of the people view any supposed infringement of their constitutional rights. . . . It is unfortunate for the cause of confederation that the break-up was brought about in the manner in which it has been. . . . Had the case not come up in this shape, we could have beaten them with great ease, but this new issue arising, it complicates matters.'[98]

⇛ VII ⇚

THERE WAS NO DOUBT about it. Gordon, who always thought that politics in New Brunswick were so easy, had once again made them just about as difficult as possible for his advisers.

Tilley and the Confederates could not afford to treat Smith's sudden, violent attack on the Governor as a spirited rearguard action; they had to regard it as a serious counter-offensive. This time they could take no chances. Everything they had must be flung into the fight; and every help they could get from Confederates outside the province must be requested frankly for a struggle that was truly British North American in its significance. In September 1865, when Tilley had been up in Quebec, the Canadian ministers had promised him aid when the test came; and now, with the cry 'We must not fail in this contest', he appealed to the Canadians for $40,000 or $50,000.[99] For a mid-Victorian general election, to a House of forty-one members, it was not a spectacularly large sum; and it was at least partly balanced by Anti-Confederate money which also came in from outside the province, certainly from Nova Scotia and possibly from the United States. 'Fellow countrymen, it is not too late,' cried the *Morning Chronicle* in Halifax. 'Be up and doing and strengthen the hands of our brethren in New Brunswick.'[100]

The rival campaign funds may not have been very unequal, though the Confederates probably possessed an advantage. What was equally important, the Anti-Confederates no longer held the near monoply of ecclesiastical favour that they had enjoyed in the election of 1865. James Rogers, Roman Catholic Bishop of Chatham, was a man of great authority and influence among the Roman Catholic Irish of the Miramichi valley. The Confederates, openly appealing to him in the press, persuaded him to issue a pastoral letter in favour of confederation.[101] He urged the people of New Brunswick to acquiesce in the wishes of the British government. He did more. He publicly rebuked Timothy Anglin for his abuse of the Lieutenant-Governor in the columns of the *Morning Freeman*. Anglin, though he continued to battle with his old vigour in the isolationist cause, was no longer the force he had been the year before; and with Archbishop Connolly of Halifax, Bishop MacKinnon of Arichat (Cape Breton), and Bishop Rogers of Chatham supporting it, union had obviously won the favour of a substantial part of the Roman hierarchy in the Maritime Provinces.

It was also likely to gain the support of New Brunswickers

who wanted to remain British subjects in a separate British America. 'I vote for the Queen,' electors were later heard to say at the polls in York County.¹⁰² The Anti-Confederates became linked with the Fenians, with the aggressive and interfering republicans to the south; sometimes they were stigmatized as the 'Annexation Antis'. The Fenian invaders had, it was true, been overawed by the tremendous armament that gathered in the waters of Passamaquoddy Bay on the 19th of April. British war-ships, British regulars, and New Brunswick militia and home guards were now joined by General Meade and a small force of Americans, which had at last been sent north-east to guard the Republic's neutrality. The victor of Gettysburg, dressed in civilian clothes and suffering from a bad cold, met and chatted pleasantly with Sir James Hope, General Doyle, resplendent in a full-dress uniform, and Lieutenant-Governor Gordon, full of consequence as the Commander in Chief of the province of New Brunswick.

The intimidated Fenians, leaving quantities of unpaid bills, slunk away from the border towns. All thought of an invasion was over. But Fenianism was to continue as a potent force in the New Brunswick general election nevertheless. In his public speeches, Killian made it perfectly clear that one of the main purposes of the Fenian movement was to defeat confederation and thus to prevent the continuation of the British monarchy in British North America. 'Republican institutions have become a necessity to the peace and prosperity of your Province,' declared a Fenian manifesto that was published in Saint John at the height of the crisis. 'English policy, represented in the obnoxious project of Confederation, is making its last efforts to bind you in effete forms of monarchism.'¹⁰³ To many British Americans this obsolete republican jargon seemed either silly or dangerous or both.

All this compromised Smith and his followers. Fenianism would unquestionably injure the Anti-Confederate cause; but it could not deal it a mortal blow. The movement's chief dis-ability was caused, not by any external force, but by its own inward deterioration – by the doubts, uncertainties, and contra-dictions that distracted and inhibited it. This weakness and irresolution had infected the whole Anti-Confederate movement in both Nova Scotia and New Brunswick; and Albert J. Smith had become their most conspicuous victim. However much he tried to shift attention to the enormities of the Lieutenant-Governor, it was obvious that he himself had been playing a double game for the past six months. If he had not made an agreement favourable to union with the Lieutenant-Governor, he would not have remained Premier of the province. The paragraph in the Speech from the Throne was the indelible pledge of his engagement. But he had refused to pay the price of his retention of office; he had declined to accept the logical consequences of his own commitment. In effect he was betraying both sides; and for a while postponement and evasion enabled him to do so with impunity. But postponement and evasion did not offer any real escape from his perplexities; and only a lucky accident could rescue him from his career of meaningless double-dealing. Gordon's brusque action on the afternoon of April the 7th gave him his last chance; and by a crude improvisation, he vastly improved upon it. He made sure that he would have a grievance over Gordon's failure to consult his Council by the simple method of preventing him from doing so. A. E. Botsford said he delivered the Lieutenant-Governor's note to Smith at the Assembly at a quarter past one; but Smith claimed that he did not receive it until after half past two. 'I own it had not occurred to me', Gordon wrote later, 'that Mr. Smith would *hide* for some hours in order that he might found a grievance on it.'[104]

Even to some of its best friends, Anti-Confederate policy in New Brunswick seemed nearly bankrupt. Smith and his followers had tried and failed to find a viable alternative to confederation. Western Extension had been stopped dead; the hopes of closer trade relations with the United States had been broken by the abrogation of the Reciprocity Treaty. There was no longer even a specious case for the only possible Anti-Confederate programme; and the weakness of the Anti-Confederate leaders was that they realized and openly or tacitly acknowledged the fact. Wilmot's conversion, Smith's agreement with Gordon, were admissions, not only that the Anti-Confederate stand was wrong, but also that the Unionist cause was substantially right. From the beginning the Anti-Unionists in both Nova Scotia and New Brunswick had been compromised by their reluctant recognition that in the end union was the only destiny of a surviving British North America. And within the last year, many of them had come to believe that it would be wise, and might be necessary, to unite at once.

As usual, the elections were strung out over a period of more than a fortnight. Northumberland County was to vote first, on the 25th of May.

CHAPTER THIRTEEN

Summer of Frustration

ROM THEIR REMOTE SEATS in the balcony, the Canadians had watched the Fredericton comedy-drama with
the most absorbed attention. For weeks they had waited
with tense expectancy for the denouement; and, as the play
gradually opened its box of tricks, they had gone through an
astonishing variety of emotions. In rapid succession, they had
experienced impatience, anticipation, gratification, surprise, per-
turbation, and bitter disappointment. On April the 17th, the
very day the Governor General learnt of the passage of the union
resolution in Halifax, he also received the news of the prorogation in Fredericton.[1] Obviously there would have to be a short
interval before New Brunswick could authorize the appointment of delegates to a conference in London; and then, as dissolution followed prorogation, it became clear that the short
interval was going to be a long pause. The vexation of the Canadians was extreme. After an unbelievable delay, they had almost
succeeded. Yet they had failed after all – and for how long and
by how great a margin they scarcely dared speculate as yet. That
cocksure Lieutenant-Governor, Gordon, was again confidently
predicting a victory in the New Brunswick general election; but
Gordon had made other prophecies – false ones – before.

The mysterious complications and astonishing mischances of
New Brunswick politics were exasperating to everybody; but of
all the Canadians it was Monck, the Governor General, who
perhaps felt the contretemps at Fredericton most keenly. As
Gordon's principal confidant in British America, he knew more
about his hopes and plans than anybody else; and as a Peelite

ex-member of the British House of Commons, he never forgot for a moment that the imperial Parliament, as well as the British American legislatures, was necessarily involved in the passage of confederation. The Canadian time-limit on general union, the approaching expiration of the Nova Scotian legislature: these were not the only perils ahead. Another danger, of which Monck was more intimately aware than any of his ministers, lay in the instability of the British government; and, ever since Gladstone had introduced the Russell ministry's new Reform Bill in March, this had been ominously increasing. Dissentient Whigs joined with Tories in attacking the franchise measure; and on April the 27th, in a crucial division, the government survived by only five votes. What was going to happen? Would the ministry be defeated? And if it was, would it resign? Or would it seek a dissolution and go to the country in a general election?

Monck watched these developments anxiously. They spelled trouble for British American confederation. A change of government in England might create difficulties in the passage of a union bill; a general election would certainly cause a long delay. The news that the Russell ministry intended to carry on and persevere with its bill – news that Monck learnt early in May – did not reassure him. The British government's decision simply postponed a possible crisis; it merely prolonged the uncertainty; and as a result it strengthened Monck's firm opinion that all the remaining preparations for imperial legislation on British North America should be completed as quickly as possible. In April, as soon as he had heard of the prorogation in New Brunswick and the success of the union resolution in Nova Scotia, he began pressing Macdonald to summon the Canadian parliament early in May.[2] Legislation providing for the local constitutions in Canada East and Canada West must be passed quickly; and then, having tied up all the dangling ends of the scheme, Canadian delegates could proceed to London to take their part in the framing of the final federal act. If, in the meantime, the Confederates won in New Brunswick, Canada would be able, without delay, to take advantage of the victory. If, on the other hand, they failed – and Monck could never quite rid himself of the presentiment that they might – Canada would be in a strong position to urge

Great Britain to complete the union despite the refusal of a single branch of one provincial legislature. 'If we are ready and present ourselves at the Colonial Office in time,' he argued persuasively to Macdonald, 'I am very much inclined to think that New Brunswick – particularly divided as she now is – would not be allowed to stop the way.'[3]

It sounded curiously like a counsel of desperation. And Macdonald remained unconvinced. He was as fully aware as Monck of the infinite harm that fifteen months of delay in New Brunswick had done to the cause of confederation. It had set the whole programme back so badly that in the future, as in the past, they would have to operate within the most perilously narrow limits of time. There were pressing circumstances – the difficulties of the British government, the approaching end of the English parliamentary session, and the inevitable expiration of the Nova Scotian legislature – all of which imperatively demanded haste. But there was another, still more crucial circumstance – the New Brunswick election – that solemnly counselled delay. If Tilley and Mitchell did not win the New Brunswick election, there would be no confederation at all. Tilley deserved all the assistance Canada could provide; and Canadians had already heavily fattened his campaign fund. But apart from this, the best help they could give him was to stay completely out of what must be at this stage a purely Maritime contest. The New Brunswick Confederates ought to be able to fight their own battle in their own way, without interference from outside. And if the Canadian parliament met before the election began, there might very well be interference – calculated and disastrous interference – from Canada.

The difficulty was simple but basic. There was no definite agreement about the nature of the proposed confederation. There was only a very general consensus about the wisdom and necessity of British American union. The Canadian parliament had adopted the Quebec Resolutions in their entirety, without altering a single comma; but in the Maritime Provinces, only the Legislative Council of New Brunswick had expressed approval of the Quebec scheme as a whole. It had not even been mentioned in the union resolution that the Nova Scotian

Assembly had passed by 31 to 19 votes.[4] Miller, Wetmore, and other prominent converts to confederation had either rejected it or had indicated forcibly that it needed a good deal of amendment; and Tupper, Tilley, and the older Confederates had hardly dared for some time to put in a word in its defence. The apparent implication of the Nova Scotian union resolution was that the making of confederation must start again, virtually *de novo* – that a new conference should assemble in London under the supervision of the imperial government and, without necessarily giving much consideration to the work of its predecessor, should arrange a scheme of union that would be satisfactory to Nova Scotia. William Miller spoke of the 'arbitrament' of the British government.[5] Tupper assured the Assembly that at this new conference the British government would have an opportunity 'of giving us an amount of consideration that otherwise we might not obtain'.[6] And he clearly implied that Nova Scotia might expect more favourable terms as a result.

The trouble was that what gave reassurance to some British Americans aroused doubts and suspicions in others. The thought of the 'imperial arbitrament' comforted the Nova Scotians; the idea of 'l'arbitrage impérial' badly frightened some French Canadians. For wavering Maritimers the hope of amendments which would improve Nova Scotia's political and financial position in union could be a real inducement to support confederation; but for apprehensive French Canadians the fear of drastic changes, which would incline the federal balance still further in the direction of centralization, might be the decisive deterrent that would drive them from the Quebec scheme. One French-Canadian newspaper, *Le Canadien* of Quebec City, became exceedingly alarmed by the great expectations of amendment which the Nova Scotians were basing on 'l'arbitrage impérial'. It proclaimed shrilly that in London French-Canadian rights would lie at the mercy of the Colonial Office, and that the British government might very well try to convert the federal system into an outright legislative union, with the purpose of submerging the French-Canadian identity for ever.[7] There was just enough evidence that these silly terrors might be catching to alarm Cartier and Macdonald. They realized anew how difficult the reconciliation of the Canadian and Maritime attitudes was going to be.

For these reasons, they rejected Monck's insistent demand for an early meeting of the Canadian legislature. It would be far too dangerous. Once parliament was in session at Ottawa, it would be only too easy for the Canadian Anti-Confederates to make public, in the most provocative fashion, the sharp difference between the union aims and commitments of the Canadians and the Maritimers. All that Holton or Dorion would have to do would be to ask the Coalition ministers whether they still adhered to the Quebec scheme. If Macdonald and Cartier replied that nothing was settled and the Quebec Resolutions were open to amendment, French Canada would undoubtedly rise in violent protest. If, on the other hand, they answered that Canada was committed to the Quebec scheme as to a compact, the Anti-Confederates in New Brunswick might exploit this assurance to Tilley's complete undoing.[8] No, there must be no repetition of that terrible blunder about the Intercolonial Railway which had so badly prejudiced Tilley's chances in the election of 1865. Macdonald remembered, with a shudder, Holton's innocent-seeming inquiry about the Intercolonial Railway guarantee, his own incautious answer, Tilley's frantic telegram of protest, and the hurried explanation he had sent off in reply. Questions asked in the Canadian parliament while a Maritime election was going on were to be avoided if possible; and the best way of avoiding them completely was to postpone the Canadian session until the election was over.

Of course, Tilley and Mitchell might lose. And if they did, would it be possible for the Canadians, by having an early session, to save the Quebec scheme from total shipwreck? Monck insisted that it would. He argued that if the Canadians did not pass the local constitution and failed to complete their part of confederation, a second reverse in New Brunswick would catch them at a terrible disadvantage. They would, he said, have the 'smaller scheme' (the federal union of the two Canadas) 'thrust' upon them, and 'in all probability have a break-up of the government upon it'.[9] If, on the other hand, they tied the whole scheme up and thus committed Canada to it, the British Parliament might be emboldened to bring the union into being, 'New Brunswick notwithstanding'. But was so heroic a course really possible? Could the Canadian government and the imperial Parliament act in tacit disregard or open defiance of a second electoral defeat? Surely all Monck's argument did was to emphasize the overwhelming importance of the New Brunswick general election. A Confederate defeat would be literally irreparable. It would mean the break-up of the Canadian Coalition and the indefinite postponement of confederation. And no imaginable political manoeuvre could prevent these inevitable consequences.

>>> II <<<

SPRING WAS AN ANXIOUS TIME for the Canadians. As in Nova Scotia and New Brunswick, the fluctuating Fenian threat kept company with the rising excitement of the general election. It was the second of the two Fenian organizations – the division led by W. R. Roberts and W. T. Sweeny – that troubled the Canadians. Roberts had always emphasized the importance of capturing Canada as an essential 'base' for further operations on behalf of Irish freedom; and Sweeny, his 'Secretary of War', a professional soldier of experience and considerable skill who had risen to the rank of brigadier in the American Civil War, was planning an elaborate three-pronged invasion of Canada.[10] Large groups of Fenians, led by former officers of the American army, patronized by American politicians, and supported by funds raised openly at public meetings, drilled and paraded, fully armed, before applauding crowds in northern American towns during the spring months.

But nothing happened. On the 7th of March, the Canadian government had called out 10,000 volunteers to defend the Province against the attacks that were threatened for St. Patrick's Day; but the dreaded 17th came and went without either incursions on the frontier or disturbances in the big cities. During April, Killian's inglorious operations at Eastport, Maine, awakened some apprehensions of a complementary invasion of Canada; but before the month was out Killian's attempt had ended in a complete fiasco, and the Fenians had fled the frontier, highly discomfited. Once again the rumours seemed to have been exaggerated and the fears unnecessary; and Canada began to sink back into a complacent feeling of security. By the end of April, most of the volunteers had gone home and the frontier was largely undefended.

Suddenly, on the last day of May, the old faded reports acquired a vivid and frightening reality. The Canadian government hurriedly called up 14,000 volunteers for border duty; but, before the troops could get to their stations, the Fenian assembly at Buffalo, which had inspired the Canadian government's order, was already on the move. On the night of the 31st of May, Colonel John O'Neill, a seasoned veteran of the Union Army, crossed the Niagara River below Buffalo with a Fenian 'army' of about 1,500; and two days later, on the morning of Saturday, June the 2nd, he took up a good position, on rising ground called the 'Limestone Ridge', not very far from the little village of Ridgeway. Here a column of about 850 Canadian volunteers – including the Queen's Own Rifles – which was attempting to make a junction with a larger force of regulars and volunteers, blundered into the Fenians. The Canadians, many of whom had had very little training, fought with spirit, and drove the Fenians from their first position. But an absurd order of their amateur commander, who feared a charge from imaginary Fenian 'cavalry', threw the column into a confusion from which it never recovered; and in the end the disordered and wavering lines of volunteers fell back under heavy fire. O'Neill himself retired soon after, for larger forces were converging upon his army; and early on Sunday morning the Fenians recrossed the river into the United States. Nine Canadian militiamen, including five of the Queen's Own, were killed, and over thirty wounded, in the meaningless little encounter at Ridgeway.[11]

A few days later, on the 7th of June, another Fenian army, about as strong as O'Neill's, established itself at Pigeon Hill, a few miles north of the Canadian boundary, in the Lake Champlain district.[12] But it got no farther; and, soon disintegrating into a formless, plundering mob, it also fled across the border. The great three-pronged Fenian invasion of Canada was over; but what had happened was enough – far more than enough –

to cause an immense sensation throughout the Province. For over a generation the Canadians had lived in profound peace; and nothing like the fight on the Limestone Ridge had happened in Canada since the most serious of former American raids, the raid on Prescott that followed the rebellions of 1837. The patriotic response which the Battle of the Windmill, near Prescott, had evoked nearly thirty years before was now called back and vastly amplified by the affair at Ridgeway. By Sunday, June the 3rd, over 20,000 militiamen had turned out eagerly to defend the Province; and in Toronto excited civilians were avidly reading 'war news' in special editions of the *Globe*.

In the days that followed, the Canadians began to reflect, with increasing amazement and indignation, upon this extraordinary series of events, and upon the American attitudes to it, both official and unofficial. Astonishment that their province had actually been invaded, grief for their fallen volunteers, anger at American politicians for encouraging the invasions, at American officials for permitting them, and at American newspapermen for jeering at Canadian alarms and exulting in the prospect of Fenian victories: these were some of the competing emotions that kept struggling for expression in the first fortnight of June.[13] The well-established contemporary American political principle that the approaching congressional elections in November justified any and every method of pandering to the Irish vote was something that the Canadians never entirely understood; and, like the editor of the Hamilton *Spectator*, they came to the simple conclusion that the American authorities had 'by their want of action become chief criminals in this great crime against the law of nations'.[14] When American newspapermen coolly described Fenian troop movements and discussed Fenian 'strategy' as if they were writing about the regular armed forces of the United States, the Canadians could hardly repress their indignation; and they were even more violently exasperated when, as frequently happened, American editors sought to use the St. Albans raid – a raid conceived in secret by twenty commissioned Confederate soldiers – as a completely sufficient justification for the open invasion of Canadian territory by a force of 1,500 Fenians, marching freely over the border with the complacent permission of the American authorities and the exultant approval of the American populace.[15] The fact that on the 6th of June President Andrew Johnson issued a proclamation commanding American neutrality did not greatly mollify the angry Canadians. By that time the battle of Ridgeway had been fought, the only fighting Fenian army had fled the province, and the dead were in their graves.

Fear and detestation of the Fenians, which were general throughout British North America, had an important effect upon the movement for confederation. The desire to unite grew out of the will to survive; survival was threatened by the marked hostility of the Americans; and dislike and distrust of the United States became a potent force in the growth of the new British American nationalism. Only a few weeks before, during the fight for union in the Nova Scotian legislature, the differences between Maritimers and Canadians – the divergence of their unionist aims – had become conspicuously, painfully apparent. The constitutional assumptions of Nova Scotians had caused tremors in Canada East, just as earlier federal plans of the Canadians had created alarm in Nova Scotia. But now this restiveness quieted down; the differences were forgotten in the struggle for the border. The threat of Fenianism was a common British American experience and the defence of the homeland was a common British American enterprise. 'Canadians have gained more in national character during the last six years than in any previous twenty,' the *Globe* wrote later, but with equal truth for 1866; 'and, if we ask, what has caused this, we shall find that the outrageous proceedings of the Fenians and their abettors have been among the chief agencies. . . . The longer these alarms continue on our borders the more will this feeling of blended indignation and patriotism be awakened, till Canada's diversified people be, through the fire of outward assault, thoroughly and unmistakably fused into one.'[16]

⇶ III ⇚

FOR DAYS the horrible obsession of the Fenian raids blotted out everything else; but as people gradually awoke from the nightmare they remembered the New Brunswick general election. It began on the 25th of May, in Northumberland County; and during the last days of the month the Canadian newspapers carried accounts of the 'glorious' Confederate victories in Northumberland, Carleton, Albert, and Restigouche.[17] The first half-dozen elections were, in fact, for fairly safe Confederate ridings; but on the 1st of June came the vote in the doubtful county of York, and the news of this and of the sequence of crucial contests that followed it was buried in newspapers crammed to the margins with 'war news'. At the end of the first week in June, when the Fenian excitement had slightly subsided, the Canadians learnt that both Saint John City and County had been captured by Confederates, and began to realize that Mitchell, Wilmot, and Tilley had won the election. They had won it, in fact, even more decisively than Smith and Wilmot had done fifteen months before.[18] Thanks in considerable measure to the Acadian vote, the Anti-Confederates had held three North Shore counties; but the whole St. John valley had gone Unionist. The Confederates captured the overwhelming number of thirty-three seats. Smith was left with a feeble minority of eight.

On the 8th of June, parliament met, for the first time in Ottawa, in a mood of mingled hope, pride, and elation. Everything combined to produce a pleasurable feeling of satisfaction. The volunteers had behaved with great 'pluck' and dash, if not with great efficiency. The Fenian raiders had been swept decisively from all the provinces. Confederation had triumphed in New Brunswick. And the new houses of parliament, spacious and splendid, were awaiting occupation. As the members strolled about the paths of the sunny forecourt, watched the view over the great river, wandered through the tall, echoing corridors of the buildings, and sat amid the vast, impressive spaces of the Assembly and Council chambers, they could not help feeling

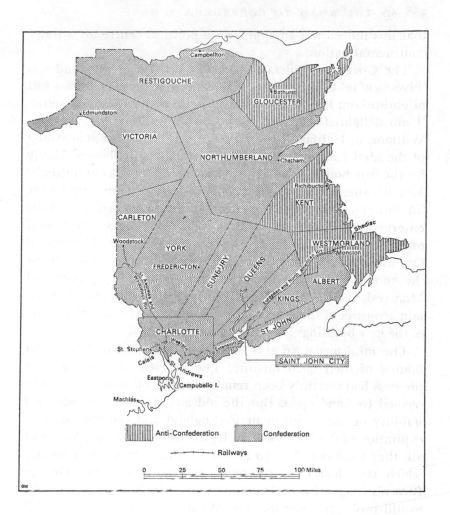

Anti-Confederation | Confederation

Railways

0   25   50   75   100 Miles

New Brunswick – General Election 1866

that this indeed was an appropriate political centre for a transcontinental nation.

The Governor General, who had come up in May and was 'bivouacking' in the original, diminutive Rideau Hall, was full of enthusiasm for the new buildings, if not for the new capital. 'I am delighted with the public buildings here,' he wrote to Williams in Halifax. 'I think they are as handsome as anything of the kind I have ever seen, and I think the halls of assembly for the two houses infinitely superior to those of Westminster.'[19] Monck's single but sweeping criticism, that the buildings were 'in the *wrong place* away from the civilization, the wealth and the enterprise of the Provinces', was echoed, of course, by a good many parliamentarians in those first weeks of June.[20] They found Ottawa an uncouth and uncivilized place, pined occasionally for the good accommodation and better cooking of Quebec and Montreal, and discovered surprising defects – such as the uncertain acoustics of the Assembly room – in the Gothic splendours of the new buildings.[21]

The ministers were also finding deficiencies in the golden bounty of their good fortune. The heaviest obstacle to their progress had certainly been removed; the road to confederation seemed free and open. But the old anxieties – the precarious stability of the government in England and the approaching expiration of the Nova Scotian legislature – remained. Worst of all, they were now face to face with a new danger – a danger which they had been privately dreading ever since George Brown's resignation in December, and which, if it came at all, would probably come quickly. What was Brown going to do? He had promised in December that if the ministers stuck to the compact they made with him when Sir Narcisse Belleau came into the government, he would give them his 'best aid in carrying out the constitutional changes we were then pledged to'. But surely this promise had its obvious limitations? Why should it necessarily include other government measures as well as the constitutional changes that still remained to be made? If it did not, and if Brown attempted to oppose important parts of the ministry's programme, what would the Reformers of Canada West do? Would they follow Brown into opposition, or would they stick by McDougall, Howland, Fergusson Blair, and the Coalition? If they followed Brown, the government could conceivably be defeated, and the whole project of confederation might collapse.

Neither the Liberals nor the Conservatives in the Coalition wanted this to happen; and they devised a rather simple, obvious stratagem by which it might be avoided or prevented. They would try, by a judicious arrangement of their programme, to keep Brown's loyalty as long as possible. The main business of the session was undoubtedly the last preparations for union. Canada East and Canada West would be separate provinces under the new dispensation; and provincial constitutions would have to be provided for both of them. But though these were the chief, they were not the only, items on the agenda. The ministry wanted to change commercial policy and it was deeply concerned over the state of provincial credit. Galt, the Minister of Finance, planned to authorize a substantial issue of provincial bank-notes, and, as a conciliatory gesture to the low-tariff Maritime Provinces, to reduce the level of the Canadian customs duties by approximately twenty per cent. In addition – and here also Galt, as the acknowledged representative of the Protestant minority of Canada East, was a powerful influence – the Coalition intended to give further protection to Protestant schools in the eastern division of the Province before it came under a separate provincial government. It was a fairly large and important programme, apart altogether from the new provincial constitutions; and the government determined to order it so as to minimize the likelihood of attack. George Brown, the ministers thought, would probably not take the risk of mounting a serious offensive against the government until the local constitutions were safely passed; and they therefore decided to postpone the local constitutions until the more controversial bills were through and the greatest danger over.[22]

The session opened with a great rush of activity. Two emergency anti-Fenian measures – the suspension of *habeas corpus* and the extension to Canada East of an old Upper Canadian statute for the trial of foreign invaders – were hurried through all stages on the opening day and presented to the Governor

General for signature before he left the parliament buildings.[23] Almost immediately, however, this rapid pace began to slacken. It was an uncertain pause between dangers, a doubtful, experimental interval in which ministers were cautiously feeling out the temper of the House; and now that the labour, the suspense, and the anxiety of the Fenian raids and the New Brunswick election were over, Macdonald sought the solace to which he sometimes went back after long periods of acute tension and fatigue. He began drinking hard and steadily.[24] There were days when he was, and other days when he ought to have been, away from the House; and the absence of his directing hand was soon evident.

The House loafed and the work dragged. Later, the *Globe* complained bitterly that the Assembly had sat only a total of seventy-eight hours in June;[25] and, after a fortnight of this inactivity, Monck became seriously alarmed. He had allowed himself to be persuaded that the opening of the session should be delayed until the election in New Brunswick was decided one way or another; but, now that Tilley and Mitchell had won their smashing victory, he became impatient for action. To leave confederation in an unfinished state any longer than was absolutely necessary seemed to him to run all kinds of risks in both British America and Great Britain. By the end of the third week in June, he had become convinced of the serious nature of the situation; and he solemnly warned Macdonald that, if the present session passed 'without the completion of our portion of the union scheme', he would be compelled to ask the British government for his recall.[26]

Monck's grave caution did not come alone. It was accompanied by equally solemn warnings and even more importunate appeals from Nova Scotia. Now that a union resolution had been passed in Halifax and was about to be passed in Fredericton, both Tupper and Archibald could see no reason why the final conference in London could not be held immediately; and they were both equally convinced that if the British Parliament did not bring the union into being that very session, the results in Nova Scotia might be complete disaster. 'We *must* obtain action during the present session of the imperial Parliament or all may be lost,' Tupper wrote urgently to Macdonald on the 17th of June. 'Our House expires by law in May next, and for reasons which it is not necessary to enter into here the result would be most disastrous to Confederation and probably defeat it altogether.'[27] Some of the reasons, which Tupper thought it unnecessary to explain in detail in a letter, were certainly just as obvious to Macdonald as they were to Tupper himself. Everybody knew that Howe was touring Nova Scotia in a passionate crusade against union, and that a monster petition to the British House of Commons was rapidly collecting signatures. But this, Archibald and McCully, Tupper's Liberal colleagues, believed, was by no means the complete explanation of Tupper's probable defeat in the next election. His whole record, including his most progressive achievement, the new provincial School Act, would be used against him with telling effect. 'Not upon Confederation so much,' McCully analysed the causes of Tupper's certain fall to Tilley, 'but all his broken promises and all his unpopular acts, and all his sins, and they are many, will be arrayed against him, and we Liberals could and would not lift a finger to save him.'[28]

Tupper and Archibald were not content to press their case by correspondence. In their minds the matter was of such desperate urgency that it demanded a personal appeal; and on the evening of the 27th of June they arrived in Ottawa.[29] They found the Canadians in a much more receptive and purposeful mood than would have been true ten days earlier. Macdonald had pulled himself together; the session was on the march again; and the day before, June the 26th, Galt had delivered his budget speech. The ministers had come to the conclusion that the chances of serious opposition were not very great; the remaining sessional business, they thought, could be speedily finished; and they agreed with Tupper and Archibald that the Canadian delegation to the London conference would sail on the 21st day of July, the Maritimers preceding them by a couple of days.

Satisfied, Archibald and Tupper departed. The Canadian members also left the capital in a body, for a few days' recess beginning on June the 28th had been decided upon. The ministers were hopeful; but on the 27th, the day before the recess, George Brown was observed canvassing his friends, the Reformers, apparently about Galt's budget proposals.[30]

→»» IV «←

DURING THE BRIEF RECESS, Brown made his great decision. He was pledged to give the government his best aid in carrying confederation; but he was not, he reasoned, under the slightest obligation to support its other measures. He had always regarded the Coalition as a mere brief truce in party warfare, justifiable only because of the imperative need of constitutional reform; and now, with Reform in sight, his reawakened political instincts and his high hopes and ambitious plans for the future of the Liberal party after confederation made him chafe within the limits of an unnatural association. He disapproved of Galt's budget, just as he had disapproved of everything that Galt had done for the past eighteen months. Worst of all, he had been nursing a sense of personal injury at the hands of John A. Macdonald, and this had now become a rankling grievance.

Two years before, when the Coalition was formed, Macdonald – so George told his wife – had given Brown his promise that he would make 'public reparation' for the personal accusations he had hurled against him on one terrible occasion years before.[31] It was an old discreditable story. The charges, uttered with a furious vehemence that had shocked the House, had been made back in the session of 1856; and they referred to a government investigation of the provincial penitentiaries that had taken place over six years earlier. Passionately Macdonald had accused Brown, as secretary of the investigating commission, of intimidating witnesses, suborning convicted criminals, and falsifying evidence. Years had passed; but to Brown this attack on his personal integrity remained unforgotten and unforgivable; and for nearly a decade it had suspended anything but 'parliamentary communication' between the two men. Then, when the work of the Coalition government brought them inevitably into a closer relationship, Macdonald, at Brown's request, had promised to make belated amends by a public retraction of his old charges. He had not done so; and, at their first meeting at the beginning of the session, Brown reminded his old antagonist of his promise and curtly told him that if he did not honour it now, there could be nothing but 'parliamentary communication' between them once more.[32] Again Macdonald apparently promised; but this time almost certainly with some surprise, a little apprehension, and considerable mental reserve.

Why had Brown renewed his request at this particular time? Was he trying to pick a quarrel? What obligation had he, Macdonald, to apologize to a man who had resigned from the cabinet six months before and who might soon be directing a frontal attack against the Coalition ministry? Why out of all the innumerable accusations that had been traded across the floor of the Assembly in the last twenty years, was it for this particular outburst and to this self-righteous and truculent man that he must make 'public reparation'? Why must Brown remain untouched and untouchable by severe criticism when all the while, in the columns of his newspaper, the *Globe*, he and his associates, without the slightest compunction, were shovelling personal abuse in cartloads upon their political opponents? No, he would not make the apology, for the conditions that alone justified it had changed in December and might change more drastically still. And he did not.

Before June was out, Brown had exactly reversed the position he had taken up two years before, at the time of the forming of the Coalition. He had broken again with Macdonald, with whom for eighteen months he had acted in the closest political association; and equally significantly, he had patched up his two-year-old quarrel with Luther Holton, with whom he had not exchanged a single friendly word since June 1864.[33] During the brief recess at the end of the month, he planned the massive offensive against Galt's budget that began immediately in the *Globe*; and as soon as he got back to Ottawa, he started organizing as broad a resistance as possible, among the old Liberal forces in both sections of the province, against the government's financial and commercial policies.[34] The onslaught which the Coalition had dreaded from the beginning, and had tried rather feebly to guard against by a special arrangement of government business, was now about to fall. Would the great mass of the Upper Canadian Reformers join it?

They did not. The angry and impetuous Brown might have been eager for a crisis; but they were far from ready. What did their old leader intend? Was he really hoping to make a big issue of a budget that actually *lowered* the tariff? Two years before he had led them into a Coalition to carry a federal union; now he was apparently trying to lead them out of the Coalition and back to the enemies of confederation, Holton and Dorion. If the attack on the budget succeeded, what was to happen to the Coalition and confederation? The western Liberals sat back unconvinced and disapproving; and by July the 10th, when Brown made his great speech in support of McGiverin's amendment to the budget, the ministers realized with delight, and Brown with disgust, that the large majority of his old followers would stand by the Coalition.[35] The debate would have to run its course; but now the result was certain.[36] Once again the ministers were out of danger; and perhaps, in two weeks, they might be on their way to England.

This sense of triumph could hardly have been more short-lived. On the same day, the hard blow which Monck had never ceased to dread fell at last. In England the Russell ministry, defeated once again in a crucial division on its Reform Bill, had resigned on the 26th of June. This was the shattering but inconclusive news that reached Government House on July the 10th;[37] and it was not until later that Monck learned that the Earl of Derby had succeeded in forming a Conservative government – a frankly minority government – and that on the 6th of July the new ministers, including the Earl of Carnarvon as Colonial Secretary, had taken office.[38] Monck had to act on the information that was available to him on July the 10th; and as a Peelite, a close acquaintance of some of the outgoing ministers, and consequently sensitive to the implications of ministerial changes, he came to the quick conclusion that the mission to England must be postponed. He could not see how he could move a step further until he had definite instructions from the new Secretary and had learnt the views of the Derby-Disraeli government on British North American union.[39] Even if the Conservatives decided to continue their opponents' confederation policy, how could they complete the union effectively before the quick prorogation they would doubtless think essential? No, there was simply not enough time. Monck wrote and then telegraphed to Gordon and Williams, warning them to postpone the departure of their delegation to England.

But delay was the last thing that the now nearly frantic Maritimers were willing to accept. 'Nova Scotia and New Brunswick delegates will leave on the nineteenth as agreed with you,' Tupper telegraphed back belligerently. 'Any delay on the part of Canada for reasons personally explained will undoubtedly be fatal to Confederation.'[40] A serious dispute over tactics – the last thing wanted in the light of the already existing divergence between Canadian and Maritime aims – loomed ahead; but Monck stuck to what seemed to him now the only sensible decision. A letter from Carnarvon, written the day after he assumed office, was already inviting the Canadian delegation to proceed according to plan;[41] but even if this unofficial note had arrived in time, Monck would probably not have changed his mind. The whole difficult and delicate business of reconciling Maritime and Canadian differences, of amending the Quebec Resolutions, must be finished to everybody's satisfaction before the union bill could possibly be introduced in the imperial Parliament; and this was a task that, as Monck now saw and Macdonald had probably realized from the beginning, 'must take weeks of anxious and constant labour'.[42] Could a new Colonial Secretary wisely undertake such a responsibility? Could he possibly carry it out in the last few days of a dying session?[43] The thing was clearly impossible. 'Please keep your people quiet, if you can,' he telegraphed to Williams in Halifax, 'and all will be right.'[44]

But Williams did not want to keep 'his people' quiet. He probably could not have kept Tupper 'quiet', even if he had wanted to. 'New Brunswick and Nova Scotia delegates go by steamer tonight and rely upon Canadian delegates meeting them promptly in London as agreed on,' Tupper telegraphed defiantly on July the 19th. This was no bluff. Sail they did; and over in London, Carnarvon, who expected them – and the Canadians as well – to arrive before the end of the month, was hurriedly preparing for their reception. There was not the slightest difference between British Conservatives and Liberals – just as there had been none between British Liberals and Whigs – about the necessity of British American union. Carnarvon was as fully aware as Cardwell had been of 'the great importance in an imperial point of view' of completing confederation that summer;[45] but he knew that if he waited until the delegates arrived to begin operations, it would certainly be too late. His only chance of success that session was to prepare a draft bill, to enlist opposition support for its quick passage in advance, and then to trust that the delegates would accept it, on sight, as a settlement of general principles, on the understanding that the details would be filled in later by Order in Council.[46]

It was an oddly rudimentary piece of legislation – an undeniable legislative abortion – that he produced.[47] Almost everything of importance in the federal plan – the organization of parliament, the administration of justice, the division of legislative powers, and the settlement of property and liabilities – was to be settled after the union, by the Colonial Secretary in consultation with British American representatives, and carried into effect by Order in Council. The first six sections, which contained the only definite provisions of the bill, were certainly fragmentary; but they indicated clearly enough that the proposed union was to be legislative in all but name and that the provincial governments were to be relegated to the status of 'councils', whose 'ordinances' would be valid only so far and so long as they were not repugnant to any act of the federal parliament.[48] The English Liberals, not without considerable misgivings about the vast amount of matter that was to be left to Order in Council, agreed to support the bill, on condition that the delegates approved it. It was likely to be an important proviso.[49]

But the news of July the 28th cut short all plans, promises, and provisos. The North American ship bearing the Maritime delegates had reached port; but the Canadians were not on board. There was nothing for Carnarvon to do but to thank Cardwell for his proffered help and cancel the Bill.[50] The imperial Parliament was prorogued on the 10th of August; and the last chance of imperial legislation in 1866 had vanished.

⋙ V ⋘

ON THE SURFACE, the prospects for confederation could hardly have seemed worse than they did at the end of July 1866. Certainly Canadian-Maritime relations had reached a depth of cold antagonism about level with that to which they had descended immediately after the cancellation of the Intercolonial Railway agreement nearly three years before. Everybody was blaming everybody else for the collapse of the grand plans for 1866; the air was frigid with recriminations and prophecies of doom. Monck indignantly repelled Williams's charge that Canada was responsible for the postponement of imperial legislation.[51] Tilley wrote Galt a long, peevish, complaining letter, full of reproaches for the past and dark forebodings for the future.[52] In the end this constant harping on the approaching danger of the defeat of confederation in Nova Scotia so exasperated the temperamental Galt that he actually proposed dropping the Quebec scheme entirely and trying instead for a legislative union with New Brunswick![53]

The Maritimers, kicking their heels resentfully in London and wondering dejectedly whether to stay or go home, felt the burden of frustration most heavily; but the excitement of a task nearly completed had vanished in Canada also, and for a while the Canadian legislature relapsed into a rather listless routine. The local constitutions for Canada East and Canada West, the only integral part of the Quebec scheme that remained to be settled, were not likely to arouse any strong constitutional convictions or to provoke a stormy debate. The resolutions concerning them, which Macdonald introduced on the 13th of July, brought no surprises; and the speeches that followed in general restated familiar views.[54] Canada West was to have a single-chamber legislature – a definite but not unexpected innovation; Canada East was to retain the bicameral parliament, with both

an assembly and a council, which had been the standard legislative equipment in British America up to that time. Each province was to have as its chief executive officer a lieutenant-
governor, appointed by the federal government; and its affairs
were to be administered according to 'the well-understood principles of the British constitution'.[55]

Cartier, who sponsored the Lower Canadian part of the resolutions, could rest his case solidly on tradition. Macdonald, who
spoke for Canada West, had to justify the reduction to a single
legislative chamber. His main theme was one that he had dwelt
on often and emphatically: under a preponderant federal parliament the local legislature must inevitably become 'more of the
nature of a municipal than a legislative body'.[56] A single-chamber
legislature was simply a sensible adjustment in the light of
British America's new political circumstances. 'Were this a
sovereign legislature there might be two houses,' he told the
Assembly, 'but for a subordinate legislature one was enough.'[57]
It was a calm but sweeping statement of Macdonald's favourite
centralist thesis; and if Cartier did not endorse it, he also did
not explicitly question it. Cartier's chief justification of the
bicameral legislature was that it was so closely identified with
what to him were the two basic principles of political perfection –
responsible government and monarchical institutions.[58]

The resolutions almost invited two obvious amendments;
A. A. Dorion proposed that Canada East should have only a
single chamber and John Hillyard Cameron moved for a bicameral legislature for Canada West. But it was George Brown
alone who struck at the heart of the government's proposals. He
was convinced that responsible, parliamentary government was
utterly unsuited to institutions so limited in scope and so simple
in structure as the provincial governments of the future ought to
be. As he had done at the Quebec Conference, he proposed that
Canada West should have an elected assembly and elected heads
of departments who would not be members of the assembly, and
that the functions of both legislature and administration should
be clearly limited and defined.[59] Fundamentally, Brown's great
object – the reduction of the local governments to the approximate level of the county councils on a larger scale – was equally

Macdonald's; and if his plan could have been carried out, it would have solved what was the central contradiction of the Quebec scheme. But in effect the issue had already been closed, though in a fumbling indecisive fashion, for British North America as a whole, at Quebec; and it was useless now to try to reopen it for one province alone. At Ottawa in 1866, as at Quebec in 1864, most people assumed that the local governments of the future would be subordinate and relatively unimportant; but neither the Quebec Conference nor the Canadian parliament could bring itself to divest them of their accustomed forms. Both Nova Scotia and New Brunswick expected to continue their bicameral legislatures. Canada East wanted a bicameral legislature. And almost everybody was a little unhappy at the thought of giving up the procedures – and the devious manoeuvres – of cabinet rule.

The uncontroversial calm, prolonged by another welcome recess, lasted for more than two weeks of blazing summer weather. Then it broke. On the 3rd of August, the day after Macdonald's resolutions on the provincial constitutions had finally passed without amendment, there came a violent outburst of that sectarian rancour which for two decades had been the curse of Canada. The occasion was the third important item in the ministry's programme for the session, the school bill for Canada East, about which Galt was so particularly concerned. His constituents, the English-speaking Protestants of Lower Canada, had for some time enjoyed the privilege of establishing and maintaining their own schools independently of the main school system of Canada East, which was under the complete and exclusive control of the Roman Catholic Church. The Protestants wanted these educational privileges slightly extended; but, even more important, they wanted them confirmed by statute before they passed under the control of a provincial legislature in which French-speaking Roman Catholics would possess an overwhelming majority. As far back as his Sherbrooke speech in November 1864, Galt had pledged the government to a revision of the Lower Canada school law.⁰⁰ Nobody expected trouble; such a revision seemed simple justice. In 1863, there had been a 'final settlement' of the school problem in Canada

West. In 1866 there would be a similar 'final settlement' for the schools of Canada East.

But the Roman Catholics of Canada West would not have it so. Led by a private member, Robert Bell of Russell, they now demanded that the Roman Catholic minority of Upper Canada should be given privileges similar and equal to those about to be granted to the Protestant minority of Lower Canada. On the face of it, this might have looked like a fair exchange; but in fact the claim to parity was completely invalid. There was not the slightest resemblance between the strictly and exclusively denominational or 'confessional' schools of the Roman Catholic majority in Canada East, and the non-sectarian, state system of public instruction of Canada West, in which, as a matter of fact, a very large portion of the Roman Catholic pupils of that section were enrolled. If Bell's bill had passed it would have gone far to ruin the public school system of Upper Canada; and it was this incredible attempt to disguise an educational revolution as a praiseworthy act of mutual religious tolerance that particularly infuriated the Reformers and strengthened the determination with which they fought Bell's bill.

With Brown and Scatcherd in this van, they contested every inch of Bell's progress. 'We will fight this bill in every possible way that parliamentary rules will permit,' Brown declared hotly.[61] Scatcherd moved the six-months' hoist; and it was clear that the great majority of the Upper Canadians of both parties would vote against Bell's measure. Unfortunately, it was equally obvious that it was gaining eager and hearty support among the French-speaking members of Canada East. Cartier announced that he could not see 'why anyone should oppose the granting of the same privileges to one minority as to another'; and Macdonald, though he was the only minister from Canada West to do so, agreed with his old colleague. Plainly the Lower Canadians would now accept the government bill for Canada East only if it were accompanied by Bell's bill for Canada West; and this obnoxious deal the Upper Canadians were determined to resist to the last. The awful spectacle of the renewal of the sectional and sectarian struggle of the past rose up before the ministers. But this was not all. An even more definite and particular apparition – the possible overthrow of the Coalition – confronted them as well. George Brown had failed to topple the ministry on the score of Galt's budget. But was not education the issue on which he would have the greatest possible chance of success? On the 6th of August, Hector Langevin wrote his brother that the cabinet had decided to withdraw its bill completely, in order to prevent Brown and the Grits from coming to power.[62] The next day, Macdonald announced that the government bill would be dropped; and Galt, who was irrevocably committed to it, resigned from the ministry.

A week later parliament was prorogued. The session of 1866 was like a miserable anticlimax to the ending of the legislature of the Province of Canada; and the last week was a final appropriate expression of its angry futility. The completion of confederation had been postponed, the educational settlement in Canada East had been abandoned; and this double frustration lay heavily on everybody's spirits. Macdonald, alarmed by the outbreak of religious strife and shocked by Galt's resignation and a virtual government defeat, had gone back to the bottle; and on the last day before the prorogation he was one of the principal actors in a blistering exchange of personalities that must have sounded like a drunken brawl.[63] He had some justification, for opposition members were commenting derisively on the political uses to which government was putting its patronage, and he hurled back some savagely frank retorts. These aspersions on the character of a worthy Liberal judge were too much for the *Globe*; and a few days after the session ended, it used them as the text for a sermon about Macdonald's scandalous intemperance.[64]

The sermon became one of a series. Sternly, but with evident relish, the *Globe* began a thorough castigation of Macdonald's bouts of drunkenness. The charitable discretion with which the newspapers had customarily treated this subject in the past was, it declared, a great mistake; tolerance merely encouraged a disgraceful licence among members of parliament. It was true, of course, that others besides Macdonald were guilty of outrageous language and shocking insobrieties; but Macdonald, 'the chief of the administration to whom the House should look for guidance', had actually been 'foremost in evil'.[65] He had been observed holding on to his desk to keep himself from falling; he had moved the passage of the same government measure twice in succession, 'with utterance so thick as to be almost incomprehensible'.[66] Worst of all, during June, before the Fenian danger was over, he had for some time been utterly incapable of transacting business. Throughout the first and last weeks of the important and critical session of 1866, his behaviour had been simply deplorable; but, the *Globe* insisted emphatically, these excesses were by no means exceptional. What had happened, it asked its readers rhetorically, at Ottawa after the Quebec Conference and at Quebec during the meeting of the Confederate Council on Trade? 'Is there any one editor of a public journal', it demanded confidently, 'who really did not understand the true meaning of the words fifty times employed on important public occasions in the dispatches of the *Globe* and other leading journals, that Mr. John A. Macdonald was *sick* and unable to be present?'[67]

Macdonald made no effort to reply. As he said later, parliament was his forum and he would answer his accuser there. But if he held back, there were others who were eager to rush to his defence. The citizens of Kingston, as if to reaffirm publicly their confidence in their member, gave a dinner in his honour; and D'Arcy McGee, who only a few years before had been a minister in a Reform cabinet, paid his new leader a handsome tribute both as the vigilant defender of the province during the Fenian raids and as the principal author of the Quebec scheme. He earnestly told the large Kingston audience that 'of the seventy-two propositions which form the basis of the union scheme agreed on at Quebec, at least fifty, either in substance or in form, owe their origin to your honourable guest, while some of those who are now crying so loudly as to his inattention to public business never enriched our conference with an idea, a suggestion or proposition; never contributed to our councils anything better than a few wild and declamatory objections abandoned almost as soon as they were made.'[68]

This was too much. The magisterial *Globe* passed summary justice on McGee. His statement about the Quebec Resolutions was, it declared, 'an unmitigated falsehood'.[69] Besides, what did D'Arcy McGee, so frequently a victim of Macdonald's infirmity, know about the matter anyway? In all probability he had been in such a condition that he had never understood how the original resolutions were prepared!

⋙ VI ⋘

FROM AUGUST ONWARDS the public affairs of British North America rested in a curious state of suspended animation. The old political life had ended; the new was still struggling, very ineffectually at the moment, to be born. And while ordinary citizens pursued their avocations in the normal way, British American politicians, however busy they might be with administrative work, had something of the air of men who were awkwardly awaiting a great event, the hour of whose arrival was completely unknown to them, and who in the meantime had not a great deal to do. The Maritime delegates in particular could hardly help but present a most embarrassing appearance. They had left their administrative jobs behind them in Halifax and Fredericton; and although there seemed to be extremely little for them to busy themselves with in England at the moment, they naturally hated the thought of going back to the old routines they had crossed the ocean to end. Even Howe and the other Anti-Confederate leaders had ceased for the moment to bother about Nova Scotia. They too had arrived in England and were busy appealing to British politicians, trying to influence British newspapers, and preparing the great petition for submission to the British Parliament. Yet the British Parliament was not in session and would not be until probably the new year. Even then, if Derby's shaky ministry fell, it might be dissolved.

Only the Canadians remained behind. And apart altogether from the prorogation of the imperial Parliament, they soon found the best of reasons for a long postponement of their departure. A new Fenian scare, supported by little concrete evidence of actual Fenian aggression, was already sweeping through the province when the Canadian session ended; and before the end of the month it had risen to the force of a panic in Canada West.[70] On Saturday, the 25th of August, the Governor General sent a strong appeal to England,[71] for substantial reinforcements of imperial troops. Only a few weeks before, the familiar slow communications between Great Britain and British America had involved British and Canadian politicians in a tangle of conflicting plans and vain hopes; but in the meantime the Atlantic cable had been successfully laid, and Monck's urgent message sped swiftly over it to the heart of the Empire. On Monday, Carnarvon was wiring Disraeli and asking for a cabinet meeting;[72] two days later he was desperately seeking transport; and in very short order two regiments of infantry, one of cavalry, with supporting artillery, were on their way to Canada.

All this kept the Canadians at home and very busy. Carnarvon, unhappily conscious of the embarrassing presence of the Maritimers in London, had hoped, early in August, that the Canadians might possibly reach England before the end of September.[73] The Maritime delegates were, in fact, in the most perplexing dilemma. In August it scarcely seemed possible for them to prolong their purposeless stay in England until the late autumn; but on the other hand they could hardly leave and come tamely back again without feeling slighted themselves and suffering serious discredit at home. Carnarvon's suggested compromise of a meeting at the end of September did not reach Ottawa until late in August; and by that time the Canadians were deep in the Fenian crisis; and the senior ministers, who would, of course, form the delegation, did not believe they could possibly leave the province until the lateness of the season ended all real danger of attack.[74]

At first the Maritime delegates were extremely annoyed; but as the summer wore on into autumn, they began to realize that they could put their enforced leisure in London to very good use. Since they could scarcely go back to the Maritime Provinces without shame, they would simply transport Maritime politics to England. At the suggestion of J. C. Pope, the Premier of Prince Edward Island, who was also in London late that summer on private business, they took the case of the reluctant Island into consideration once again; and they pledged themselves to support a grant of $800,000 for the purchase of the absentee proprietors' rights, provided the Island would send delegates to the London conference.[75] By that time it was September, and Howe had published his anti-union pamphlet, *Confederation considered in Relation to the Interests of Empire.*[76] At Carnarvon's suggestion, Tupper replied, first in a letter to the *Daily News*, which had published an unexpectedly favourable review of Howe's effort, and then in a pamphlet of his own, *A Letter to the Rt. Hon. Earl of Carnarvon.*[77] William Annand, who had come with Howe to England, fired off a rejoinder to Tupper; Archibald and McCully published rebuttals to Annand. Several of the delegates and their opponents – Howe, Tupper, Annand, and McCully – were journalists – part-time journalists at least. Carrying on a brisk pamphlet warfare was a familiar and meritorious occupation; it almost made one feel one was back in the political mêlée in Halifax!

Yet, as Carnarvon kept anxiously repeating, too prolonged delay might yet do irreparable damage to union. The reconciliation of the Canadian and Maritime points of view – the adjustment of the Quebec scheme by whatever amendments the Maritimers felt they must insist upon – was the one great remaining task. Nobody could tell precisely how difficult it would be or how long it would take, for, apart from the New Brunswick demand for an Intercolonial Railway guarantee, the Maritime bill of complaints had never been set down in detail. But the work, whatever its difficulties, must be successfully completed by the beginning of the New Year, in time to take immediate advantage of the opening of the British Parliament; and this final conference – the London Conference – could not be approached with much hope of easy success if the Maritimers had been seriously offended by what looked like studied neglect.

Nobody could be certain. But the Canadians never lost their confidence. The Maritimers were committed; they themselves were committed. There was no turning back for anybody now. On the 7th of November, McDougall and Langevin sailed for England; and a week later, Macdonald, Cartier, and Howland followed.

CHAPTER FOURTEEN

Achievement

ON SATURDAY, the 17th of November, when McDougall and Langevin docked at Liverpool, Wilmot and Mitchell of New Brunswick were waiting to greet them.[1] That night Langevin slept gratefully at the Westminster Palace Hotel, in a bed that neither pitched nor rolled; and next morning, when he had lit the little gas fire in his frigid bedroom, he looked out through the streaming window on a typical English November day of wind and heavy rain. Only the New Brunswickers were in town that day; but Tupper, Archibald, and Ritchie of Nova Scotia, who, with their wives, had been visiting Paris, returned to London on Monday. Monday was a fine day, and McDougall and Langevin set out to pay their respects to Lord Carnarvon at the Colonial Office; but the bad weather – 'brumeux, humide, malsain, un vrai temps de Londres' – closed in again;[2] and by the end of the week Langevin was waiting almost as impatiently as the Maritimers for the arrival of his fellow Canadians. It was late on Sunday night, the 25th of November, when Macdonald, Cartier, and Howland reached the capital.[3] Only Galt – a delegate, and an important one, though no longer a minister – was absent now; but Galt's knowledge would be vital in the discussions of federal and provincial finance, and the Canadians did not want the conference to begin without him. They waited; and the second night he was in London Macdonald went off to the theatre.

Appropriately enough, the Maritime and Canadian delegations were separated. The Canadians occupied two sets of rooms in the Westminster Palace Hotel, at the corner of Victoria and

Tothill streets. It was a convenient place, close to the Houses of Parliament, with Whitehall, Downing Street, and the Colonial Office only a short distance away. The Maritimers, more distant from Parliament and government, were all living in the Alexandra Hotel, near Park Lane and overlooking Hyde Park. Maritimers and Canadians often visited and entertained each other at their respective hotels; but for these first discussions, which were exclusively among the delegates themselves, without participation by any member of the British government, the Westminster Palace Hotel became the official place of meeting, and in the end gave its name to the conference. On its ground floor was a long, spacious room, handsomely decorated in white and gold in a rather ornate Corinthian style, and normally used as a lecture room or concert hall. The delegates secured this for the meetings, and here the third and last of the union conferences was held.

At about noon on Tuesday, the 4th of December, the delegates were assembling for the first of their formal sessions.[4] It was a different company from that of either the Charlottetown or the Quebec Conference, smaller in size and slightly but significantly altered in membership. The Nova Scotian delegation, again five in number, had changed least. J. W. Ritchie, who had replaced Robert Dickey, was a new delegate; but the four familiar faces – the incisive, aggressive Tupper; the impulsive McCully; Archibald, calm and reflective; and Henry with his strongly marked features, his hearty, genial ways, and his gout – were all back again.[5] R. D. Wilmot, whom Langevin thought extremely ugly, was the only new New Brunswick delegate. Johnson, Fisher, Mitchell, and Tilley had all been to Quebec; but striking personalities such as E. B. Chandler and the fashionably dressed, rather elegant John Hamilton Gray had not been sent to London; and in their places, the principals, by luck or accident, of the crisis of 1865-6 had taken on a new prominence. Fisher was, if possible, more voluble than ever, and the saturnine Mitchell went around in a way that suggested an untroubled view of his own importance.[6]

A year of crisis at Ottawa had similarly affected the Canadian delegation less seriously than might have been expected. With six members, three from Canada East and three from Canada West, it was smaller than the delegation that had gone to Charlottetown and only half the size of that which had represented Canada at Quebec. Langevin and McDougall had been present both at Charlottetown and Quebec; and three of the 'big four' – Macdonald, Cartier, and Galt –were in their accustomed places. Only Brown was absent. Like Galt, he had been invited to go, though no longer in the ministry; but the invitation had offended him as unsuitable and he had declined.[7] The absence of his huge frame, his robust personality, his immense enthusiasms, violent dislikes, and rough, fervid eloquence left the biggest gap, literally as well as metaphorically, in the conference. It was amusingly emphasized by his replacement, the Reformer W. P. Howland, a cautious, prudent man, reserved to excess.

As soon as they were all seated around the table, Tupper, seconded by Tilley, proposed Macdonald as chairman.[8] The nomination was unanimously accepted. Nobody now thought of questioning Macdonald's pre-eminence. After nearly three years, during which the leadership of the union movement had never been definitely settled, he had finally taken his place at the front. The 'ablest man in the Province' Monck had called him, without qualification;[9] and Tupper and Tilley were ready freely to acknowledge him as the foremost politician in British North America. A few months before, his lapses into drunkenness, his abusive language, and his neglect of public affairs had been the scandalous subjects of public criticism; but as he sat at the conference table that morning, the delegates may well have wondered how these preposterous accusations could ever have been invented. He was in complete command of the entire situation. As George Brown himself had said on the journey over to England in the spring of 1865, he was as 'steady as a rock'.[10] On all great occasions – the Charlottetown Conference, the Quebec Conference, the mission to England, and now the London Conference, he had been – he would always be – 'steady as a rock'. For him the trivial fag-end of a parliamentary session, the placid sequel to prolonged toil and tension, the irremediable collapse of plans and hopes, were times when he could let himself go with utter recklessness. But for the great moments – the moments of preparation and achievement – he kept and gave everything he had. 'C'est *l'homme* de la conférence,' Langevin said soberly.

The conference was about to open; and the dangerous moment when the Quebec scheme, to which the Canadians were committed, would meet the criticisms and amendments of the Maritimers was at hand. It was the one great unknown peril that the union movement yet had to encounter, and the Canadians had been dreading it; but the moment went by so easily and naturally that afterwards they were hardly aware of the significance of its passage. Tilley reminded the conference – in accordance with the terms of New Brunswick's union resolution – that his Province was in London on condition that provision be made in the union plan for the construction of the Intercolonial Railway;[11] Tupper recounted the abortive efforts that had been made to bring Prince Edward Island in at the last;[12] and then, without a pause, as if it were the most natural thing in the world, as if it had been the only possible way to set about their business, the delegates settled down to a systematic review of the Quebec Resolutions.

There was, in fact, nothing else for them to do. Despite all that had been said and hinted in Halifax and Fredericton, it would have been impossible for them to start all over again; and they knew it. The creative energies of British America had exhausted themselves in those few months of inspired planning and improvisation in the summer and autumn of 1864. With what aims, and on what principles, could they begin anew? Even the sharpest critics of the Quebec scheme had never put forward a definite list of precise amendments. And Tupper, Tilley, and the rest had never been the foremost critics of the plan; they had been its apologists and, in part, its creators.

The Quebec Resolutions would stand. They would constitute the foundation and the greater part of the superstructure of the federal constitution. But if no major changes were conceivable, minor amendments were possible and likely; and one of the most important of them, on the perilous subject of education, came up for discussion on the second day of the conference.

Already, in a single day's brisk work, the delegates had made remarkable progress. They had got down to the twenty-ninth resolution, which set out the powers of the general parliament; and next day, December the 5th, they took up the powers of the local or provincial legislatures. The sixth section of Resolution 43 gave education to the provinces, 'saving the rights and privileges' – so ran D'Arcy McGee's amendment at Quebec – 'which the Protestant or Catholic minority in both Canadas may possess as to their denominational schools at the time when the union goes into operation'. It was a comparatively narrow proviso, which would affect only two of the future provinces of the union; but the forces that were to broaden it had been gaining in strength, particularly since the previous summer.

The pressure came from two main sources. On the one hand, the defeat of the Lower Canadian schools bill in the summer session of 1865 had left a natural demand that its unfulfilled aim must be realized in some other fashion. On the other hand, the drastically limited scope of Resolution 43 had inspired the hierarchy of the Maritime Provinces, led by the energetic and influential Thomas L. Connolly, Archbishop of Halifax, to demand that similar protection should be given to the Roman Catholics of Nova Scotia and New Brunswick. All that the existing Resolution 43 did was to safeguard the rights of the two minorities in the Canadas as they were at the time when the union went into effect. It would not protect the new rights and privileges which the Protestants of Canada East had hoped, and failed, to acquire by the school legislation of the summer of 1866, but which they might gain in the future; and it would not protect the Roman Catholics of the Maritime Provinces at all. In fact, for Maritime Roman Catholics, the educational subsection had an even more serious defect. In Nova Scotia and New Brunswick, education was not exclusively provided by the churches as in Canada East, nor organized by the state, with Roman Catholic separate schools as an integral part of the provincial system, as in Canada West. Most of the privileges that the Maritime – and particularly the Nova Scotian – Roman Catholics possessed in respect to education were extra-legal and acquired simply by usage and custom.

By the time the Canadian delegates were ready to leave for England, it had become an open secret that in the new constitution the religious minorities in both the Canadas would be granted the right to appeal to the central government against any law of a provincial legislature that prejudicially affected their educational interests.[13] At Halifax, where McDougall and Langevin stopped on their way from Boston to Liverpool, they met the determined clerics who were intent upon extending all possible educational privileges to the Roman Catholic minority of the Maritime Provinces. Archbishop Connolly, Bishop Rogers of Chatham, even poor Bishop Sweeney of Saint John – looking properly embarrassed, Langevin thought, at the thought of his notorious Anti-Confederate stand in the election of 1865 – were there in a formidable phalanx to greet him.[14] Archbishop Connolly had already been in England that autumn discussing education with the Maritime delegates; and now that the Canadians were at last on their way and the conference was obviously about to begin, he had booked a passage on the *China* and sailed with Langevin and McDougall for Liverpool. In London he haunted the delegates and the Colonial Office; he was persistent, tenacious, talkative, a little egotistical, and inclined to place a high value upon his contribution to the success of confederation in the Maritime Provinces. The idea of an appeal to the central government against provincial legislation affecting minority educational privileges pleased him; but in his view it did not go nearly far enough. He wanted something much more formidable – to have Maritime Roman Catholics placed in approximately the same position as the Protestants of Canada East with respect to education.[15]

But this was something the delegates in conference at the Westminster Palace Hotel could not possibly grant. They were redistributing legislative power in British America, not exercising it themselves. If the school laws of Nova Scotia and New Brunswick were to be altered for the benefit of the Roman Catholics, it could only be done by the legislatures of those provinces, and probably after confederation; and to get the denominational schools of Canada East accepted as a pattern for the whole of British America – which was what Archbishop

Connolly hoped for – was a quite impossible task. Bell of Russell had tried, and dismally failed, to apply the Lower Canadian system to Canada West; and if a similar attempt could have been made in either Nova Scotia or New Brunswick, it almost certainly would have been an equally complete failure. Connolly was asking for something no legislature, outside of Canada East, would be willing or able to give; and all that the delegates in London could do, at Galt's suggestion, was to extend the limits of their right of appeal in both space and time. All provinces were now to share in the privilege; and it was to apply to separate or dissentient schools that might be established after, as well as to those that had been established before, the union went into effect.[16] The defect, serious from the point of view of the Maritime bishops, remained that the appeal was granted with respect to educational rights and privileges instituted by law, not those sanctioned by use and custom.

By the end of the first week, the delegates had completed their initial review of the Seventy-two Resolutions. Galt's amendment – the right of appeal – to the educational clause was the only important amendment they had agreed upon. A number of resolutions, however, including all those relating to property and finance, had been left for further consideration; and a special committee, composed of the financial experts of the three provinces, had been appointed to deal with them.[17]

≫ II ≪

ON TUESDAY, December the 11th, when the London Conference had been in session a week, Macdonald, Cartier, and Galt took the train to Newbury to pay a visit to a person with whom they were to be very closely associated for the next few months, the new Colonial Secretary, Lord Carnarvon. A comparatively young man of thirty-five, Henry Howard Molyneux Herbert, fourth Earl of Carnarvon, brought to the problems of British American union a warmer interest than Edward Cardwell had ever displayed, if not as great a critical or executive ability. He had Cardwell's firm belief in a strongly centralized British

American union, and all Cardwell's eagerness to see it realized
as quickly as possible; but he looked on confederation, not as
an incident in the unravelling of British colonial problems in
North America, but as the significant beginning of a potentially
great British American nation. In his quiet, unassertive, but
convinced fashion, he was that preposterous oddity of the 1860s,
an enthusiast for the future of the Empire. Slight in build, of
middle height, with fine-cut features, dark brown eyes, wavy
hair, and a short, rather wispy moustache, he could be a gracious
host and a charming companion;[18] and his country house, High-
clere Castle, with its lovely setting of rolling parkland and noble
beech trees, became, on the night of December 11th, an informal conference chamber for the discussion of British American
union.

Wednesday, when Macdonald, Cartier, and Galt returned to
London, was a day of accidents, one narrowly averted, and one
only too real. The brief, dreary December day – it ended in mid-
afternoon – was thick with fog; and at one point on the journey
back to London, the three travellers and their carriage nearly
crashed off the rails and into a ditch.[19] It was well past eleven
o'clock at night before they got back to the Westminster Palace
Hotel; but for Macdonald the day was never finished until he
had gone through the newspapers. With his candle by his side,
he settled down, as usual, to read in bed, fell asleep, and woke
in consternation to discover that the bed, bed-clothes, and curtains were blazing about him. He characteristically kept his
head, and, with Galt's and Cartier's help, smothered the flames
in feathers from his pillows and bolster, and water from the jugs
in the three adjoining bedrooms.[20]

Only then, when the three of them sat looking at the ruined
bed and the pile of feathers on the floor, did Macdonald realize
that his hair, forehead, and hands were scorched and that his
right shoulder-blade was rather seriously burned. 'So I got it
dressed,' he said airily, later on, 'and thought no more of it.'[21]
He was in his usual place as chairman next morning, as if nothing had happened; and it was well that he felt so little affected,
for the discussion quickly took a critical turn. On that day,
Thursday, December the 13th, the delegates began their second

review of the constitution, taking up and settling, one by one, the points they had left for further consideration. They arrived at the seventh resolution, which established the regional composition of the legislative council; and there they stopped.

Everybody had expected the problem of the upper house to emerge again. The basic disagreements over its nature had never been really reconciled; and even if a dispute over fundamentals could have been avoided, one particular point would have to be clarified before the scheme was complete. What was to happen to the four places in the council which, by the eighth Quebec Resolution, were to be given to Prince Edward Island? The latest suggested inducement – the $800,000 grant proposed by the Maritime delegates to buy up the absentee proprietors' rights – was obviously not going to bring Prince Edward Island into confederation. The Canadian government, approaching this proposal in a very cautious and legalistic spirit, insisted that all that Canada and the Maritime Provinces could do in the matter would be to make a strong representation to the future federal parliament recommending the payment of the suggested sum.[22] The Islanders had not shown any great enthusiasm for the idea, even when it was assumed to imply a firm commitment; and when the guarded Canadian reply arrived, the Island government seized on it in some relief as the welcome end to a doubtful business. Prince Edward Island was not going to take up its four places in the legislative council, at least not for the present; and the Maritime delegates had devised a simple solution for the vacant seats. The Maritime regional representation in the council must not be reduced, they argued, pending Prince Edward Island's final decision. It should remain a representation of twenty-four members, to be divided equally between Nova Scotia and New Brunswick.[23]

In the end this obvious solution seemed reasonable to everybody; but this unfortunately did not mean that the conference was finished with the upper house. The eighth of the Quebec Resolutions determined the number of members in the legislative council, the eleventh provided for their appointment for life by the central government; and together these raised a far more serious issue, which some delegates believed had never yet been satisfactorily resolved. At Quebec, the protest against appointment for life had been cut short by the sterner struggle over regional representation; but the Reformers from Canada West continued stubbornly to prefer election; and they had been greatly encouraged when, in his dispatch of the 3rd of December, 1864, Edward Cardwell had picked out the legislative council for one of his few criticisms of the Quebec scheme.[24] What was to happen if this upper house with its rigid total of life members – this body of seventy-two unremovable oligarchs – was to come into collision with the lower chamber, henceforth to be known as the House of Commons? In the British parliamentary system, where the upper house had come by convention to occupy a subordinate position, particularly in finance, it had always been possible to overcome its resistance by adding new members. New peers could be created in the United Kingdom; new councillors could be appointed in British North America.

But this, as things stood, would not be possible in the legislative council of the future confederation. In British North American history, it was a new kind of upper house. Its number was fixed at seventy-two; the tenure of its members was limited only by death. The delegates, with their long parliamentary experience and their settled belief in the primacy of the lower house, looked at these facts, and their possible consequences, with some dismay.[25] The two western Liberals, Howland and McDougall, protesting against this 'irresponsible chamber of crown appointees', suggested election for a term of years by the provincial legislatures; and their proposal won considerable support from the New Brunswick delegation, and even some from Nova Scotia. 'Do you wish to stereotype an upper branch irresponsible both to the Crown and the people,' Henry of Nova Scotia asked rhetorically, 'a third body interposed unaccountable to the other two? The Crown unable to add to their number. The people unable to remove them. Suppose a general election results in the election of a large majority in the lower house favourable to a measure, but the legislative council prevent it from becoming law. The Crown should possess some power of enlargement.'[26]

Nobody could deny the force of Henry's argument; but neither could anyone forget that the legislative council – the future Senate – had been regarded from the first as the heart of the proposed federal system. With its regional rather than provincial representation, and its members appointed by the central government, it could be criticized – and was criticized by those disgruntled Reformers Howland and McDougall – as a very anomalous embodiment of the federal principle. But to both Maritimers and Lower Canadians it was their sole protection against the brute force of numbers that would determine the House of Commons. 'I feel that we are now touching the very life of the whole scheme,' Jonathan McCully said earnestly;[27] and the delegates agreed with him. The Crown, it was admitted on all sides, could not be given an unlimited power to appoint; the grant of authority to swamp the council would imperil its essential character. But, on the other hand, would it not be possible, in order to avoid a deadlock between the two houses, to provide for the addition of a small number of members, 'in equal proportions from each division', so as to preserve the regional equality of the house? The suggestion, made by McCully, was tacitly accepted by the delegates; but it was left for the drafting stage. And without making any further changes in the legislative council, the conference went on with its review of the Quebec scheme.

For another full week, the delegates continued their work. There were no night sessions; but equally there were no days off. At Quebec, George Brown, not noticeably laconic himself, had complained that the Maritimers indulged in too much 'talkee-talkee'; and at London Galt told his wife that 'our friends from the Maritime Provinces are excessively fond of talking.'[28] Yet the thorough discussions did not make any serious impression on the Quebec scheme. The abrogation of the Reciprocity Treaty had terminated American privileges in the inshore fisheries of British America and had thus raised the problem of their future protection against the depredations of American fishermen. At Tupper's suggestion, the subject 'sea coast and inland fisheries' was removed from the list of provincial powers and transferred to the enumerated powers of the federal parliament. This was the only amendment of importance in the distribution of legislative authority; and even the changes in the financial arrangements of the Quebec scheme were fewer than might have been expected or than the Maritimers probably desired. Rather more money was to be provided for the provinces, but without disturbing either the debt allowance system or the basic subsidy rate. Each province would receive a special grant 'for the support of their local governments and legislatures'; and for Nova Scotia and New Brunswick, the subsidy of eighty cents per head of population according to the census of 1861 was to be increased with the increase of each new census, 'until the population of each of those Provinces shall amount to four hundred thousand souls, at which rate it shall thereafter remain'.

By Friday, the 21st of December, the delegates had nearly finished their work; and late on Monday, the day before Christmas, Macdonald informed Lord Carnarvon that the 'London Resolutions' were ready to be sent to the Colonial Office.[29]

≫ III ≪

CHRISTMAS DAY was dull with December gloom: 'le temps est sombre aujourd'hui,' Langevin wrote resignedly to his wife. Most of the delegates, both Maritime and Canadian, had friends or relatives in Great Britain; and for the last twelve hours they had been eagerly departing, by half a dozen different railway stations, to various parts of England and Scotland for the holidays. Only Langevin and Macdonald remained. Langevin, who had neither English relatives nor his colleague Cartier's convivial talent for improving acquaintanceships, had nowhere to go; and Macdonald, who had more invitations that he would have known what to do with, could accept none of them. The burn on his shoulder, which he had treated so nonchalantly, had taken on an ugly look. A doctor was consulted; and the unwilling patient had to keep to his bed for a few days, and stay carefully inside the hotel for a few more. 'I had a merry Xmas alone in my own room, and my dinner of tea and toast,' he reported cheerfully to his sister.[30] Langevin, pondering with sober pride on the historic achievements of the London Conference, went off to hear Archbishop Manning preach.[31]

In a few days, when the delegates had returned from their Christmas visits, the conference nominated a small committee to prepare a first rough draft of a bill;[32] and its members, the attorneys general of the different provinces, set to work to adapt the revised resolutions to the legal language of enactment. For the first time, the British Americans were conscious of a slight feeling of relaxation. The imperial Parliament would not meet until the 5th of February; and it would probably be another ten days at least before the Colonial Office began to busy itself seriously about Confederation. Langevin went off on a pious pilgrimage to Rome, and even Macdonald slipped across to the Continent for a few days' holiday. After the first week in January, the pace quickened again. Carnarvon returned to town; the Governor General, Lord Monck, who had followed the Canadian delegates across the ocean, came over from his country seat in Ireland and settled down in his town house in Hill Street, Berkeley Square;[33] and F. S. Reilly, the professional legal expert, was at work on the second draft of the bill. There were delays in drafting and printing; and, with the worst of ill luck, Carnarvon was confined to his room for a few days, with a bad attack of gout.[34] But by the 24th of January, the bill was ready, and copies reached the delegates.[35] And on Saturday, the 26th, along with the Parliamentary Under-Secretary, C. B. Adderley, the Permanent Under-Secretary, Sir Frederic Rogers, and the draftsman, Reilly, they assembled at Lord Carnarvon's house in Grosvenor Street for their first formal conference on the draft.[36] With the ailing Carnarvon, who could not yet leave his house, in the chair, they began to go systematically over its tentative provisions.

Both Carnarvon and Monck were ardent centralists, whose 'foremost object', as Carnarvon put it, was undoubtedly 'to strengthen, as far as is practicable, the central government against . . . the encroachments of the local administrations'.[37] Their inspiration may very well have helped to shape some of the new and distinctive features of Reilly's draft. Up to then, in the Quebec Resolutions, the London Resolutions, and the local government resolutions passed by the Canadian parliament in the previous summer, the chief executive officer of each province had been invariably called the lieutenant-governor or governor. Now, in the new draft bill, he was styled by the humble designation of 'superintendent' and the local assemblies were empowered to pass 'ordinances' only.[38] Much more important than these was the change in the position of Macdonald's major interest, the residuary clause, and the enormous improvement in its wording. It was placed – its only logical position – at the head of the section dealing with the powers of the federal parliament; the specific enumerated powers were then listed; and their significance, as mere examples which illustrated but by no means covered the vast range of the residuary authority, was expressed with admirable clarity.[39]

The delegates accepted the new residuary clause with gratitude; they had to reject the local 'superintendents', perhaps with some regret. But these were not the only changes that confronted them in the draft. There was another, extremely startling innovation, much more provocative and contentious than any of the others. It provided that the legislative council – or Senate, as they were now beginning to call it – would not remain a body of lifetime oligarchs; instead, after a period when there would be no change, one-eighth of its members were to retire by rotation every year. As certain delegates had feared, and as the Reformers McDougall and Howland had frankly hoped, the British cabinet, as well as the Colonial Secretary and the Colonial Office officials, strongly objected to a Senate with fixed numbers, appointed for life, on the ground of a possible deadlock with the House of Commons; and, as Carnarvon explained, the proposed change, a frank departure from the Quebec scheme, was the imperial government's device for avoiding the danger. Once again, the whole intractable and harassing subject had been opened. The barely suppressed conflicts of opinion within the conference – the divisions between Upper and Lower Canadians, between Nova Scotians and New Brunswickers, even between the different members of a single delegation – trembled on the edge of a final explosion.[40]

For the next three days the delegates struggled to reach agreement. On Monday and Tuesday, the 28th and 29th, they talked the problem over with Carnarvon and his officials at the Colonial

Office. It was obvious, with the weight of British disapproval added to the large measure of dissent inside the conference itself, that the Quebec plan for the Senate would have to be changed; and the only remaining questions were how far the change would go and by what means it would be effected. The resistance of the Senate in a possible conflict with the House of Commons could be weakened in various ways; its composition could be altered annually, as the draft bill envisaged, by the change of a certain proportion of its membership; or, as McCully and Macdonald had suggested, a small number of additional members, equally representative of the three divisions, could be appointed in the case of a deadlock; or finally, as was done in the British Parliament Act of 1911, the House of Commons might be empowered, under certain conditions, to pass money bills or other legislation notwithstanding their rejection by the Senate. The last two methods were combined in the original counter-proposal that the delegates presented to the British officials;[41] but in the end they retained only the right of the Crown to appoint additional senators, without specifying the circumstances that would justify the appointments. Lord Carnarvon and the cabinet believed that no fewer than twelve additional members were necessary to guard against a possible deadlock; but the majority of the delegates, strong in their belief that the Senate was the final safeguard of sectional interests and 'racial' customs, reduced the number to six.[42]

This, the last crisis in the framing of the British North America Act, was also a brilliant revelation of Macdonald's extraordinary powers of statesmanship. They were well known – perhaps too well known – to the Canadians; the Maritimers were becoming acquainted with them; but to onlookers at the Colonial Office, such as Sir Frederic Rogers, the Permanent Under-Secretary, they were impressive as well as new. Sir Frederic, who had a civil servant's normally critical attitude to his political chief, thought Carnarvon a rather disappointing chairman of the meetings. 'Macdonald was the ruling genius and spokesman,' he observed, 'and I was very greatly struck by his power of management and adroitness. The French delegates were keenly on the watch for anything which weakened their securities;

on the contrary, the Nova Scotia and New Brunswick delegates were very jealous of concessions to the *arrière* province; while one main stipulation in favour of the French was open to constitutional objections on the part of the home government. Macdonald had to argue the question with the home government on a point on which the slightest divergence from the narrow line already agreed on in Canada was watched for – here by the French, and there by the English – as eager dogs watch a rat hole; a snap on one side might have provoked a snap on the other, and put an end to the concord. He stated and argued the case with cool, ready fluency, while at the same time you saw that every word was measured, and that while he was making for a point ahead, he was never for a moment unconscious of the rocks among which he had to steer.'[43]

By the 2nd of February – with the opening of Parliament only three days away – the problem of the Senate had been settled. There remained a far from merely formal question – the question of nomenclature. The two sections of the Province of Canada gave up their old, rather cumbrous titles and became Ontario and Quebec. There was no difficulty about these changes; there was no difficulty even about the name of the new nation. It was to be 'Canada'; a Maritime delegate proposed the name and it was unanimously accepted.[44] Only one problem – the determination of the rank or style of the new nation – was left; but it was nearly the most delicate and significant of all. The fulfilment of the delegates' hopes hung upon it. The fundamental nature, and perhaps even the ultimate destiny, of the nation they were creating depended upon it.

There was no doubt about the choice of the British Americans. They wanted to call their new nation a kingdom. At Halifax, at the time of the Charlottetown Conference, Macdonald had talked of 'founding a great British monarchy, in connection with the British Empire';[45] the delegates had come to the Quebec Conference, Frances Monck reported, to create a 'United Kingdom of Canada'.[46] 'There exists in Canada and I think also in the other provinces', Monck informed Carnarvon in September 1866, 'a very strong desire that Her Majesty would be graciously pleased to designate the union a "Kingdom" and so give to her representative the title of "Viceroy". The wish is based on a consciousness of their increasing importance and a desire on their part to reconcile their highly prized position in reference to the Crown of England with the natural yearning of a growing people to emerge, at least in name, from the provincial phase of existence.'[47] The 'natural yearning' was just as strong in London as it had ever been before; and in their revision of the Colonial Office draft, the delegates changed the insipid title 'United Province' to 'Kingdom'.

But they were not going to get their way. Already the reception at the Colonial Office of Monck's dispatch of the previous September had shown how strong and instinctive was the opposition of the English governing class to the Canadian proposal. The proud title 'kingdom' was both premature and pretentious, the Colonial Office clerks considered; but their disapproval was not founded solely, or perhaps even mainly, on the astonishing impropriety of this colonial attempt to eliminate national class distinctions. 'Kingdom' and 'viceroy' were terms to be avoided, C. B. Adderley believed, for they were 'too open a monarchical blister on the side of the United States';[48] and British fear of incurring the displeasure of the irascible republic was probably one of the main causes for the rejection of the delegates' request.

There was some reason for this fear. American attitudes to the creation of a separate and united British America, so far as they had been shown at all, had been unsympathetic, if not hostile; but it was clear by this time that this unfriendliness was not going to find expression in action. The struggle between President Andrew Johnson and Congress over the problems of postwar reconstruction had come to monopolize American political energies to the exclusion of almost everything else. In the congressional elections of 1866, the Radical Republicans had sought to win the Irish-American vote by a reckless patronage of Fenianism; and as a result British America had endured six months of border terrorism. But once the Radicals had consolidated their majority in Congress, interest in the North and concern for the future of British North America largely died away in the obsessive violence of the controversy over the fate of the conquered South.

Yet there were a few public protests. On the 27th of February, H. J. Raymond attempted to introduce into the House of Representatives a resolution requesting the President to inform the House 'whether any remonstrance has been made by this government against the proposed consolidation of all the British North American Provinces into a single confederation under the imperial rule of an English prince . . .'.[49] Exactly a month later, N. P. Banks, for the committee on foreign affairs, reported a resolution that declared that 'the people of the United States cannot regard the proposed confederation of the Provinces on the northern frontier of this country without extreme solicitude; that a confederation of states on this continent, extending from ocean to ocean . . . and founded upon monarchical principles, cannot be considered otherwise than in contravention of the traditions and constantly declared principles of this government, endangering its most important interests, and tending to increase and perpetuate embarrassments. . . .'[50] The resolution passed the House of Representatives; but that was as far as the matter went. The United States made no further official protest against the northern union; and, by that time, its most offensive feature, in the eyes of good republicans, had disappeared. Sir Frederick Bruce, the British Minister at Washington, had sent home a copy of the Raymond resolution and had reported to the Foreign Office that the title 'Kingdom of Canada' had aroused 'much remark of an unfriendly character in the United States'.[51] He was promptly informed that he might deny the rumour that any such designation was to be conferred on the new union.

The first desire of the British Americans had been denied; they found a second-best alternative in the title 'Dominion'.[52] It was perhaps Tilley who discovered how appropriate to the ultimate territorial limits of confederation were the words of the Seventy-second Psalm, 'He shall have dominion also from sea to sea and from the river unto the ends of the earth'. By the second-last of the Quebec Resolutions, the Queen had been requested to determine 'the rank and name' of the federal union; but the daring suggestion of 'kingdom' had been successfully stifled in the Colonial Office, with some help – if help were needed – from the Foreign Office; and neither the Queen nor the Prime Minister, the Earl of Derby, was informed of the delegates' first choice. The Queen wanted more information and further assurances before she made a definite pronouncement; but she approved 'Dominion of Canada', though without much enthusiasm, apparently feeling that the style 'Dominion' was not a very happy addition to the title.[53] Derby, who, like Disraeli, showed remarkably little interest in British American union, was a good deal more outspoken. 'I do not know that there is any objection to the term "Dominion",' he wrote to Disraeli, 'though it strikes me as rather absurd.'[54]

By the end of the first week in February, the British North America Bill was ready for printing. Carnarvon sent a copy to the Queen on Monday, the 11th of February, and next day it was read for the first time in the House of Lords.

⇛ IV ⇚

O N SATURDAY, February the 16th, the British American colony in London gathered at St. George's Church, Hanover Square, for what was certainly the most important social event of the delegates' stay in England. John Alexander Macdonald, the chairman of the London Conference and the probable future Prime Minister of the Dominion of Canada, was to marry Miss Agnes Bernard. The Bernards were an English family that had given two generations of service to the British colonial Empire. Agnes's father had for some time been Attorney General of Jamaica; her brother, Colonel Hewitt Bernard, had become Macdonald's private secretary and had also acted as secretary to both the Quebec and London conferences. Macdonald's close association with Hewitt Bernard had not led directly, however, to a growing friendship with his sister. Mrs. Bernard and her daughter had gone back to live in England over a year earlier; and it was not until Macdonald met them, quite by chance, in Bond Street, during the early days of the London Conference, that the rapid courtship began.[55] Though she was considerably younger than Macdonald, Agnes Bernard was a mature woman, tall and handsome like her brother, with grace and poise and dignity. And Macdonald, at fifty-two, with his tall, slight frame, strongly marked features, and dark, bushy hair, had his own odd, attractive air of distinction.

Everybody was at St. George's, Hanover Square. It was a British North American occasion that called back the crowded events of that other busy assembly, the Quebec Conference. The Bishop of Montreal, Metropolitan of Canada, read the marriage service;[50] and four of the daughters of the delegates, the Misses Tupper, Archibald, McGee, and McDougall, attended the bride. Seventy people sat down to the wedding breakfast that Colonel Bernard gave for his sister at the Westminster Palace Hotel. There was a bouquet of violets at every place; and Francis Hincks, now Governor of British Guiana, who had helped Macdonald form the Liberal-Conservative coalition twelve years before, proposed the toast to the bride. It was mid-afternoon before the newly-married couple left for the briefest of honeymoons, at Oxford. Lord Carnarvon was expected to move the second reading of the British North America Bill early in the next week; and Agnes knew as well as John Alexander that they could not possibly miss that.

On Tuesday afternoon, February the 19th, they were both in their places in the gallery of the House of Lords. A row of British Americans watched and waited, with little flutters of excitement and apprehension when the Earl of Carnarvon rose for his great effort. Now the final realization of their plan might seem to be completely assured; but they had endured so much uncertainty and faced so many reverses that only the passage of the bill through Parliament could bring them satisfaction. In the meantime, there were certain disquieting circumstances which it was beyond their power to change and which they could not forget. Joseph Howe, who had haunted the Colonial Office earlier in the winter, had failed entirely to move the British government; but his famous petition, supposedly bearing thirty thousand signatures and begging the imperial Parliament to delay consideration of the bill until after the approaching general election in Nova Scotia, was about to be presented; and through some independent-minded member, such as the Radical John Bright, he still might have a considerable influence upon Parliament.

Even if the Derby-Disraeli ministry had possessed a solid majority and the session had been an ordinary one, there still would have been the possibility of some appalling misfortune. But in fact the question of electoral reform was dividing an already shaky cabinet and completely monopolizing the interest of an excited Parliament. The Derby government might fall over its Reform Bill, just as the Russell government had fallen nine months before; and the crisis of the spring of 1867 might be worse and more prolonged than the crisis of the summer of 1866.

The delegates badly needed reassurance; and the debate on Tuesday in the House of Lords was definitely reassuring.[57] Carnarvon was at his lucid and persuasive best; and his speech, which showed a sensitive appreciation of the varied interests that had been reconciled in the bill, was also a skilful and comprehensive defence against all the chief criticisms that could be directed against it. Monck, the Governor General, who spoke later, added the testimony of his experience in favour of the measure; Normanby, who a few years before had been Lieutenant-Governor of Nova Scotia, gave his fellow Lords the benefit of his knowledge 'of the way in which petitions were got up' in that province; and Earl Russell, though he would have preferred a thorough legislative union, declared his hearty approval of the bill and thereby largely ensured its support by the opposition.

It was a practical, useful debate, carefully managed by experts who were both forewarned and forearmed. Its intended audience was wider than the House of Lords; its chief purpose was to remove doubts and to quiet apprehensions. In the main it was a humdrum affair; but, at one point in his peroration, Carnarvon suddenly lifted the pedestrian argument to the heights of enthusiasm and prophecy; and for a few telling moments he spoke for the great nation of the future which the British Americans hoped and believed they were creating. 'In geographical area,' he told the Lords, 'this Confederation of the British North American Provinces is even now large – it may become one day second only in extent to the vast territories of Russia – and in population, in revenue, in trade, in shipping, it is superior to the Thirteen Colonies when, not a century ago, in the Declaration of Independence, they became the United States of America. We are laying the foundation of a great state – perhaps one which at a future day may even overshadow this country. But, come what may, we shall rejoice that we have shown neither indifference to their wishes nor jealousy of their aspirations, but that we honestly and sincerely, to the utmost of our power and knowledge, fostered their growth, recognizing in it the conditions of our own greatness.'[58]

On Friday, the 22nd of February, when the bill was in the committee stage, Carnarvon disposed, with easy dexterity, of a couple of half-hearted inquiries. The third reading was on Tuesday, the 26th; and it was not to pass without a dismaying foretaste of the kind of protest the delegates had been dreading in the Commons. Lord Campbell argued strongly that the bill ought 'to stand over' until after the general election in Nova Scotia.[59] Why should that province be hurried into an unwanted union with Canada? Why should it not join with Newfoundland and Prince Edward Island, which had declined to enter the Canadian confederacy, in a rival Maritime union? Lord Campbell's was a lone protesting voice; and in the end he withdrew his amendment in a rather shamefaced fashion. But Carnarvon felt it necessary to restate his former argument that the union measure was in the nature of a treaty, that it had been brought about only at the sacrifice of great personal and local interests, and that if the imperial Parliament postponed and thereby imperilled the realization of the agreement, it would incur a terrible responsibility.[60]

By this time, the crisis over British electoral reform had reached its climax in both cabinet and Parliament. Carnarvon, who, with General Peel and Lord Cranborne, was one of the three moderate ministers who wished to limit the scope of Disraeli's Reform Bill, had already threatened resignation. Carnarvon knew that at the next twist of the government's devious, harassed course he might be out of office; he knew too that the House of Commons, obsessed with the problem of parliamentary reform, did not particularly want to give its attention to British North America. But, as Campbell had said satirically in the

Lords, 'he had embarked on a career of irresistible velocity'; and he was determined to get his bill through in time if he possibly could. On Tuesday, February the 26th, the very day on which it had passed the Lords, it was read for the first time in the Commons. The second reading was fixed for Thursday, the 28th; and on Wednesday Hadfield got up to protest against the unseemly haste with which a bill affecting four millions of people was being rushed through the House without any real opportunity for consideration.[61] The government replied soothingly; but the order was not changed.

On Thursday afternoon the delegates were all waiting in a row in the gallery of the House of Commons. They were feeling excited and uplifted. On the previous day, their five leaders – Macdonald, Cartier, Galt, Tilley, and Tupper – had had the privilege of a private audience of the Queen.[62] She had had a few words to say to each of them and she had shown an obvious interest in the success of their bill. The sympathy of the Crown, together with the already granted approval of the House of Lords, seemed somehow to guarantee that now the imperial Parliament could not fail them. It would, of course, have been more flattering to British American self-esteem if a minister or at any rate somebody more prominent and talented than the Parliamentary Under-Secretary for the Colonies, C. B. Adderley, had been given the task of piloting the bill through the Commons. Carnarvon told Derby frankly that Adderley's 'incurable inaccuracy and confusion of mind' made him highly unreliable;[63] he could not, he said, answer for the management of affairs in the Commons if Adderley were left in charge; and at the last moment Derby rather belatedly considered asking a cabinet minister to take over.[64]

But it was Adderley who on Thursday, the 28th of February, moved the second reading of the bill. His speech was adequate – if no more than adequate – to the occasion.[65] He emphasized Carnarvon's point that the measure was a 'delicate treaty and compact', the final product of much 'mutual concession and compromise'. Like Carnarvon, he tried to discourage sympathy for the protests of British American Anti-Confederates and at the same time to enlist support on the ground of genuine imperial interests. Cardwell, upon whose informed assistance Carnarvon had counted, came strongly to Adderley's aid. England's colonial policy, he declared, could only be to assist in the growth – under the Crown of England, under the flag of England – 'of great and powerful communities'.[66] His speech, which committed an already willing opposition, ensured the passage of the bill. The only remaining question was whether Bright's expected intervention would be so effective as to prolong the debate, cause an adjournment, and upset Carnarvon's timetable.

But it did not do so. This was one cause for which John Bright felt neither enthusiasm nor conviction. He had no real interest in British America; his indifference to it was the reverse side of his profound sympathy for the American union. His speech showed far more concern for the sensibilities of American republicans and the pockets of British taxpayers than it did for the plight of the Nova Scotians.[67] He repeated the 'ill-natured' opinion that Canadian loyalty had its price; he indulged in a covert sneer at the 'nation' the British Americans imagined themselves to be creating. That British America should desire a political existence separate from that of the United States, that it should wish for institutions different from those of the United States, that it should actually prefer to call these institutions by such British titles as the 'House of Commons', seemed to Bright to be both perverse and preposterous. In his view, both the bill and the Nova Scotian petition against it were irrelevant to the manifest destiny of North America; and though he began by protesting against Parliament's forcing an unwilling Nova Scotia into union, he ended by declaring that he would not oppose the second reading. He raised no real issue and did not lift the debate from the level of satisfied acquiescence. The bill passed second reading with ease.

On Saturday, the 2nd of March, when the cabinet decided to revert to the original, more radical plan of parliamentary reform, Carnarvon, along with Peel and Cranborne, resigned. But by that time his measure was through in safety. On Monday, March the 4th, while he was explaining his resignation in the Lords, the bill went through the committee stage in the Commons with only trifling amendments. It passed third reading, without a word of debate, on the 8th of March; and on the 29th received the royal assent. England had finished all that she was to do for the union of British North America. She had not played her part with any great enthusiasm, or even much interest. She had played it with considerable relief. 'I am more than ever disappointed at the tone of feeling here as to the colonies,' Galt wrote sadly to his wife; 'I cannot shut my eyes to the fact that they want to get rid of us.'[68] *The Times* voiced Galt's suspicions openly and with blunt directness. 'We look to Confederation as the means of saving this country from much expense and much embarrassment,' it declared.[69] Englishmen put a low estimate on Canadian loyalty and a high valuation on freedom from American entanglements. Canada had been set on the road to nationhood which might soon end in the goal of independence; and in the meantime the Dominion was a possibly viable unity on which British responsibilities in North America could be conveniently deposited. Yet Great Britain's withdrawal from the new world had not been abrupt or selfishly thoughtless. She had delayed her departure until the British Americans had themselves decided upon union; and during their difficult and dangerous period of nation-making, she had repeatedly given her military aid. Her retreat had been unhurried, deliberate, dignified; and she had left behind a nation she hoped might endure.

⤜⤜ V ⤜⤜

THE DELEGATES could go home. The task of bringing the new Dominion of Canada into existence was now theirs and must be carried out in British America. The Maritimers, after eight months' stay in England, were ready enough to go back; but, in addition, there was a special political reason for their prompt return. The legislatures of both Nova Scotia and New Brunswick would have to meet for a last session, in order to provide, among other things, for any desired changes in their local constitutions. Tupper, whose eye was still fixed a little nervously on the approaching expiration of the Nova Scotian

Assembly, wanted as early a meeting as possible. He enjoyed the novel thrill of sending his recommendation to the Lieutenant-Governor by cablegram, caught the first available ship, and on the 16th of March, when the legislature met at Halifax, he was in his accustomed place.[70] Tilley, whose lease of power was not yet a year old, could afford to be more leisurely; the provincial parliament did not meet in Fredericton until nearly two months later.[71] The Canadians, who had decided to avoid the dangers of still another session by the simple expedient of not calling one, lingered longest of all in England. Macdonald did not return to Canada until early in May. Lord Monck, who had been asked to serve an extended term as Governor General, was not expected to be back until shortly before the union was inaugurated.

This, by Royal Proclamation, was to take place on the 1st of July. By that day, the first Dominion Day, a large number of important decisions would have to be made. The first senators would have to be chosen, the new lieutenant-governors appointed, and the new provincial governments set up. Of all the tasks, however, that faced the now victorious Confederates the formation of the first federal cabinet was without a doubt the most difficult. For public men who believed devoutly in the doctrine that the cabinet was the 'efficient secret' of parliamentary government, the structure of the federal ministry, though it could not be recorded in the constitution, was among the most important issues that they had to settle. It was generally agreed that the cabinet ought not to be too large, that if possible it ought not to be any larger than the former Canadian cabinet, which was normally composed of twelve ministers. In the end it turned out to be slightly larger, with thirteen rather than twelve members; but this approximate equality of numbers was the only point in which it at all resembled the Canadian cabinet of the past. The vast change that confederation brought was expressed as clearly in the organization of federal executive power as it was in any other part of the law or custom of the new constitution.

The former Canadian cabinets had been based upon a frank recognition of the dual character of the Province of Canada. The first cabinet of the Dominion definitely and explicitly rejected this dualism. Sectional representation would continue, of course, to be the guiding principle in the formation of the ministry; but henceforth three, not two sections, would be involved. The primacy of Ontario was to be acknowledged in the concession of five cabinet positions; Quebec was to have four; and Nova Scotia and New Brunswick two each. The Maritime region was to stand on an equality with Quebec; and while Lower Canada had occupied half the places in the old Canadian cabinet, Quebec would have less than a third in the new. Moreover, the number of French-speaking ministers had been correspondingly reduced. The parity of Canada East and Canada West had been sectional, not 'racial'; but, with four of the six Lower Canadian ministerial posts, French Canadians had held a third of the total. Now, with three cabinet positions at most, they would have less than a quarter.

But there was more than this. Still another distinctive feature of the first Canadian federal cabinet signified, with even sharper clarity, the radical nature of its departure from the past. In the Province of Canada the duality that prevailed in both the legislature and the cabinet had had its crowning expression in the dual premiership. There had been a long succession of 'double-headed' premiers; Baldwin-Lafontaine, Macdonald-Cartier, Brown-Dorion, Taché-Macdonald – the hyphenated leadership had been unbroken. But now this, like all the other conventions of dualism, was to be ended deliberately. By the time the delegates were ready to leave London it was known that Macdonald was to be the first Prime Minister of the new union. 'In authorizing you to undertake the duty of forming an administration for the Dominion of Canada,' Monck wrote to Macdonald later, 'I desire to express my strong opinion that, in future, it shall be distinctly understood that the position of First Minister shall be held by *one* person, who shall be responsible to the Governor General for the appointment of the other ministers, and that the system of dual First Ministers, which has hitherto prevailed, shall be put an end to. I think this is of importance, not only with reference to the maintenance of satisfactory relations between the Governor General and his cabinet, but also with a view to the complete consolidation of the union which we have brought about.'[72]

At the end of May, with a month before the union went into effect, Macdonald began to grapple seriously with the problems of cabinet-making. There was less difficulty with the Maritime Provinces than with either Ontario or Quebec; and least trouble of all with Nova Scotia. Tupper was a certainty; so also was Archibald, Tupper's chief Liberal associate. 'You will, of course, come on with Tupper,' Macdonald wrote casually to Archibald, as if there had been no doubt about the matter from the beginning.[73] Tilley's presence in the first federal cabinet was also a foregone conclusion; but there was some uncertainty about the second New Brunswick minister. 'I leave to you to select an associate from New Brunswick,' Macdonald wrote to Tilley. 'Is it to be Mitchell, Fisher, Wilmot, or who?'[74] Tilley confessed himself a little puzzled. Mitchell, whom Langevin had described as a good fellow with a badly swelled head, wrote to Macdonald with an elaborate affectation of detachment, to recommend himself as the representative of the important North Shore interests.[75] Tilley agreed that the consensus of opinion favoured Mitchell.[76] And the Maritime contingent was complete.

It was composed of both former Liberals and Conservatives, Liberals predominating. From the first the Confederate movement had been a union of both parties; and this principle, which was accepted everywhere, had been formally recognized in the Coalition government of the Province of Canada. The Coalition still continued, though for nearly a year Brown had been trying to break it up and was even then planning a monster convention of anti-Coalition Liberals, to be held in Toronto at the end of June. These attacks had certainly weakened the solidarity of Liberalism; but in the session of 1866, the majority of the western Reformers had stood by the Coalition; and there was good reason for assuming that in the first federal election the great mass of Ontario voters would remain faithful to the union that had given them confederation. This record and these expectations gave McDougall his bargaining power; he insisted that of the five Ontario members in the cabinet, three must be Liberals, 'your position as premier', he argued to Macdonald, 'equalizing the preponderance of Liberals in that Province.'[77] Macdonald, who had accepted the principle that there must be an approximately equal number of former Liberals and Conservatives as ministers, agreed.

But it was Quebec, rather than Ontario or the Maritime Provinces, that created the greatest problem. The first cabinet of the Dominion must represent 'racial' and religious, as well as regional, interests; and in the Province of Quebec the three categories became a tangle of conflicting claims. Cartier, under pressure from McDougall and Howland, was ready to concede that Ontario should have one more place than Quebec; but he insisted that three out of the four Quebec ministers must be French Canadians. This left the English-speaking Protestant minority, which was already worried about its prospects in confederation, and the Irish Roman Catholics, who were powerful in New Brunswick as well as in Quebec, competing for the sole remaining ministerial post. Galt, who was generally thought to be one of the ablest public men of his generation, was the acknowledged leader of the Protestant English of Quebec. D'Arcy McGee, who was known throughout British America as a prophet of confederation, was an influential Irishman who was fully aware of his own enormous popularity. 'I certainly have no desire to embarrass future arrangements which will naturally be under your direction,' McGee had written to Macdonald early in April, 'but in a Confederation government, founded on principles which I have always zealously advocated, I will, if in Parliament, give way neither to Galt, nor to a third Frenchman, "nor any other man".'[78]

For nearly a week, with the first Dominion Day only a fortnight away, Macdonald struggled to fit the intractable pieces of his puzzle together. He was almost ready to throw the whole business up in despair, when Tupper suggested a way out. Charles Tupper may have been a domineering man with a sharp tongue and a bullying manner; but he had far more generosity and public spirit than his many enemies would ever allow. He offered to surrender his own strong claims to office; and provided McGee would do as much, he could see a possible, if not a very impressive, solution to the difficulty. In the room their joint withdrawal would leave, another, a Roman Catholic, Nova Scotian could be appointed; and he would at one and the same time fill Tupper's place as a sectional representative and McGee's place as a representative of the Irish Roman Catholics of the Dominion. The initiative was Tupper's; he proposed the plan to McGee; and McGee accepted it with the same generosity of spirit.[79] Edward Kenny, who was a Nova Scotian and a Roman Catholic, and who had few other claims to distinction or to office, received, out of the blue, a telegram inviting him to become a minister of the Crown at Ottawa. The first Dominion government had been formed.

On the 27th of June, the list of cabinet members was published in the newspapers.[80] The next day, Friday, the ministers, who were now all assembled in the capital, went down in a body to greet Lord Monck who had arrived in Canada only two days before and had come up the Ottawa by steamer.[81] The executive government of the Dominion of Canada was now complete.

⫸ VI ⫷

IN 1867, THE LAST DAY of June was a Sunday; and in Christian British North America Sunday was a day of quiet, and rest and reflection, and church-going. It was also a day of visits and family parties and discreet jollification; and since Monday, Dominion Day, was to be a holiday, the Canadians had been granted that rare gift of their generation, a long week-end. Tomorrow there would be picnics, parades, and sports; and today farmers and their wives and children were driving down dusty country roads to pay calls, have dinner, or stay the night with friends or relatives in the next concession, or the near-by village, or the neighbouring township. The big table in the spacious winter-kitchen – all culinary arrangements had, of course, been transferred to the summer-kitchen late in May – was crowded with six or eight extra places; and there had been a piece of fresh beef, and a ham from the smoke-house, and new potatoes and new peas. In the afternoon they all went to church, the women and girls in their best summer crinolines, the men in rather rusty top hats. It was so bright and hot that the women had worried a little about their dresses sticking to the varnished oak pews.

And the minister preached about confederation and the future of Christian Canada.

In the towns and cities, the clergy and the journalists, those two groups that were expected to have great thoughts for public occasions, were busy at their respective callings. The journalists were writing inspiring leading articles for the first Dominion Day; and in many pulpits prayers were being offered and sermons preached for confederation. In St. Paul's Church, Montreal, the Rev. Mr. Jenkins, apologizing that he could scarcely do justice to his theme in fifty minutes, preached a fine sermon, divided, in good Presbyterian fashion, under four main heads, on the text 'Blessed is the nation whose God is the Lord'.[82] Church services were, of course, over by the time George Brown, hot, perspiring, and extremely thirsty, arrived at the *Globe* office on King Street, Toronto. He drank copiously, took off his coat, waistcoat, and collar, retired to his inner editorial office, and began to compose the enormous leading article, nine thousand words in length, which was to be the *Globe*'s salute to the 1st of July, 1867.[83] It flowed over into a second huge page of statistics on the population, trade, and navigation of the different uniting provinces.[84] Other editors were impressively reviewing the new Dominion's human and natural resources and speculating generously about its prospects of material advancement. They were also making sober appeals to the new nation's consciousness of maturity and its sense of obligation. 'Colony implies the political status of adolescence,' reflected the Montreal *Gazette*, 'but Dominion implies power and the political status of manhood; it implies also responsibility.'[85]

As midnight and the new day drew closer, people were thinking a good deal less about responsibility and much more about celebration, in even the soberest of Canadian towns and cities. In the central streets of Toronto, strangely gay Sunday groups began to gather; and in Ottawa, an hour before twelve o'clock, large crowds were beginning to assemble on Major's Hill and on the Ordnance Lands beyond the Cathedral. The bells of St. James' Cathedral in Toronto began to peal at midnight; impromptu parades of citizens, led by fifes and drums, were march-

ing happily up and down; and in King Street a huge bonfire was
kindled.[86] An even more splendid bonfire, a 'huge, pyramidal
pile', constructed of firewood, packing-cases, and tar barrels, had
been reared, the previous Saturday, on the Ordnance Lands in
Ottawa; and at the Cathedral clock's final stroke of twelve, it was
fired. There were cheers for the Queen and the Dominion; the
church bells chimed; rockets soared into the air and fell in
showers of coloured lights; and the Ottawa Field Battery – the
capital might be forgiven a rather grandiose expression of enthusiasm – wakened the whole town with the prolonged din of a
one-hundred-gun salute.[87]

Little by little, the laughing crowds came home. The gaslit
streets grew silent; and one by one, the house lights went out.
Long before that, oil lamps had been turned down and candles
blown out in the parlours and bedrooms of farm-houses. Still
earlier, the trundle beds had been pulled out, and the children,
including perhaps a few small visitors from across the townline
or the county boundary, had been put to bed. For a while their
elders had sat on in the big winter-kitchen, enjoying the cool of
the summer night and gossiping about the future. Everybody
was eager for tomorrow; everything was ready for the picnic that
was to be held in the near-by fair grounds, or on the common
under the elm trees beside the drowsy inland river. The children
had picked a great mound of wild strawberries; bottles of the
best raspberry cordial had been selected; two plump chickens
had been roasted and were waiting in the cellar; there were pans
of gingerbread, and crocks of lemon biscuits and twisted fried
cakes; and two of the girls had been deputed to start a freezerful
of frozen cream immediately after breakfast. All the preparations had been made. The lights were out now along the quiet,
starlit concession roads. And for a few hours, on that brief
summer night, the Canadians slept.

Their land slept too. They had occupied such a small part –
such a mere fringe of its grand totality. The great wheat-lands
of the North-West, which only the stars looked down on, had
never been touched by the plough; and beneath the unbroken
prairies and the scarred, primordial contours of the Precambrian

Shield there lay untouched and sunk in far more profound slumbers the undreamed-of mineral riches of the future. No young people had ever looked forward to such a vast inheritance. No new nation had ever begun its existence with such an enormous patrimony. It stretched so far from ocean to ocean that on these longest, richest days of summer, the sun ceased to shine on it for only a few hours; and for the whole land the last night before nationhood was brief indeed. It was still bright daylight in the Rocky Mountains and on the Pacific Coast when dusk began to settle down over Nova Scotia and New Brunswick. And it would still be deep night in the far West when the skies began paling over Eastern Canada.

They were paling now; and from Halifax to Sarnia, the Canadians were beginning to bestir themselves. The military – British regulars, volunteers, and home guards – were among the first to rise, for it was their duty to greet the day with gun salutes. All over the country, by forts, on grand parades, barrack squares, and garrison grounds, the great cannon would, as *Le Journal des Trois Rivières* put it, announce to the world 'que nous pouvions maintenant prendre place parmi les nations de la terre'.[88] The volunteers were putting the last touches to their dress uniforms. 'Nos volontaires sont sortis en grande tenue,' the St. Hyacinthe journalist declared proudly.[89] The streets were still nearly deserted in some places as the soldiers moved quickly towards the rendezvous; but in other towns the citizens had risen early to greet the day and watch the guns go off. At Saint John, New Brunswick, the streets were crowded with people before dawn.[90] The shops and houses were ablaze with flags; and great transparencies promised 'success to the Confederacy' and 'Bienvenue à la nouvelle Puissance'.

It was very early yet, the morning was still dull; but though the sky was pale and ashen, it was clear, and there was no doubt that the day would be warm and brilliant. Now the soldiers were all at their posts, beside the guns, waiting for the moment; and from a score of different stations scattered across Canada they looked out over the varying landscapes of their country – past rocky headlands towards the sea, down the St. Lawrence, the River of Canada, over the Great Lakes, or into the green abundance of orchards and farm lands. The sun had risen now; daybreak was on their faces; and the great guns roared their salute into the pale blue sky of morning.

A Note on Sources

This book is based on contemporary documents in manuscript or print, a body of material that is large in amount and varied in character. Since *John A. Macdonald: The Young Politician* was published twelve years ago, a number of collections of private papers have been made available for the first time; and the evidence for the history of British North America during the four crucial years 1863-7 is now both large in quantity and high in quality. The story of the making of Canadian Confederation can be told almost from day to day and with a wealth of circumstantial detail that would have been impossible a quarter-century earlier.

It is true that certain breaks in the chain of evidence – breaks that are not likely ever to be repaired – exist; and it is particularly unfortunate that some of the worst of these gaps in our information occur in the records of the Charlottetown, Quebec, and London conferences, the three intercolonial meetings in which the scheme of union was gradually worked out. These gaps in the official record are regrettable; but to some extent they can be filled in from unofficial sources, in manuscript or print. And for all other phases of the union movement, the available material is extremely rich.

A book such as this, which attempts to explain the ideas, aims, and conduct of the leaders in the making of Confederation, necessarily depends, for both completeness and vitality, upon the uninhibited expression of private letters. It is extremely fortunate that so much survives of the private correspondence

of this period in British American history. The Fathers of Confederation wrote freely and frequently to each other about their
common interests, and a large part of this invaluable material
has been preserved. At the Public Archives of Canada, undoubtedly the most important repository for the history of the union
movement, are to be found collections of the private papers of
John A. Macdonald, George Brown, Charles Tupper, A. T. Galt,
and William McDougall. A part of S. L. Tilley's correspondence
for the period has been acquired by the New Brunswick Museum
at Saint John, and there are other Tilley letters at the Bonar
Law–Bennett Library at the University of New Brunswick,
Fredericton. Finally, the private papers of H. L. Langevin are
included in the Chapais Collection at the Archives Publiques
de Québec, Quebec City.

The governors of British North America and the members of
both Liberal and Conservative governments in the United Kingdom also kept up a fairly active private correspondence on
various aspects of British American union. The Papers of Lord
Monck, at the Public Archives of Canada, are disappointing;
but, in compensation, the correspondence of Arthur H. Gordon,
at the Bonar Law–Bennett Library, Fredericton, is very reward-
ing; and the Williams Papers, at the New Brunswick Museum,
are also useful for the latter part of the story. Edward Cardwell
and Lord Carnarvon held office in succession as Secretary of
State for the Colonies during this period; and their Papers are
deposited in the Public Record Office in London. They are
supplemented, on the Liberal side of politics, by the Russell
Papers, also at the Public Record Office, by the Gladstone Papers,
at the British Museum, and by the Palmerston Papers, now in
the possession of Admiral of the Fleet the Earl Mountbatten of
Burma. Carnarvon's letters to Queen Victoria are at the Royal
Archives, Windsor Castle, and his correspondence with Disraeli
is to be found in the Beaconsfield Collection, Hughenden Manor,
High Wycombe.

Less outspoken and revealing, but essential, is the official
correspondence between the imperial authorities and the colonial
governments. The first side of this correspondence – the dispatches sent by the Governor-in-Chief and the Lieutenant-Gov-

ernors of British North America to the Secretary of State for the
Colonies in England – is much the more copious of the two. It
is divided among the various Colonial Office series – C.O. 42
for Canada, C.O. 188 for New Brunswick, C.O. 194 for Newfoundland, C.O. 217 for Nova Scotia, and C.O. 226 for Prince
Edward Island. The originals for these dispatches are kept in
the Public Record Office, London; but microfilm copies are
available at the Public Archives of Canada in Ottawa. The other
side of this official correspondence – the dispatches sent by the
Secretary of State for the Colonies to the different colonial
governors – may be consulted in the various divisions of the
G. Series in the Public Archives of Canada. The G. Series also
includes the greater part of the official correspondence among the
different governors; the Nova Scotian division of these dispatches
is deposited in the Public Archives of Nova Scotia at Halifax.

Other official sources, manuscript or printed, are the Executive
Council Minutes, and the *Journals* and *Debates* of the Legislative
Assemblies and Legislative Councils of the British American
provinces. The Minutes of Council do not provide much help
for this study; but the *Journals*, with their appendices, and the
Debates are extremely valuable. During this period Nova Scotia,
New Brunswick, and Prince Edward Island usually printed their
legislative debates; but Canada and Newfoundland, the richest
and the poorest of the colonies, did not. Fortunately Canada
made an exception for the debate on Confederation held in the
legislative session of 1865, which was officially printed; but otherwise the record of the debates in the legislatures of Canada and
Newfoundland can be found only in the newspapers of the time.
Hansard's Parliamentary Debates have been used for debates in
the Parliament of the United Kingdom, and the *Congressional
Globe* for debates in the Congress of the United States.

Contemporary newspapers are very useful, both as a record
of events – of election campaigns, for example – and as an
expression of public opinion. No attempt has been made in this
book to go over the ground so thoroughly covered in P. B. Waite's
*The Life and Times of Confederation, 1864-1867, Politics, News-
papers, and the Union of British North America.* Here attention
is focused rather upon a substantial group of representative

newspapers, both for and against Confederation, in most of the provinces and in both sections of Canada. The Canadian Library Association has microfilmed a number of the newspapers of the period; but in most cases the original files were consulted in the preparation of this book. Useful collections of newspapers, and of the *Journals* and *Debates* of the different colonial legislatures, are to be found in the following archives and libraries: the Public Archives of Canada and the Library of Parliament, Ottawa; the British Museum, London; the University of Toronto Library, and the Legislative Library, Toronto; the Public Archives of Nova Scotia, Halifax; the New Brunswick Museum and the Saint John Public Library, Saint John, New Brunswick; the Bonar Law–Bennett Library, Fredericton; and the Charlottetown Public Library, Prince Edward Island.

REFERENCES

Chapter 1 – Maritime Initiative

(pages 1-38)

1. J. Morley, *The Life of William Ewart Gladstone* (Toronto, 1903), vol. I, p. 597.
2. J. B. Conacher, 'A Visit to the Gladstones in 1894', *Victorian Studies* (December 1958), pp. 155-60; J. K. Chapman, *The Career of Arthur Hamilton Gordon, First Lord Stanmore, 1829-1912* (Toronto, 1964), pp. 12-13.
3. Chapman, *Gordon*, p. 14.
4. P. B. Waite, *The Life and Times of Confederation 1864-1867* (Toronto, 1962), p. 231.
5. Public Archives of Canada, Newcastle Papers (microfilm), Gordon to Newcastle, 13 October 1862.
6. *Ibid.*, Gordon to Newcastle, 16 March, 27 April, 1863.
7. University of New Brunswick Library, Stanmore Papers, Gordon to Newcastle, n.d., 1863.
8. Newcastle Papers, Gordon to Newcastle, 16 March 1863.
9. Stanmore Papers, Newcastle to Gordon, 29 May 1863.
10. Public Record Office, Colonial Office 188, vol. 137, Gordon to Newcastle, 31 December 1862.
11. J. Pope, *Correspondence of Sir John A. Macdonald* (Toronto, 1921), p. 29.
12. Newcastle Papers, Gordon to Newcastle, 22 December 1862.
13. *Ibid.*, Gordon to Newcastle, 27 April 1863.
14. Public Record Office, Cardwell Papers, vol. 39, Gordon to Cardwell, 24 October 1864.
15. W. L. Morton, 'British North America and a Continent in Dissolution, 1861-71', *History*, vol. 47, pp. 139-56.
16. W. S. MacNutt, *New Brunswick, a History: 1784-1867* (Toronto, 1963), pp. 396-7.
17. Newcastle Papers, Gordon to Newcastle, 22 November 1862.

18. Canada, Legislature, *Sessional Papers*, 1863, vol. 4, no. 14, L. V. Sicotte and W. P. Howland to Secretary of State for the Colonies, 23 December 1862.
19. Newcastle Papers, Gordon to Newcastle, 17 January 1863.
20. C.O. 188, vol. 137, Gordon to Newcastle, 31 December 1862.
21. Newcastle Papers, Gordon to Newcastle, 23 June 1863.
22. F. W. P. Bolger, *Prince Edward Island and Confederation, 1863-1873* (Charlottetown, 1964), pp. 24-6.
23. *Ibid.*, p. 25.
24. Newcastle Papers, Gordon to Newcastle, 23 June 1863.
25. C.O. 188, vol. 138, Gordon to Newcastle, 6 July 1863.
26. Newcastle Papers, Gordon to Newcastle, 22 November 1862.
27. J. K. Chapman, 'The Mid-Nineteenth Century Temperance Movement in New Brunswick and Maine', *Canadian Historical Review*, vol. 35, pp. 43-60; MacNutt, *New Brunswick*, p. 362.
28. C.O. 188, vol. 138, Gordon to Newcastle, 6 July 1863.
29. R. W. Winks, *Canada and the United States; the Civil War Years* (Baltimore, 1960), pp. 128-9.
30. *Nova Scotian* (Halifax), 14 September 1863; *British Colonist* (Halifax), 24 October 1863; *Morning News* (Saint John), 13 November 1863.
31. *Gazette* (Montreal), 3 July 1863.
32. *Leader* (Toronto), 2 July 1863.
33. *Gazette*, 7 July 1863.
34. *British Colonist*, 14 July 1863.
35. *Globe* (Toronto), 7 July 1863; *Evening Times* (Hamilton), 6 July 1863.
36. *Leader*, 7 July 1863.
37. *Globe*, 10 July 1863.
38. *Gazette*, 10 July 1863.
39. *Morning News*, 16 October 1863.
40. Newcastle Papers, Gordon to Newcastle, 29 July 1863.
41. *Ibid.*, Gordon to Newcastle, 14 September 1863.
42. C.O. 188, vol. 139, Gordon to Newcastle, 29 August 1863.
43. Newcastle Papers, Gordon to Newcastle, 14 September 1863.
44. Public Archives of Canada, G.8, B., vol. 43, Newcastle to Gordon, 31 July 1863.
45. E. M. Saunders (ed.), *The Life and Letters of the Rt. Hon. Sir Charles Tupper* (London and Toronto, 1916), vol. I, p. 7.
46. W. M. Whitelaw, *The Maritimes and Canada before Confederation* (Toronto, 1934), p. 184.
47. C.O. 188, vol. 139, Gordon to Newcastle, 28 September 1863.
48. *Ibid.*
49. New Brunswick, Assembly, *Journals*, 1864, Appendix, Correspondence Relating to the Intercolonial Railway, pp. 16-18.
50. *Morning News*, 19 October 1863.
51. *Ibid.*, 26 October 1863.
52. *Morning Chronicle* (Halifax), 27 October 1863.
53. New Brunswick, Assembly, *Journals*, 1864, Appendix, Correspondence relating to the Intercolonial Railway, p. 22.
54. *Morning Chronicle*, 27 October 1863.

55. *Morning Freeman* (Saint John), 20 October 1863.
56. *Morning Chronicle*, 8 October 1863.
57. *Ibid.*, 27 October 1863.
58. *Ibid.*, 27 October, 5, 21 November, 1, 3 December, 1863.
59. C.O. 188, vol. 139, Gordon to Newcastle, 7 December 1863.
60. *Ibid.*
61. Stanmore Papers, Doyle to Gordon, 9 January 1864.
62. *Ibid.*, Newcastle to Gordon, 28 November 1863.
63. Winks, *Canada and the United States*, pp. 244-63.
64. Public Record Office, C.O. 217, vol. 233, Doyle to Newcastle, 23 December 1863.
65. Saunders, *Tupper*, vol. I, p. 91.
66. *British Colonist*, 14 July 1863.
67. C.O. 217, vol. 233, Doyle to Newcastle, 23 December 1863.
68. Winks, *Canada and the United States*, p. 258.
69. MacNutt, *New Brunswick*, pp. 398-9.
70. Public Archives of Nova Scotia, Lieutenant-Governor's Correspondence, Monck to Doyle, 19 February 1864.
71. P. B. Waite, 'A Chapter in the History of the Intercolonial, 1864', *Canadian Historical Review*, vol. 32, pp. 356-69.
72. *Morning Freeman*, 5 March 1864.
73. Stanmore Papers, Doyle to Gordon, 14 February 1864.
74. Lieutenant-Governor's Correspondence, N.S., Gordon to Doyle, 18 February 1864.
75. C.O. 188, vol. 140, Gordon to Newcastle, 18 January 1864.
76. Nova Scotia, Assembly, *Debates*, 1864, pp. 179-84 (28 March).
77. *Morning Telegraph* (Saint John), 12 April 1864.
78. Prince Edward Island, Assembly, *Debates*, 1864, p. 32 (18 April).
79. *Ibid.*, pp. 33-5.
80. *Ibid.*, p. 32.
81. *Ibid.*, p. 41.
82. Prince Edward Island, Legislative Council, *Debates*, 1864, p. 114 (30 April).
83. New Brunswick, Assembly, *Journals*, 1865, Appendix 10, Gordon to Dundas, 11 April 1864.
84. *Ibid.*, Dundas to Cole, 4 May 1864.
85. Stanmore Papers, Doyle to Gordon, 17 November 1864.
86. New Brunswick, Assembly, *Journals*, 1865, Appendix 10, Monck to Doyle, 30 June 1864.

Chapter 2 – The Astonishing Agreement

(pages 39-69)

1. J. M. S. Careless, 'George Brown and the Mother of Confederation', Canadian Historical Association, *Report*, 1960, pp. 57-73.
2. Public Archives of Canada, George Brown Papers, Brown to Anne Brown, 3 March 1864.

3. Careless, 'George Brown and the Mother of Confederation', p. 59.
4. Brown Papers, Brown to Anne Brown, 27 February 1864.
5. Canada, Assembly, *Journals*, 1864, pp. 91-4 (14 March).
6. *Leader*, 15 March 1864.
7. *Globe*, 15 March 1864.
8. Brown Papers, Brown to Anne Brown, 15 March 1864.
9. *Leader*, 15 March 1864.
10. *Globe*, 15 March 1864.
11. Brown Papers, Brown to Anne Brown, 15 March 1864.
12. Public Record Office, C.O. 42, vol. 640, Monck to Newcastle, 31 March 1864.
13. Brown Papers, Brown to Anne Brown, 11 May 1864.
14. D. Smalley and B. A. Booth (eds.), *North America by Anthony Trollope* (New York, 1951), p. 51.
15. *Ibid.*, p. 55; S. P. Day, *English America: or Pictures of Canadian Places and People* (London, 1864), vol. I, pp. 16-17.
16. Brown Papers, Brown to Anne Brown, 13 May 1864.
17. *Ibid.*, Brown to Anne Brown, 18 May 1864.
18. *Leader*, 20 May 1864.
19. Canada, Assembly, *Journals*, 1864, pp. 223-6 (19 May).
20. *Globe*, 21 May 1864.
21. Brown Papers, Brown to Anne Brown, 13 June 1864.
22. *Leader*, 14 June 1864.
23. Canada, Assembly, *Journals*, 1864, pp. 383-4 (14 June).
24. *Ibid.*, p. 387.
25. *Globe*, 15 June 1864; *Leader*, 15 June 1864.
26. Canada, Assembly, *Journals*, 1864, p. 390 (14 June).
27. A. Morris, *Nova Britannia; or Our New Canadian Dominion Foreshadowed* (Toronto, 1884), pp. 98-9.
28. Waite, *Life and Times of Confederation*, p. 41.
29. Public Archives of Canada, Macdonald Papers, vol. 191, Brydges to Macdonald, 22, 24 February, 1864.
30. Macdonald's intentions are revealed in the protests he received from friends and associates; Macdonald Papers, vol. 338, Patton to Macdonald, 19 November 1863; vol. 247, Macpherson to Macdonald, 27 February 1864.
31. C.O. 42, vol. 641, Taché to Governor General, 15 June 1864, enclosed in Monck to Cardwell, 30 June 1864.
32. *Ibid.*
33. Cardwell Papers, vol. 39, 14 January 1866.
34. Stanmore Papers, Monck to Gordon, 15 October 1863.
35. *Ibid.*, Monck to Gordon, 24 February 1864.
36. *Ibid.*
37. C.O. 42, vol. 641, Monck to Taché, n.d., enclosed in Monck to Cardwell, 30 June 1864.
38. *Ibid.*
39. *Leader*, 16 June 1864.
40. C.O. 42, vol. 641, Monck to Taché, n.d.
41. *Globe*, 16 June 1864.

42. *Ibid.*
43. Ministerial Explanations, enclosed in C.O. 42, vol. 641, Monck to Cardwell, 30 June 1864; also in Macdonald Papers, vol. 46; and published in Joseph Pope, *Memoirs of the Right Honourable Sir John Alexander Macdonald, G.C.B.* (Toronto, n.d.), appendix 5, pp. 681-7. There are minor differences between the texts; the version in C.O. 42, vol. 641, Monck to Cardwell, 30 June, is accepted here as the final authority.
44. T. D. McGee, *Speeches and Addresses chiefly on the Subject of British American Union* (London, 1865).
45. J. C. Taché, *Des Provinces de l'Amérique du Nord et d'une Union Fédérale* (Quebec, 1858).
46. *Globe*, 15 March 1864.
47. Canada, Assembly, *Journals*, 1864, p. 384 (14 June).
48. *Globe*, 15 March 1864.
49. *Ibid.*
50. Frances E. O. Monck, *My Canadian Leaves, an Account of a Visit to Canada in 1864-1865* (London, 1891), pp. 37-8.
51. *Globe*, 18 June 1864.
52. Ministerial Explanations.
53. *Ibid.*
54. *Ibid.*
55. *Ibid.*
56. *Globe*, 18 June 1864.
57. *Ibid.*
58. *Leader*, 18 June 1864.
59. Brown Papers, Brown to Anne Brown, 18 June 1864.
60. Monck, *My Canadian Leaves*, p. 39.
61. Brown Papers, Brown to Anne Brown, 20 June 1864, 5:30 p.m.
62. Ministerial Explanations.
63. Brown Papers, Brown to Anne Brown, 20 June 1864.
64. Ministerial Explanations.
65. *Leader*, 22 June 1864.
66. Ministerial Explanations.
67. Brown Papers, Brown to Anne Brown, 23 June 1864.
68. *Leader*, 23 June 1864.
69. *Globe*, 23 June 1864.
70. *Leader*, 23 June 1864.

Chapter 3 – First Responses

(pages 70-103)

1. New Brunswick, Assembly, *Journals*, 1865, Appendix 10, pp. 7-8, Cole to Monck, 12 July 1864; Whitelaw, *The Maritimes and Canada*, p. 216.
2. New Brunswick Museum, Tilley Papers, Tupper to Tilley, 15 July 1864.
3. C.O. 217, vol. 234, MacDonnell to Cardwell, 18 July 1864.
4. Tilley Papers, Tupper to Tilley, 26 July 1864.

5. New Brunswick, Assembly, *Journals*, 1865, Appendix 10, p. 8, Mac-Donnell to Cole, 11 July 1864.
6. C.O. 217, vol. 234, MacDonnell to Cardwell, 18 July 1864.
7. New Brunswick, Assembly, *Journals*, 1865, Appendix 10, Cole to Mac-Donnell, 25 July 1864.
8. C.O. 217, vol. 234, MacDonnell to Cardwell, 18 August 1864.
9. Prince Edward Island, Assembly, *Journals*, 1865, Appendix E, Dundas to Cole, 25 July 1865; Cole to Dundas, 26 July 1864.
10. C.O. 226, vol. 100, Dundas to Monck, 25, 28 July, 1864.
11. *Monitor* (Charlottetown), 4, 11, 25 August, 1864; *Examiner* (Charlottetown), 22 August 1864.
12. *Morning Chronicle*, 4 August 1864.
13. *Acadian Recorder* (Halifax), 30 July 1864.
14. Waite, *Life and Times of Confederation*, pp. 62-3.
15. *British Colonist*, 6 August 1864.
16. *Morning News*, 18 July 1864.
17. *Ibid.*, 12 August 1864.
18. *Ibid.*, 18, 25 July, 24 August, 1864.
19. *Globe*, 23 June 1864.
20. *Ibid.*, 27 July 1864.
21. *La Minerve* (Montreal), 21 June 1864.
22. *Le Pays* (Montreal), 27 June 1864.
23. *La Minerve*, 9 July 1864.
24. *Le Courrier du Canada* (Quebec), 6 July 1864.
25. *La Minerve*, 9 July 1864.
26. *Leader*, 15 July 1864.
27. *Gazette*, 22 June 1864.
28. *Ibid.*, 25 June 1864.
29. *Ibid.*, 8 July 1864.
30. *Leader*, 2 July 1864.
31. *Globe*, 28 July 1864.
32. *Ibid.*, 29 July 1864.
33. Macdonald Papers, vol. 188, Brown to Macdonald, 15 July 1864.
34. A. B. Erickson, *Edward T. Cardwell: Peelite*, Transactions of the American Philosophical Society, New Series, vol. 49, Pt. 2 (Philadelphia, 1959), pp. 96-7.
35. G. E. Marindin (ed.), *Letters of Frederic, Lord Blachford, Under-Secretary of State for the Colonies, 1860-1871* (London, 1896), p. 252.
36. Erickson, *Cardwell*, p. 36.
37. *Times* (London), 29 June 1864, quoted in *Morning News*, 20 July 1864.
38. C. P. Stacey, *Canada and the British Army, a Study in the Practice of Responsible Government* (London and Toronto, 1936), pp. 160-2.
39. *Ibid.*
40. British Museum, Additional MSS. 44118, Gladstone Papers, vol. 33, Gladstone to Cardwell, 25 July 1864.
41. Public Record Office, Russell Papers, vol. 27, Palmerston to Russell, 29 July 1864.
42. Public Archives of Canada, G.1, vol. 160, Cardwell to Monck, 6 August 1864.

43. Palmerston Papers, Memorandum on the Defence of Canada by W. E. Gladstone, 12 July 1864.
44. Monck, *My Canadian Leaves*, p. 43.
45. Brown Papers, Brown to Anne Brown, 20 July 1864.
46. *Leader*, 5 July 1864.
47. *Gazette*, 12 July 1864.
48. *Morning News*, 15 July 1864.
49. *Globe*, 5 August 1864.
50. *Ibid.*, 24 June 1864; *Gazette*, 25 June 1864.
51. Brown Papers, Brown to Anne Brown, 5 August 1864.
52. *Ibid.*, Brown to Anne Brown, 8 August 1864.
53. J. W. O'Brien, *Excursion aux Provinces Maritimes* (Quebec, 1864).
54. *Morning Freeman*, 4 August 1864.
55. O'Brien, *Excursion aux Provinces Maritimes*, p. 4.
56. *Leader*, 12 August 1864.
57. *Globe*, 15, 16 August, 1864.
58. *Leader*, 16 August 1864.
59. *Globe*, 23 August 1864; *Leader*, 23 August 1864.
60. *Leader*, 20 August 1864; *Globe*, 20 August 1864.
61. *Globe*, 18 August 1864.
62. *Ibid.*, 20 August 1864.
63. *Ibid.*
64. C.O. 217, vol. 234, MacDonnell to Cardwell, 18 August 1864.
65. C.O. 188, vol. 141, Gordon to Cardwell, 15 August 1864.
66. C.O. 217, vol. 234, MacDonnell to Cardwell, 18 August 1864.
67. *British Colonist*, 8 September 1864.
68. *Morning News*, 12, 24 August, 1864.
69. *Examiner*, 22 August 1864.
70. *La Minerve*, 16 July 1864.
71. *Globe*, 1 August 1864.
72. *Morning Chronicle*, 16 August 1864.
73. *Gazette*, 24 August 1864.
74. *La Minerve*, 30 August 1864.
75. *Gazette*, 2 September 1864.
76. *La Minerve*, 6 September 1864.
77. Brown Papers, Brown to Anne Brown, 26 August 1864.
78. *Ibid.*, Brown to Anne Brown, 28 August 1864.
79. *Gazette*, 1 September 1864; Brown Papers, Brown to Anne Brown, 29 August 1864.
80. Monck, *My Canadian Leaves*, pp. 79, 85, 95.
81. Brown Papers, Brown to Anne Brown, 13 September 1864.

Chapter 4 – Mission to Charlottetown

(pages 104-31)

1. *Examiner*, 22 August 1864.
2. *Vindicator* (Charlottetown), 7 September 1864.

3. *Islander* (Charlottetown), 2 September 1864.
4. *Morning Telegraph*, 5 September 1864.
5. *Examiner*, 5 September 1864.
6. *Islander*, 9 September 1864.
7. *Vindicator*, 7 September 1864.
8. Brown Papers, Brown to Anne Brown, 13 September 1864.
9. *Ibid.*
10. *Islander*, 9 September 1864.
11. *Morning News*, 29 August 1864.
12. *Leader*, 10 September 1864.
13. Brown Papers, Brown to Anne Brown, 13 September 1864.
14. *Ibid.* Brown's account of the order in which the Canadians addressed the Charlottetown Conference differs from the reports in the newspapers of the day. Brown's account has here been followed.
15. *Ibid.*
16. *Ibid.*
17. C.O. 188, vol. 141, Gordon to Cardwell, 12 September 1864.
18. *Morning Chronicle*, 10 September 1864; *Gazette*, 26 September 1864.
19. *Vindicator*, 7 September 1864.
20. Brown Papers, Brown to Anne Brown, 13 September 1864.
21. *Globe*, 16 September 1864.
22. Brown Papers, Brown to Anne Brown, 13 September 1864.
23. *Morning Telegraph*, 8 September 1864.
24. Brown Papers, Brown to Anne Brown, 13 September 1864.
25. *Gazette*, 25 June 1864.
26. *Morning Chronicle*, 10 September 1864.
27. C.O. 188, vol. 141, Gordon to Cardwell, 10 September 1864.
28. *Morning Chronicle*, 10 September 1864; *Gazette*, 26 September 1864; C.O. 188, vol. 141, Gordon to Cardwell, 26 September 1864.
29. *Vindicator*, 7 September 1864.
30. C.O. 188, vol. 141, Gordon to Cardwell, 26 September 1864.
31. Brown Papers, Brown to Anne Brown, 13 September 1864.
32. *Islander*, 9 September 1864.
33. *Morning Chronicle*, 10 September 1864.
34. C.O. 188, vol. 141, Gordon to Cardwell, 12 September 1864.
35. *Ibid.*
36. *Morning Chronicle*, 10 September 1864.
37. Brown Papers, Brown to Anne Brown, 13 September 1864.
38. *Examiner*, 5 September 1864.
39. *Morning Telegraph*, 12 September 1864.
40. Brown Papers, Brown to Anne Brown, 13 September 1864.
41. *Ibid.*
42. *Examiner*, 12 September 1864.
43. *Islander*, 16 September 1864.
44. Brown Papers, Brown to Anne Brown, 13 September 1864.
45. D. C. Harvey (ed.), *Edward Whelan's Union of the British Provinces* (Gardenvale and Toronto, 1927), pp. 10-13.
46. *Morning Telegraph*, 12 September 1864.
47. *Islander*, 23 September 1864.

48. *Ibid.*
49. *Globe*, 20 September 1864, quoting *Evening Express* (Halifax), 10 September 1864.
50. *Morning Chronicle*, 12 September 1864.
51. *Gazette*, 19 September 1864, quoting *Morning Telegraph*.
52. Brown Papers, Brown to Anne Brown, 12 September 1864.
53. Macdonald Papers, vol. 51, Macdonald to Taché, 12 September 1864.
54. Harvey, *Whelan's Union of British Provinces*, p. 40.
55. *Ibid.*, p. 25.
56. *Ibid.*, pp. 28-39.
57. *Ibid.*, pp. 45-50.
58. *Evening Express*, 14 September 1864; *Gazette*, 19 September 1864, quoting *Morning Telegraph*.
59. *Courier* (Saint John), 17 September 1864.
60. Brown Papers, Brown to Anne Brown, 19 September 1864.
61. Harvey, *Whelan's Union of British Provinces*, p. 58.
62. *Ibid.*
63. *Morning Freeman*, 19 November 1864.
64. *Courier*, 17 September 1864.
65. Brown Papers, Brown to Anne Brown, 19 September 1864.
66. C.O. 188, vol. 141, Gordon to Cardwell, 12 September 1864.
67. C.O. 188, vol. 141, Gordon to Cardwell, 26 September 1864.
68. Cardwell Papers, vol. 39, Cardwell to Gordon, 10 December 1864.
69. *Ibid.*, vol. 39, Gordon to Cardwell, 15 January 1865.
70. Brown Papers, Brown to Anne Brown, 12 September 1864.
71. *Ibid.*, Brown to Anne Brown, 19 September 1864.

Chapter 5 – The Bases of Nationhood

(pages 132-57)

1. Public Archives of Canada, Diary of Mercy Ann Coles, 5 October 1864.
2. Harvey, *Whelan's Union of British Provinces*, pp. 62-3.
3. Mercy Coles Diary, 8 October 1864.
4. Harvey, *Whelan's Union of British Provinces*, p. 62.
5. C.O. 217, vol. 234, MacDonnell to Cardwell, 31 August 1864.
6. *Gazette*, 20 October 1864.
7. Harvey, *Whelan's Union of British Provinces*, p. 62.
8. *Ibid.*, p. 63.
9. Public Archives of Canada, Canada, Provincial Secretary's Office, Russell to Provincial Secretary, 10 January 1865.
10. Mercy Coles Diary, 9 October 1864.
11. *La Minerve*, 13 October 1864.
12. Harvey, *Whelan's Union of British Provinces*, p. 65.
13. *Gazette*, 28, 31 October, 1864.
14. Macdonald Papers, vol. 46, p. 17837; Joseph Pope, *Confederation: being a Series of Hitherto Unpublished Documents bearing on the British North America Act* (Toronto, 1895), pp. 4-5. In this and in subsequent

references to the minutes and discussions of the Quebec Conference, attention is directed first to the manuscript records kept by Hewitt Bernard, now in the Macdonald Papers, and secondly to Sir Joseph Pope's *Confederation Documents*, in which these records were first published. Bernard's notes of the discussions at Quebec were condensed and elliptical; and Pope supplied 'here and there such small words as are clearly necessary to bring out the sense'. In this book, all quotations have been taken from the Pope version, as being the more readily intelligible; but in each case the quoted passage has been compared for meaning with the original in Bernard's manuscript notes.

15. A. C. Doughty (ed.), 'Notes on the Quebec Conference', *Canadian Historical Review*, vol. I, p. 27.
16. Macdonald Papers, vol. 46, p. 17851.
17. *Gazette*, 26 September 1864.
18. Macdonald Papers, vol. 46, p. 17838; Pope, *Confederation Documents*, p. 5.
19. Doughty, 'Notes on the Quebec Conference', p. 28.
20. *Ibid.*
21. *Ibid.*, p. 30.
22. P. B. Waite, 'Edward Whelan Reports from the Quebec Conference', *Canadian Historical Review*, vol. 42, p. 29.
23. *Gazette*, 22 October 1864.
24. *Globe*, 29 August 1864; *Gazette*, 2 September 1864.
25. Macdonald Papers, vol. 46, p. 17853; Pope, *Confederation Documents*, p. 55.
26. Macdonald Papers, vol. 46, p. 17853; Pope, *Confederation Documents*, pp. 58-9.
27. J. H. Gray, *Confederation: or the Political and Parliamentary History of Canada* (Toronto, 1872), p. 56.
28. Macdonald Papers, vol. 46, p. 17853; Pope, *Confederation Documents*, pp. 54-5.
29. Macdonald Papers, vol. 46, p. 17862.
30. *Globe*, 12 October 1864.
31. Brown Papers, Brown to Anne Brown, 17 October 1864.
32. *Globe*, 12 October 1864; *Leader*, 13 October 1864.
33. Mercy Coles Diary, 11 October 1864.
34. Waite, 'Edward Whelan Reports from the Quebec Conference', p. 32.
35. Mercy Coles Diary, 12 October 1864.
36. *La Minerve*, 15 October 1864.
37. Macdonald Papers, vol. 46, p. 17884; Pope, *Confederation Documents*, p. 12.
38. *Ibid.*
39. Macdonald Papers, vol. 46, pp. 17888, 17893; Pope, *Confederation Documents*, p. 12.
40. Macdonald Papers, vol. 46, pp. 17888, 17894; Pope, *Confederation Documents*, p. 13.
41. Doughty, 'Notes on the Quebec Conference', p. 34.
42. Waite, 'Edward Whelan Reports from the Quebec Conference', p. 36.
43. *Gazette*, 19 October 1864.

44. Brown Papers, Brown to Anne Brown, 15 October 1864.
45. Waite, 'Edward Whelan Reports from the Quebec Conference', p. 35.
46. *Globe*, 15, 17 October, 1864; *Leader*, 15 October 1864.
47. Waite, 'Edward Whelan Reports from the Quebec Conference', p. 36.
48. Mercy Coles Diary, 14 October 1864.
49. Brown Papers, Brown to Anne Brown, 17 October 1864.
50. Macdonald Papers, vol. 46, pp. 17890-1, 17895-6; Pope, *Confederation Documents*, p. 14.
51. Doughty, 'Notes on the Quebec Conference', p. 35.
52. *Ibid.*
53. Macdonald Papers, vol. 46, pp. 17801, 17898; Pope, *Confederation Documents*, p. 14.
54. William McDougall's copy of the Canadian *Confederation Debates*, University of Toronto Library, p. 35.
55. Doughty, 'Notes on the Quebec Conference', pp. 36-7.
56. Macdonald Papers, vol. 46, pp. 17913-14; Pope, *Confederation Documents*, p. 19.
57. Macdonald Papers, vol. 46, pp. 17933-5; Pope, *Confederation Documents*, pp. 66-8.
58. *Ibid.*
59. Macdonald Papers, vol. 46, p. 17936; Pope, *Confederation Documents*, p. 68.
60. Macdonald Papers, vol. 46, pp. 17936-7; Pope, *Confederation Documents*, p. 69.
61. *Monitor*, 22 December 1864; E. Palmer to Editor, 19 December 1864.
62. Macdonald Papers, vol. 46, p. 17938; Pope, *Confederation Documents*, pp. 69-70.
63. *Monitor*, 29 December 1864, J. H. Gray to Editor, 24 December 1864.
64. Macdonald Papers, vol. 46, p. 17939; Pope, *Confederation Documents*, p. 70.

Chapter 6 – The Design Completed

(pages 158-86)

1. Brown Papers, Brown to Anne Brown, 17 October 1864.
2. Waite, 'Edward Whelan Reports from the Quebec Conference', p. 39.
3. *Ibid.*, p. 41; *Globe*, 22 October 1864.
4. Waite, 'Edward Whelan Reports from the Quebec Conference', p. 41.
5. Mercy Coles Diary, 19 October 1864.
6. Waite, 'Edward Whelan Reports from the Quebec Conference', p. 41.
7. Brown Papers, Brown to Anne Brown, 15 October 1864.
8. *Ibid.*, Brown to Anne Brown, 17 October 1864.
9. Mercy Coles Diary, 18 October 1864.
10. *Ibid.*, 22 October 1864.
11. Bolger, *Prince Edward Island and Confederation*, pp. 76-7.
12. Macdonald Papers, vol. 46, pp. 17949-50; Pope, *Confederation Documents*, pp. 71-2.

13. Macdonald Papers, vol. 46, p. 17951; Pope, *Confederation Documents*, p. 72.
14. Macdonald Papers, vol. 46, p. 17952; Pope, *Confederation Documents*, p. 73.
15. Macdonald Papers, vol. 46, p. 17951; Pope, *Confederation Documents*, p. 72.
16. Macdonald Papers, vol. 46, p. 17952; Pope, *Confederation Documents*, p. 73.
17. Macdonald Papers, vol. 46, p. 17945; Pope, *Confederation Documents*, p. 21.
18. Macdonald Papers, vol. 46, p. 17879; Pope, *Confederation Documents*, p. 9.
19. Macdonald Papers, vol. 46, p. 17881; Pope, *Confederation Documents*, pp. 9-10.
20. Macdonald Papers, vol. 46, p. 17948; Pope, *Confederation Documents*, p. 22.
21. Frances Monck, *My Canadian Leaves*, pp. 211-12.
22. Macdonald Papers, vol. 46, pp. 17954-5; Pope, *Confederation Documents*, pp. 74-5.
23. *Ibid.*
24. Macdonald Papers, vol. 46, p. 17947; Pope, *Confederation Documents*, p. 22.
25. Macdonald Papers, vol. 46, p. 17956; Pope, *Confederation Documents*, pp. 75-6.
26. Macdonald Papers, vol. 46, p. 17957; Pope, *Confederation Documents*, p. 76.
27. Macdonald Papers, vol. 510, Macdonald to M. C. Cameron, 19 December 1864.
28. Brown Papers, Brown to Anne Brown, 17 October 1864.
29. Macdonald Papers, vol. 46, pp. 17964-5; Pope, *Confederation Documents*, pp. 24-5.
30. Macdonald Papers, vol. 46, p. 17975; Pope, *Confederation Documents*, p. 81.
31. Macdonald Papers, vol. 46, p. 17973; Pope, *Confederation Documents*, p. 80.
32. Macdonald Papers, vol. 46, pp. 17978-9; Pope, *Confederation Documents*, pp. 25-6.
33. Macdonald Papers, vol. 46, p. 17984; Pope, *Confederation Documents*, p. 83.
34. Macdonald Papers, vol. 46, p. 17984; Pope, *Confederation Documents*, p. 84.
35. Doughty, 'Notes on the Quebec Conference', pp. 41-2.
36. *Globe*, 24 October 1864.
37. *Ibid.*, 25 October 1864.
38. Macdonald Papers, vol. 46, pp. 17987-8; Pope, *Confederation Documents*, p. 27.
39. Macdonald Papers, vol. 46, p. 17991; Pope, *Confederation Documents*, p. 84.

40. Macdonald Papers, vol. 46, p. 17989; Pope, *Confederation Documents*, p. 27.
41. Macdonald Papers, vol. 46, pp. 17990, 17993-4; Pope, *Confederation Documents*, pp. 27, 85.
42. Macdonald Papers, vol. 46, pp. 17991-2; Pope, *Confederation Documents*, pp. 84-5.
43. Macdonald Papers, vol. 46, p. 17994; Pope, *Confederation Documents*, p. 86.
44. Macdonald Papers, vol. 46, p. 17995; Pope, *Confederation Documents*, p. 86.
45. Macdonald Papers, vol. 46, pp. 17996-7; Pope, *Confederation Documents*, p. 87.
46. Macdonald Papers, vol. 46, p. 18010; Pope, *Confederation Documents*, p. 28.
47. Macdonald Papers, vol. 46, p. 18005; Pope, *Confederation Documents*, p. 31.
48. Macdonald Papers, vol. 46, p. 18021; Pope, *Confederation Documents*, p. 88.
49. *Ibid.*
50. *Ibid.*
51. Macdonald Papers, vol. 46, p. 17997; Pope, *Confederation Documents*, p. 87.
52. Macdonald Papers, vol. 46, pp. 18025, 18038; Pope, *Confederation Documents*, p. 33.
53. MacNutt, *New Brunswick*, p. 367.
54. Macdonald Papers, vol. 46, pp. 18025-7; Pope, *Confederation Documents*, p. 34.
55. Doughty, 'Notes on the Quebec Conference', p. 45.
56. Prince Edward Island, Assembly, *Debates*, 1865, p. 68 (31 March).
57. Doughty, 'Notes on the Quebec Conference', p. 46.
58. *Ibid.*
59. Prince Edward Island, Assembly, *Debates*, 1865, p. 68 (31 March).
60. Macdonald Papers, vol. 46, p. 18063.
61. *Ibid.*, p. 18048; Pope, *Confederation Documents*, p. 37.
62. Brown Papers, Brown to Anne Brown, 27 October 1864.
63. *Gazette*, 29 October 1864.
64. *Ibid.*
65. *Ibid.*, 31 October 1864.
66. *Globe*, 2 November 1864.
67. Harvey, *Whelan's Union of British Provinces*, p. 137.
68. *Ibid.*, p. 139; *Globe*, 2 November 1864.
69. Mercy Coles Diary, 26 October 1864.
70. Harvey, *Whelan's Union of British Provinces*, p. 147.
71. *Globe*, 3 November 1864.
72. *Ibid.*
73. Harvey, *Whelan's Union of British Provinces*, p. 66.

458 ->>> THE ROAD TO CONFEDERATION

Chapter 7 – Uncertain Reception

(pages 187-219)

1. Royal Archives, Windsor, P. 22, Colonies, 1851-65, vol. I, Monck to Cardwell, 11 November 1864.
2. W. G. Ormsby, 'Letters to Galt concerning the Maritime Provinces and Confederation', *Canadian Historical Review*, vol. 34, pp. 166-9.
3. *Monitor*, 22 December 1864, Palmer to Editor, 19 December 1864; Tilley Papers, Chandler to Tilley, 31 October 1864.
4. Harvey, *Whelan's Union of British Provinces*, pp. 147, 195-6.
5. *Ibid.*, pp. 199-218.
6. Whitelaw, *Maritimes and Canada before Confederation*, p. 265.
7. *Monitor*, 10 November 1864.
8. *Spectator* (Hamilton), 10 November 1864.
9. *Globe*, 5 November 1864.
10. Macdonald Papers, Additional, vol. I, Macdonald to Amsden, 1 December 1864.
11. *Le Courrier du Canada*, 14 November 1864.
12. *Le Pays*, 12 November 1864.
13. *Le Courrier du Canada*, 5, 7, 9, 12, 14, 16, 18, 21, 23, 26, 30 December, 1864; 2, 4, 9, 11, 13, 16, 18, 20, 25 January, 1865.
14. *Ibid.*, 11 November 1864.
15. *Le Canadien* (Quebec), 9, 14 September, 14, 26 October, 1864; 9 January 1865.
16. J. Cauchon, *L'Union des Provinces de l'Amérique Britannique du Nord* (Quebec, 1865).
17. *Le Courrier du Canada*, 11 November 1864.
18. *Ibid.*, 26 December 1864.
19. C.O. 42, vol. 643, Monck to Cardwell, 7 November 1864.
20. Gladstone Papers, vol. 33, Cardwell to Gladstone, 27 October 1864.
21. Russell Papers, vol. 38, Lyons to Russell, 28 October 1864.
22. *Globe*, 10 November 1864.
23. Public Archives of Canada, Canada, Executive Council Minutes, E. 1, vol. 89, pp. 403-11 (11 November 1864).
24. *Ibid.*, pp. 427-43 (16 November 1864).
25. Pope, *Correspondence of Macdonald*, p. 16, Brown to Macdonald, 12 November 1864.
26. *Islander*, 9 December 1864, Letter of W. H. Pope, 5 December 1864.
27. Public Archives of Canada, Tupper Papers, vol. I, J. H. Gray to Tupper, 7 January 1865.
28. *Islander*, 18 November 1864, Letter of J. H. Gray, 16 November 1864.
29. *Ibid.*
30. *Ibid.*, 18 November 1864.
31. Harvey, *Whelan's Union of British Provinces*, pp. 195-6.
32. *Monitor*, 1 December 1864, Letter of E. Palmer, 28 November 1864.
33. *Islander*, 9 December 1864, Letter of W. H. Pope, 5 December 1864; *Examiner*, 12 December 1864, Letter of Coles, 5 December, and A. A. Macdonald, 6 December, 1864; *Monitor*, 22 December 1864, Letter of

E. Palmer, 19 December 1864; *ibid.*, 29 December 1864, Letter of J. H. Gray, 24 December 1864.

34. Ormsby, 'Letters to Galt concerning the Maritime Provinces and Confederation', p. 168.
35. *Islander*, 23 December 1864, Gray to Dundas, 17 December 1864.
36. Tilley Papers, Chandler to Tilley, 31 October 1864.
37. Waite, *Life and Times of Confederation*, p. 236.
38. Macdonald Papers, vol. 51, Tilley to Galt, n.d. [April, 1865].
39. *Ibid.*
40. Brown Papers, Tilley to Brown, 21 November 1864.
41. Cardwell Papers, vol. 39, Gordon to Cardwell, 7 November 1864.
42. *Ibid.*, Cardwell to Gordon, 14 October 1864.
43. C.O. 188, vol. 141, Gordon to Cardwell, 11 October 1864.
44. Macdonald Papers, vol. 51, Tilley to Galt, n.d.
45. Brown Papers, Tilley to Brown, 21 November 1864.
46. *Daily Evening Globe* (Saint John), 18 November 1864.
47. *Morning Freeman*, 19 November 1864.
48. *Morning Telegraph*, 18 November 1864.
49. *Ibid.*, 23 November 1864.
50. *Daily Evening Globe*, 23 November 1864.
51. *Morning News*, 18 November 1864.
52. *Morning Telegraph*, 22 November 1864.
53. *Ibid.*, 25 November 1864.
54. *Daily Evening Globe*, 24 November 1864.
55. Macdonald Papers, vol. 51, Tilley to Macdonald, 23 November 1864.
56. Tilley Papers, Tilley to Tupper, 8 December 1864.
57. *The Newfoundlander* (St. John's), 1 December 1864.
58. Ormsby, 'Letters to Galt concerning the Maritime Provinces and Confederation', p. 167.
59. Public Record Office, C.O. 194, vol. 173, Musgrave to Cardwell, 27 December 1864.
60. Waite, *Life and Times of Confederation*, pp. 162-3.
61. *Newfoundlander*, 8 December 1864.
62. *Ibid.*, 5 December 1864, Letter of C. F. Bennett, 2 December; *ibid.*, 12 December 1864, Letter of C. F. Bennett, 9 December.
63. *Halifax Citizen*, 19, 22 November, 1864.
64. *British Colonist*, 22 November 1864.
65. Stanmore Papers, MacDonnell to Gordon, 14 November 1864.
66. *Ibid.*, MacDonnell to Gordon, 24 November 1864.
67. *Ibid.*, MacDonnell to Gordon, 10 December 1864.
68. Tilley Papers, Tupper to Tilley, 4 December 1864.
69. Macdonald Papers, vol. 188, Tupper to Macdonald, 13 December 1864.
70. Tilley Papers, Tupper to Tilley, 4 December 1864.
71. *Acadian Recorder*, 11 December 1864.
72. Macdonald Papers, vol. 188, Tupper to Macdonald, 13 December 1864.
73. *Morning Chronicle*, 12 December 1864.
74. *Ibid.*, 20 December 1864; *British Colonist*, 20 December 1864.
75. *Morning Chronicle*, 24 December 1864.
76. *Ibid.*, 12 December 1864.

77. *British Colonist*, 27 December 1864; *Morning Chronicle*, 27 December 1864.
78. Macdonald Papers, vol. 188, Tupper to Macdonald, 13 December 1864.
79. *Gazette*, 14 December 1864.
80. *Ibid.*
81. *Ibid.*, 15 December 1864.
82. Pope, *Correspondence of Macdonald*, p. 19, Macdonald to Swinyard, 19 December 1864.
83. *Globe*, 28 December 1864.
84. Russell Papers, vol. 38, Burnley to Russell, 27 December 1864.
85. *Daily Telegraph* (London), 25 November 1864.
86. *Times*, 24 November 1864.
87. Cardwell Papers, vol. 39, Cardwell to Gordon, 1 October 1864.
88. Marindin, *Letters of Lord Blachford*, pp. 252-3, Rogers to Miss Rogers, 23 December 1864.
89. *Ibid.*
90. Public Archives of Canada, G. 1, vol. 160, Cardwell to Monck, 3 December 1864.
91. *Ibid.*
92. Macdonald Papers, vol. 188, Brown to Macdonald, 22 December 1864.
93. Brown Papers, Brown to Anne Brown, 5 December 1864.
94. Tilley Papers, Brown to Tilley, 8 December 1864.
95. Macdonald Papers, vol. 188, Brown to Macdonald, 22 December 1864.
96. Marindin, *Letters of Lord Blachford*, pp. 252-3, Rogers to Miss Rogers, 23 December 1864.
97. Macdonald Papers, vol. 188, Brown to Macdonald, 22 December 1864.

Chapter 8 – The Hard Check

(pages 220-52)

1. C.O. 217, vol. 237, MacDonnell to Cardwell, 5 January 1865.
2. *Monitor*, 22 December 1864, Letter of E. Palmer, 19 December 1864.
3. *Ibid.*
4. Bolger, *Prince Edward Island and Confederation*, pp. 95-6.
5. C.O. 226, vol. 101, Dundas to Cardwell, 9 January 1865.
6. *Ibid.*, vol. 100, Dundas to Cardwell, 30 December 1864.
7. *Morning Chronicle*, 10 January 1865.
8. Macdonald Papers, vol. 51, Tupper to Macdonald, 4 January 1865.
9. Saunders, *Tupper*, vol. 1, pp. 100-1.
10. *Globe*, 20 August 1864.
11. J. A. Chisholm, *The Speeches and Public Letters of Joseph Howe* (Halifax, 1909), vol. 2, pp. 268-95.
12. E. M. Saunders, *Three Premiers of Nova Scotia* (Toronto, 1909), p. 371.
13. *Morning Chronicle*, 16 January 1865.
14. *Ibid.*
15. *Ibid.*, 11 January 1865.
16. *British Colonist*, 17 January 1865.

17. *Morning Chronicle*, 20, 23, 27 January, 1865.
18. *Ibid.*, 10 February 1865.
19. *Ibid.*, 18 January 1865.
20. Stanmore Papers, MacDonnell to Gordon, 15 January 1865.
21. Cardwell Papers, vol. 39, Gordon to Cardwell, n.d. [December 1864?].
22. *Ibid.*, vol. 39, Gordon to Cardwell, 2 January 1865.
23. *Ibid.*
24. *Ibid.*, 15 January 1865.
25. *Ibid.*, 19 December 1865.
26. *Morning Telegraph*, 9 January 1865.
27. *Ibid.*, 13 January 1865.
28. *Ibid.*, 16, 17 January, 1865.
29. *British Colonist*, 7 January 1865.
30. *Morning Telegraph*, 13 January 1865.
31. C.O. 188, vol. 143, Tilley to Gordon, 30 January 1865.
32. Stanmore Papers, Cardwell to Gordon, 7 January 1865.
33. C.O. 188, vol. 143, Gordon to Tilley, 14 January 1865.
34. *Ibid.*
35. *Ibid.*, Gordon to Cardwell, 30 January 1865.
36. *Morning News*, 23 January 1865.
37. *Morning Freeman*, 24 January 1865.
38. Public Archives of Canada, Monck Papers, Monck to Henry Monck, 20 January 1865.
39. C.O. 226, vol. 100, Dundas to Cardwell, 30 December 1864.
40. *Leader*, 20 January 1865.
41. *Ibid.*, 25 January 1865.
42. *Ibid.*, 20 January 1865.
43. Newfoundland, Assembly, *Journals*, 1865, pp. 5-6 (27 January).
44. *Newfoundlander*, 2 February 1865.
45. *Ibid.*, 6 February 1865.
46. *Gazette*, 10 February 1865.
47. Brown Papers, Brown to Anne Brown, 7 February 1865.
48. Canada, Legislature, *Parliamentary Debates on the Subject of the Confederation of the British North American Provinces* (Quebec, 1865), pp. 25-45 (6 February).
49. *Ibid.*, pp. 53-62 (7 February).
50. *Spectator*, 21 January 1865.
51. Brown Papers, Brown to Anne Brown, 7 February 1865.
52. *Canadian Confederation Debates,* pp. 84-115 (8 February).
53. *Spectator*, 8 February 1865.
54. *Canadian Confederation Debates*, p. 62 (7 February).
55. Macdonald Papers, vol. 51, Tupper to Macdonald, 4 January 1865.
56. *Morning Journal and Commercial Advertiser* (Halifax), 13 January 1865.
57. Stanmore Papers, MacDonnell to Gordon, 15 January 1865.
58. *Newfoundlander*, 16 March 1865.
59. Prince Edward Island, Assembly, *Debates*, 1865, p. 5 (2 March).
60. *Ibid.*, p. 5.
61. *Canadian Confederation Debates*, pp. 245-69 (16 February).

62. *Le Courrier du Canada*, 20 February 1865.
63. Brown Papers, Brown to Anne Brown, 28 February 1865.
64. *British Colonist*, 10 November 1864; *Evening Express*, 28 November 1864.
65. G. E. Buckle (ed.), *Letters of Queen Victoria* (London, 1926), Series 2, vol. I, pp. 248-9, Palmerston to the Queen, 20 January 1865.
66. *Ibid.*
67. G. 1, vol. 161, Cardwell to Monck, 21 January 1865.
68. Macdonald Papers, vol. 51, Macdonald to Gray, 27 March 1865.
69. United Kingdom, Parliament, *Debates*, 3rd Series, vol. 127, pp. 416-20 (20 February 1865).
70. *Ibid.*, pp. 429-35 (20 February 1865).
71. *Times*, 21 February 1865.
72. *Morning News*, 21 November 1864.
73. *Ibid.*, 1 February 1865.
74. *Ibid.*
75. *Morning Telegraph*, 26 January 1865.
76. *Ibid.*, 23 January, 1 February, 1865.
77. MacNutt, *New Brunswick*, p. 413.
78. *Morning Freeman*, 21 January 1865.
79. *Morning Telegraph*, 1 February 1865.
80. *Ibid.*, 3 February 1865.
81. *Canadian Confederation Debates*, p. 18 (3 February).
82. *Morning Freeman*, 14, 16, 18 February, 1865.
83. Macdonald Papers, vol. 51, Tilley to Macdonald, 13 February 1865.
84. *Ibid.*, Macdonald to Tilley, 20 February 1865.
85. MacNutt, *New Brunswick*, p. 427.
86. Stanmore Papers, Tilley to Gordon, 24 February 1865.
87. Cardwell Papers, vol. 39, Gordon to Cardwell, 27 February 1865.
88. *Morning News*, 6 March 1865.
89. C.O. 188, vol. 143, Gordon to Cardwell, 6 March 1865.

Chapter 9 – Appeal to Caesar

(pages 253-83)

1. *British Colonist*, 9 March 1865.
2. *Halifax Citizen*, 7 March 1865.
3. *Canadian Confederation Debates*, pp. 648-50 (6 March 1865).
4. *Ibid.*, p. 650.
5. *Ibid.*, p. 703 (7 March 1865).
6. *Ibid.*
7. *Le Courrier du Canada*, 10 March 1865.
8. *Gazette*, 9 March 1865.
9. *Canadian Confederation Debates*, p. 962 (10 March 1865).
10. Brown Papers, Brown to Anne Brown, 14 March 1865.
11. Stanmore Papers, Cardwell to Gordon, 4 February 1865.
12. Cardwell Papers, vol. 39, Gordon to Cardwell, 13 March 1865.
13. *Ibid.*, Gordon to Cardwell, 10 April 1865.

14. C.O. 188, vol. 143, Gordon to Cardwell, 8 April 1865.
15. *Ibid.*
16. MacNutt, *New Brunswick*, p. 43.
17. Brown Papers, Gray to Brown, 27 March 1865.
18. *Morning Telegraph*, 28 March 1865.
19. *Morning Freeman*, 30 March 1865.
20. *Ibid.*
21. Public Archives of Canada, Watkin Papers, 29 March 1865.
22. Stanmore Papers, Cardwell to Gordon, 13 May 1865.
23. Cardwell Papers, vol. 39, Gordon to Cardwell, 5 June 1865.
24. Prince Edward Island, Assembly, *Debates*, 1865, pp. 39-44 (24 March).
25. *Ibid.*, p. 40 (24 March).
26. *Ibid.*, pp. 44-5.
27. *Ibid.*, p. 66 (29 March).
28. *Ibid.*, 44-5.
29. *Ibid.*, pp. 70-1 (31 March).
30. Prince Edward Island, Legislative Council, *Debates*, 1865, p. 68 (1 April).
31. C.O. 226, vol. 101, Dundas to Cardwell, 3 April 1865.
32. Pope, *Correspondence of Macdonald*, p. 25, Tupper to Macdonald, 9 April 1865.
33. Stanmore Papers, MacDonnell to Gordon, 7 March 1865.
34. Public Archives of Nova Scotia, Lieutenant-Governor's Correspondence, N.S., Tupper to MacDonnell, May 1865.
35. Nova Scotia, Assembly, *Debates*, 1865, pp. 203-17 (10 April).
36. Stanmore Papers, MacDonnell to Gordon, 14 April 1865.
37. *Ibid.*
38. C.O. 217, vol. 237, MacDonnell to Cardwell, 30 March 1865.
39. Nova Scotia, Assembly, *Debates*, 1865, pp. 297-8 (21 April).
40. Brown Papers, Brown to Anne Brown, 13 March 1865.
41. *Ibid.*, Brown to Anne Brown, 9 March 1865.
42. *Ibid.*, Brown to Anne Brown, 28 February, 20 March, 1865.
43. *Ibid.*, Brown to Anne Brown, 6 March 1865.
44. *Globe*, 22 March 1865; Brown Papers, Brown to Anne Brown, 21 March 1865.
45. *Ibid.*, Brown to Anne Brown, 20 March 1865.
46. *Ibid.*
47. Waite, 'Edward Whelan Reports from the Quebec Conference', p. 44.
48. Brown Papers, Brown to Anne Brown, 23 March 1865.
49. *Globe*, 10 August 1865; Macdonald Papers, vol. 188, Brown to Macdonald, 5 August 1865.
50. Great Britain, Parliament, *Debates*, 3rd Series, vol. 128, pp. 104-5 (23 March 1865).
51. *Ibid.*, p. 175.
52. *Ibid.*, p. 170.
53. *Morning Post* (London), 24 March 1865; *Daily Telegraph*, 24 March 1865.
54. *Daily News* (London), 23, 24 March, 1865; *Times*, 23, 24 March, 1865.
55. *Times*, 25 March 1865.
56. *Daily News*, 25 March 1865.

57. *Gazette*, 20 January 1865.
58. *British Colonist*, 10 November 1864.
59. *Ibid.*, 24 October 1863, 3 September 1864; *Morning News*, 13 November 1863, 13, 15 July, 1864; *Nova Scotian*, 14 September 1863.
60. Brown Papers, Brown to Anne Brown, 23, 24 March, 1865.
61. *Ibid.*, Macdonald to Brown, 11 April 1865.
62. *Unionist* (Halifax), 17 April 1865; *Citizen*, 18 April 1865.
63. *Citizen*, 18 April 1865.
64. *British Colonist*, 18 April 1865.
65. *Citizen*, 18 April 1865.
66. *Times*, 5 April 1865.
67. *Ibid.*, 13 April 1865.
68. *Ibid.*
69. *Ibid.*, 7 April 1865.
70. *Ibid.*
71. *Daily News*, 6 April 1865.
72. Macdonald Papers, vol. 161, Memorandum of an Interview with Mr. Cardwell, 26 April 1865.
73. *Ibid.*
74. *Ibid.*, Unofficial and Confidential Memorandum of an Interview with Mr. Cardwell, 27 April 1865.
75. Brown Papers, Brown to Anne Brown, 6 May 1865.
76. Gladstone Papers, Gladstone to Gordon, 11 July 1865.
77. O. D. Skelton, *The Life and Times of Alexander Tilloch Galt* (Toronto, 1920), p. 382, Galt to his wife, 25 May 1865.
78. Palmerston Papers, Cardwell to Palmerston, 27 April 1865.
79. Macdonald Papers, vol. 100, Memorandum of the Defence Committee on the Report of Lieut. Col. Jervois on the Defence of Canada, 17 May 1865.
80. Brown Papers, Brown to Anne Brown, 6 May 1865.
81. *Ibid.*, Brown to Anne Brown, 13 May 1865.
82. Palmerston Papers, Palmerston to Cardwell, 21 May 1865.
83. *Ibid.*
84. Macdonald Papers, vol. 161, Canadian Memorandum, June 2, 1865.
85. Gladstone Papers, vol. 33, Gladstone to Cardwell, 23 May 1865.
86. *Ibid.*
87. Brown Papers, Brown to Anne Brown, 1 June 1865.
88. Skelton, *Galt*, p. 382, Galt to his wife, 25 May 1865.
89. Public Archives of Canada, G. 1, vol. 162, Cardwell to Monck, 17 June 1865.
90. Brown Papers, Brown to Anne Brown, 3 June 1865.

Chapter 10 – Imminence of Failure

(pages 284-315)

1. C.O. 188, vol. 143, Gordon to Cardwell, 10 April 1865; MacNutt, *New Brunswick*, p. 439.
2. C.O. 188, vol. 143, Gordon to Cardwell, 10 April 1865.
3. *Ibid.*
4. *Ibid.*, Gordon to Cardwell, 8 May 1865.
5. *Morning Freeman*, 17 November 1864.
6. Public Archives of Canada, B. 2, vol. 2, Cardwell to MacDonnell, 1 April 1865.
7. New Brunswick, Assembly, *Debates*, 1865, pp. 87-9 (22 May).
8. C.O. 217, vol. 237, MacDonnell to Cardwell, 7 June 1865.
9. New Brunswick, Assembly, *Journals*, 1865, pp. 13-15 (27 April).
10. New Brunswick, Assembly, *Debates*, 1865, pp. 7-8 (29 April–1 May).
11. *Morning Freeman*, 20 January 1865.
12. *Morning News*, 10 March 1865.
13. New Brunswick, Assembly, *Debates*, 1865, p. 15.
14. New Brunswick, Assembly, *Journals*, 1865, p. 223 (6 June).
15. *Ibid.*
16. Stanmore Papers, MacDonnell to Gordon, 15 January 1865.
17. *Ibid.*, Cardwell to Gordon, 4 March 1865.
18. *Ibid.*, Cardwell to Gordon, 13 May 1865.
19. *Ibid.*, Gordon to Cardwell, 22 May 1865.
20. *Ibid.*, Cardwell to Gordon, 9 June 1865.
21. *Ibid.*
22. Cardwell Papers, vol. 39, Cardwell to Gordon, 8 July 1865.
23. Stanmore Papers, Cardwell to Gordon, 9 June 1865.
24. *Ibid.*, Monck to Gordon, 22 June 1865.
25. Cardwell Papers, vol. 39, Gordon to Cardwell, 5 June 1865.
26. Bolger, *Prince Edward Island and Confederation*, p. 129.
27. *Ibid.*, p. 136.
28. Public Archives of Canada, G. 8, B., vol. 45, Cardwell to Gordon, 24 June 1865.
29. New Brunswick, Assembly, *Debates*, 1865 (30 May–5 June).
30. Waite, *Life and Times of Confederation*, p. 250.
31. C.O. 188, vol. 145, Gordon to Cardwell, 15 July 1865.
32. Stanmore Papers, Smith to Gordon, 7 July 1865.
33. Nova Scotia, Lieutenant-Governor's Correspondence, Tupper to MacDonnell, May 1865.
34. *Morning Chronicle*, 2 March 1869.
35. Cardwell Papers, Gordon to Cardwell, 17 July 1865.
36. Stanmore Papers, Smith to Gordon, 7 July 1865.
37. *Morning Chronicle*, 2 March 1869.
38. Russell Papers, vol. 26, Cardwell to Russell, 15 July 1865.
39. Howe Papers, vol. 4, Russell to Howe, 21 July 1865.
40. Monck Papers, Monck to Henry Monck, 7 July 1865.
41. *Times*, 20 June 1865.

42. *Daily News*, 21 June 1865.
43. Macdonald Papers, vol. 51, Ministerial Negotiations for the Reconstruction of the Government Consequent on the death of Sir Etienne Taché; Pope, *Memoirs of Macdonald*, pp. 700-6, Appendix 9.
44. Macdonald Papers, vol. 74, Monck to Macdonald, 3 August 1865.
45. Brown Papers, Brown to Anne Brown, 4 August 1865.
46. *Ibid.*
47. *Ibid.*
48. Macdonald Papers, vol. 51, Ministerial Negotiations; Pope, *Memoirs of Macdonald*, Appendix 9, pp. 700-6.
49. C.O. 42, vol. 641, Monck to Cardwell, 30 June 1864, Ministerial Explanations.
50. Brown Papers, Brown to Anne Brown, 4 August 1865.
51. Macdonald Papers, vol. 51, Ministerial Negotiations; Pope, *Memoirs of Macdonald*, pp. 700-6, Appendix 9, Brown to Macdonald, 5 August 1865.
52. Brown Papers, Brown to Anne Brown, 4 August 1865.
53. Macdonald Papers, vol. 51, Ministerial Negotiations; Pope, *Memoirs of Macdonald*, pp. 700-6, Appendix 9, Brown to Macdonald, 5 August 1865.
54. *Globe*, 10 August 1865.
55. Stanmore Papers, Monck to Gordon, 22 June 1865.
56. Brown Papers, Brown to Monck, 25 December 1865.
57. N. M. Rogers, 'The Confederate Council of Trade', *Canadian Historical Review*, vol. 7, pp. 277-86.
58. *Ibid.*
59. *Daily Evening Globe*, 14 March 1866, Wilmot to Gordon, 4 January 1866.
60. New Brunswick, Assembly, *Debates*, 1866, p. 34 (20 March).
61. *Globe*, 25 September 1865.
62. Russell Papers, vol. 26, Cardwell to Russell, 15 August 1865.
63. Gladstone Papers, Gladstone to Russell, 6 September 1865.
64. Russell Papers, vol. 31, Russell to Gladstone, 4 September 1865.
65. Richard Cartwright, *Reminiscences* (Toronto, 1912), pp. 40-1.
66. Brown Papers, Brown to Anne Brown, 13 July 1865.
67. *Globe*, 4 September 1865.
68. Brown Papers, Brown to Anne Brown, 16 September 1865.
69. *Globe*, 29 September 1865.
70. *Gazette*, 3 October 1865; *La Minerve*, 21 October 1865.
71. *Gazette*, 3 October 1865.
72. *Spectator*, 25 September 1865.
73. *Globe*, 29 September 1865.
74. *Spectator*, 30 September 1865.
75. *Globe*, 3 October 1865.
76. *Spectator*, 3 October 1865.
77. *Globe*, 9 October 1865.
78. *Ibid.*, 12, 16 October, 1865.
79. *Ibid.*, 17 October 1865.
80. *Ibid.*
81. *Spectator*, 23, 24 October, 1865.
82. *La Minerve*, 27 October 1865.

83. *Leader*, 19 October 1865.
84. *La Minerve*, 27 October 1864.
85. *Le Canadien*, 20 October 1865.
86. *Ibid.*, 27 October 1865.
87. *Leader*, 28 October 1865.
88. Pope, *Memoirs of Macdonald*, p. 305, McDougall to Macdonald, 19 October 1865.
89. *Leader*, 30 October 1865.
90. *Spectator*, 30 October 1865.

Chapter 11 – The Calculated Risk

(pages 316-45)

1. *Morning Freeman*, 31 October 1865.
2. *New Brunswick Reporter*, 18 August 1865.
3. Cardwell Papers, vol. 39, Gordon to Cardwell, 28 August 1865.
4. *Ibid.*, Gordon to Cardwell, 12 October 1865.
5. Chapman, *The Career of Arthur Hamilton Gordon*, p. 36.
6. Cardwell Papers, vol. 39, Gordon to Cardwell, 5 October 1865.
7. *Ibid.*, Gordon to Cardwell, 14 October 1865.
8. *Ibid.*, Gordon to Cardwell, 26 October 1865.
9. Macdonald Papers, vol. 51, Tilley to Macdonald, 13 September 1865.
10. MacNutt, *New Brunswick*, p. 388.
11. Macdonald Papers, vol. 51, Tilley to Macdonald, 13 September 1865.
12. *New Brunswick Reporter*, 3 November 1865.
13. *Ibid.*, 10 November 1865.
14. *Daily Evening Globe*, 28 October 1865.
15. *Ibid.*, 3 November 1865.
16. *Ibid.*, 30 October 1865.
17. *New Brunswick Reporter*, 3 November 1865.
18. *Ibid.*
19. *Ibid.*, 10 November 1865.
20. *Unionist*, 6 November 1865.
21. *Daily Evening Globe*, 7 November 1865.
22. *Citizen*, 7 November 1865.
23. *New Brunswick Reporter*, 10 November 1865.
24. *Unionist*, 8 November 1865.
25. Brown Papers, Brown to Anne Brown, 8 November 1865.
26. *Ibid.*
27. *Ibid.*, Gordon to Brown, 9 November 1865.
28. *Ibid.*, Brown to Anne Brown, 13 November 1865.
29. *Ibid.*, Brown to Monck, 25 December 1865.
30. *Ibid.*, Brown to Anne Brown, 13 November 1865.
31. *Ibid.*, Brown to Anne Brown, 18 November 1865.
32. *Ibid.*
33. Cardwell Papers, vol. 39, Gordon to Cardwell, 15 January 1865.
34. *Ibid.*, Gordon to Cardwell, 20 November 1865.

35. Stanmore Papers, Williams to Gordon, 6 January 1866.
36. *Morning Chronicle*, 15 November 1865.
37. *British Colonist*, 21 November 1865.
38. *Ibid.*
39. *Unionist*, 20 November 1865.
40. Nova Scotia, Assembly, *Debates*, 1866, p. 236 (13 April).
41. *Ibid.*, p. 237 (14 April).
42. *Newfoundlander*, 6 November 1865.
43. C.O. 194, vol. 174, Musgrave to Cardwell, 14 November 1865.
44. Waite, *Life and Times of Confederation*, p. 173.
45. *Newfoundlander*, 9 November 1865.
46. *Ibid.*, 20, 27 November, 1865.
47. C.O. 194, vol. 174, Musgrave to Cardwell, 14 November 1865.
48. Brown Papers, Gordon to Brown, 21 December 1865.
49. *Ibid.*
50. *Morning Freeman*, 21 January 1865.
51. C.O. 188, vol. 144, Gordon to Cardwell, 20 November 1865.
52. Waite, *Life and Times of Confederation*, p. 253.
53. C.O. 188, vol. 144, Gordon to Cardwell, 4 December 1865.
54. *Daily Evening Globe*, 14 March 1866, Wilmot to Gordon, 4 January 1866.
55. *Ibid.*
56. C.O. 188, vol. 144, Gordon to Cardwell, 4 December 1865.
57. Cardwell Papers, vol. 39, Gordon to Cardwell, 20 November 1865.
58. Brown Papers, Brown to Anne Brown, 14 December 1865.
59. Pope, *Memoirs of Macdonald*, p. 308, Macdonald to Louisa Macdonald, 28 September 1865.
60. Brown Papers, Brown to Anne Brown, 16 December 1865.
61. *Ibid.*, Brown to Monck, 25 December 1865.
62. Macdonald Papers, vol. 145, Printed 'Memorandum' on the Reciprocity Negotiations.
63. *Ibid.*
64. Macdonald Papers, vol. 145, Galt's Draft Report on the Reciprocity Negotiations, 19 December 1865.
65. Brown Papers, Brown to Monck, 25 December 1865.
66. Canada, Executive Council Minutes, vol. 91, 22 December 1865.
67. Brown Papers, Brown to Monck, 25 December 1865.
68. Manuscript Autobiography of Sir William Howland, p. 20.
69. Pope, *Memoirs of Macdonald*, p. 708, Brown to Cartier, 19 December 1865.
70. *Ibid.*
71. Brown Papers, Brown to Anne Brown, 19 December 1865.
72. Howland's Autobiography, p. 21.
73. C.O. 217, vol. 238, Williams to Cardwell, 18 December 1865.
74. *Morning Chronicle*, 28 December 1865.
75. *Daily Evening Globe*, 14 March 1866, Wilmot to Gordon, 13 January 1866.
76. *Ibid.*, Wilmot to Gordon, 4 January 1866.
77. C.O. 188, vol. 145, Gordon to Cardwell, 12 February 1866.

78. *Daily Evening Globe*, 14 March 1866, Gordon to Wilmot, 12 January 1866.
79. C.O. 188, vol. 145, Gordon to Cardwell, 12 February 1866.
80. Macdonald Papers, vol. 51, Tilley to Macdonald, 13 February 1866.
81. *Morning Chronicle*, 24 January 1866.
82. *Ibid.*, 1 February 1866.
83. *Unionist*, 29 January 1866.
84. Stanmore Papers, Williams to Gordon, 15 February 1866.
85. Brown Papers, Brown to Monck, 25 December 1865.
86. Macdonald Papers, vol. 145, Report of the Conferences between the Colonial Delegation and the Committee of Ways and Means of the House of Representatives.
87. *New Brunswick Reporter*, 16 February 1866.
88. C.O. 188, vol. 145, Gordon to Cardwell, 12 February 1866.

Chapter 12 – The Last Chance

(pages 346-76)

1. C.O. 194, vol. 175, Musgrave to Cardwell, 21 March 1866.
2. *Ibid.*, *Royal Gazette*, 30 January 1866, enclosed in Musgrave to Cardwell, 20 February 1866.
3. *Ibid.*, Musgrave to Cardwell, 20 February 1866.
4. Tilley Papers, McCully to Tilley, 8 June 1866.
5. C.O. 188, vol. 145, Gordon to Cardwell, 21 February 1866.
6. New Brunswick, Assembly, *Journals*, 1866, pp. 205-6, Minute of the Lieutenant-Governor, 12 April 1866.
7. *Ibid.*, pp. 217-18, Mr. Smith's Memorandum of Conversations with His Excellency the Lieutenant-Governor.
8. C.O. 188, vol. 145, Gordon to Cardwell, 21 February 1866.
9. *Ibid.*
10. Public Archives of Nova Scotia, Nova Scotia, Lieutenant-Governor's Telegraph Book, Gordon to Williams, 20 February 1866.
11. Nova Scotia, Assembly, *Debates*, 1866, pp. 1-2 (22 February).
12. Cardwell Papers, vol. 39, Gordon to Cardwell, 25 February 1866.
13. New Brunswick Museum, Williams Papers, Monck to Williams, 2 March 1866.
14. *Ibid.*, Cardwell to Williams, 6 January 1866.
15. C.O. 217, vol. 239, Williams to Cardwell, 1 March 1866.
16. *Ibid.*, Williams to Cardwell, 24 February 1866.
17. Stanmore Papers, Monck to Gordon, 16 February 1866.
18. *Ibid.*, Monck to Gordon, 15 February 1866.
19. C.O. 188, vol. 145, Gordon to Cardwell, 5 March 1866; New Brunswick, Assembly, *Journals*, 1866, pp. 207, 218.
20. C.O. 188, vol. 145, Gordon to Cardwell, 12 March 1866.
21. New Brunswick, Assembly, *Journals*, 1866, p. 12 (8 March).
22. C.O. 188, vol. 145, Gordon to Cardwell, 12 March 1866.
23. Macdonald Papers, vol. 237, McMicken to Macdonald, 12 March 1866.

24. Stanmore Papers, Gordon's manuscript Account of the Events of 1866.
25. New Brunswick, Assembly, *Debates*, 1866, p. 26 (16 March).
26. *Ibid., Journals*, 1866, p. 21 (12 March).
27. *Ibid., Debates*, 1866, pp. 12-13 (13 March).
28. *Daily Evening Globe*, 9 March 1866.
29. New Brunswick, Assembly, *Debates*, 1866, p. 23 (15 March).
30. *Ibid.*, p. 34 (20 March).
31. *Morning Telegraph*, 21 March 1866.
32. C.O. 188, vol. 145, Gordon to Cardwell, 25 March 1866.
33. New Brunswick, Assembly, *Debates*, 1866, p. 14 (13 March).
34. *Ibid.*, p. 23 (15 March).
35. *Ibid.*, p. 19 (14 March).
36. C.O. 188, vol. 145, Gordon to Cardwell, 25 March 1866.
37. Nova Scotia, Lieutenant-Governor's Telegraph Book, Williams to Monck, 1 March 1866.
38. Nova Scotia, Assembly, *Debates*, 1866, p. 53 (7 March).
39. *Ibid.*, pp. 53-4.
40. *Ibid.*, p. 55.
41. Waite, *Life and Times of Confederation*, p. 227.
42. Stanmore Papers, Williams to Gordon, 12 March 1866.
43. Nova Scotia, Lieutenant-Governor's Telegraph Book, Monck to Williams, 12 March 1866.
44. *Morning Chronicle*, 23 March 1869.
45. C.O. 217, vol. 239, Williams to Gordon, 18 March 1866 (enclosed in Williams to Cardwell, 27 March).
46. Waite, *Life and Times of Confederation*, p. 227, Annand to Smith, 20 March 1866.
47. *Ibid.*
48. Stanmore Papers, Williams to Gordon, 20 March 1866.
49. *Morning Chronicle*, 25 May 1866.
50. Nova Scotia, Lieutenant-Governor's Telegraph Book, Williams to Gordon, 19 March 1866; *ibid.*, Gordon to Williams, 19 March.
51. Waite, *Life and Times of Confederation*, pp. 226-7, Annand to Smith, 20 March 1866.
52. Howe Papers, vol. 12, Howe to Cardwell, 29 March 1866.
53. *Ibid.*, Cardwell to Howe, 14 April 1866.
54. *Citizen*, 8 April 1869.
55. Howe Papers, Howe to Cardwell, 12 April 1866.
56. *Citizen*, 8 April 1869.
57. *Morning Chronicle*, 23 March 1869.
58. Nova Scotia, Assembly, *Debates*, 1866, p. 186 (3 April).
59. Nova Scotia, Lieutenant-Governor's Telegraph Book, Williams to Monck, 3 April 1866.
60. Nova Scotia, Assembly, *Debates*, 1866, p. 190 (3 April).
61. *Ibid.*
62. New Brunswick, Legislative Council, *Journals*, 1866, pp. 61-2 (4 April).
63. *Ibid.*, pp. 14-16 (14 March).
64. New Brunswick, Legislative Council, *Speeches on Confederation and the Resignation of the Government*, April 1866.

65. New Brunswick, Legislative Council, *Journals*, pp. 77-9 (6 April).
66. C.O. 188, vol. 145, Gordon to Cardwell, 23 April 1866.
67. New Brunswick, Assembly, *Journals*, 1866, p. 204. Memorandum of Conversation between His Excellency and Mr. Smith.
68. *Ibid.*, p. 210, Lieutenant-Governor's Reply to Minute of the Executive Council, 12 April 1866.
69. *Ibid.*, p. 204, Memorandum of Conversation between His Excellency and Mr. Smith.
70. *Ibid.*, p. 210, Lieutenant-Governor's Reply to Minute of the Executive Council.
71. New Brunswick, Legislative Council, *Journals*, 1866, pp. 80-1 (7 April).
72. *Daily Evening Globe*, 10 April 1866.
73. *Ibid.*
74. Nova Scotia, Assembly, *Journals*, 1866, p. 60 (10 April).
75. *Ibid.*, *Debates*, 1866, pp. 233-4 (14 April).
76. *Ibid.*, p. 237 (14 April).
77. *Ibid.*, pp. 237-40 (14 April).
78. C.O. 188, vol. 145, Gordon to Cardwell, 12 March 1866.
79. H. A. Davis, 'The Fenian Raid on New Brunswick', *Canadian Historical Review*, vol. 26, pp. 316-34.
80. *Citizen*, 17 April 1866; *British Colonist*, 17 April 1866.
81. Nova Scotia, Assembly, *Debates*, 1866, pp. 202-3 (17 April).
82. *Ibid.*, p. 295 (17 April).
83. *Citizen*, 19 April 1866.
84. *Morning Chronicle*, 19 April 1866.
85. *British Colonist*, 19 April 1866.
86. New Brunswick, Assembly, *Debates*, 1866, pp. 108-17 (13 April).
87. *Ibid.*, p. 108.
88. C.O. 188, vol. 145, Gordon to Cardwell, 14 April 1866.
89. New Brunswick, Legislative Council, *Speeches on Confederation and the Resignation of the Government*, April 1886, pp. 34-54.
90. New Brunswick, Assembly, *Debates*, p. 118 (13 April).
91. *Ibid.*, pp. 118-21 (16 April).
92. New Brunswick, Legislative Council, *Speeches on Confederation and the Resignation of the Government*, pp. 51-2 (16 April).
93. New Brunswick, Assembly, *Journals*, 1866, pp. 227-8, Petition to the Queen, 17 April.
94. Macdonald Papers, vol. 51, Tilley to Macdonald, 17 April 1866.
95. C.O. 194, vol. 175, Musgrave to Cardwell, 21 March 1866.
96. Prince Edward Island, Assembly, *Debates*, 1866, pp. 100-21 (7-8 May); Bolger, *Prince Edward Island and Confederation*, pp. 145-7.
97. New Brunswick, Assembly, *Debates*, 1866, p. 119 (16 April).
98. Macdonald Papers, vol. 51, Tilley to Macdonald, 17, 20 April, 1866.
99. *Ibid.*, Tilley to Macdonald, 14 April 1866.
100. *Morning Chronicle*, 21 April 1866.
101. MacNutt, *New Brunswick*, pp. 451-2.
102. *New Brunswick Reporter*, 8 June 1866.
103. Davis, 'The Fenian Raid on New Brunswick', p. 322.
104. Cardwell Papers, vol. 39, Gordon to Cardwell, 23 April 1866.

Chapter 13 – Summer of Frustration

(pages 377-405)

1. Macdonald Papers, vol. 51, Monck to Macdonald, 17 April 1866.
2. *Ibid.*, Monck to Macdonald, 17, 18 April, 1866.
3. *Ibid.*, Monck to Macdonald, 17 April 1866.
4. Nova Scotia, Assembly, *Journals*, 1866, p. 60 (10 April).
5. Nova Scotia, Assembly, *Debates*, p. 189 (3 April).
6. *Ibid.*, p. 222 (10 April).
7. *Le Canadien*, 6, 20 April, 16, 18 May, 1866.
8. Pope, *Memoirs of Macdonald*, p. 324, Macdonald to Tilley, 8 October 1866.
9. Macdonald Papers, vol. 51, Monck to Macdonald, 10 May 1866.
10. C. P. Stacey, 'Fenianism and the Rise of National Feeling in Canada at the Time of Confederation', *Canadian Historical Review*, vol. 12, pp. 238-61.
11. G. F. G. Stanley, *Canada's Soldiers, 1604-1954. The Military History of an Unmilitary People* (Toronto, 1954), pp. 224-7.
12. *Ibid.*, pp. 228-9.
13. *Globe*, 2, 9 June, 1866; *Spectator*, 5, 7 June, 1866.
14 *Spectator*, 7 June 1866.
15. *Ibid.*, 5 June 1866; *Globe*, 11 June 1866.
16. Stacey, 'Fenianism and the Rise of National Feeling', p. 261.
17. *Spectator*, 26, 28 May, 1866.
18. *Daily Evening Globe*, 26, 31 May, 8, 10, 13 June, 1866.
19. Williams Papers, Monck to Williams, 6 May 1866.
20. *Ibid.*
21. Brown Papers, Brown to Anne Brown, 14 June 1866.
22. *Globe*, 7 September 1866; *Leader*, 7 September 1866.
23. *Globe*, 9 June 1866.
24. Brown Papers, Brown to Anne Brown, 26 June 1866.
25. *Globe*, 8 September 1866.
26. Pope, *Memoirs of Macdonald*, p. 317, Monck to Macdonald, 21 June 1866.
27. Macdonald Papers, vol. 51, Tupper to Macdonald, 17 June 1866.
28. Tilley Papers, McCully to Tilley, 8 June 1866.
29. *Leader*, 28 June 1866.
30. *Ibid.*
31. Brown Papers, Brown to Anne Brown, 22 June 1866.
32. *Ibid.*
33. *Ibid.*, Brown to Anne Brown, 26 June 1866.
34. *Ibid.*, Brown to Anne Brown, 4 July 1866.
35. *Ibid.*, Brown to Anne Brown, 10 July 1866.
36. *Leader*, 14 July 1866.
37. Williams Papers, Monck to Williams, 10 July 1866.
38. Cardwell Papers, vol. 40, Cardwell to Monck, 7 July 1866.
39. Stanmore Papers, Monck to Gordon, 10 July 1866.
40. Macdonald Papers, vol. 51, Tupper to Macdonald, 14 July 1866.

41. Public Record Office, Carnarvon Papers, Carnarvon to Monck, 7 July 1866.
42. Pope, *Memoirs of Macdonald*, p. 326, Macdonald to Tilley, 8 October 1866.
43. Carnarvon Papers, vol. 151, Monck to Carnarvon, 21 July 1866.
44. Pope, *Memoirs of Macdonald*, p. 323, Monck to Williams, 14 July 1866.
45. Cardwell Papers, vol. 40, Carnarvon to Cardwell, 23 July 1866.
46. *Ibid.*, vol. 40, Carnarvon to Cardwell, 19, 20 July, 1866.
47. *Ibid.*, vol. 40, Heads of a Bill for the Union of the British North American Colonies and the Government of the United Province.
48. *Ibid.*
49. Cardwell Papers, vol. 40, Cardwell to Carnarvon, 27 July 1866.
50. *Ibid.*, vol. 40, Carnarvon to Cardwell, 28 July 1866.
51. Williams Papers, Monck to Williams, 16 July 1866.
52. Macdonald Papers, vol. 51, Tilley to Galt, 9 August 1866.
53. *Ibid.*, vol. 51, Galt to Macdonald, 31 August 1866.
54. Canada, Assembly, *Journals*, 1866, pp. 141-2 (13 July).
55. *Ibid.*
56. *Globe*, 14 July 1866.
57. *Leader*, 14 July 1866.
58. *Globe*, 14 July 1866.
59. *Ibid.*
60. A. T. Galt, *Speech on the Proposed Union of the British North American Provinces, Delivered at Sherbrooke, Canada East* (Montreal, 1864), pp. 14-15.
61. *Globe*, 4 August 1866.
62. Archives Publiques de Québec, Chapais Papers, Langevin to Edmond Langevin, 6 August 1866.
63. *Globe*, 15 August 1866.
64. *Ibid.*, 17 August 1866.
65. *Ibid.*, 22 August 1866.
66. *Ibid.*
67. *Ibid.*, 5 September 1866.
68. *Ibid.*, 11 September 1866.
69. *Ibid.*
70. Carnarvon Papers, vol. 151, Monck to Carnarvon, 24 August 1866.
71. *Ibid.*, vol. 151, Monck to Carnarvon, 27 August 1866.
72. Hughenden Manor, High Wycombe, Beaconsfield Papers, vol. 12, Carnarvon to Disraeli, 27 August 1866.
73. Carnarvon Papers, vol. 151, Carnarvon to Monck, 10 August 1866.
74. Macdonald Papers, vol. 74, Monck to Macdonald, 29 August 1866.
75. Bolger, *Prince Edward Island and Confederation*, p. 157.
76. Joseph Howe, *Confederation Considered in Relation to the Interests of the Empire* (London, 1866).
77. Charles Tupper, *Recollections of Sixty Years in Canada* (London, 1914), pp. 46-50; *Letter to the Right Honourable Earl of Carnarvon* (London, 1866).

Chapter 14 – Achievement

(pages 406-39)

1. Chapais Papers, Langevin to H. Langevin, 19 November 1866.
2. *Ibid.*, Langevin to Justine Langevin, 23 November 1866.
3. *Ibid.*, Langevin to Justine Langevin, 27 November 1866.
4. Macdonald Papers, vol. 47, pt. 1, pp. 18238-41; Pope, *Confederation Documents*, pp. 94-5 (4 December 1866).
5. Chapais Papers, Langevin to Jean Langevin, 4 December 1866.
6. *Ibid.*
7. Brown Papers, Brown to Anne Brown, 14 June 1866.
8. Macdonald Papers, vol. 47, pt. 1, pp. 18239-40; Pope, *Confederation Documents*, p. 94 (4 December 1866).
9. Carnarvon Papers, vol. 151, Monck to Carnarvon, 27 September 1866.
10. Brown Papers, Brown to Anne Brown, 28 April 1865.
11. Macdonald Papers, vol. 47, pt. 1, p. 18255; Pope, *Confederation Documents*, p. 111.
12. *Ibid.*
13. Waite, *Life and Times of Confederation*, pp. 291-2.
14. Chapais Papers, Langevin to Justine Langevin, 18 November 1866.
15. *Ibid.*, Connolly to Langevin, 15 December 1866.
16. Macdonald Papers, vol. 47, pt. 1, p. 18270; Pope, *Confederation Documents*, p. 112 (5 December 1866).
17. *Ibid.*, vol. 47, pt. 1, p. 18244; Pope, *Confederation Documents*, p. 96 (6 December 1866).
18. A. Hardinge, *The Life of Henry Howard Molyneux Herbert, Fourth Earl of Carnarvon*, 1831-1890 (London, 1925), vol. 1, p. 67.
19. Chapais Papers, Langevin to Justine Langevin, 12 December 1866.
20. Pope, *Memoirs of Macdonald*, pp. 335-6, Macdonald to Louisa Macdonald, 27 December 1866.
21. *Ibid.*
22. Bolger, *Prince Edward Island and Confederation*, p. 158.
23. Chapais Papers, Langevin to Justine Langevin, 27 November 1866.
24. McDougall Papers, McDougall to Monck, 27 January 1867.
25. Macdonald Papers, vol. 47, pt. 1, pp. 18282-9; Pope, *Confederation Documents*, pp. 115-19 (13 December 1866).
26. Macdonald Papers, vol. 47, pt. 1, p. 18286; Pope, *Confederation Documents*, p. 118.
27. Macdonald Papers, vol. 47, pt. 1, p. 18288; Pope, *Confederation Documents*, p. 119 (13 December 1866).
28. Skelton, *Galt*, p. 408, Galt to his wife, 19 December 1866.
29. Macdonald Papers, vol. 51, Macdonald to Carnarvon, 24 December 1866.
30. Pope, *Memoirs of Macdonald*, p. 336, Macdonald to Louisa Macdonald, 27 December 1866.
31. Chapais Papers, Langevin to Justine Langevin, 25 December 1866.
32. Macdonald Papers, vol. 47, pt. 1, p. 18281.
33. *Ibid.*, vol. 75, Monck to Macdonald, 10 January 1867.
34. Carnarvon Papers, Carnarvon to Grey, 29 January 1867.

35. Macdonald Papers, vol. 51, Macdonald to Carnarvon, 24 January 1867.
36. Hardinge, *Carnarvon*, vol. 1, p. 303.
37. Cardwell Papers, vol. 40, Carnarvon to Cardwell, 19 July 1866.
38. Pope, *Confederation Documents*, p. 150, Draft of a Bill for the Union of the British North American Colonies and for the Government of the United Colony.
39. *Ibid.*, pp. 152-3.
40. McDougall Papers, McDougall to Monck, 27 January 1866.
41. Macdonald Papers, vol. 51, Macdonald to Carnarvon, 30 January 1867; Pope, *Memoirs of Macdonald*, pp. 727-8.
42. Carnarvon Papers, vol. 169, Carnarvon to the Cabinet, 2 February 1867.
43. G. E. Marindin, *Letters of Lord Blachford*, pp. 301-2.
44. Royal Archives, B 23, Carnarvon to Grey, 6 February 1867.
45. *Globe*, 21 September 1864.
46. Frances Monck, *My Canadian Leaves*, p. 175.
47. C.O. 42, vol. 656, Monck to Carnarvon, 7 September 1866.
48. *Ibid.*, Minute by C. B. Adderley, 28 September 1866.
49. United States, 39th Congress, 2nd Session, *Congressional Globe*, p. 1617 (27 February 1867).
50. *Ibid.*, 40th Congress, 1st Session, *Congressional Globe*, p. 392 (27 March 1867).
51. L. B. Shippee, *Canadian-American Relations*, 1849-74 (New Haven and Toronto, 1939), p. 196.
52. Royal Archives, B 23, Carnarvon to Grey, 7 February 1867.
53. Carnarvon Papers, vol. 144, Grey to Carnarvon, 9 February 1867.
54. *Ibid.*, vol. 139, Derby to Carnarvon, 7 February 1867.
55. Pope, *Memoirs of Macdonald*, p. 334.
56. *Times*, 21 February 1867.
57. Great Britain, Parliament, *Debates*, 3rd Series, vol. 185, pp. 557-82 (19 February 1867).
58. *Ibid.*, p. 576 b.
59. *Ibid.*, pp. 1011-17 (26 February 1867).
60. *Ibid.*, pp. 1019-20.
61. *Ibid.*, pp. 1090-1 (27 February 1867).
62. Pope, *Memoirs of Macdonald*, pp. 337-8, Macdonald to Louisa Macdonald, 21 March 1867.
63. Carnarvon Papers, vol. 139, Carnarvon to Derby, 7 January 1867.
64. *Ibid.*, vol. 139, Carnarvon to Derby, 22 February 1867.
65. Great Britain, Parliament, *Debates*, 3rd Series, vol. 185, pp. 1164-74 (28 February 1867).
66. *Ibid.*, pp. 1174-80.
67. *Ibid.*, pp. 1180-5.
68. Skelton, *Galt*, p. 410, Galt to his wife, 14 January 1867.
69. *Times*, 1 March 1867.
70. Saunders, *Tupper*, vol. 1, pp. 145-6.
71. Macdonald Papers, vol. 51, Tilley to Macdonald, 6 May 1867.
72. Pope, *Correspondence of Macdonald*, p. 46, Monck to Macdonald, 24 May 1867.
73. Macdonald Papers, vol. 51, Macdonald to Archibald, 30 May 1867.

74. *Ibid.*, vol. 51, Macdonald to Tilley, 30 May 1867.
75. *Ibid.*, vol. 51, Mitchell to Macdonald, 27 May 1867.
76. *Ibid.*, vol. 51, Tilley to Macdonald, 5 June 1867.
77. *Ibid.*, vol. 230, McDougall to Macdonald, 5 June 1867.
78. Pope, *Correspondence of Macdonald*, p. 43, McGee to Macdonald, 9 April 1867.
79. Tupper, *Recollections of Sixty Years in Canada*, pp. 53-4.
80. *Gazette*, 27 June 1867.
81. *Globe*, 29 June 1867.
82. *Gazette*, 3 July 1867.
83. J. M. S. Careless, *Brown of the Globe*, vol. 2, *Statesman of Confederation, 1860-1880* (Toronto, 1963), pp. 251-2.
84. *Globe*, 1 July 1867.
85. *Gazette*, 1 July 1867.
86. *Leader*, 1 July 1867.
87. *Citizen* (Ottawa), 5 July 1867.
88. *La Minerve*, 6 July 1867.
89. *Ibid.*, 8 July 1867.
90. *Morning News*, 3 July 1867.

INDEX

at London Conference, 406, 407, 408, 409, 416; and first federal cabinet, 433, 434-5

Uniacke, Andrew, 210

Unionist (Halifax), 238, 321, 326-7, 343

United States of America: fear of, in Great Britain and British North America, 83, 91, 213-14, 244, 273; and St. Albans raid, 195, 212-14; and the *Alabama*, 304; and Reciprocity Treaty, 336-7, 344; and confederation, 422-3

Wade, George, 28, 29

Wallbridge, T. C., 243

Wells, David, 336

Western Extension, 30-1, 249-50, 287-9, 296, 318, 319, 332, 340, 375

Westminster Palace Hotel, 279, 406-7

Wetmore, A. R., 318, 355, 380

Whelan, Edward, 233; criticism of the Charlottetown Conference, 122; at the Quebec Conference, 140, 147, 150, 151, 159, 160; opinion of Edward Palmer, 197; admits defeat of confederation, 199; and reliance of Lower Canada on the Maritime Provinces, 271-2

Williams, Sir William Fenwick, 340, 357, 361, 369, 395; character and career, 324-5; his belief in confederation, 325-6; his cautious policy, 342-3, 348, 350-1; negotiations with Annand, 358-9

Wilmot, Lemuel Allen, 318, 333

Wilmot, Robert Duncan, 284, 285, 294, 310, 323, 330, 372; forms Anti-Confederate government with Smith, 258, 260; his dislike of federalism, 258-9, 286, 317; his visit to Canada, 307-8; becomes Confederate, 308, 355-6; and office of auditor general, 318, 333; resigns, 341-2, 348-9; wins election, 386; at London Conference, 407

York by-election, 318-20